History
of
Greenup County, Kentucky

by
Nina Mitchell Biggs
&
Mabel Lee Mackoy

Southern Historical Press, Inc.
Greenville, South Carolina

Please Direct All Correspondence and Book Orders to:

**Southern Historical Press, Inc.
1071 Park West Blvd.
Greenville, SC   29611**

Originally printed: KY 1951
ISBN #978-163914-607-9
Printed in the United States of America

TO

The memory of those pioneers
who braved the dangers
of an unknown wilderness
and paved the way
for the families and homes
of today

DEDICATION

This reprinting is dedicated to Mrs. Nina Mitchell Biggs, who was born in Greenup, Kentucky on September 28, 1867, and died September 28, 1969. She lived a busy and productive life raising five children, teaching school — although she was 68 years of age before she received her high school diploma.

In 1951, at the age of 84, she published a History of Greenup County, Kentucky, as co-author with Miss Mabel Mackoy, and later published a supplement to the first history in 1962.

In 1968, she moved from her old farm home, to a new house built from the Frost Schoolroom where she had taught for 10 years, and where she resided in her daughter's home until her death at 102 years.

The Greenup Woman's Club takes great pleasure in sponsoring the reprinting of these history books and dedicating their reprinting to Mrs. Nina Mitchell Biggs.

Preface

There comes a time in the life of every thinking person when he wonders about his forefathers, who they were, where they came from, how they were occupied, and many other things concerning them.

Fortunate, indeed, are those who have listened to the words of the old grandparents they knew when they were children. Some people were thoughtful enough to preserve family Bibles and old records; but others, in removing from one section of the country to another, may have lost or misplaced them, or the records may have been destroyed by fire.

Some members of families may have had valuable information that they might have imparted to others, had an occasion presented itself, or if they had had the proper encouragement to talk of earlier days; many folk, however, are more prone to live in the present than in the past or the future.

One may go to public records and learn general facts, but personal items of interest are rarely recorded in writing. The reason for this bit of history is an earnest desire to aid future seekers in such a quest.

Acknowledgments

We are indebted to many sources for the material contained in this book—a history of the past for the future. Much of this material has been obtained from old records in the county and circuit court offices and from Collins' *History of Kentucky*, Evans' *History of Scioto County, Ohio*, and Ely's *History of the Big Sandy Valley*, all of which contain material pertaining to Greenup County.

We are indebted to all who have aided us in this work, especially to those descendants of our pioneers for the use of scrapbooks and records from family Bibles; to James Watt Womack and William Alexander Biggs for past history; to Professor B. F. Kidwell for early educational material; to Miss Rebecca Wentworth Spalding of New York for books of which she is the author and which contain much interesting material of early days of the county; to Mrs. Elizabeth Warnock Womack for "Notes of Early Greenup," compiled by Mr. John Myers but preserved by her; to Miss Elizabeth Mead for history of the eastern section of the county and also for the loan of the James Gilruth Letters written to her kinsman, General W. H. Kelly; to Hon. Joseph B. Bates for records obtained from Frankfort; to Mr. Forest Holdercamper, of Washington, D. C., for record of postmasters; and to the Editor of the *Russell Times* for the use of material from the "Special Edition of the *Times* of 1942."

And to those who read this HISTORY OF GREENUP COUNTY we would say, "Be tolerant of the composition and rhetoric, and of any errors that may have crept in; look only to the spirit that prompted its compilation."

THE AUTHORS

Contents

HISTORY OF GREENUP COUNTY, KENTUCKY

" . . . . . and he went out, not knowing whither he went. By faith he sojourned in the land of promise . . . . . "

HEBREWS 11: 8-9

One

A NEW LAND

From the settlement of Virginia in 1607 to the coming of the first pioneers from there to Kentucky in the early 1770's, more than one hundred and sixty years had passed. Many changes had taken place in Virginia and most of the desirable land had been taken. Many people were dissatisfied with conditions and so were ready to try the new land of which they had heard much from the early fur traders and adventurers. These had told of the many rivers, great forests, and wide grassy plains.

Many of the pioneers followed the windings of the rivers, and, on coming to a big bend in the Ohio, with a broad valley enclosed by green hills, decided that the northeastern section of the new land would be a pleasant place to live. Apparently there were no Indians nor many savage animals here and it would be an ideal location for these English and Scotch-Irish farmers, whose ancestors had come to Virginia.

When the Revolutionary War was over in Virginia, many who had received grants of land in this section either came or sold their grants to others. Some came overland with necessities on horseback and in wagons, while others came down the river on flatboats. Many of these first comers settled in the Ohio Valley, and others made their way up the Little Sandy River and Tygart Creek. This creek was named for Thomas Tygart, an early settler of the valley.

An abundance of timber was found on the hills suitable for every need, such as houses, barns, and mills. Here were trees of oak, poplar, beech, sycamore, pine, chestnut, and hickory. Also *in* the hills were coal for fuel, stones of many kinds for building purposes, veins of iron ore, and other minerals.

EARLY SETTLERS

Under the title of Early Settlers it is hardly appropriate to write of Daniel Boone, although he was in Greenup County a great deal, staying at the home of his brother, Jesse. It is said that he lived above Greenup for a while at one time. Daniel was of a restless nature and did not tarry long at any one place. Many interesting stories are told of him in connection with the county, such as the one about a carving on a tree at Little Sandy Falls, which said, "Daniel Boone killed a bar." Another was told by Mr. John Warnock, who said that he saw Daniel Boone in 1799, at the Falls of Little Sandy, cutting a tree to make a canoe for his wife, Rebecca, and himself to go down the Ohio River on their way to Missouri. Although we later read of his being at Limestone (Maysville) helping his cousin, Jacob Boone, to build a tavern, he did reach Missouri in 1820.

Jesse Boone, unlike Daniel, was active in all of the early affairs of the county and town. As one of the town fathers, he aided in the organization of the courts, both quarter sessions and circuit, and also in the planning of roads. He owned much land above Greenup, and Mrs. Juliet Hockaday Collins has two deeds given by Jesse Boone to her great-grandfather, John Hockaday. The Boone family has been widely scattered and little is known of their descendants. Jesse Boone is buried in the Shuff Graveyard near East Fork, having died at the home of Matilda Hood Davidson, a daughter of the pioneer, Andrew Hood.

Simon Kenton was not a resident, although he owned much land in the county. One deed in the clerk's office shows that he owned land west of the Little Sandy River; another shows that he owned land along Tygart Creek, and records of deeds still call for Simon Kenton Lines.

Andrew Hood was a true pioneer, having lived within the present bounds of the county before it was organized. He and his wife, Mary Kane, came from Virginia and lived two miles above the Little Sandy River. It was in Andrew Hood's home that the town fathers met to organize the county; and also where they met to organize both the quarter sessions and the circuit courts. Thomas Hood, a brother of Andrew, was also one of the town fathers. Hood's Creek, below Ashland, was named for Andrew Hood, and Hood's Run, in the Tygart Valley, was named for Thomas Hood.

2

Seriah Stratton came from Mason County to Greenup and was one of the town fathers. Nothing can be learned about his family, but we find among the old marriage license records that Ann Stratton married Jacob Friend in 1808; that Jane Stratton married Nelson Brown in 1810; and that James Stratton married Elizabeth McGuire in 1815. These three were no doubt the children of Seriah Stratton, as his name appears on the marriage records as the parent.

Captain Moses Fuqua, a descendant of the French Huguenots in Virginia, and a Revolutionary soldier, bought more than one thousand acres of land above the mouth of Tygart Creek in 1799. Being an old man at that time, he sent his son, Moses Fuqua, Jr., to see the land and to arrange for a place for the family to live. There being no settlement in Kentucky near there at that time, he stayed at the tavern of John Collins at Alexandria, the settlement at the mouth of the Scioto River in Ohio. Soon he fell in love with the tavern keeper's sixteen-year-old daughter, Cynthia, and proposed marriage. But John Collins insisted he needed Cynthia as his housekeeper, his wife being dead, and because of her youth he suggested that at some future time such a proposition might be agreeable. Moses Fuqua, Jr., returned to Virginia, made his report of the land to his father, and in due time the large family with their many slaves came to Kentucky. Moses Fuqua, Sr.'s wife, Judith Woodson, died just before they left Virginia. As soon as the family was settled in the new home, Moses Fuqua, Jr., went to Alexandria and claimed Cynthia Collins as his bride. They made their home on Tygart Creek and raised a family of ten daughters and one son. Some of their descendants still live in that neighborhood.

John and James Mackoy came from Campbell County, Virginia, and settled in Kentucky about 1800. They both had large families. James established the first mill near Dover in Mason County while John made his home in what is now the Siloam neighborhood near the Fuqua family. His wife was Lavinia, daughter of Moses Fuqua, Sr. He was interested in all the early affairs of the county and he, with Josiah Davidson, Andrew Hood, and Andrew Wolf were, on the motion of Jesse Boone, appointed to view the necessary and best way for a road to be opened from the county line opposite the mouth of the Scioto River to the mouth of the Big Sandy River. This was probably the first road to be made in the county.

Hon. Thomas Truman Greenfield Waring's father, Thomas Waring, came to Mason County from Virginia about 1783. In 1799 he bought one thousand acres of land on Tygart Creek where Lynn now is. This section became known as the Waring Settlement because of the numerous Waring families living there. Thomas Waring was one of the organizers of the county and was prominent in all the early affairs in both the town and the county of Greenup.

Other early settlers' names are found in numerous wills, deeds and other court records. These will be mentioned further on in this work, and there will be sketches of the early pioneer families as obtained from descendants. Some of these families are: Howe, Clark, Daugherty, Lowery, Rucker, and many others.

There were some men who were not settlers, but who should be mentioned, as they had a part in the early settling of the county. They did not live in the county, nor do they seem to have had families there. Two of these men, John and Lewis Craig, were active in land deals in various counties of Virginia, also in church affairs. A Mason County history has similar accounts of them, and Greenup County records many deeds by them and to them, all of which leads us to believe they were what we call today real estate agents. They were probably known as land agents then. The name of Lewis Craig is appended to a plat made of the town and placed on record in the second year book of the county. There were two other men, John and Dan Young, who seemed to work together. John Young built the courthouse that was finished in 1816, and we learn from records that he built a courthouse in Portsmouth, Ohio, the same year. John and Dan Young lived near Concord, Ohio (Wheelersburg). They bought the cotton carding machinery from the mill in Greenup, moved it to Concord and used it in building a woolen mill. Dan Young was a preacher, as records show he conducted religious services both in Greenup and Scioto Counties.

FORMATION OF GREENUP COUNTY

Greenup County was formed from Mason County in June, 1803, and it extended from the Mason County line on the west to the Big Sandy River on the east, along the Ohio River for forty miles. It had an average width of twelve miles which included those counties later formed from it, these being Lewis (1806), Lawrence (1821), Carter (1838), and Boyd (1860). The

4

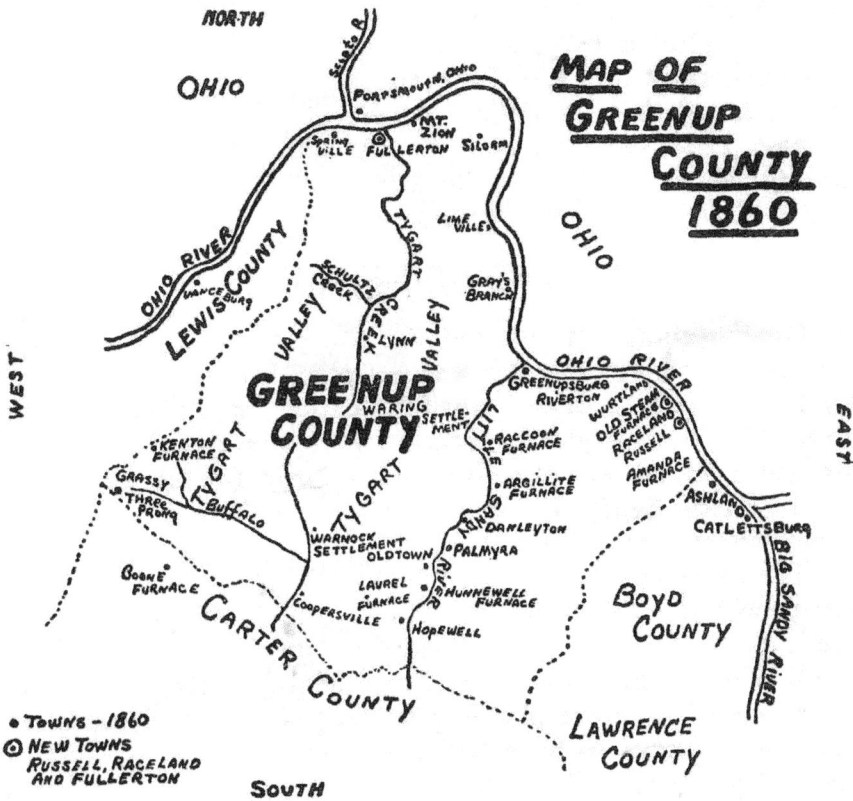

MAP OF GREENUP COUNTY 1860

NORTH

OHIO

• TOWNS - 1860
◉ NEW TOWNS
  RUSSELL, RACELAND
  AND FULLERTON

WEST

EAST

SOUTH

new county was named for Christopher Greenup, who was born in Virginia in 1750, fought in the wars against the Indians, and was a colonel in the Revolutionary War. He was prominent in the organization of the district of Kentucky, was a member of the first Congress, Clerk of the Senate and became Governor of Kentucky in 1804.

Greenup County occupied the most northeastern section of the state until 1860 when Boyd was formed from it in that section. It is crossed from southeast to northwest by the Little Sandy River and Tygart Creek, and includes the foothills of the Cumberland Mountains.

The following is taken from an early account of the county's resources as contained in Collins' *History of Kentucky*: "Greenup County is rich in mineral resources, the iron ore being of a superior character and seemingly inexhaustible. Coal is also found in abundance. The hills are covered with timber and the water power is not excelled in the state. Seven varieties of iron ore

5

were analysed by Professor Robert Peter in connection with the Geological Survey, and it was found that Big Block Ore was the richest and Red Ocre was the poorest. At the furnaces it was found that the richest ore yielded 60.9 per cent and the poorest 11.35 per cent of iron." At that time Greenupsburg, Springville, and Lynn were the largest villages, although Oldtown and Fulton were important ones.

GREENUPSBURG

Greenupsburg was platted the same year that the county was organized, but the plat was not placed on record until 1815 by Lewis Craig. A more beautiful location for a town could not have been found anywhere, situated as it is on the banks of "The Beautiful River" and extending from Town Branch on the east to the Little Sandy River on the west with a background of symmetrically rounded hills.

The town was laid off around a central square with the square courthouse exactly in the center, the clerk's office being on the north side facing the river, and the jail on the south side facing Main Street. Those who were instrumental in the organization of the county and the planning of the town did their work well and they deserve to have had a memorial erected to them on the public square. These town fathers were Thomas Waring, Seriah Stratton, Jesse Boone, Andrew and Thomas Hood.

A temporary frame courthouse was built in 1806 and the brick one, which was in use for one hundred and twenty-three years, was begun in 1811 by John Young, but was not finished until 1816. The jail was built in 1811 by Jesse Boone and probably the clerk's office was built at the same time. The brick used in these buildings was made on the Rankins farm below the Little Sandy River. The town was incorporated in 1818.

The streets were named: Water, Elizabeth, Main and Perry, from the river to the rear of the town. The street below the Court Square was named Washington and the one above was Harrison. From Washington to the Little Sandy River the alleys were named: Cedar, Walnut, and Cherry, while along the Ohio River and Little Sandy was Ferry Lot. From Harrison to the upper part of the town the alleys were Laurel, Hickory, and Boston. The plat of the town shows that Lot No. 1 began at the Stark corner and ended at Lot No. 11, at the Ferry Lot, also that Lot No. 12 began at the Kouns House corner and ended at

NORTH

OHIO RIVER

WATER STREET

JONES 114 105 104		
JONES 103		
JONES 102		
JONES		
LAUDERS 101		ABBOTT 106 115
		ABBOTT 107 105
		STEVENS 108
		L. LOCKE
BOSTON		ALLEY
J WARNOCK		J. MORTON
KIMBAL		J. MORTON
C SWEET		WARNOCK
CHAPMAN		WARNOCK
HICKORY		ALLEY
J. CHAPMAN	40 FEET WIDE	DAWSON
Wm. RICE		C. LEVEIT
Wm. RICE		C. LEVEIT
Wm. RICE		C. LEVEIT
LAUREL		ALLEY
		CHITWOOD
J. MORTON 14 15		J.R. CHITWOOD 33 34
HALEY 13		MAY JONES 35
WARNOCK 12		

ALLEY 112	ALLEY 113
ALLEY	T. MAY 74
J. MORTON	T. MAY 75
CRUMP	MAY 76
WHEELER	MAY 77
ALLEY	ALLEY
CORUM	MAY 78
REYNOLDS	MAY 79
REYNOLDS	MAY 80
B HOBBS	MAY 81
ALLEY	ALLEY
B.H. GAINES 56	82
B.H. GAINES 57	
R. DAVIS 58	WARNOCK
WHEELER	WARNOCK

HARRISON STREET   ST.   ST.

66 FEET WIDE

| C.O. | PUBLIC SQUARE C.H. | JAIL |

SCHOOL	LAND
O.L. TIMBER LAKE	86
TIMBER LAKE	87

MAIN STREET   PERRY STREET

SOUTH

WASHINGTON STREET   ST.   ST.

ELIZABETH STREET

J. McGUIRE		36	62	88
J. McGUIRE 2		37	63	89
3		38	64	90
VALADY*		39	65	91
CEDAR 5	ALLEY	40	ALLEY 66	ALLEY 92
DAUGHERTY 6		41	67	93
WARNOCK		42	68	94
WARNOCK 7		43	69	95
JONES				
WALNUT 9	ALLEY	44	ALLEY 70	ALLEY 96
		45	71	97
J. McGUIRE 10		46	72 73	98 99
J. McGUIRE 11				
CHERRY	ALLEY		ALLEY	ALLEY
FERRY LOT	100		109	100

LITTLE SANDY R.

STATE OF KENTUCKY
GREENUP COUNTY Yct

I do hereby certify that this plan of the Town of Greenupsburg was produced to me as Clerk of the County Court of said County on the 29th day of June 1815 by Lewis Craig who desired the same might be recorded which has been accordingly done.

Als Att. John Hockaday.

7

Lot No. 23 at Boston Alley. These mentioned lots were on Water, later known as Front Street. Main and Perry Streets were laid off according to the same plan. Much later, lots were laid off above and below, numbering to one hundred and eleven, that being the number of the Ferry Lot. The names of the streets (except Water which was changed to Front), and the alleys have never been changed. A later expansion of the community above Town Branch is now known as East Greenup. Bridges over Town Branch and the Little Sandy were built very early in the settlement of the town. A ferry was in use for crossing the Little Sandy River until a wooden bridge was built in the 1830's which was badly damaged in the flood of 1883. This was repaired, but in 1884 it was destroyed entirely by the flood, and the present iron bridge was erected under the supervision of the County Judge, Lewis Nichols, and Commissioners Robert Johnson, James D. Biggs, and John Rhoades. Their names appear on a plate on each end of the bridge and are still legible.

EARLY GREENUP COUNTY BY JAMES GILRUTH
Letters written in 1872

The following material is taken from a series of letters written by James Gilruth of French Grant, Scioto County, Ohio, to General W. H. Kelly, who was connected with the Mead and Powell families. James Gilruth was the son of Thomas and Mary Ingles (Ingalls) Gilruth. He writes, "Vincent Furguson settled on Lot No. 2 in the French Grant and next below him settled Peter Van Bibber, whose children were Jesse, Jacob, John, and Tice. In the family was a niece, Olive Van Bibber, who married Nathan, the youngest son of Colonel Daniel Boone. After the Van Bibbers left, Gabriel Neff occupied the place." (Mr. Gilruth does not say where the Van Bibber family went, but it was probably across the river to Greenup County, as there were a number of Van Bibber families in the county.)

Mr. Gilruth continues, "I think it proper now to cross the river and come up on the Kentucky side, beginning below Little Sandy. Between the narrows and Little Sandy, about 1803, settled John Nichols (or Nicholson). His wife was Cassandra Wilcoxen and their children were John, Patty, Nicholas, James, Mary, Cassandra, and Alfred. Patty married Benjamin Chinn and Cassandra married James Bartley. About the same time that Nichols settled below, Lewis Wilcoxen, an uncle of Mrs. Nichols, settled above the point of Little Sandy.

"Lewis Wilcoxen built a hewed log house with a clapboard roof, the first house built on the present site of Greenupsburg. He had slaves and cleared the land of beech, poplar, and oak trees. About a half mile above Little Sandy settled Andrew Hood, who was called Major. His wife was Mary Kane of Virginia, and the children were named Sarchet, Elizabeth, Patty, Andrew, Rachel, Catherine, and Henry. Major Hood was the first settler in this *part* of the county, if not the first in the county. His son, Thomas, married Sarah Pickey; Sarchet married Jesse Griffith; Andrew, Jr., married a Miss Crain; and Rachel married Joseph Howe.

"Hood's Run forked two or three hundred yards from the mouth and the left hand fork lay parallel with the river up through the bottoms for a mile, then it came at nearly right angles from the hill. At some period, at this angle, the water had found a passage through to the river and it became known as Howe's Run. When the Little Sandy Salt Works began to export salt by wagons down to the Ohio River, Hood built a high frame bridge over this Run for the salt wagons and also for his own convenience. This bridge was the first frame bridge built on either side of the Ohio River between Big Sandy and Big Scioto Rivers that had any connection with public utility.

"After Greenup County was organized court was held for several years in a rough plank shed attached to the north end of Hood's house. The judges' seats were on a rough plank scaffold raised sufficiently high for them to look over the bar, jury, and audience. In those days such a thing as a bolt for flour was never heard of being connected with any grist mill in these parts. Hood bought a fine brass wire sieve 18 inches in diameter, for which he paid $2 and he fixed up a little room adjoining the court room, with all the convenience necessary for sifting. He gave all the neighbors the free privilege of fetching their grist there to sift their flour. The opportunity was readily embraced by all who had any wheat ground, though it cost them hours of weary labor to get a little coarse flour. In a shed attached to the end of his house was kept for some time the first dry goods store on either side of the Ohio River between Big Sandy and Big Scioto. It was kept by Benjamin Chinn.

"Major Hood owned no slaves, but he owned the largest breed of hogs in the county, kept a large flock of geese, the first kept in these parts, and set out the first apple orchard in Greenup County. He was a respected and good citizen.

"Near the hill on the bank of Hood's Run, in a rough log cabin built for the purpose, was kept the first school between Big Sandy and Tygart Creek, and I am certain that it was the first school in Greenup County. It was made up of scholars from both sides of the Ohio River and was kept by Silas Wooten. His wife's name was Theba, and they had two children, Rhoda and William. Wooten was a teacher of the true backwoods type, as to literary qualifications.

"The Boone family settled above the Hoods and next came John Hockaday, who settled there before 1803. He was a single man and taught school for one term in a cabin between Jesse Boone's and Thomas Hood's. He bought a tract of land, probably a part of the Boone tract, and built a hewed double log house with an open entry between, a shingle roof, and a brick chimney. He obtained the clerkship of the county and kept his office in his house. He married Margaret Donathan after coming here. Few men sustained a more amiable or worthy character than John Hockaday.

"About 1803 or 1804 John How settled next above John Hockaday. His children were Joseph, Rebecca, Ellenore, Sarah, William, Daniel, and John. Joseph married Rachel Hood, Rebecca married James Warnock, and Ellenore married Roland Comelius. After living here some years How moved back a few miles among the hills and opened a new farm which they named "Willow Cave" (Way). After How moved, Reuben Dawson came. The Dawson children were Gabriel, Fanny, Arthur, Henry, and Joseph. About 1807 Reuben Dawson built the first keel boat ever built on either side of the river between Portsmouth and Gallipolis.

"Next above the Dawsons was a 1000-acre tract bought and settled by Lewis Wilcoxen, who had built the first house in Greenupsburg. Two of the children were Leven and Lloyd. Failing to make payment for the land, Wilcoxen moved west to Scioto River. After Lewis Wilcoxen, Martin Smith bought the land. His children were Robert, William, Woodson, Nancy, Elizabeth, and John. Elizabeth married John C. Kouns and Nancy married William Ward. Martin Smith owned more slaves than any other man in the county. Next above settled Benjamin Ulen, whose children were Benjamin, John, Nancy, and Samuel.

10

"Josiah Davidson (known as Short Si) was the next settler, with two children, Reuben and Jesse. This family moved to East Fork of Little Sandy. (Name must have been Davisson.) Next above settled Steven Colvin, whose son, John, married Margaret Davidson. Josiah Davidson (known as Long Si) settled next and his children were Lizzie, Maply, and Samuel. They did not remain long and William Roby moved here.

"On the next tract of land settled Joseph Powell, whose children were Vincent, Catherine, and Benjamin. Vincent married Polly Kelly, and Benjamin married Rev. John Young's daughter, Nancy Now I shall go up no farther but return and give you some of the early settlement of Greenupsburg.

"In a former letter I said Lewis Wilcoxen settled and cleared part of the land where Greenupsburg now stands. Robert Johnson with whom Daniel Boone had a law suit, built a small tub mill at the Falls of Little Sandy. He was the father of Vice-president of the United States, Richard Johnson, and it was said both of them were here at one time. James McGuire put up the first carpenter shop in Greenupsburg, Oba S. Timberlake kept the first tavern, Reason Davis kept the first hat shop, lived in the Lewis Wilcoxen house, and ran the first ferry. Robert Daugherty had the first dry goods store, Jones and Noble built a small cotton factory, Mr. Seaton established the first school in the form of an academy in Greenup. The first doctor was Henry Green, the first lawyer was a man named Fishback, the first sermon was preached by R. Lindsey. Benjamin Locke built the first Courthouse, a frame building of white pine, and he received $900. The first prisoner was a man named Byrman, a hatter, who in a quarrel with William Webb struck him with his fist in the pit of the stomach, killing him at once.

"Colonel Boone, in a conversation with my father, gave the following account of his land failure:

"He had gotten his warrant and laid it on a tract of four thousand acres of choice land lying on the waters of a stream called Elkhorn. Apprehending no danger, he omitted for some time to get his warrant and survey recorded. In the meantime Robert Johnson, father of the Richard Johnson, afterward Vice-president of the United States, laid his warrant on the land covered by Boone's warrant, and got his warrant recorded. Suit was entered to decide who should hold the land and after litigating the matter for some time Johnson said to Boone, 'To settle the matter and end our lawing I will give you for your claims four hundred acres on the Ohio River, one mile above the mouth of Little Sandy for which I will give you a warranty deed.' Boone rejected this proposition, but when he told his lawyer what Johnson had proposed he advised him to accept the offer, which he ultimately did.

"Boone left Kentucky with his family and moved to the Big Kanawha. He lived there and then moved back here about 1800. His children were Daniel, Jr., Jesse, and Nathan. Daniel, Jr., had gone to Missouri some time before this; Jesse had married Chloe Van Bibber and had two children, Harriet and Alphonso, when they came to Kentucky. Three children, Minerva, Panthea, and Mattison, were born in Kentucky. Nathan, the youngest son of Daniel, married Olive Van Bibber after they came here. I remember being at Boone's with my father one day when their attention was attracted to an object on the other side of the river and Colonel Boone got his spectacles to see what the object was, remarking that he used these glasses in shooting. While he lived here he did not hunt much, though game was plentiful. What hunting he did was for pastime. Jesse and Nathan were both good hunters but took no special interest in it further than convenience.

"Mrs. Boone, as I remember her, was a little taller than the common size, rather spare, slightly aquiline nose, fine forehead, good countenance, and genteel manners. The Colonel said she was a better horseman than he was. Colonel Boone was a little over common size, of well-proportioned figure, neither spare nor corpulent, features formed on the Grecian countenance; in manners what we might call one of Nature's gentlemen. While the Colonel lived here, he and my father spent much of their leisure time together, recounting the adventures of past life. He expressed dissatisfaction with the land policy and his treatment. This led him to determine to quit the country here and accordingly he formed the resolution to go to Missouri which at that time belonged to Spain. Not long after this time, accompanied by his wife, his son, Nathan, and his wife, he left for Missouri. I heard that the Spanish Governor made the Colonel a grant of ten miles square, but when the country was ceded to the United States he failed to establish the grant. The United States granted it to him anyway. For this I cannot vouch.

"Jesse Boone remained on the place above Greenup, farmed, owned several slaves, became judge of the court, was active in promoting schools, and was in every way a first class citizen.

His daughter, Minerva, married Wynekoop Warner. Colonel Boone's last Kentucky cabin was converted into a schoolhouse, in which a Mr. Johnson taught a common English school for three months. In 1819, Jesse Boone and family moved to Missouri. When they were aboard their keel boat and about to shove off, I stepped on board to bid them farewell. This is the last time I ever saw one of this much respected family. Nathan Boone came back to Greenup County some years after they had moved to Missouri.

"Some years ago when I was at the French Grant, I visited. Major John C. Kountz (Kouns) who was living in Greenupsburg. In speaking of the Boone family he said he wondered that none of the writers of Colonel Boone's life have mentioned the fact of his having lived in this county. I spoke doubtingly of the report that he had once gone to the Big Kanawha. Kountz replied, 'There is no mistake about it, I know he did go.' "

Note: Much material has been taken from the letters written by James Gilruth to General W. H. Kelly. Kentucky histories have told much of Daniel Boone's early life at Boonesboro and along the Kentucky River. We have read of his activities at Limestone and at Washington in Mason County; of the friendship between him and Simon Kenton and of his being taken and held prisoner by the Indians at Chillicothe, Ohio. We have read of James, the Colonel's eldest son, being killed when a party attempted to come through Cumberland Gap; also of his son, Israel, being killed at Blue Licks; of Jemima being captured by Indians with the two Calloway girls; and of her marriage to Flanders Calloway and their moving to Missouri. All this we have read and much more of his life; but now we *know* from the old letters of James Gilruth that Daniel Boone was really a citizen of Greenup County the last years of his life in Kentucky. Since he did not take an active part in the early affairs of the county, one might assume that he was only an occasional visitor to the Jesse Boone family above Greenup, or, perhaps, he was getting too old; but on counting up various dates, he could not have been more than sixty-six years of age when living in Greenup County. So it is probable that he did not care to settle down to a routine of court duties, the principal affairs of that early day.

Mr. Gilruth says that in 1819, Jesse Boone and family went to Missouri, yet Matilda Hood Davisson states that Jesse Boone died at her father's home on East Fork and was buried in the Shuff Cemetery nearby. It is possible that he could have come back to Greenup County in later years. Jesse Boone was one of the first three justices of the county; he was postmaster March 11, 1814, and his son, Alphonso, was postmaster July 11, 1814.

(Mr. Gilruth does not always adhere to the correct spelling of names.)

LAND GRANTS

The most important person to have received a land grant in what is now Greenup County, from Virginia, was Patrick Henry, the famous orator. He was given four hundred acres in the western part of the county. He never came to view his grant of land.

The records in the clerk's office at Maysville show that a grant of ten thousand acres in Mason County was owned by Edmund Taylor, John Harvey, and Charles M. Thurston, probably of Jefferson County, Kentucky. Edmund Taylor's part of the ten thousand acres became the property of his three daughters, Sarah Christy, Martha Easton, and Hannah Easton. They sold twelve hundred and twenty-three and one-half acres to Moses Fuqua, Sr., December, 1799. This land extended from "Tygart Creek up the Ohio River." Part of this became the property of Benjamin Cook, of Virginia, who had married the daughter of Moses Fuqua. Benjamin Cook deeded his land "From Tygart Up" to Thomas B. and Nancy Cook King, October 16, 1812.

Abraham Buford received a grant of five thousand acres of land which, after a law suit, was given to his son Charles. Charles Buford sold the land in farm tracts to the Mead, Chinn, and Powell families. Russell and Raceland are built on the original Buford grant.

Josiah Morton received a grant of land extending from Tygart Creek on the east, to the west end of what is now Fullerton. Mr. Morton is buried near the village of Taylor on this land. Descendants of Josiah Morton still own a part of the original grant.

Charles Womack received a tract of two thousand acres near Oldtown in a Virginia Land Grant. He was a bachelor and rented out his land. When he died he left the land to a nephew, Charles Womack of Virginia, who sold it to the Womack Brothers at Oldtown. Orin and Ward Womack sold some of it in farm tracts but still own part of the original tract.

William Lindsay Pogue patented a large parcel of land in the eastern part of Greenup County joining the Buford Grant. This land was sold to the Means and Russell Iron Company.

John Young patented a tract of land lying between the Big Sandy and the Little Sandy Rivers and settled, in 1784, near the Little Sandy at what is now Palmyra.

The land at Wurtland that was bought by the Hon. John C. McConnell about 1819 was patented by Peter Taylor.

George Mason of Caroline County, Virginia, received a Treasury Warrant, No. 12101, in 1783, of 2748 acres on Tygart Creek near where Enterprise now is located. Part of this land was given to Henry C. Coleman of Caroline County, Virginia, by George Mason, and he with his family lived on the land. It was later divided into farms.

Peter Mason and John Kenton patented 2748 acres of land on Tygart Creek in the early days.

INDIANS

The early settlers of the county had no Indian troubles to contend with. That there had been Indians within its present limits is known, because of the many relics, mounds and fortifications found. At this time there were not many wild animals for food, and it may be that as game became scarce the Indians went to some other locality. Animals found by the pioneers were wolves, wildcats, deer, and an occasional bear.

Kentucky was never a home for the Indians, but it was a game preserve, a happy hunting ground, and a battlefield where hostile tribes chanced to meet, hence the name "Dark and Bloody Ground." There were many tribes north of the Ohio River and also south of the river, and these had two routes of travel—The Great Warrior Paths—one of which crossed the western part of the county.

Early records state that the French traders and Shawnee Indians lived on the plains of the Scioto River in Ohio and were driven from there to higher ground by the floods. Some of them came across the Ohio River where they remained until they learned of the coming of the English.

The early settlers of Oldtown found so many relics and traces of Indians there that they concluded there must have been a town there at one time. These relics consisted of pipes, tomahawks, and flints. Similar relics have been found in various parts of the county and it is probable that some tribes may have remained for a long period.

In Collins' *History of Kentucky* and Evans' *History of Scioto County* there is a drawing and description of a Temple Mound on the John Johnston farm at Siloam. This is described as having had three walls around a central mound, with an opening in each wall facing different directions. On the William Biggs farm at Frost is a fort which is located in what has always been known as the fort field, where many relics have been found. On the King farms below the fort field are other mounds, some of which have been opened and shells, beads, and a skeleton have been found. At Springville there is a large enclosure with walls plainly discernible, and it is said to have been an Indian town having an underground opening to the Ohio River.

SLAVERY IN GREENUP COUNTY

The pioneers who came from Virginia to Greenup County brought their slaves with them, and as these pioneers were mostly farmers the slaves were useful on the farms and in building the new homes. The Negroes were well mannered and they were well treated by their masters. There were none of the evils of slavery that existed in some sections of Kentucky, no slave auction block nor whipping post. It is true they were bought and sold, as elsewhere in the South, but it was done in a decent and orderly manner.

The Waring, Warnock, and Howland families brought slaves to the Tygart Valley, and along the Ohio River the Biggses, Lawsons, Mackoys, Fuquas, and Mortons owned slaves. Those people who came from Pennsylvania and other eastern states to work at the furnaces had no use for Negro labor. This was fortunate for the farmers, as there was no discontent among the slaves. These eastern people lived here a long time before they ever became used to having Negro servants.

When the Emancipation Proclamation went into effect and the Negroes could go where they pleased, some left their masters overnight and went to Ohio, which was to them a "Promised Land," while others chose to remain with their masters and work for them as they had always done. Some of the masters who were made poorer by the War, felt relieved of a burden when the Negroes could earn wages elsewhere and the owner was no longer responsible for their food and clothing. We hear of descendants of these slaves who went to Ohio, bearing the names of their masters in Greenup County. Some free Negroes chose to come from the farms to Greenup, and their descendants are as well mannered and as capable as were their ancestors. In the old days the mistress of the household would oversee and perhaps cut out the clothes for the Negroes to be finished by the Negro women. Those early "uncles and aunties" have passed out of the picture with their "white" folks, but between the descendants of both there is the most kindly feeling.

After the Civil War the Waring Negroes came into Greenup to live. They were very black in color, as were also Uncle Nelse Warnock and his wife, Amanda, who lived in their own home on the corner of Perry and Washington Streets. Beyond them lived Uncle Charlie and Aunt Delilah Green. Next to their home was the frame building used for both church and school. Across the street was the home of Uncle Harrison and Aunt Mary Wheatley. All these folks owned their homes and made a living for themselves. Uncle Harrison was janitor of the Christian Church and also of the Academy, while Aunt Mary did washing for the "white folks." Perry Thomas lived on Perry Street and was porter for the Kouns House for many years.

On upper Main Street lived Uncle Nelse and Aunt Evaline Jackson, who owned their home, had beautiful flowers and a nice garden. Uncle Nelse was the preacher at the Negro church, and janitor of the Southern Methodist Church. On Tuesday evenings at the prayer meeting the leader, Mr. Jimmie Winters, often called on Uncle Nelse to pray, which he did very well.

In East Greenup lived the McConnell Negroes, who had belonged to the Hon. John McConnell on a large farm above Greenup. When the McConnell family sold the farm to the Wurts family, the Negroes came to Greenup to live and have owned their own homes ever since. The Martin Negroes also came from the James Martin farm above Riverton to East Greenup, while the King Negroes remained near the original King land near Riverton.

Belle and Sadie McMullan were among the first teachers in the Negro church-school building. They were the daughters of James McMullan, who lived on the southeast corner of Perry and Washington Streets. Before this, Miss Mary Hollingsworth (later Mrs. W. J. Sands) taught Negro children in the old Kouns home on Elizabeth and Main Streets. Fannie Carter was one of the first Negro teachers in the schools.

When the Stark family moved from Oldtown to Greenup in 1858 they brought Aunt Sukey and her children with them and some of them lived near "Miss Betsy" as long as she lived. Aunt Sukey took care of "Miss Betsy's" three children always, and when the Mitchell family moved to the Stark farm at Oldtown in 1868, Aunt Sukey's Kate went along to take care of "Miss Fannie's" children. Georgeann, Aunt Sukey's granddaughter (Kate's daughter), was living with the Mitchell family near Ashland when "Miss Fannie" died, and then she went to the home at Greenup where she died of the same fever.

Another case of loyalty of slave to master was that of Uncle Harrison Wheatly. When Aunt Mary died, he went up in Ohio to live with his son, but was not satisfied and came to the William Biggs home at Mt. Zion, Kentucky. When he told the family how he felt, Mr. Biggs told him to get some of his things together and fix up the old house in the yard, and there Uncle Harrison lived contentedly until he died. William Biggs, Sr., had bought Uncle Harrison from the Wheatly family in slavery days, but his name was never changed from Wheatly.

At Wurtland Dick Rawlings had bought his freedom from the Rawlings family and owned his home. Another of the Rawlings Negroes fought in the Civil War.

John Young came to Palmyra in 1784 with his wife, two children, a Negro man, and three Negro women. They were the first settlers of that community. Christina Young, one of the three Negro women, lived at Young Ford on Sandy and was said to have been one hundred and eleven years of age when she died.

In Greenup, in the 1880's, lived Maria Black, who was a milliner. She was started in the business by Mrs. Eliza Vandyke, and was a woman of excellent taste, patronized by the best people of the town.

Notices printed in the *Telegraph*, a Portsmouth, Ohio, newspaper, concerning runaway slaves from Greenup County owners:

(Evans' *History of Scioto County*)

In 1820 Thomas B. King offered a reward of $50 for the return of a runaway Negro from his farm four miles above Portsmouth.

Tignal Womack advertised for the return of his Negro, Daniel, in 1826.

In 1831 Henry Blake advertised a reward of $50 for the return of a Negro boy, Edward Ringo, from the Greenup Iron Works.

In 1832 H. Blake and Company offered a reward of $50 for a Negro named Isaac.

In 1836 James Martin offered $50 reward for the return of William, a Negro man.

Nathaniel Morton advertised in 1846 for the return of a black boy, Sam, and offered a $100 reward.

In 1855 a reward of $100 was offered by Mrs. Hannah Parker for the return of a Negro, George.

Two

COURT RECORDS

GREENUP COUNTY COURT RECORDS OF 1804

On the 20th day of February, 1804, a small group of men met at the home of Andy Hood for the purpose of establishing a Court of Sessions for the new County of Greenup. Thomas Waring, Jesse Boone, and Seriah Stratton were the first Justices of the Court.

John Nichols, Reuben Rucker, John Davis Poage, Charles N. Lewis, Moses Fouquay (Fuqua), Jr., John Chadwick, George Hardwick, and Jacob Lockwood produced a commission from His Excellency, the Governor of Kentucky, constituting and appointing them Justices of the Peace in and for the said County of Greenup. Whereupon the said Reuben Rucker administered the Oath of Fidelity to the Commonwealth of Kentucky, the pledge to support the Constitution of the United States, and the oath of office as Justice of the Peace to the said John Nickols, who then administered the said oath to the said Reuben Rucker, John Davis Poage, Charles N. Lewis, Moses Fuqua, Jr., John Chadwick and Jacob Lockwood.

Thereupon a court was held for the County of Greenup, agreeable to an act, establishing a new county out of Mason County. Josiah Davidson produced a commission from the governor appointing him Sheriff of Greenup County. Whereupon he took the necessary oath and entered into bond with Jesse Boone and Reuben Rucker, his securities, as the law directs. The court then appointed Isaac Hockaday as the Clerk pro tem. Whereupon he took the necessary oath and entered into bond with John Nichols and Jesse Boone, his securities. It was ordered that James Howe be appointed Commissioner of the Revenue

Tax for the present year. Whereupon he took the necessary oath with Robert Poage as his security. On the motion of Isaac Hockaday, Clerk of the Court, John Hockaday is permitted to take the necessary oath, with John Nichols, Moses Fuqua and William Lowery bound to Governor James Garard in the sum of 1000 pounds.

On the motion of Jesse Boone it is ordered that John Mackoy, Andrew Hood, Josiah Davidson and Andrew Wolf be appointed to view the necessary and best way for a road to be opened from the county line opposite the mouth of the Scioto River to the mouth of the Big Sandy and make report of same to the court.

Court ordered that Thomas Waring be exempted from payment of a county levy for his Negro woman, named Nelly, on account of age and infirmities.

James Clark and Thomas Daugherty qualified as attorneys-at-law. James Clark was appointed Commonwealth Attorney.

The first grand jury was composed of Robert Poage, Robert Davidson, John Davis Poage, William Lowery, David Ellington, Benjamin Uling, Thomas Hood, Absolom Burton, James Lowery, James Norton, Jesse Griffith, James McGinness, James Warnick, John How, John Terrill, Andrew Hood and William Dupuy.

The first case in court was Christopher Stump, plaintiff, against Aaron Littlejohn.

In July, 1804 a Negro slave, property of John How, was charged with stealing, taking and carrying away, a pair of overalls, the property of William Robinson, to the value of nine shillings. He was found not guilty.

New names appearing in this court were: John Davisson, Tilman Short, Moses Kibby, Reuben Rucker, Daniel Wilford, Robert Kirkpatrick and Lewis Davisson. Fifty pence was allowed each witness for two days.

October 15, 1804—The Commonwealth against Nancy Bailey, Ann Foster, and Robert Kirkpatrick for breach of the peace.

October 16, 1804—The following cases were tried: Solomon Saveall of the demise of David White, plaintiff, against Simpleton Spendall, defendant. Josiah Davidson, Sheriff. Hugh McGary, plaintiff, against George Shortridge and received judgment to the amount of 450 pounds, 10 shillings with interest from November 1, 1797.

January 19, 1805—William McClure was tried for having counterfeit money.

FIRST COURTHOUSE

The first courthouse was built of logs on the same site as the present one. At the June 1, 1807 session of the court it was ordered that the following repairs be made: "An addition to the west end, a door with shutters, seats therein sufficient for twenty-four men, a wooden chimney at the west end, a puncheon floor, and seats to be done in such a manner as the superintendent may direct. It is further ordered that J. D. Poage, John Poage, and Francis Waring be appointed to superintend and let out the foregoing addition and repairs upon the best terms that can be done, the expense thereof to be laid in the next county levy. Ordered that court be adjourned with court convenes.

"ROBERT D. DAWSON, J. P."

A square brick courthouse was built in 1811-1816 on the same site as the log one. The judge sat on the south side of the room about four feet above the bar where the lawyers sat. His platform was sixteen feet long and four feet wide, bannistered off, and had steps at each end. The main floor was about twenty inches below the bar and was laid with brick. This building was improved later. It was the courthouse that was in use for one hundred and twenty-three years and was badly damaged in the 1937 flood. In 1939 it was torn down and the present courthouse was built on the old site.

The clerk's office was a small brick building that stood on the bank of the river north of the courthouse and contained but two rooms.

The jail was built of brick and stood on the south side of the courthouse, facing Main street. This was torn down in the 1890's and the present jail at the corner of Elizabeth Street and Cedar Alley was built.

CIRCUIT COURT

May 6, 1806—Circuit Court was established with Hon. John Colwin, Circuit Judge; Thomas Waring and Jesse Boone, Assistant Judges; John Hockaday, Clerk; Thomas Grayson, Commonwealth Attorney; Thomas Daugherty, David Trimble, Robert Grayson, James Clark, and William Roper, Attorneys-at-law; Amos Kibby, Charles Lewis and William Lowery, Security.

In the circuit clerk's office there is a letter written by Abraham Lincoln, reporting a survey made by him. A receipt signed by him shows his fee to have been $5.00. (1831)

There is also a letter from Henry Clay, relating to a fee due him by members of the Grayson estate (1819). There is another of Albemarle County, Virginia, a deposition in an action against Samuel Bell. (1812)

The following records were copied from the original by Mr. Robert Robb, now deceased.

A court record of July 7, 1806 reads "Ordered that Jacob Kouns, Moses Fuqua and Charles N. Lewis let out and superintend the building of a temporary courthouse in the Public Square."

At a court held for Greenup County on Monday, June 2, 1806, present John Davis Poage, Charles N. Lewis, Robert D. Poage, Robert D. Dawson, Francis Waring, and John Poage, Gentlemen: "Ordered that a public jail for Greenup County be built of the following description: First, that a bed of stone be laid six inches thick, fourteen feet square, for the foundation of said jail. The outside wall made of square hewed logs 12 inches square, let down close together with a half dufftale, a wall built on the inside of said wall of shaved logs, seven inches by twelve inches, set on their edge, let down in the same manner as the outside wall, leaving a space of four inches between the two said walls to be filled with flat stones or gravel; to be laid with hewed logs, twelve inches thick, seven feet between the lower and second floor. The second floor to be laid with two tier of square logs twelve inches thick crossing each other. The second story to be raised with logs twelve inches square plumb with the outside of the lower story, seven feet high with a floor made of logs twelve inches thick. The roof to be made of joint shingles. The doors, etc. to be made as commissioners direct. The commissioners to superintend and let out the building of said jail, either by private or public contract as they may think proper. Also stocks and whipping post."

This first jail was situated in the center of the town on the site where the Methodist Episcopal Church now stands.

In 1811 John Young had a contract to build a courthouse, which was probably the one finished in 1816.

Also in 1811 Jesse Boone was allowed £3.8 for building a jail. It is known that the brick used in the construction of these buildings, also the clerk's office, was burned on the Rankins farm below the town.

A very early marriage license was issued September 16, 1804, by the county clerk, John Hockaday, to Jacob Neal and Sallie Kouns, daughter of Jacob Kouns. Jacob Kouns and John

Hockaday were great-great-grandfathers of Mrs. Juliet Hockaday Collins of Greenup.

There is found under date of 1817 a record of an action wherein a "girl of color," named America, was the plaintiff in action against Thomas Ward, defendant, for her freedom from slavery. This action was based upon the claim made by America, a slave girl, because of her departure from Kentucky, a slave state, to Ohio, then a free state; that by virtue of this act she had become free and was therefore entitled to her freedom. This action was tried by Judge Kouns and Samuel McKee, which in their opinion sustained the contention of the plaintiff and granted her her freedom.

The principal acts set out and proven in this case were that the slave, America, went as a nurse with her mistress from the town of Greenup, Kentucky, to the village of Haverhill, Ohio, to attend a party. After the party she refused to return to Kentucky and maintained as aforesaid that by reason of her entering a free state she had obtained her freedom. It is interesting to note that the question involved in this case, and the circumstances stated, present the question decided to the contrary in the Dred-Scott case by the Supreme Court of the United States immediately preceding the Civil War. It is maintained by many older citizens that they were advised by their forebears that the suit was, if not the first, among the first, to present this question in a Court of Justice of the United States.

COURT RECORDS 1813—1818

1813 Moses Fuqua, Jr., was the sheriff, with Jacob Kouns and Thomas Ward his deputies.

The law was administered by justices of the peace and the following men were the justices (judges) in the years from 1813 to 1818:

Francis Waring	David Brown (Removed)
John Poage	James Van Bibber (Resigned)
—Benjamin Chinn	John R. Chitwood
Jonathan Morton (deceased)	~James Ward, Sr.
Jacob M. Ham (deceased)	Thomas B. King
Robert G. Grayson	Martin Smith (Resigned)
Robert Henderson	Nimrod Canterbury
Richard Wheatly (Removed)	William Lowry
Levi Shortridge	

Jailers in these years were John Bartley, Joshua Bartley, Oba Timberlake, and Andrew Biggs.

There were three voting precincts, Greenupsburg, Sandy Licks (Raccoon), and Big Sandy.

John Hockaday, James Van Bibber and Martin Smith were appointed commissioners to let the contract for finishing the courthouse.

James Van Bibber was given permission to operate a ferry across Little Sandy near the Falls. Rates were 6¼ cents for man and same for a horse.

Bounties were paid at the November term of court on thirty wolf heads at $1.50 and $2.00 each.

Jonathan Morton and James Van Bibber were appointed judges of the ensuing election at Greenupsburg precinct with Irvine Hockaday, clerk; David Brown and Robert Henderson were appointed judges at the Sandy Licks precinct, with Benedict Bacer their clerk; Jacob M. Ham and Reuben Canterbury were appointed judges at Big Sandy precinct with Levi Shortridge their clerk.

Of the men mentioned above the Waring families lived on Tygart Creek and at Gray's Branch; the Poage families, in the eastern part of the county; the Chinn families, near Wurtland (Oil Works); Jonathan Morton and his wife, Letitia, at Gray's Branch; Jacob M. Ham, Reuben Canterbury, and the Shortridge families, near Big Sandy; James Van Bibber, at the Falls of Little Sandy; the Chitwood and Ward families, below Greenupsburg; Thomas B. King, at the mouth of Tygart; Martin Smith, below the Fulton Oil Works; the Hockaday and Jesse Boone families, above, and Andrew Biggs, in Greenupsburg.

1814   William Bradshaw was permitted to operate a ferry "from his lands, across the Ohio River to the opposite shore." Rates 12½ cents for man and same for a horse.

Samuel Demint produced credentials as to his being in regular communion with the Methodist Society and having taken the necessary oaths was permitted to solemnize the "rights of matrimony" according to the rules of said church. Jacob Kouns was sheriff and Nathan Kouns, deputy. At this time many new roads were opened and old ones were changed. Bounties were paid on eighteen wolf heads at $1.50 each.

1815   (Jacob Kouns, sheriff, and Nathan Kouns was his deputy.) Ordered that David Brown, Justice of the Peace, be authorized to solemnize the "rights of matrimony," there not being enough ordained ministers.

Ordered that the sheriff pay Benjamin Locke and Amos Kimball for finishing the courthouse $258.00.

That Roland Gaines, on motion of the Commonwealth, purchase *Littell's Laws of Kentucky* in four volumes, paying $15.00 collected from fines, and the sheriff is ordered to furnish such sum as is necessary in addition to said sum.

That Joseph Gardner be permitted to keep tavern at his dwelling house in this county for one year from date hereof.

That William L. Gholson be permitted to keep tavern at his dwelling house in this county for one year from this date.

That a writ of *ad quod damnum* be granted to Levi Johnson for the erection of a water grist mill on the east fork of Little Sandy.

That Richard S. Wheatly be summoned to the court to show why he should not be "fined and tribble taxed" for failure to give in his list of taxable property.

That John Young be appointed Commissioner "in the room of" Robert Poage, deceased, for the purpose of Dividing and Conveying land between residents and nonresidents of the county.

1816   January. Andrew Biggs is appointed Jailer "in the room of" Oba Timberlake, resigned.

Oba Timberlake is permitted to keep tavern at his dwelling house in this county for one year from date hereof.

Reuben Canterbury produced a Commission appointing him sheriff of this county and entered into bond with Amos Kibby, Armistead C. Bragg, Horatio Catlett, George N. Davis, Aaron Young and Alex Catlett, Jr.

On motion of Reuben Canterbury, George N. Davis is permitted to qualify as his deputy.

On motion of Alex Catlett, Jr., he is permitted to keep tavern at his dwelling house for one year from date hereof.

A writ was granted to Turner Crump for the erection of a water grist mill on Clay Lick Creek.

On motion of William Dupuy, a ferry was established from his land across the Ohio River to the opposite shore. Rates as follows: "for a single man 12½ cents, and for a horse the same."

On motion of Jacob Kouns, he is permitted to keep tavern at his dwelling house in this county for one year from the date hereof.

On motion of George N. Davis, deputy sheriff of this county, proof being made of the absence of Reuben Canterbury, sheriff of the county, it is ordered that William Ward be permitted to qualify as deputy.

November. The court proceeded to lay the county levy for the present year to wit: Claims allowed bounties paid on two "wolf scalps at $1.50 each," salaries and fees allowed.

Ordered that a ferry established across the Ohio River from the mouth of Little Sandy be discontinued on motion of James McGuire, since a ferry is established across the Ohio River to the opposite shore from his Lot No. 1 in Greenupsburg. Rates were established as follows: each man 12½ cents and for each horse the same.

John M. McConnell took the necessary oaths and the duelling oath as Attorney-at-law whereupon he was permitted to practice as such in this Court.

John Young, surveyor of the county, returned a "Platt" of the County and it is ordered to be recorded.

1817 January. Lucy, a Negro woman slave of Stephen Wilson's, was summoned to appear this day on charge of "feloniously and burglariously" breaking open a trunk, taking, stealing, and carrying away, to the amount of $196 in bank notes from Elisha Catlett, to be tried by a Jury of twelve good and lawful men.

On motion of Horatio Catlett it is ordered that the Clerk of this Court bind out to the said Catlett, George W. White, an orphan, to learn Bookkeeping, as the law directs.

Ordered that Martin Smith and Benjamin Chinn be appointed Judges of the ensuing election and John Hockaday their Clerk in the Greenupsburg precinct.

That Nimrod Canterbury and William Buchannon be appointed Judges and Levi Shortridge Clerk at the Big Sandy precinct.

That James Ward and Robert Henderson be appointed Judges and Richard Hampton Clerk in the Little Sandy precinct.

Richard Deering is permitted to establish a ferry across Little Sandy from the lands of said Richard Deering to Lowry's Falls on the opposite shore, with rates 6¼ cents for a man and 12½ cents for man and horse.

June. The Court proceeded to fix tavern rates as follows: For breakfast 37½ cents, dinner 37½ cents, and supper 37½ cents, for good brandy one half pint 50 cents, for good rum, wine or Holland 50 cents, for whiskey per one half pint 12½ cents, for cider and beer per quart 12½ cents, for lodging per night 12½ cents, for horse feed per gallon oats or corn 12½ cents, for horse to stay twelve hours 25 cents, for horse to stall and feed 50 cents, and for horse to pasture 12½ cents for twelve or twenty-four hours.

Ordered that the several Ordinary Keepers of the county take and receive the above rates and no more.

The writ of *ad quod damnum* granted to Robert Daugherty for the erection of a water grist mill near the Falls of Little Sandy.

The writ of *ad quod damnum* is granted to Richard Deering for the erection of a water grist mill on Little Sandy.

Ordered that it be certified to the Judge of the Court of Appeals and General Circuit Court of this Commonwealth that Benjamin Aills of this county is a gentleman of honesty, probity and good demeanor.

An instrument of writing from under the hand and seal of George N. Davis purporting to emancipate a Negro slave named Jack; the property of the said George N.

Davis was this day accounted and ordered. It is therefore ordered that the said Negro man named Jack be emancipated and set at liberty and that the clerk of the Court issue him a certificate to that effect, it appearing to the Court that the said Negro is not aged and infirm and is not likely to become chargeable to the county.

This Court doth receive a post and rail pen built by John Littlejohn as the publick stray pen for this County. John Hockaday is directed to pay over to the said John Littlejohn $13.50 the amount of money in his hands and George N. Davis, Sheriff of the county, to pay over to the said John Littlejohn $4.50 in full payment.

November. The Court proceeded to lay a levy for the present year and to receive claims to wit:

To William Dupuy for two young wolf heads $2.00

To John Wilson for one old wolf head $1.50

To officials of the county salaries and claims against the County allowed.

To James Warnock for ferrying Grand Jurymen across the mouth of Little Sandy for the year 1818, $6.00. Fines collected $75.03½, total income $273.46½ and $75.03½ combined makes a total of $348.50 less $277.15½ expenses which leaves a deposition of $71.34½.

Ordered that $50.50 be placed in the hands of John Hockaday for the purpose of procuring a stove for the use of the Greenup County Courthouse out of the fines collected and paid by George N. Davis and Andrew Biggs.

Ordered that the Jailor make the necessary repairs to the Jail door. The sheriff enters his objections to the sufficiency of the Jail of this county.

Ordered that Francis Waring and John Poage Gentlemen be nominated to his excellency the Governor of the Commonwealth of Kentucky as proper persons to fill the office of Sheriff of this county.

January 19th. Cynthia and Nathan Fuqua, orphans of Mary Fuqua, came into Court and made choice of Moses M. Fuqua as their guardian, they being over the age of fourteen years. Moses M. Fuqua entered into bond with Thomas B. King as security.

On motion of John Young, Surveyor of Greenup County, John Powell is permitted to qualify as his Deputy.

On motion of Thomas B. King as Justice of the Peace of Greenup County he is permitted to celebrate the rite of matrimony in this county.

On motion of Francis Waring, Sheriff of Greenup County, George Washington Ward is permitted to qualify as his deputy.

Ordered that James H. Waring be appointed Commissioner of the Revenue Law for the present year.

On motion of Lewis M. N. Reason he is permitted to keep a tavern at his dwelling house in the county for one year from date hereof.

On motion of Mordacai Williams he is permitted to keep tavern at his dwelling house in this county for one year from date hereof.

1818   May 25th. The last Will and Testament of Thomas Waring was produced in Court and was ordered to be recorded. Lydia Waring, widow of said deceased, and Clement H. Waring entered into bond with Francis Waring, Thomas T. G. Waring and Bazil Waring as their securities.

June. Ordered that Thomas B. King and John Poage be Judges of the ensuing election, with George Bartley Clerk, at the Greenupsburg precinct.

Ordered that Levi Shortridge and Nimrod Canterbury be appointed Judges at the Big Sandy precinct with Richard W. Price their Clerk.

Ordered that James Ward and Robert Henderson be appointed Judges at the Big Sandy precinct with Richard Hampton their Clerk.

Ordered that the Court be adjourned until Court in Course.

JOHN POAGE

NOVEMBER COURT 1813

Jacob Kouns and Reuben Canterberry the two Senr. Justices of this county as proper persons to fill that office.

The Court proceeded to lay the county levy, to wit,

	$	¢
To Matthew Small one old wolf	1.	50
To Gabriel Scott one young Do (Ditto)	1.	-
To Daniel Perry one Do Do	1.	-
To James Warnock one old Do	1.	50

To Robert Smith one old Do	1.	50
To Aaron Short two old Do	3.	-
To Johnson Warnock one old Do	1.	50
To Thomas Hood one old Do	1.	50
To Same Same	1.	50
To Johnson Warnock one old Do	1.	50
To Thomas Hood one old Do	1.	50
To Same Same	1.	50
To Josiah Morton one old Do	1.	50
To Samuel Warnock one old Do	1.	50
To Francis Waring Jr. one old Do	1.	50
To Andrew Mefford two old Do	3.	-
To Clement H. Waring one old Do	1.	50
To Thomas T. G. Waring two old Do	3.	-
To Andrew Zornes one young Do	1.	-
To Thomas Sammons one old Do	1.	50
To Josiah Davisson one old Do	1.	50
To William Bradshaw two old Do	3.	-
To James Waring Sr. two old Do	3.	-
To Thomas Hood one old wolf	1.	50
To Peter Jones one old Do	1.	50
To Pleasant Ellington eight young wolves	8.	-
To Same two old wolves	3.	-
To John W. Howe one old wolf	1.	50
To Martin Smith acc't. filed and sworn to	4.	-
To Benj. Chinn and Francis Waring, Judges of last election, 2 days each in Greenupsburg Precinct	4.	-
To their clerk 2 days	2.	-
To Jacob Kouns and Francis H. Gaines, judges of last election, 2 days each in Sandy Lick precinct	4.	-
To their clerk 2 days	2.	-
To Reuben Canterberry and William Buchhannon judges of last election 1 day each in Big Sandy precinct	2.	-
To their clerk one day	1.	-
	$75.	-
To the Sheriff for ex officio services for the present year	40.	-
To the Clerk for same	40.	-
	$155.	-
To Richard S. Wheatly as Commonwealth Commissioner in County Court for the last four months of his services as such	16.	16¼
	$171.	16¼ ¢
To Oba S. Timberlake for attending this court as Jailor 5 days	5.	-
	$176.	16¼
By $18. fines collected and paid by Thomas Richards, Constable to Irvine Hockaday and Thomson Ward in Lieu of their claims	18.	-
	$158.	16¼
By 515 tithes at 37½ per tithe	193.	12½
	158.	16¼
To a deposition of	**$34.**	96¼

Ordered that the Court be adjourned until Court in Course.

JACOB KOUNS

COUNTY COURT NOTES
December Term 1851
Loaned by J. B. Merrill.

The Hon. James Bryan, presiding.

Upon the death of Thomas Bagney, Esq., Justice of the Peace of the First District, Robert Gilbert was appointed by the Court to fill the vacancy.

On motion of R. W. Waring, sheriff, Obadiah Mackoy was permitted to take necessary oath as his deputy.

On motion of William Corum, Clerk, James Van Bibber was permitted to take the oath as deputy in his office.

On motion of George Chinn, one of the heirs of Benjamin Chinn, deceased, it was ordered that A. H. Meade, E. J. Hockaday, A. Cole, and T. Roach be appointed to divide the estate of the deceased in pursuance of the last will of the said Benjamin Chinn.

Ordered that Henry Hardwick, I. R. Poynter, and Benjamin King be appointed overseers of roads and their hands (workmen), in opening and cutting out the new road leading from Argillite to Laurel Furnace.

Ordered that Alexander Rankins be allowed the sum of $10.00 for ferrying the grand jurors and militiamen for the last year.

CIRCUIT COURT
July 1853

Allen Myers was jailor of Greenup County at this time. Marshall Baker and Cyrus Van Bibber were his deputies.

Zachariah Richards, James Howland, and George Howland have produced in open court certificates of having killed wild cats in the county and were allowed one dollar each per head for the same.

In the case of the Commonwealth against Elijah Artist, colored, charged with petit larceny, on trial by a jury, was sentenced to thirty lashes on the bare back at the public whipping post, the same to be administered by the sheriff of the county.

At the jury trial the following gentlemen served as Grand Jurors: (sixteen in number served then where now we have twelve) James McMullen, foreman, Calvin Carnifax, John Howe, Joseph Davidson, Jesse Davidson, John Hartley, H. A. Poage, Edward Brooks, Daniel Iliff, Vincent Colvin, Acy Billow, Elza Allison, William Jones, N. F. Thom, George Womack and Jabez Z. Coe.

The examining trial judge in the case prior to the trial in Circuit Court was Judge James Bryan.

William Guilky convicted on the charge of operating a tippling house for the thirsty element was fined in the sum of $60.00.

William Wills produced in open court the certificate of John E. Dunn, Esq., of his having killed three wild cats and was allowed one dollar each per head for the same.

The *Big Sandy News*, a newspaper owned and published by E. C. Thornton and G. W. Smith, was commissioned by the court to do all the public printing at this time for Greenup County. (This paper was edited in Catlettsburg, then in Greenup County).

November 1854

At the November term of court came John McKee and made formal application for citizenship in the United States and was admitted. He was a subject of Great Britain and had resided in this county for a period of five years prior to his admission. Also John Mock was admitted. He came from Grand Duchy of Baden, in Germany.

March 1857

In pursuance to an act of the legislature Joshua Oaks and John C. Kouns appeared in court and executed bond as Ferry Keepers across the Ohio River.

After many adjournments and disagreements among the court officials it was finally decided to carpet the floor of the courtroom. Allen Myers was directed to purchase twenty spittoons for the room after the laying of the carpet. The spitting proposition held up the purchase of the carpet for several days, but the spittoons being offered as a compromise, carried the day.

On motion of William Corum, clerk, John Seaton was sworn in as his deputy.

On motion of Robert Galbraith, surveyor, S. H. Walcott took the oath of deputy.

Ordered that G. W. Darlington be appointed committee to procure a standard of measures for Greenup County and that Robert Galbraith be appointed as keeper of the same.

Sanford Hurn was allowed the sum of $17.00 for the making of a judges' stand in the courtroom.

John Schmutz was allowed $4.25 for plastering the courthouse.

Ten per cent interest was considered reasonable on borrowed money, the county having borrowed at that rate for the building of Tygart bridge.

August 1858

In the county election, August, 1858, William Corum was reelected clerk, S. H. Walcott was elected surveyor, Allen Myers was reelected jailor, John C. Adams was elected county judge and George E. Roe was elected county attorney.

John Myers produced in court his plan for the building of a new clerk's office and for the same was allowed $5.00.

James A. Sneed and Fielding Hardin having produced satisfactory evidence to the court of being in regular communion with the Methodist Protestant and the Baptist Churches, respectively, upon giving the usual bond, were permitted to celebrate the rites of matrimony.

S. H. Walcott and Jesse Dupuy were appointed road commissioners, the former for that part of the county above Little Sandy and the latter for the western half of the county.

John M. Powell, deputy sheriff, was fined $3.00 by the court for failure to attend its sessions. Upon reconsidering, the court ordered the above order rescinded.

Upon the application of Jesse Corum to lease from the county a portion of the public square for the erection of an office building for himself at the corner of Main and Washington Streets, the court did lease him the ground for a period of thirty-five years, the building to be brick and at no time to be used other than for an office building, he to pay the county at the rate of $10.00 annually. (No brick building was erected there.)

H. M. Rust entered into a similar lease with the county for that part of the public square that fronts on Main and Harrison Streets.

January 1859

At the January term of court George M. Darlington produced to the court a certificate of his election to the office of sheriff of Greenup County and together with C. M. Wilson, A. L. Reid, J. L. Waring, and James Bryan, as his sureties, entered into a covenant to the Commonwealth of Kentucky for bonds, etc.

Upon motion of George W. Darlington, sheriff, James Morton and O. W. Martin took the necessary oaths as his deputies. The newly elected Justices of the Peace of the county were:

W. A. Womack, Samuel Powell, Jefferson Keeton, James Rouse, George W. McClure, Hugh A. Poage, P. B. Byrne, John Miller, John T. King, Francis Waring, and Charles Pearce.

The then presiding Judge, John C. Adams, is responsible for the excellent bell which now rests in the cupola of the courthouse. Having made a trip to Pittsburgh, as special commissioner, he bought the bell, the old bell being exchanged with much extra currency for the new one.

John C. Adams, the presiding judge, was granted permission to build a law office on one of the corners of the public square near the river front.

Front Street was then known as Water Street and John E. Winn conducted a "Saddler Shop" thereon.

W. C. Ireland, Lewis D. Ross, and George E. Roe were appointed special commissioners to buy a poor farm for the county. They were instructed to expend $1000.00 and the land not to be more than ten miles from the courthouse. (This was bought at Wurtland.)

COUNTY COURT JUSTICES AND JUDGES
1804-1949

Court of Sessions was organized February 20, 1804. Authority was vested in justices of the peace who were appointed as needed to enforce the law and these justices served unless removed by death, moved from the county, or resigned. There were eight justices appointed in 1804, by the Governor of Kentucky. The first justice was Reuben Rucker, who administered the oath of fidelity to the others, who were John Nicholls, John Davis Poage, Charles N. Lewis, Moses Fuqua, Jr., John Chadwick, George Hardwick, and Jacob Lockwood.

Justices were appointed until about 1850, when James Bryan, a justice, became the first judge of the county. Besides those justices named above, others from 1804 to 1850 were:

Thomas Waring	David Brown	John Hollingsworth	William Hampton
Jesse Boone	James Van Bibber	Samuel Bartley	Jesse Poynter
Seriah Stratton	John R. Chitwood	Basil Waring	Clement H. Waring
John Poage	James Ward, Jr.	Jehu Rice	Abraham Crooks
Benjamin Chinn	Thomas B. King	George Naylor Davis	Robert Laughlin
Jonathan Morton	Martin Smith	Samuel Gammon	Christian Spangler
Jacob Ham	Nimrod Canterbury	Jesse Corum	James Stewart
Robert H. Grayson	William Lowry	Robert J. Harrison	Benjamin F. King
Robert Henderson	Levi Shortridge	John Brown	James Bryan
Richard Wheatly	John C. Kouns	William Kouns	William A. Womack

From 1850 to the present time the county judges were:

James Bryan	1850	William T. Cole	1900
John Poage	1854	W. J. A. Rardin	1908
John Seaton	1858	J. Watt Womack	1912
J. D. McCoy	1862	Lewis Nicholls	1916
William J. Worthington	1866	Dow Quillen	1922
A. L. Reid	1870	Robert Parsons	1926
Lewis Nicholls	1884	William H. Wheatly	1930
J. W. Kouns (Billy)	1892	J. R. Shepherd	1934
Joseph B. Bennett	1898	Jacob Fisher	1938
		G. W. Burchett	1942

CIRCUIT JUDGES

This list of judges was furnished by Judge James R. Sowards.

1804	Thomas Waring	1823	Adam Beatty
	Jesse Boone	1824	William Roper
	Seriah Stratton	1833	Walker Reed
1805	John Coburn	1835	Silas Robbins (Special)
	Thomas Waring	1851	James W. Moore
	Jesse Boone	1856	Elijah C. Phister
1811	William McClung	1864	L. W. Andrews
	Thomas Waring	1868	R. H. Stanton
	Jesse Boone	1874	George Morgan Thomas
1815	Adam Beatty	1876	William H. Wadsworth (Special)
	Thomas Waring	1882	Alfred E. Cole
1816	W. T. Barry	1893	James P. Harbison
1818	Samuel McKee	1906	Stephen G. Kinner
	Benjamin Miller	1912	William C. Halbert
1819	Eli Shortbridge	1931	Harvey Parker
1822	Silas Robbins	1946	James R. Sowards

CIRCUIT CLERKS

In 1870 a law separating the county and circuit court clerks was passed. The circuit clerks were as follows:

Charles Davidson	1870-1912	Kelly Spears	1922-1928
Charles B. Bennett	1912-1916	John Setser	1928-1934
James D. Atkinson	1916-1922	William Coldiron	1934-1940
		Maynard Bush	1940-1949

COUNTY CLERKS

Isaac Hockaday	1803	John Prichard	1916-1916
John Hockaday	1804-1836	Alva Cochran	1916-1922
William Corum	1836-1876	Joseph B. Bates	1922-1938
George Corum	1876-1908	John Millis	1938-1950
Stephen Howland	1908-1916 (Died)	J. L. O'Bryan	1950-

SHERIFFS

In the early days of the county the sheriff had to cover a great deal of territory, as parts of what is now Lawrence, Carter, and Boyd Counties were included in Greenup County. At that time the high sheriff had but one deputy. In 1812, because of the War with Great Britain, two deputies were appointed to serve under Sheriff Moses Fuqua, Jr. In 1842, before the War with Mexico, Sheriff Samuel S. Gammon had three deputies. There was a great deal of trouble at this time because of runaway slaves. For this reason James Morton and Adolphus Reid had four deputies in 1861-1864.

At this time a great deal of ill feeling arose between slave owners and those men who had come from the North to operate furnaces in the county. It was the sheriff's business to protect the furnaces. Also, the illegal sale of liquor caused much trouble between those who made it and the government. In the 1870's when the making of liquor became more commercialized, the government took vigorous action. From 1870 until recent years there has been but one deputy sheriff.

SHERIFFS OF GREENUP COUNTY

Listed below are all of the sheriffs and deputies since the county was organized. This list was compiled by William Adkins, while he was sheriff. You will notice that the first sheriff was Josiah Davidson, and there was a very interesting tale in regard to Davidson. He had been in office but a short time when he was obliged to deliver a prisoner to the state prison at the capital of Kentucky. He took two deputies with him on the trip and was gone twelve days. He was paid a dollar a day for himself and ninety cents for his two deputies.

Another gentleman on the list who is well known and respected by all in Greenup is Mr. J. Watt Womack. "Mr. Watt" was a mere stripling when he was elected sheriff, the youngest in the state of Kentucky, and he established a record for efficiency in the state.

Taylor Lawson, George Biggs, Thomas Meyers, William Corum, Jr., Marshall Baker, John C. Kouns, and many others have descendants who are still living in the county.

The following are sheriffs and deputies and the years served in that order:

Sheriff	Deputy	Years Served
Josiah Davidson	Benjamin Ulin	1804-1805
Reuben Rucker	Ambrose Rucker	1806-1807-1808-1809
Charles Lewis	James Ward	1810-1811
Moses Fuqua, Jr.	Jacob Kouns, Jr.	1812-1813
	Thomas Ward	
Jacob Kouns	Nathan Kouns	1814-1815
Reuben Canterberry	Geo. N. Davis	1816-1817
Francis Waring	William Ward	1818-1819

Sheriff	Deputy	Years Served
John Poage	William Ward	1820-1821-1822
Ben Chinn	Geo. N. Davis	1823-1824
	John Rice	
Robert Henderson	James Ward	1825-1826
	William Ward	
James Ward	Geo. N. Ward, Jr.	1827
Thomas B. King	Geo. Garrett	1828-1829
	Clifton A. Garrett	
Thomas T. G. Waring	John Culver	1830-1831
John Culver	William Biggs	1832-1833
Thomas H. Poage	Romulus E. Culver	1834-1835
John C. Kouns	Harris W. Thompson	1836-1837
James Bartley	R. M. Biggs	1838-1839
G. N. Davis	James W. Davis	1840-1841
Sam'l W. Gammon	Geo. W. Darlington	1842-1843
	Thos. B. King	
	Roger W. Waring	
Clement H. Waring	Andrew Biggs	1844-1845
	Clem Swearingin	
	William Waring	
Basil Waring	James H. Waring	1846-1847
	Truman S. Waring	
	Chas. N. B. Raison	
Samuel Ratliff	Thos. Lawson	1848-1849
	Roger W. Waring	
John Brown	R. W. Waring	1850
	Jas. H. Waring	
	J. S. Gammon	
	Elba Ulen	
Roger Waring	Cyrus Vanbibber, Jr.	1851
	Thos. Waring	
	Robert Laughlin	
	James H. Waring	
Marshall Baker	Cyrus Van Bibber	1852-1853-1854-1855
	James I. Allen	
Geo. W. Darlington	James Morton	1856-1857-1858-1859-1860
	Oliver W. Martin	
James Morton	Mellon P. Willard	1861
	Evan D. Thomas	
	Augustus C. Van Dyke	
	Moses F. Dupuy	
Adolphus L. Reid	William Corum, Jr.	1862-1863-1864
	Moses F. Dupuy	
	George Rice	
	Stanford Hurn	
Robert McAllister	B. B. Roberts	1865-1866-1867-1868
	John E. Brooks	
John Brooks	Thos. E. Myers	1869-1870
John D. Russell	Geo. N. Biggs	1871-1872-1873-1874
Geo. N. Biggs	B. F. Warnock	Appointed Sept. 1, 1874 Served 4 months
B. F. Warnock	J. Watt Womack	1875-1876-1877-1878
	J. W. Kouns	
J. W. Kouns	J. Watt Womack	1879-1880-1881-1882
J. Watt Womack	W. B. Taylor	1883-1884-1885-1886
W. B. Taylor	John T. Womack	1887-1888-1890
John T. Womack	Taylor Lawson	1891-1892
Matthew Warnock	Denny Warnock	1893-1894
	James E. Morton	
James E. Morton	Patrick Artis	1895-1896-1897

Sheriff	Deputy	Years Served
John W. Collins	Samuel Bailey	1898-1899-1900-1901
Samuel Bailey	George Patterson	1902-1903-1904-1905
	Patrick Artis	
Patrick Artis	Geo. Patterson	1906-1907-1908-1909
Taylor Lawson	R. T. Lawson	1910-1911-1912-1913
W. M. Arthurs	J. Harve Elam	1914-1917
J. Harve Elam	William Anderson	1918-1921
Vernon Callihan	Ed. Tinsley	1922-1925
	J. R. Shepherd	
Ed Tinsley	George Crisp	1926-1929
	Ben Rowland	
George Crisp	William Adkins	1930-1933
	Jacob Fisher	
	Green Howard	
Jacob Fisher	William Adkins	1934-1937
	Green Howard	
	Robert Bradford	
G. W. Burchett	J. G. Nichols	1938-1941
	Mayo Stallard	
	Jim Timberlake	
Earl McKenzie	William Adkins	1942-1945
	Trace A. Rice	
William Adkins	J. O. Womack	1946-1949
	Delbert McKenzie	
	Brook Large	

EARLIEST MARRIAGE LICENSES

John Walker	and	Rachel McCool	Feb. 20, 1804
Rowland Cornelius	and	Ellenor Howe	Oct. 6, 1804
John Snedgar	and	Rosanna Shope	Oct. 13, 1804
John Deatly	and	Nancy McKenny	Oct. 16, 1804
Jacob Neal	and	Sally Kouns	Sept. 16, 1804
William Crank	and	Susanna Biggs	Mar. 4, 1805
John Briant	and	Catherine Shope	Apr. 1, 1805
Daniel Ratcliff	and	Stacy Frazier	May 12, 1805
James Ford	and	Elizabeth Fisher	May 17, 1805
Lewis Frazier	and	Elizabeth Ratcliff	May 18, 1805
James Gilkerson	and	Malinda Mayhew	Sept. 10, 1805
Jacob M. Ham	and	Sallie Stephenson	Nov. 27, 1805

EARLY MARRIAGE LICENSES OF LOCAL INTEREST

John C. Kouns	and	Elizabeth Smith	Nov. 21, 1818
Archer Womack	and	Miriam Kouns	July 4, 1823
John McCoy	and	Judith Morton	Nov. 20, 1820
Cyrus Van Bibber	and	Mary Timberlake	Dec. 26, 1821
Alex Rankins	and	Elizabeth Saunders	Feb. 2, 1825
Edwin Heisler	and	Rebecca Corum	Oct. 24, 1826
William Biggs	and	Lucy Davis	Oct. 15, 1827
Henry Blake	and	Martha Ann Hockaday	Dec. 1, 1830
William Corum	and	Edith Passmore	Dec. 3, 1834
William Kouns	and	Nancy Womack	Nov. 3, 1836
William Woodrow	and	Theresa Sophia Green	June 26, 1836
William Smith Kouns	and	Caroline Van Bibber	Oct. 21, 1841
John Seaton	and	Mary Elizabeth Rice	Nov. 19, 1845
John Hollingsworth	and	Elizabeth Ann Kouns	Dec. 1, 1845
Joseph Pollock	and	Sarah Kouns	Oct. 20, 1850

MARRIAGE LICENSE PAID FOR WITH WHISKEY

Zephaniah Bryan   and   Rachel Roman................July 11, 1807

Issued upon the permit of the bride's guardian, David Hogan. This was the first recorded license that was paid for with whiskey. The payment amounted to two barrels of whiskey.

CENSUS OF GREENUP COUNTY 1811

Alexander, John
Allison, John
Anglin, Gabriel
Anglin, John
Bacon, Benedict
Bainfield, Thomas
Ball, James
Ball, Robert
Bar, Henry
Barklow, Ruth
Barley, Wiatt
Barnes, Robert
Bartley, John
Bartley, Joshua
Baset, Amos
Bean, Stephen
Bell, Thompson
Benough, George
Biggs, Douglas
Blackburn, William
Blake, Kenneth
Blankenship
Boone, Jesse
Boone, Nathan
Bradshaw, George
Bradshaw, William
Bragg, Armstead
Barklow, Ruth
Broomfield, Skinner
Brown, Davis
Brown, John
Brown, Nelson
Brubaker, Abraham
Bruce, John
Bruce, William
Bryan, John
Bryan, Zephaniah
Bryson, William
Buckhannon, William
Buckles, Robert
Burbridge, Robert
Cain, John
Cam, Jacob
Cam, Job
Cam, Thomas
Campbell, Jesse
Campbell, Johnson
Cannon, John
Canterbury, Benjamin
Canterbury, John

Canterbury, Nimrod
Canterbury, Reuben
Carter, George
Carter, Hebe
Cartwright, Thomas
Cathwell, Robert
Catlett, Alex
Catlett, Alex, Jr.
Catlett, Horatio
Catlett, Elisha
Chadwick, John
Chaffin, Christopher
Chaffin, Nancy
Chapman, Reuben
Chinn, Benjamin
Chitwood, John R.
Clark, John
Clark, John, Jr.
Cob, John
Cohlin, Gideon
Colvin, John
Colvin, Samuel
Comelius, Austin
Craig, William
Crank, Jacob
Crank, John
Crank, Joseph
Craycraft, Charles
Creekpaun, Michell
Culp, Conlas
Culp, Tilman
Curren, Joseph
Curry, Henry
Cummings, Henry
Davis, George N.
Davis, Rezin
Davis, Samuel
Davisson, Josiah
Deering, Anthony
Deering, Richard
Demint, Samuel
Downs, John
Duncan, Alexander
Duncan, Charles
Drury, Salson (Lawson)?
Dummit, William
Dupuy, William
Durbin, Amos
Easom, Edward
Edwards, John

Ellington, John
Ellington, Pleasant
Evans, William
Everman, Jacob
Everman, John
Farmer, Jeremiah
Farmer, Joshua
Flaugher, Christian
Foster, Job
Friend, Andrew
Friend, Jacob
Friend, Jonas
Fuqua, David
Fuqua, Mary
Fuqua, Moses
Fuqua, Samuel
Fuqua, William
Gaine, Francis H.
Gammon, Richard
Garrett, Ignatius
Garden, Joseph
Gibson, James
Gholson, William
Gilkey, Edward
Goble, Abram
Goble, Daniel
Goble, Ephriam
Gorman, William
Grayson, Alfred
Grayson, George
Grayson, Robert
Greene, Robert H.
Greenslate, John
Hamm, Jacob
Hannah, Gabriel
Hannah, Robert
Hatch, Edward
Hatton, William
Hatton, Elijah
Hardwick, George
Hargus, John
Hedges, Solomon
Henderson, Robert
Henderson, Robert, Jr.
Hensley, George
Hitchcock, Caleb
Holland, Wright
Hockaday, John
Hood, Andrew
Hood, Thomas

Horseley, Taylor
Howe, James
Howe, John
Howe, Joseph
Huffman, Jacob
Huson, James
Jackson, Charles
Johnson, Levi
Jones, Peter
Jordan, William
Kibbee, Amos
Kibbee, Moses
Kilgour, David
Kiser, Jacob
Kite, James
Knap, Joshua
Kouns, Jacob
Kouns, John
Lacy, John
Lawson, Thomas
Lewis, Charles
Littlejohn, John
Littlejohn, Valentine
Lockwood, Jacob
Lowry, James
Lowry, John
Lowry, Melvin
Lowry, William
Lyons, Hezakiah
Mayhew, Ezra
Mayhew, Elijah
Mackoy, John
Madden, Nathan
McAlester, James
McCallister, James
McCallister, Luke
McGlone, Owen
McGlone, Andrew
McGuire, James
McGuire, John
McLaughlin, William
Meadow, James
Meek, Samuel
Meek, James
Miller, John
Miller, William
Morton, Jonathan
Morton, Josiah
Nicholls, Cassandra W.
Nicholls, John
Norman, Joseph
Norton, James
Osborne, William
Oscar, James
Parker, David

Parker, Elias
Parker, Robert
Perry, Daniel
Pettit, Matthew
Pettit, Samuel
Pickett, Younger
Pogue, Allen
Pogue, James
Pogue, Mary
Pogue, John
Porter, Jacob
Powell, Joseph
Price, Edmund
Price, Mordacai
Price, Sampson
Radcliffe, Daniel
Reason, Lewis
Rice, James
Richards, Thomas
Riddle, John
Roberts, Jesse
Robertson, Winslow
Rucker, Ambrose
Rucker, Ephriam
Rucker, Reuben
Scott, David
Scott, James
Scott, John
Scott, Thomas
Shelton, Joseph
Shields, John
Short, Aaron
Shortridge, Levi
Shortridge, Margaret
Skidmore, Joseph
Skidmore, Polly
Skidmore, Samuel
Slawter, Samuel
Smith, Martin
Smith, Robert
Smith, Randall
Smith, Samuel
Smith, Thomas
Solliday, Samuel
Sperry, James
Sperry, Samuel
Spriggs, Samuel
Starr, Koonrad
Stephenson, Richard
Stewart, Charles
Stewart, Matthew
Storey, John
Stratton, Seriah
Stratton, Jeremiah
Stump, Christopher

Terry, Thomas
Terry, William
Thompson, Andy
Thompson, James
Thompson, Samuel
Thompson, Waddy
Throckmorton, Joseph
Throckmorton, William
Timberlake, Oba
Tolbert, Thomas
Tyree, William
Ulen, Benjamin
Van Bibber, Jacob
Van Bibber, James
Van Bibber, Peter
Vice, Enoch
Virgin, Rezin
Virgin, Thomas
Ward, James
Ward, John
Ward, Thomas
Warnock, James
Warnock, Johnson
Warnock, Samuel
Warnock, William
Waring, Clement H.
Waring, Francis
Waring, James
Waring, Thomas
Waring, Thomas Truman
  Greenfield
Wells, John
Wheatly, Richard
White, David
White, William
White, Solomon
Wilcox, Lewis
Willit, Joseph
Williams, Eli
Wilson, Alexander
Wilson, Thomas
Woods, Andrew
Woolford, John
Wooten, Charles
Wooten, Silas
Womack, Archer
Young, Fountain
Young, John
Zane, Andrew
Zane, Philip

1813

Biggs, Andrew
King, Thomas B.

MEMBERS OF THE LEGISLATURE
FROM GREENUP COUNTY

This list was furnished by Mr. Frank K. Kavanaugh of Frankfort, Ky.

MEMBERS OF THE SENATE

Thompson Ward..........1820-1826
John M. McConnell.......1826-1830
William Conner..........1830-1834
William G. Carter........1834-1838
William Conner..........1842-1846
John C. Kouns...........1850-1857

Henry M. Rust...........1857-1861
Wm. J. Worthington......1865-1869
George T. Halbert........1878-1882
J. B. Hannah..............1890-1894
Thomas H. Paynter.......1905-1909
J. Howard Williams.......1914-1918
Dr. Henry T. Morris......1918-1926

REPRESENTATIVES

Charles N. Lewis..........1813-1815
Thompson Ward......1815-1818-1830
Francis H. Gaines.........1816-1820
Thomas T. G. Waring......1819-1821
John M. McConnell.......1822-1825
William Conner......1825-1827-1847
John C. Kouns............1828-1831
Samuel Seaton.......1831-1833-1845
John C. Hollingsworth.....1823-1835
David Trimble............1836-1840
Basil Waring.............1840-1841
Robinson M. Biggs........1841-1842
Joseph D. Collins.........1842-1843
Jesse Corum..............1844-1846
Jefferson Evans...........1846-1848
James W. Davis...........1848-1849
Richard Jones........1849-1855-1857
Marcus L. Williams........1850-1851
William C. Grier..........1851-1853
Christopher C. Chinn......1853-1855
Joseph Patton............1857-1859
William C. Ireland........1859-1863
Edward F. Dulin..........1863-1865
John D. Russell..........1865-1869
James C. Waring..........1869-1873
Dr. Samuel Ellis..........1873-1875
Marshall Baker...........1875-1877

W. H. H. Callihan.........1877-1879
George W. Thompson......1879-1880
B. F. Warnock............1880-1882
John T. King..............1882-1884
Wm. J. Worthington......1884-1886
W. J. A. Rardin...........1886-1890
J. Watt Womack..........1890-1892
B. F. Bennett.............1892-1896
D. J. McCoy..............1896-1898
R. C. Myers..............1898-1900
Benj. F. Meadows........1900-1902
Wm. J. Worthington......1902-1906
C. W. G. Hannah.........1906-1910
J. Howard Williams.......1910-1914
James A. Scott...........1914-1916
A. S. Cooper.............1916-1920
C. C. Oney..............1920-1924
Henry J. Kegley.........1924-1926
J. G. Swearingen.........1926-1930
Russell O. Miller.........1930-1932
Earl R. Stephens.........1932-1934
Mary Breckinridge.......1934-1936
C. C. Byrne.............1936-1940
Henry Stewart..........1940-1942
E. R. Hilton............1942-1944
R. C. Holbrooks.........1944-1946
E. R. Hilton............1946-1950

Three

TRAVEL

EARLY TRAVEL

Early settlers came to Greenup County either by the Ohio River or overland by horseback and wagons. When they reached here there were no good roads anywhere. Even in the dry season the travel was very rough going. The first passable road at all seasons was probably from the Big Sandy River down the Ohio. Shortly after the county was organized a road was laid off from Greenupsburg, the county seat, down the Ohio River to a line across from the mouth of the Big Scioto River in Ohio. The present highway practically follows the old road. When the furnaces were in operation the roads near them were improved by using the slag from the furnace on them.

Streams were either forded or crossed by rude bridges constructed for temporary use. Later, wooden bridges were built, and some of the covered ones are still in use. Three of these are at Bennett's Mill, at Enterprise, and at Oldtown, but most of this kind have been replaced either by iron or concrete.

Early means of travel by horseback and wagons were followed by buggies and spring wagons. When trucks and automobiles came into use, better roads were necessary. With the road building under the jurisdiction of the state and national government, bad roads, save in some of the isolated sections, will soon be a thing of the past.

The Ohio River played such an important part in the early transportation and settlement of Greenup County that it is fitting to give a detailed history of river travel.

FIRST BOATS

The first travel on the Ohio River was by canoes which brought hunters and adventurers; but when settlers came, they wanted to bring their possessions with them, so rafts came into use. These were roughly made with little or no shelter on them. The rafts soon gave way to the flatboats, large enough to accommodate several families with their household necessities, and with shelter against the sun and rain. These were the boats that brought the pioneer settlers to Greenup County.

Several years after the settlements were established there began to be a surplus of products of different kinds. In order to market these, a farmer and his neighbors had a flatboat built, loaded it with their products and took it to Memphis or New Orleans where they sold both the boat and cargo. They had to make their way back home as best they could, either afoot or on horseback, up the Natchez Trace to Kentucky. Due to the dangers and perils that lurked along the way, some of these men were never heard of again. But many did manage to get home safely, with the proceeds of the sales intact.

After the flatboats came the keelboats which were one step in advance because they could be poled or rowed back up stream instead of being sold at New Orleans. Flatboats and keelboats, carrying settlers and cargoes, became so numerous that one might count as many as sixty of these crafts passing a given point in one day.

Another type of boat seen on the river about 1825 was the storeboat coming from Pittsburgh loaded with merchandise which called at the settlements to sell and trade with the people. Later as the china and glassware industry in Pittsburgh expanded, the Raike family, which lived a few miles below Greenup, built up quite a business. They brought floatboats loaded with china and glass down the river and traded these articles to the eager farmers' wives for castoff products, such as scrap iron and rags. These dishes and glassware are valued antiques in this section today.

When the steamboats came they carried both passengers and freight and the towboats carried large cargoes of different products so that the hand propelled boats soon passed out of existence.

STEAMBOAT TRAVEL AND TRAFFIC

The following notes are taken from the book, *Steamboats and Steamboat Men*, by Captain Ellis C. Mace.

In 1810 an Ohio Steamboat Company was organized at Pittsburgh for the purpose of building boats for use in the western waters. The first boat, the "New Orleans," was launched at Pittsburgh in March 1811, and taken to New Orleans for the southern trade. This strange craft created intense excitement among the people living along the banks of the Ohio River as she passed down stream. The second boat, the "Comet," was launched at Pittsburgh, also, and taken south in 1814. These first boats had but one deck, the boilers being placed in the hold.

The "Washington" was the first boat with two decks, with the boilers placed on the lower deck. She was also the first boat to have separate rooms for the passengers, each being named for a state instead of being numbered as in a hotel. This is the origin of "State Rooms" on boats. The "Washington" went to Louisville and on to New Orleans in September 1816 and returned to Louisville in November. This proved the ability of a boat to make headway against the current of the Ohio River.

The steamboat proved so successful that by 1820 there were a number of boats running on the river, carrying both passengers and freight. The first towboat was the "Condor" and this was soon followed by other towboats. Steamboat traffic continued to increase until it reached its peak in usefulness, elegance, and luxury in the 1870's and 1880's.

Washington Honshall of Catlettsburg was one of the most prominent rivermen of this section. He began his river life on a flatboat. Later, on the steamboats, he advanced from watchman and mate to captain and to commander of a large fleet. In 1872 when Collis P. Huntington wanted a river connection between Cincinnati and the Chesapeake and Ohio Railroad, completed only as far as Huntington, West Virginia, he found in Captain Honshall the man he needed to carry out his plan. With the help of Thomas and John Means and several others, Captain Honshall organized the Cincinnati-Portsmouth-Big Sandy and Pomeroy Packet Company. When the trains came into Huntington, Captain Honshall was there to meet them with two fine sidewheel steamers, the "Bostona" and the "Fleetwood," and they moved all freight, mail, and passengers to Cincinnati in record time. These two boats continued in this so-called railroad trade until the Chesapeake and Ohio Railroad was completed to Cincinnati in the late 1880's.

Another line of boats managed by Captain Honshall was the famous "White Collar Line," so named for the white collar painted on each smokestack. In this line there were both passenger and towboats. Commodore Honshall's career as an Ohio Steamboat Commander covers a long period; his boats made trips twice a week promptly for a quarter of a century.

Names of boats familiar to the people of Greenup County were the "Telegraph," "Henry M. Stanley," "Bonanza," "Sunshine," "Courier," "Tacoma," "Shirley," "St. Lawrence," "City of Ironton," "Keystone State," and the palatial "Queen City" and "Virginia." There were more than two hundred in all.

Two other prominent men in early history of steamboating were the Bay brothers, George and William. They came down the river on a storeboat during the Civil War, and located near Proctorville, Ohio. They built many boats, among them several named for members of their own family—the "Minnie Bay," the "Ruth," the "Lizzie Bay," and the "Lizzie Johnson." In 1872 they built the "Fashion" to carry the mail and deliver it at all the villages between Portsmouth and Proctorville every day. In 1874 they built the "Scioto" to carry the mail faster, making the trip in five hours including fifteen to twenty landings.

Perhaps one of the best loved boats ever known on the Ohio River was the "Fannie Dugan," built in 1872 at Portsmouth by Captain John McAllister of Springville. She was named for the daughter of Thomas Dugan, a prominent banker of Portsmouth, and in appreciation he presented the boat with a grand piano. She ran between Portsmouth and Proctorville and she also carried the mail. Captain McAllister died and his widow placed his brother, Captain Jack McAllister, in charge of the boat. In 1876 Mrs. McAllister pooled her interests with the Bay Brothers, and they formed the Portsmouth and Pomeroy Packet Company. The "Fannie Dugan" was sold later to a Jacksonville, Florida, company to be used on the St. Johns River. There she was wrecked in a storm.

Probably the best known and most useful boat to all the local people after the turn of the century was the small sternwheel packet, owned by the Bay Brothers, which made daily trips between Portsmouth and Huntington, stopping at all landings for freight and passengers. The "Chevalier" ran in this trade for many years and she was followed by the "Greyhound" with Thomas Roush as Captain and 1st Pilot, Peter Lallance as 2nd Pilot, and Frank Rolf as Clerk. The "Greyhound" ran for more than twelve years and in 1917 when she sank at Huntington, this particular period of river traffic closed.

LIGHT POSTS

For the safety of the boats there were lighthouses at intervals along the river on both banks. These lights guided the boats into the channel of the river; they were placed so that one light was always in sight.

The lighthouse, or light posts as they were called, consisted of a lantern enclosed in a glass box set on the top of a tall white post; it was reached by climbing a flight of steep, narrow steps. The keeper put the lighted lantern in the box each evening and took it down each morning. The farmer on whose land the light post was located was the custodian of the light, and it was his responsibility to make sure that the light burned brightly throughout the night. For this service he received six dollars per month.

Once every six months a government boat, carrying officers and supplies, visited each light and summoned the keeper with a series of short blasts of the whistle. At this signal he left his work immediately and went aboard the boat to accept the supplies and receive his pay.

The steamboat, "Goldenrod," served in this capacity for more than thirty-five years. After the "Goldenrod" retired, the "Greenbrier" served until the light posts were electrified. Now the lights are kept in order by Coast Guard officers who make their rounds in a small launch.

Mrs. Eva Winkler Duduit, a retired keeper of the light, takes pride in telling that she performed this service continuously for forty-five years. A former resident of Greenup County, she now lives at Wheelersburg, Ohio, across the river from Siloam.

FERRIES

The first ferries were run by man power and these were followed by ferries run by horsepower. Space was provided for the horses and sweep to move in a circular fashion. Then came the steam power which was in use on the ferries for many years. Gasoline is used now for propelling ferries.

The first ferryman at Greenup is said to have been Reason Davis, who also kept a hat shop. May 14, 1813, James Van Bibber was permitted to establish a ferry across Little Sandy below the Falls. Benjamin Smith, son of Godfrey Smith, was an early ferryman near the mouth of Little Sandy. Thomas Richards, who lived in a "hewed log house on Water Street," was a ferryman at the same place.

May 16, 1814. On motion of William Bradshaw, he was permitted to establish a ferry across the Ohio River from his land to the opposite shore.

November 18, 1816. On motion of James McGuire the ferry at Lot No. 11 was discontinued, as a ferry had been established from his Lot No. 1 across the Ohio River to the opposite shore.

November 17, 1817. James Warnock was given a contract by the court to ferry the grand jurymen across the Little Sandy River in 1818 for $6.00.

Alexander Rankins was probably the last ferryman at Little Sandy before the bridge was built.

Horatio Catlett was the earliest ferryman in the northeastern part of the county, operating a ferry across the Big Sandy River near its mouth.

March 1857. John C. Kouns and Joshua Oakes executed bond as "Ferry Keepers" at Greenup across the Ohio River at Haverhill.

In the 1870's Thomas Carr was the ferryman at Greenup and in the 1880's and 1890's George Sanders was the ferryman there. He operated the ferryboat "Royal" from Greenup to Haverhill, Ohio. One winter night when the ice was floating in the river the "Royal" broke from her landing and floated down the river. Captain Sanders was drowned. The "Royal," which had been in use for many years, was replaced by the "O'Neil," which was later placed in the Fullerton-Portsmouth trade by George D. Winn.

The "Royal" and the "O'Neil" were the last steam ferries to ply the Ohio River between Greenup, Kentucky, and Haverhill, Ohio.

Early ferryboats between Russell, Kentucky, and Ironton, Ohio, were the "Elwood," owned and operated by Peter Boynton, and the "Eva," built by Captain Wayne Carner. A later ferryboat was the "H. A. Mead," built and operated by Benjamin F. Young in 1880. This boat was sold to Captain Carner and J. M. Kirker and they sold it to the Chesapeake and Ohio Railroad in 1889.

This company operated the ferry between Russell and Ironton until the Russell-Ironton Bridge was built and opened to traffic in 1922.

The first ferry between Springville and Portsmouth was a flatboat, forty feet long and fifteen feet wide, owned by William Dupuy, and operated first by man power and later by horsepower. An earlier ferry may have been operated by members of the Thomson family. In 1813 the rates for crossing on the ferry were ten cents for foot passengers, six and one-fourth cents for horses and cattle, one dollar for a loaded wagon and team, seventy-five cents for an empty wagon or a four-wheeled carriage.

In 1838 ferry rates were fifty cents for a one-horse vehicle, seventy-five cents for two or more horses, twenty-five cents for a riding horse, and ten cents for foot passengers.

In 1842 the rates were five cents for foot passengers, thirteen cents for horse and rider, thirty cents for a one or more horse conveyance up to four horses, and more would be fifty cents. (Ref. Evans' *History of Scioto County*.)

After William Dupuy, the record of the next owner of the Springville ferry is that of John Mackoy of Siloam, who also owned a number of lots in Springville. After his death in 1842, his son, Thomas, inherited the ferry and also a negro slave, Armstead Faucet. When the steam ferry came into use, Armstead was the engineer. An obituary, cut from a Portsmouth newspaper and found in an old scrapbook, says: "Armstead Faucet was the engineer on the ferries for forty years, outliving four boats. He was honest, industrious, and trustworthy. Having ferried for many years over the Ohio River, when the waters lay tranquil and blue, and in storm when the waters were turbulent and white with foam, in the sunset of life he has been ferried over death's dark river."

The ferry remained in the Mackoy family and was operated by Obadiah F. Mackoy, a brother of Thomas, until he went to Missouri in the early 1870's. A nephew of Obadiah, John Lawson Mackoy, operated the ferry until it was sold to Captain W. W. Little. In the 1880's he traded the ferry to Captain Samuel Brown for a farm at Siloam. Captain Brown was the last local ferry owner, as he sold it to the Chesapeake and Ohio Railroad and went to Newport, Kentucky. The railroad operated the ferry until the Grant Bridge was completed in 1922.

Captain George Winn was the first ferryman at Fullerton. In 1893 he took the "O'Neil" to Fullerton and operated it from there to East Portsmouth until the boat sank in 1895. The "Belle of Ashland" was the ferry there until 1900, when the "B. F. Bennett," which was being built at Point Pleasant, was finished and brought to Fullerton. Captain Winn died in 1902 and the "Bennett" was sold to the Captain George W. Davis family of Big Sandy Valley. They operated the ferry many years. Since that time several different ferryboats, among them the "Emily" and "Captain John," have been operated by Captain John Davis, son of Captain George W. Davis.

RAILROADS

The first railroad in the county was begun in 1845 by a Boston, Massachusetts, company. It was to be used as an outlet for furnace products which were carried to Riverton and from there shipped by boat on the Ohio River. It was to serve as an outlet for farm and mine products, carrying passengers and mail to all the smaller places in that section.

The Kentucky Improvement Company was formed in 1865 by two Thayer brothers and Walter Hunnell of Boston, Massachusetts. This company purchased twenty-five thousand acres of land south of Riverton on the Little Sandy River. In 1866 six miles of track were built to Argillite, and in 1868 the track was extended to Hunnewell. This railroad was constructed as an outlet for the iron products of Argillite and Hunnewell Furnaces.

In 1870 the Eastern Kentucky Railroad took over the property of the Kentucky Improvement Company and built the road to Grayson in Carter County in 1871.

The first superintendent of the Eastern Kentucky Railroad was Mr. Goodwin of Boston, Massachusetts. He was succeeded by Horace W. Bates, also from Boston, Massachusetts, and at his death his son, Sturgis Bates, became Superintendent, continuing in that office until the Eastern Kentucky Railroad was abandoned in 1928. The first engineer was James Schooly of Pittsburgh, Pennsylvania, and the last one was Hugh Craynon of Riverton. The first conductor was Samuel Weaver and the last one was William McKee of Riverton. Daniel Weaver was the first master mechanic at Riverton and also at Hunnewell when the shops were moved there. His son, Charles Weaver, was one of the first station agents at Hunnewell.

HISTORY OF THE CHESAPEAKE AND OHIO
RAILROAD IN GREENUP COUNTY

The day after Christmas, December 26, 1888, the first train ran from Huntington, West Virginia, into Cincinnati. President M. E. Engalls and the Chesapeake and Ohio's former president, Collis P. Huntington, both were on this trial run. Regular operation of train service began January 1, 1889, although accommodation trains had been operating on the first section, from Huntington to South Portsmouth, six months earlier. These trains carried two orange-colored coaches, one for baggage and mail, and the other for passengers. In May, 1889, two new passenger trains, the Fast Flying Virginians (F. F. V.) began their run. They had orange-colored vestibule coaches, steam heat, dining cars, and electric lights, as modern then as the streamlined trains of today.

This fulfillment of railroad transportation along the Ohio River brought into reality plans that had engaged the attention of Greenup County and northeastern Kentucky since 1850.

On December 18, 1850, an act was approved by the general assembly of the Commonwealth of Kentucky to incorporate the Maysville and Big Sandy Railroad Company.

"(1) For the object and purpose and with the full power to construct and maintain a railroad, with all such appendages, fixtures, buildings, and machinery as may be deemed necessary for the use of the same, commencing at or near the said city of Maysville in Kentucky, thence to the Big Sandy River by such route as may be found practicable and means raised to construct same.

"(2) The Capital Stock of said company shall be $1,000,000.

"(3) That Thomas Y. Payne, Thomas P. Stevens, Charles B. Coons, A. M. January, and James B. Robinson, of Mason County, Samuel Stevenson, T. J. Walker, William Ireland, and R. Lobb, of Lewis County, *Charles M. Wilson, John C. Kouns, William Corum,* and *George Darlington,* of *Greenup County,* shall be commissioners, with power to open books and receive subscriptions of stock in this corporation."

The first meeting of the board of directors was held in Maysville July 24, 1852. The Scioto and Hocking Valley Railroad Company, which terminated at Portsmouth, subscribed to the stock on the express condition that Springville on the Ohio River, opposite Portsmouth, should be a point on the railroad.

In April, 1853, the board of directors authorized that the whole interest in the ferry operating between Springville and Portsmouth should be acquired, and that a contract be let immediately for a bridge across the Little Sandy River at Greenupsburg. That same year Greenup County was asked to take a vote on July 4th upon a proposal that the county subscribe to $125,000 of the railroad's capital stock, in county bonds payable thirty days after date with six per cent interest. Rights of way were purchased and approximately $300,000 expended. By July 1854 the money had run out and work on the road was suspended. The two tracts of land in Springville and the ferry rights attached therewith were ordered to be mortgaged. Under a decree of foreclosure the property, rights, and franchises of the Maysville and Big Sandy Railroad Company were sold.

After about fifteen years of litigation and reorganization a special act of the general assembly of the State of Kentucky approved the incorporation of the Great Eastern Railway Company which bought the Maysville and Big Sandy Railroad for $57,007. The new owner would immediately commence construction of a railroad from Catlettsburg to Maysville. About seven miles of rails were laid the following year and the work was stopped. After about ten more years of litigation the Supreme Court of the United States decided the property should revert to the Maysville and Big Sandy Company.

In 1879 Greenup County was asked to subscribe the further sum of $100,000 to the railroad's capital stock. Collis P. Huntington was president of the Chesapeake and Ohio Railroad from 1869 to 1888. In 1886, having already completed a railroad westward from White Sulphur Springs, West Virginia, to Huntington, he had dreams of a transcontinental line. In order to further his plans he acquired the control of several Kentucky railroads, among them the Maysville and Big Sandy line. In 1888-1889 the rail line was finally completed and in 1907 it was merged with the Chesapeake and Ohio Railroad.

The bridge across the Ohio River at Siloam was begun in 1914 and finished in 1917 at a cost of $1,500,000. By way of this bridge Greenup County is afforded transportation to Northern Ohio, Michigan, and the great northwest.

Note: This information was furnished by Laura E. Armitage, Research Analyst of the Chesapeake and Ohio Railroad of Richmond, Virginia.

EARLY TAVERNS OF GREENUP

South of the house built by Major David Trimble on the corner of Water and Washington Streets, was a tavern kept first by Richard Crump, then by Denby Timberlake, and later by Andrew Biggs, who had a store nearby.

On the southeast corner of Main and Washington Streets stood a large frame house where Jeremiah Davidson kept a tavern. This house was next occupied by the Jacobs family, who later moved to Texas.

Jesse Corum lived in a house on Main Street below Washington at one time. It was later known as the Andes House and was kept by Robert Callihan. The house finally burned.

In 1827 Major John C. Kouns built the Kouns House, and it was for many years the leading tavern of the town. Later it was kept by John Winn, who had married Nancy, the daughter of Major Kouns and his wife, Elizabeth. After Mr. and Mrs. Winn died their daughters, Mrs. Hattie Alexander, Kate, and Sallie Winn, kept the tavern for years.

Circuit Court time was an event in the lives of the Greenup folk in the early days. The judge and prominent lawyers lived in Maysville. Before 1890 these officials traveled by boat and usually arrived on the fast boat, the "Telegraph," about noon on Sunday. Many citizens came to the river bank every day to see the boats land, but on this particular Sunday the crowd was doubled in number.

It was indeed a grand sight to see the dignified judge and lawyers in their tall silk hats walk up the grade, escorted by Perry, the hotel porter, with all the luggage he could possibly carry. At the top of the river bank the party turned east and then north, arriving at their destination, the Kouns House, where a warm welcome and an elegant repast awaited them.

Perry began young and grew old in the service of the Kouns House.

U. S. MAIL IN EARLY DAYS

In early days the mail was carried on horseback from the Big Sandy River to the Mason County line. There were no stamps or envelopes, the written page being folded and sealed with wax. When the steamboats began to run they carried the mail to all points along the river. When the Norfolk and Western Railroad was built on the Ohio side of the river the mail was carried on the trains and was brought from the station at Haverhill, Ohio, across the river on the ferry to Greenup. In the late 1860's the Eastern Kentucky Railroad was built and those trains carried the mail to that section of the county. In 1889 the Chesapeake and Ohio Railroad was completed and the mail was carried along that route.

At the present time all the post offices in the county receive a daily mail.

POSTMASTERS OF GREENUP

According to the records of the Post Office Department in Washington for the period 1789 to 1934, now in the National Archives, a post office was established in Greenup shortly before July 1, 1811. Names of postmasters and dates of their appointment were:

Joshua Bartlett.........July 1, 1811	Wm. M. Stevens..December 26, 1882
(Date of first return)	Benj. F. Brown........July 16, 1885
Samuel L. Crawford.....April 1, 1813	Leonidas Callon......August 21, 1888
(Date of first return)	Wm. M. Stevens........April 2, 1889
Jesse B. Boone........March 21, 1814	Herbert Reid.........March 24, 1893
Alphonso Boone........July 11, 1814	Thomas Myers........May 26, 1897
Joseph Gardner.........May 20, 1816	Charles Taylor.........July 24, 1905
Henry E. Green.........May 11, 1818	(Declined)
Wm. W. Bunnel......August 22, 1828	Thomas Myers....December 13, 1905
Chas. M. Wilson..December 11, 1833	Charles Taylor..........July 3, 1909
C. L. Raison............July 8, 1844	J. D. McCoy..........August 2, 1913
Joseph Pollock.......March 19, 1850	Eunice D. Taylor....August 30, 1916
Benj. F. Brown.....August 29, 1859	Wm. I. Myers.......March 1, 1922
Joseph Pollock.........July 9, 1861	Ernest Warnock......May 27, 1929
Benj. F. Brown...September 25, 1866	Mrs. Maggie Warnock.October 1, 1932
Francis C. Robb.....March 6, 1867	Mrs. Rebecca Forsythe..April 1, 1934
John Moran............July 8, 1872	

Four

INDUSTRIES & PROFESSIONS

INDUSTRIES

Farming was, of course, the principal industry of the county in the early days, as it is still. Corn and wheat were the first crops raised, although there were some oats and rye, and some livestock. Farming was slow work in the days of the scythe, cradle, and the plow of that day. Besides the farming tools the pioneer fathers brought their axes, saws, and other necessities to the new home, while the pioneer mothers brought the old customs in the shape of their black iron kettles for boiling clothes, dyeing, and making soap outdoors, their wheels for spinning various materials for clothing, and their looms for weaving. Many such kettles may be seen in the yards of farmers today. Looms are still being used to weave rugs and carpets, and the spinning wheels are often prized as family heirlooms.

When the furnaces were built they began producing pig iron. There were two iron foundries in the county, and on the banks of Little Sandy at Argillite, George and James Hoop had built a flour and grist mill. On Tygart Creek at Coopersville, there was a grist mill, a lumber mill, and a stave mill. Farther down on Tygart Creek the Bennett family had a mill where they sawed lumber and ground grain, and on Town Branch in Greenup there was a lumber and grist mill. Two men named Jones and Noble built a cotton mill in Greenup, but it was not a success. On the Rankins farm below the Little Sandy River were two brick yards, which furnished the brick for most of the buildings in Greenup.

Another industry in the county was the operation of tanneries, which were located at Little Sandy Falls, at Oldtown, at Lynn, and one at Springville, which was said to have been operated by President Ulysses S. Grant's father.

There was a factory for making shoes at Lynn in 1846, but this was not in operation very many years. In Greenup a chair factory and a cooper shop were active for some time. At Limeville there were lime kilns and a thriving business was carried on by the Tong family and later by the Merrills. Lime was shipped by boat to both Cincinnati and Pittsburgh and the limestone was used in the construction of the Chesapeake and Ohio Railroad.

FURNACES

The following is a list of the old charcoal furnaces of Greenup County and the years that they were built, with the names of the builders:

Name	Year	Builder
Argillite	1818	Richard Deering
		John Trimble
		David Trimble
Old Steam	1824	Shreves Brothers
Pactolus	1824	McMurty and Ward
Bellefonte	1826	A. Paul and George Poage
Amanda	1829	Lindsay Poage
Enterprise	1832	Clingman and others
Hopewell	1832	John Campbell and others
Caroline	1833	Henry Blake and Company
Globe	1833	George Darlington
Raccoon	1833	David Trimble and others
New Hampshire	1838	Samuel Seaton and Company
Hunnewell	1844	Campbell, Peters and Co.
Sandy	1847	D. Young and Gilruth
Laurel	1848	Wurts Brothers
Pennsylvania	1848	Wurts Brothers
Buffalo	1851	Hollister and Ross Company
Kenton	1856	John Waring and others

Copied from *The Rise and Growth of the Iron Industry in and About Ashland, Kentucky*, by Kendall Gordon Seaton

Early settlers soon found that the county was rich in iron ore, coal, timber, and water power. It was not long before men from Pennsylvania interested in iron making were coming down the Ohio River, and with material at hand for building, furnaces were soon constructed. The machinery for making pig iron was brought down the river from Pittsburgh to be installed in the furnaces.

In the building of a furnace, these things had to be considered. There had to be plenty of ore, timber, limestone, and hard rock to use for building the stack. Before a furnace could begin operation the "Ax Men" would be engaged in cutting wood into four-foot lengths and in cording it. Then the colliers prepared the charcoal pits by leveling the ground and placing the wood so that when finished it would be shaped like a cone and usually ten to twelve feet high. This was covered with leaves and dirt. Openings made at the bottom were for firing while openings near the top were for escaping gases. These pits had to be watched closely to see that they might not become too hot and yet hot enough so that the wood was charred through. When ready, the charcoal was hauled to the furnaces in high flaring wagon beds drawn by oxen.

It was the foundryman's duty to see that the furnace was kept in repair, that it was properly charged with ore, sandstone, and charcoal. It was also his duty to know when the iron was ready for the discharge, and to discharge the slag. It was a wonderful sight, as many people will remember, to see the red hot metal run down the alleys, then into the sand grooves made for the purpose. This was the way the pigs were made.

Engineers were needed to care for the engines and boilers. They had two helpers whose duty it was to open the doors for the discharge of the iron.

Laurel Furnace was in operation about thirty-four years. Joshua Kelly, of Ironton, Ohio, bought the furnace lands and it was the Kelly home for many years, the land being turned into a stock farm.

When Buffalo Furnace shut down, the land was sold to a man named Armstrong, from Illinois, who used it for raising stock. Kenton Furnace, the last one built in the county, was named in honor of Simon Kenton. Over the border, in Carter County, Boone Furnace was built and named for Simon Kenton's companion in many Indian fights and in hunting, Daniel Boone. It was fitting that the two furnaces were named for the men who traveled together over that territory many times, no doubt. Ruins of some of the old furnaces may still be seen covered with vines.

In June 1937 the *Ashland Independent* published an address, which was made by Dr. George Bell, of Ashland, before a meeting of the American Institute of Mining and Metallurgical Engineers at Columbus, Ohio, in which he gave an interesting and vivid account of the iron industry in Greenup and Boyd Counties. His description of Laurel Furnace and the ruins are worthy of particular notice. Lack of space forbids the giving of much of the valuable information it contained.

When the furnaces of Greenup County were no longer operating, charcoal was still made and shipped by flatboat and oxen
drawn wagons to the Kelly Mills in Ironton, Ohio. At one time
the Kelly firm had a coaling store at Kellyville, two miles below
Greenup. When the industry was discontinued at Smith and Coal
Branches, the store was moved to the old foundry building in
Greenup, on Elizabeth Street. At that time the charcoal was
burned on Little Sandy and shipped to Ironton.

The iron industry brought many different kinds of labor to
this section, among them mining, charcoal burning, and hauling.
This created a demand for many things that farmers had been
accustomed to produce on their land for their own use. As there
was more travel, more and better roads were needed, also bridges
instead of fords, and more mills to supply food from grain and
lumber for building. In a few years after the furnaces came to
Greenup County it became a busy and thriving place.

EARLY BUSINESS CONCERNS

The first merchants of the county were Benjamin Chinn and
Robert Daugherty. Samuel Seaton kept a general store in the
building on Front Street, long known as the Dr. Spalding home.
John King kept a store on Main Street in a frame building later
occupied by James P. Winters. It was moved to the rear of the
lot when the Columbia Hotel was built in 1893.

The father of Charles Hertel had a shoe shop on Washington
Street below the corner of Main Street. George Roe kept a clothing
store next door to the Hertel shoe shop. John F. Day and
Dupoultee Valodine each had a tailor shop on Main Street
below the corner of Washington. Jesse Corum was jailer and had
a tailor shop in one room of the old brick jail (1811) on Main
Street. Later James P. Winters was jailer for almost twenty
years and part of the time had his saddle shop in a room of the jail.

Charles Stringles had a shoe shop on Washington Street.
Benedict Hobbs and William Lewis kept a halter shop in a
building where the Womack Store has stood so long. Major David
Trimble, a furnace man, built the large frame house on Lot No. 1.
He had a store in the corner room for the Argillite and Buffalo
Furnaces. This was kept by Charles Wilson, a relative of the
Trimbles, and was bought by Cardinal F. Stark in 1858. Cardinal
Stark built a store and house combined on the corner of Wash-
ington and Elizabeth Streets and began keeping store there.

Jehu Sydenstricker, who married Maria Kouns, was one of the early merchants of Greenup.

The Pratt and Brooks store was operated by Benjamin Pratt and Thomas Brooks, of Lynn. They had two large storerooms on Washington Street and had a very large country trade. James McMullan was a tinner and kept a shop on Washington Street. Benjamin Brown had a large store on the corner of Main and Washington Streets. For a time the business was known as Brown and Reid, but Mr. Reid later withdrew from the firm and went into business on Harrison Street.

On lower Main Street was a flour and lumber mill built by Major John C. Kouns. On Washington Street were three small offices generally occupied by lawyers. One was occupied by William Beatty, a "very shrewd lawyer." Some time later one of these offices was occupied by Benjamin Smith, who operated the ferry across Little Sandy River and lived in the ferryhouse. This ferryhouse was occupied in 1810 by Thomas Richards, who had come from Belmont County, Ohio. He ran the ferry for several years.

There was a carding machine and a gristmill on Front Street built by Noble and Jones. William Biggs had a storeroom near the mill on lower Front (or Water Street, as it was then known). At one time he had this room full of ginseng root which he had bought to ship to Cincinnati.

Alexander Rankins had a brick yard on the land below Little Sandy and furnished the brick for a number of the buildings in Greenup. At Lynn on Tygart Creek there were tanneries and a shoe factory that ran for a time. John W. Timmonds had a tannery at the Falls of Little Sandy in the 1840's. At Oldtown there were a tannery, a grain mill, and a general store. At Coopersville there were a cooper shop and a lumber mill built by the Cooper family. Benjamin Chinn had a general store near Old Pond Run.

BANKS

The first bank in Greenup was the Greenup Deposit Bank located on Harrison Street between Front and Elizabeth Streets. William Ireland was the first president and Joseph Pollock was the cashier.

The second bank was the Farmers' and Merchants' Bank owned and operated by James Sowards at the present site of the Dr. Henry Morris home and office.

Since then there have been the Citizens Bank and the First National Bank, the latter on the corner of Main and Harrison Streets.

EARLY HOUSES AND BUILDINGS IN GREENUP
(*From notes by Mr. John Myers*)

Beginning at Lot No. 1, where James McGuire built a log cabin, the next house was built and occupied by a man named Halley from Ohio. Thomas Richards built a hewed log house below these two on Water Street. Across Cedar Alley stood the home of John Passmore Tanner, who had a cabinet shop which burned about 1869 or 1870 and was not rebuilt. Next to the Tanner house was a frame building used by William Biggs as a storeroom. A log building near by was used for storing salt made at Hopewell and brought down Little Sandy.

Below the houses already mentioned there were two houses, one in which Guy Wilson lived, and a family named Barney lived in the other. Farther down was another house, and then the ferryhouse where the Little Sandy ferryman lived.

On Main Street next to the old Jacobs place stood a one-story building where Major Van Bibber lived. On the north side of Main Street was the B. F. Brown home, which had belonged to the Day family, relatives of Mr. Brown. The house at the rear of the Brown store building was built in 1838 or 1839 by Nicholas Thom, a carpenter.

There was a one-story house on the south side of Main Street next to Little Sandy that was built by George Malone. The next house was built by Robert McCallister and was the John Riggs home for many years. An old frame house stood at the corner of Walnut Alley and Main Street which was occupied by the Benjamin Smith family. The John Powell home stood next to the Benjamin Smith home. It is said that the brick house on the corner of Main Street and Cedar Alley was built by John Kaut in 1846. It was occupied by the Dr. Samuel Ellis family in the 1860's and 1870's, and later was sold to the John Schmutz family. It is said to have been the site of the Nathan Seaton family home in the 1820's and 1830's.

For many years John B. Norris lived in the small brick house next to the Andes Tavern and taught school in his home. John Myers built this house and also the Presbyterian Church. The house just above the church was built by Frank York, the father of Sallie and Belle York, who lived with their grandparents,

Mr. and Mrs. Benjamin Smith, after their parents died. The house on the south side of Main Street and Cedar Alley (later the Scott Warnock and Fullerton home) was built by George Darlington, a furnace man.

We have mentioned those houses in the lower part of the town, and now beginning at Lot No. 12 we learn that a house was built on the corner by Johnson Warnock in 1813. He married Lucy Forrester and they went to housekeeping there. A few years later Samuel Seaton, who was a teacher, a merchant, and later a furnace man, built the home just above the Johnson Warnock home. Next to the Seaton home was the Myers home, which has been owned and occupied by members of the Myers family ever since. Mrs. India Callihan Myers kept a millinery store in a room of the building for many years, and in the rear there still is in use the blacksmith shop built by Allen Myers.

Across Laurel Alley from the Myers home was a frame house that was occupied by a lawyer named Chetwood. It was later owned by Martin Morris, but was razed, and Dr. A. G. Sellards built the present house on the site. The Martin Morris house was the last one on Water Street. On the northeast corner of the Court Square stood a one-story frame house used as a storeroom where the mail was taken care of. Joshua Bartley built a house on the site of the Patton Hotel, which was built in the 1880's by Nicholas Bergmeyer of Ironton, Ohio.

In 1827 Major John C. Kouns built the Kouns House on the corner of Front and Harrison Streets and this house has been owned and occupied by members of the Kouns family to the present time. Jesse Corum, at one time, lived in the house on Main Street which was later a tavern and called the Andes House. William Corum's father lived in the house on the corner of Main and Laurel Alley which was for a long time the home of the Edwin Heisler family. Mr. Heisler was an undertaker who had married Rebecca Corum. Their family consisted of Edward, Benjamin, George, Amanda, Josephine, and Nancy Pugh.

James Van Bibber lived on the south side of Main Street where the John Moran house and store stood for many years. The Chillison property stood on Main Street, on both corners of Laurel Alley. The lower property consisted of a store and house combined and was sold to John Hoffman in the 1880's. The upper property was long the home of the David Mitchell family. His wife was Sophia Chillison.

Farther up Main Street Samuel Osenton built a house on Lot No. 29. Here also lived Dr. Henry Green, who moved to Alcorn. The house was then occupied by William Corum until bought by Edward Dulin, a lawyer, and it was the Dulin home for many years. This property was the home of James Watt Womack and wife for many years. On Perry Street, where the George Pratt house stood so long, there was originally a small log house. Another resident of Perry Street was Chris Kinsler, who had a house and a small store just above the school ground. Mr. Kinsler built the brick house across the street from there in the early 1880's.

On the corner of Washington and Perry Streets was the James McMullan home. He was a tinner. At the lower end of Perry Street, next to Sandy, was a frame house where the John Schmutz family lived until they bought the Dr. Ellis home on Main Street. On the corner of Perry and Walnut Streets stood the Joseph Pollock home, and it is still a wonderfully preserved house. The large brick house at the head of Elizabeth Street was also built very early and was long the home of the Hollingsworth family. It was the homestead of the Major John C. Kouns family. He not only built this house, but also the Kouns House, and the brick house on Front Street and Hickory Alley which was later owned by the Womack family and then by the Owen Kendall family. Edward Hollingsworth married Elizabeth, daughter of Major John and Elizabeth Kouns, and they lived in the old homestead.

In 1842 and 1843 several houses were built, among them a two-story frame built by Dupouletee Valodine, which was owned successively by John Russell, Frank B. Trussel, Adolphus Reid, Miss Bessie Brugh, and A. S. Cooper. The Van Dyke house was built by Charles Wilson about this time and was later owned and occupied by the Van Dyke and Pollock families. It is now owned by Frederick and Rebecca Biggs Forsythe. The Pierson McCoy cottage was built by Mr. Chillison. The Dr. William Kouns house was built in 1856 by A. W. Wood, a carpenter. This has been the home of the Cole and Leslie families for many years.

There were not many houses built in East Greenup before 1880. On the southwest corner beyond Town Branch was the Walters home. Mrs. Walters married Jacob Urban and for a long time many Greenup citizens went "over the Rhine" as it was called, to the Urban Saloon.

At Riverton, the Hockaday family built a store and house combined and there the Edwin Hockaday family lived for a long time. Upon the hill near the store was another Hockaday farmhouse where the George Hockaday family lived. The Corum family built and occupied the brick house, later sold to Colonel William Worthington, and now owned by the Crawfords. Here were the Jesse Corum and the John Seaton homes, both of which burned.

Besides the John Hockaday home on the river there were not many houses until the coming of the Eastern Kentucky Improvement Company and later the Eastern Kentucky Railroad. Probably the first house to be built by that company at Riverton was the H. W. Bates home, where members of that family lived for sixty years. Another house built was the large frame house on the corner above the Bates home, and in between these two stood the red brick office building. The house on the corner was occupied by the George Gibbs family. Mr. Gibbs was the Civil Engineer for the Eastern Kentucky Railroad Company.

The Tibbitts and Crawford houses were built much later. At Riverton, near the river, stood the John Hockaday farmhouse, which was destroyed by fire and rebuilt only to be burned again. On the rear of this farm was built a store and dwelling house combined, which was the home of some of the Hockaday families for many years. Up on a hill from here stood a farmhouse occupied by the George Hockaday family and they lived here until Mr. Hockaday built the house on the river where the William McKee family lived. Some of the family are still living there. The Hockaday storehouse was bought by J. W. Kouns, who remodeled it into a dwelling.

NEWSPAPERS

The first newspaper in Greenup County was published at Catlettsburg in the 1850's by G. W. Smith and Ezra C. Thornton. In 1853 it was commissioned by the court to do all the public printing at that time for the county.

The *Independent* was the first newspaper published in Greenupsburg. It was edited by George A. Creel in the early 1870's and later by Karl B. Grahn. In 1879 and 1880 Carlisle H. Callon was the editor of this paper.

The next paper was the *Greenup Gazette* started by H. B. Woodrow in the late 1870's, and the office was located in the

Masonic Building. In the early 1880's W. J. A. Rardin bought the press and fixtures and edited the *Gazette* for many years. In 1913 the press was badly damaged by the flood of that year and the *Gazette* was discontinued.

In 1892 the *Democrat* was started and edited by Samuel Callon and Robert Wilson. The office was over the present post office on Washington Street. Later the *Democrat* was edited by J. Frank Hutchinson of Corbin, Kentucky, for a short time. It was moved to the Myers building on Front Street, where it was edited by Walter Callon for five or six years. After that time it was discontinued.

About 1915 Seneca X. Swimm brought a press from Olive Hill, Kentucky, and edited a newspaper called the *Republican* for one year. Leo Thompson was the editor for the next two years, A. S. Cooper for a short time, and James M. Richardson, of Ironton, was the editor until 1922, when it was bought by William I. Myers, and he was the editor until 1934, when it was discontinued. The *Greenup News* is the current newspaper.

The Register of the Kentucky Historical Society of July 1938 gives:

Newspapers in Ashland—1856—*Ashland Kentuckian* weekly until 1859

1857—*Democratic Battery* weekly

1860—*Sandy Valley Advocate* weekly

Newspapers in Catlettsburg—1852—*Big Sandy News* weekly until 1853

Newspapers in Greenupsburg—1859—*Sandy Valley Advocate* weekly until 1860

PHYSICIANS

Dr. Henry Green was the first physician in Greenup and he came there from Mt. Sterling, Kentucky. His wife was Miss Evelyn Gardner, whose family came from the Island of San Domingo, having left there because of the insurrection of 1799. The Gardners came first to Barboursville, West Virginia, and later to Greenup, where they kept a hotel that stood near the place where the Kouns House was built later. Dr. Green was the great-grandfather of Mrs. Lucy Sellards Taylor. He lived on Main Street on the lot where Edward Dulin built the house later occupied by James Watt and Ida Osenton Womack. Dr. Green later moved to Alcorn.

In 1830 James Van Bibber was a practicing physician in Greenup. Very little is known of him, but he probably lived on Main Street below John Moran's home.

Dr. Alfred Spalding was born in 1815 at Amherst, New Hampshire, a son of Dr. Matthias Spalding. He graduated in medicine from Dartmouth College, New Hampshire, and came to Greenupsburg to practice his profession soon after his graduation in 1843. The Spalding and Seaton families were both from Amherst. Dr. Spalding married Rebecca, daughter of Samuel Seaton, who lived on Water Street, where the Spalding family lived later. In December 1878 Dr. Spalding died, having been a practicing physician of Greenup County for thirty-five years. Two sons, George and Alfred, are both physicians in New York.

Dr. Samuel Ellis came from Lewis County to Greenup about 1850. He had married Lucy Bruce of Vanceburg, and their children were Elizabeth, Thomas, and Samuel Bruce (Hal). The Ellis family owned and occupied the brick house on the corner of Main Street and Cedar Alley. He sold this house to John Schmutz and built the frame house above it which was later sold to the James Clifton family. Miss Lydia Bell, a relative of the Waring family, made her home with the Ellis family. Several of the family developed lung trouble and went to Colorado seeking the western climate for their health. Later all the family went there.

Dr. Alfred Davis DeBard was a son of Dr. James and Eliza Lewis DeBard. He was born in Carter County in 1833, and learned his profession in Louisville, Kentucky, coming to Greenup as a partner with Dr. Alfred Spalding in 1857. Here he met Augusta Seaton and they were married in 1859. He established a home and office on upper Front Street, where he lived and practiced for many years both in Greenup and in the county. They were the parents of six children, Alfred, Mary, Helen, Harriet, Margaret, and Eunice.

Dr. Abram Goble Sellards was a son of Andrew and Mary Hartley Sellards of Greenup County. He studied his profession in Cincinnati and in Philadelphia. He began practicing in Greenup in 1872 and continued there until 1893, when he moved to Portsmouth, where he practiced until his death. He married Emma Woodrow and they were the parents of Dr. Howard, a physician in Portsmouth, Dr. Ernest of Ashland, Kentucky, Margaret, and William, a druggist.

Dr. John Sellards, a brother of Dr. A. G. Sellards, came to Greenup about 1880 to practice. Before coming to Greenup he had practiced in Powellsville, Ohio. He married Mary Woodrow, a sister of Dr. A. G. Sellards' wife. They had four children: Dr. William, who practiced in Greenup, married a Miss Armstrong, and died while yet a young man; Lucy Taylor, Thomas, George, and an adopted daughter, Rose.

Dr. Alonzo Carnahan was born in Boyd County in 1841. His parents were Dr. James and Delilah Hopkins Carnahan. He studied medicine at Johns Hopkins University and settled at Oldtown, where he married Virginia Anglin Kendall. Besides practicing his profession he was a farmer and one of the first growers of tobacco in the county.

Dr. Benjamin Bennett practiced in the Tygart Valley during the 1870's and 1880's. He married Miss Maude Holbrook of Tygart and moved to Fullerton, where he lived the last years of his life.

Dr. Charles Secrest practiced at Lynn in the 1870's and 1880's. He had married Miss Polly Warnock of Tygart and they were the parents of Edna Jones, William, Charles, Elizabeth Graham, and Laura Stricklett.

Dr. James L. Gibson was the physician at Laurel Furnace and the surrounding country in 1850 and 1860. He had served in the Mexican War, and gave his sword to the family of Benjamin King, brother-in-law of the Wurts brothers of Laurel Furnace. This sword is a relic in the Biggs home at Frost, Kentucky, Mrs. William Biggs having been a daughter of Benjamin King. He died in 1867 at the age of fifty and was buried in the Laurel Graveyard.

Dr. Martin Samuel Leslie was born in Pike County, Kentucky, and studied his profession in Lexington, Kentucky. He located in Greenup in 1882 and shortly afterward married Florence Hunt of Lexington. They were residents of Greenup for many years and were the parents of Ralph, Samuel, Philip, and Robert G.

Dr. Henry Thomas Morris was born in Lawrence County, Kentucky, in 1868, son of Richard and Emily Edwards Morris. He received his education in the rural schools and attended the Kentucky School of Medicine. He received his degree in 1879 and located at Lynn, Greenup County. In 1901 he married Caroline Carnahan, and in 1905 moved to Greenup, where he was a leading physician until he retired from active practice a few years ago.

Dr. Morris has an award from the Kentucky School of Medicine for more than fifty years of continuous practice. For years he has been a member of the Greenup County Medical Association, the Kentucky Medical Association, and the American Medical Association. Dr. Morris served two terms in the State Senate and was the author of the Anti-Loafing Bill, an act compelling every man from sixteen to sixty years of age to work, the only exceptions being bona fide students of colleges and universities. This bill was passed during World War I.

Dr. Morris is a York Rite Mason and a Noble of the Mystic Shrine.

Dr. William Morris, a brother of Dr. Henry Thomas Morris, was born in 1866. He attended the county schools of Lawrence County and the Kentucky School of Medicine at Louisville. On receiving his degree he practiced in Lawrence County, where he married (1) Maud Hensley. They were the parents of Dr. Hurston Morris of Portsmouth, Ohio. Dr. Morris came to Greenup County about 1900 and located at Oldtown. He married (2) Alma Womack of Oldtown, and moved to Fullerton, where he practiced until his death.

Dr. Morris was a member of the Masonic fraternity.

Dr. Ellis Raike was born in Greenup in 1874, the son of Jasper and Martha Nichols Raike. The family had come from Pennsylvania to Ohio and from there to Greenup County. Dr. Raike received his education in the Greenup schools and attended the Kentucky School of Medicine. After receiving his degree he married Lenore Carnahan of Oldtown and located at Lynn. A daughter, Anna Carnahan, was born while they lived there.

After a few years of practice at Lynn the family moved to Leavenworth, Kansas, where Dr. Raike was connected for many years with the Government Hospital. He and his wife returned to Greenup, where he is now practicing.

Anna Carnahan Raike married Professor Edwin Clark, who is connected with the State University at Iowa City, Iowa.

Dr. Albert S. Brady came from Jackson, Ohio, to Greenup County and practiced medicine on Tygart Creek. He married Cora, daughter of Edward and Mary Mearns Warnock of Warnock. They came to Greenup to live in 1895 and purchased the home of Dr. Abram G. Sellards, who moved to Portsmouth just previous to that time.

Dr. Brady was a progressive citizen and had a large practice. He owned the second automobile brought to Greenup.

Dr. and Mrs. Brady were the parents of three daughters, Marie, Maude, and Grace.

LAWYERS

The following names appear as lawyers in the county:

1805

Thomas Grayson
Thomas Daugherty
James Clark
David Trimble
William Roper

1815-1830

Thompson Ward
John M. McConnell
William Connor

1834-1840

John Hollingsworth
William J. Sands
William Ireland

1850-1860

Edward Dulin
F. B. Trussell
William Worthington

1860-1870

George Roe
Benjamin F. Bennett
Jeremiah Davidson

1880

Benjamin E. (Bud) Roe
George Halbert
Thomas H. Paynter
Joseph B. Bennett

1890

William T. Cole

1925-1950

Thomas E. Nickell
J. D. Atkinson
Lovell Lyles
C. H. Bruce
John Coldiron

Five

CHURCHES & BURIAL GROUNDS

CHURCHES

William Cullen Bryant said in his beautiful poem, "The groves were God's first temples," and such were used as places of worship by the pioneers, most of whom were deeply religious. Traveling preachers came to isolated settlements and word would be sent far and near that a meeting would be held on the Sabbath Day in a convenient grove. Settlers came on horseback and in wagons, bringing well-filled baskets of food and also provender for the teams. There were happy meetings of the people so far from their former homes and much preaching, praying, and singing,

Religious services were often held in the homes of the settlers. Schoolhouses built of logs cut from the groves nearby were used for church meetings as well as for teaching. Now every community has one church and sometimes more according to creeds.

Among the early traveling preachers was Samuel Demint, who married Deborah, daughter of Garret G. Harsin, in 1811, and settled on Little Sandy River. He organized the first Methodist Church in Greenup County. Another Methodist preacher was Dan Young, an ordained minister of New Hampshire, who came with others, overland to the Ohio River, and to Concord (Wheelersburg), Ohio. He preached many sermons and funerals in Greenup County. The Rev. Lindsay was a Presbyterian preacher of the county in the 1820's. The followers of Alexander Campbell organized the Christian Church in the county in the 1840's.

CATHOLIC CHURCH

In the 1870's a meeting was held in the Methodist Church in Greenup, at which much was said against dancing and card playing. A discussion arose which resulted in the Dr. William S.

Kouns family withdrawing their membership. The Kouns families had been prominent members of the Methodist Church since its beginning. The Dr. Kouns families adopted the Catholic faith, erected an altar in the home, and had a priest from Ironton, Ohio, to hold services. These were attended by the John Schmutz family of Greenup, and by the German families of Harris, George, and others of Coal Branch. In the 1890's a church was built on the Dr. Kouns land.

GREENUP CHRISTIAN CHURCH

The Christian Church in Greenup was built in 1855 on land donated by Mrs. Rebecca Seaton Spalding. The first building was razed some years ago and the present one erected on the original site on Main Street. Early members of this church were the Seaton, Spalding, Hockaday, Ireland, Halbert, Stark, Mitchell, Morton, Pratt, and Chillison families. Two early ministers were George Dorsey and J. R. Pinkerton, the latter serving the church for many years.

LYNN CHRISTIAN CHURCH

The Christian Church at Lynn was organized in 1850 and called the Liberty Christian Church. The land was donated by Rival D. Jones to the following members: Samuel B. Pugh, Edward Brooks, William F. Pratt, Eliza Pratt, Mary Jones, Mary Ann Pugh, Amanda Brooks, Daniel Mosely, Mildred Mosely, Oratio Nelson Jones, Martha Jones, and Elijah Pugh. This church was served for many years by Oratio Nelson Jones, who also served the Siloam Christian Church.

SILOAM CHRISTIAN CHURCH

Keyes's *History of Scioto County, Ohio*, states that Siloam Church was the first religious organization in Greenup County.

The original records of the church are still in existence and the first legible date is that of 1819, with the minutes signed by John Mackoy. The congregation met as the "Regular Baptist Church of Tigerts Creek" until 1834, when, evidently through the influence of the teachings of Alexander Campbell, they embraced his doctrine and assumed the name of "The Church of Christ of Tigerts Creek."

Under date of January 1840, the minutes state that a meeting was held at Siloam Meeting House, which was probably the house built by Nicholas Fisher Thom, an elder of the church, on the ground given by John Mackoy. This is the present location of the church and cemetery.

Families listed as members of the church are Fuqua, Mackoy, Smith, McCall, Hoytt, Medaugh, Osborn, and Thom. Past ministers who served the church were "Brother" Ashley, Moses Mackoy, Oratio Nelson Jones of Liberty, and Thomas Degman of Springdale, Kentucky. The Rev. Oaks served as minister of the church in later years.

METHODIST EPISCOPAL CHURCH, SOUTH, OF GREENUP

The Methodist Episcopal Church was the first church built in Greenup. It was built on Main Street on Lot No. 27, donated by Major John C. Kouns and his wife, Elizabeth Smith Kouns, in 1845. Near the present building there stood at that time a small building used for both a school and a "Preaching House." The first trustees were John F. Day, Joseph Taylor, George Wurts, John Myers, and John C. Stuart. The original church had two front doors, and the pulpit was located on the north side of the room. One of the front doors has been eliminated and the pulpit is now on the west side, but the foundation, walls, windows, and color are the same as the original.

Early members besides those mentioned above were the Hollingsworth, Winn, Sands, Rankins, Winters, Womack, Reid, Martin, and Kouns families. Some of the early preachers were Medley, Armstrong, Mitchell, Carter, and Madison.

SECOND METHODIST CHURCH

This Methodist Church was organized and built in 1880 on land donated by A. C. Van Dyke, and is situated on Perry Street. The early members were Dr. A. G. Sellards, Heislers, Hodges, Woodrows, Taylors, Crawfords, and Sowards families. Some of the early ministers were Pollard, Frenger, and Riffle.

BETHLEHEM METHODIST CHURCH

Bethlehem Church was organized and built in 1892. Mrs. Hattie Bryson collected the money to build the church from people all over the county. Thomas McNeal gave the ground for it on the west side of the highway just above Rocky, and James W. West and Maurice Edmund Cartwright did carpenter work.

The Rev. Gosling was the presiding elder at that time and the Rev. Isaac Newton Fannin was the first pastor. The pastors who followed him were the Rev. McKinster, Dr. Johnsy Glover, the

Rev. Switzer, the Rev. Bush in 1902, the Rev. James F. Pennybacker in 1903, the Rev. Surgeon, and the Rev. Mallory.

Some of the charter members were Lawson Bryson and his family, Smith Herbert, and James W. West. Among other families who became members were McClave, Cartwright, and Fitch.

Lawson Bryson was the first Sunday school superintendent. Simeon Fitch served the church as Sunday school superintendent for forty-five years.

LIMEVILLE CHURCH

The Limeville Methodist Church was organized and built in 1909, on land donated by the Merrill family. Early members were the John Merrill, James West, Cyrus Cartwright, and Tong families. It is a part of the Mt. Zion Circuit and is served by the same ministers.

MT. ZION CHURCH

A Methodist Church was organized at Mt. Zion in 1820. On May 23, 1839, Thomas Lawson and wife, Ada, Pleasant Savage and wife, Susan, deeded land for a church. The deed reads, "Being the lot or parcel of land on which the meeting house now stands (1839)." When the log church was razed to make room for the present frame building it was rebuilt on the farm of William Biggs (1873). The trustees were William Dupuy, Wilson Lee, Jane Walker, Nathaniel Warner, Benjamin F. King, Cyrus Lawson, and J. Burton. Of these the Lawsons, Warners, and Kings have descendants still living near Mt. Zion.

The first preacher was Samuel Demint, of whom it was said, "This is the first preacher in the county, a great man, God-fearing and fearless, his name is Samuel Demint." By whom this was said no one knows. He served until 1826. C. F. Harbour, who served in 1939, was the last minister to serve before it was joined with the Methodist Episcopal Church, North, and after his name are these words: "This is the last year of the Methodist Church, South. It has been one hundred years since the deed was made."

BENNETT'S CHAPEL

Bennett's Chapel, on Shultz Creek, was built about one hundred years ago on land belonging to Colonel Thaddeus Bennett. It is of the Methodist persuasion and the early members were the Greenslate, Anderson, Clary, and Hunt families.

OLDTOWN CHURCH

The Oldtown Church was organized before 1820. Samuel Demint, "a regular communicant of the Methodist Society," organized several Methodist Churches in Greenup County. He lived on the Little Sandy River near Oldtown. John Howe, who lived above Greenup in 1804 and moved to Oldtown a few years later, gave the land for "the erection of a Methodist Church." A log church was built which was in use until 1890, when the present frame church was built. Early members were Womacks, Kouns, Starks, Kendalls, Carnahans, Downs, Osentons, Cliftons, Howes, Virgins, and Hartleys, all of whom lived at Oldtown. Other members were Deerings, Norrises, Hannahs, and Anglins, who lived near Hopewell. A churchyard surrounds the church and many of these old families are buried there.

RUSSELL METHODIST CHURCH

The first Methodist Church at Russell was a frame building known as the Mead Chapel, the Mead family having been instrumental in building it. Henry Mead paid off a debt on the old church, and the new one, Mead Memorial, was named in honor of the family. Mrs. Belle Mead Prichard, who was born and reared at the Mead farm, gave generously to the erection of the new church.

SPRINGVILLE METHODIST CHURCH

In 1820 the Methodists of Springville held their services in a small log building. The Rev. Samuel Demint served the people of several communities. He was one of the old-time circuit riders.

In 1876 the members began to plan the erection of a suitable church building. Anthony and Elizabeth Thomson donated a lot for the purpose, the members raised the money for material, and the men gave their services toward the building. The church was built on the corner of Main and Spruce Streets. There were but thirty-five members at the time and the Rev. Hiram Moore was the pastor.

After a number of years the church building was raised above flood stage and the Sunday school rooms were added. For many years the Springville Church was a part of the Mt. Zion Circuit but this has been changed and it is now a part of the Carlisle Circuit.

GREENUP UNION PRESBYTERIAN CHURCH

One of the first churches in the county was organized January 14, 1829, at the home of John Lawson, by the Rev. Eleazer Brainard of the Portsmouth Presbyterian church. It was named the Greenup Union Presbyterian Church. Three trustees were appointed to superintend the building of a meeting house in the "Lawson Settlement": John Lawson and Josiah Morton, elders of the Portsmouth Church, and Clement H. Waring.

Later, in the same year, John Culver deeded one acre of ground "in the forks of the roads leading to Portsmouth and to Osburn's Mill on Tygart Creek five or six miles below Greenup, for the purpose of building the Greenup Union Meeting House." The first minister was the Rev. Lindsley and the first families to become members were Lawson, Morton, Waring, Reid, Pogue, Powers, Burton, Bryson, Hill, and Merrill.

In 1881 James D. Biggs, Thomas W. Jones, and the Rev. A. D. Tadlock were appointed a committee to erect a new church building. It was built of red brick and Gothic style of architecture, and, probably at this time, the church became known as Brick Union instead of Greenup Union.

This was a Southern Presbyterian Church and served the people of the community for almost one hundred years. In 1919, however, the building was sold to the Christian congregation, which still worships here.

Ministers who served the Presbyterian Church were J. H. Condit, A. A. Case, John C. Bayliss, Faris Brown, William Condit, A. D. Tadlock, Samuel D. Boggs, William M. Mebane, M. V. P. Yeaman, David L. Lander, and J. L. Irvin.

In the cemetery around the church many of the early settlers of the county are buried. One grave is that of George Naylor Davis, a soldier of the War of 1812.

GREENUP PRESBYTERIAN CHURCH

In 1859 a Northern Presbyterian Church was organized in Greenup, and a church built by John Myers on land donated by the Kouns family. The original members of the congregation were Debards, Pollocks, Warnocks, Paynters, and those members of the Greenup Union Church who lived in Greenup. Ministers who served the Greenup Church in the early days were the Rev. Brown, the Rev. Condit from the Catlettsburg Presbyterian Church, the Rev. Barbour, and the Rev. Tait.

UNION CHURCH

The Wurtland Union Church is one of the oldest in the county. It was built about 1860 and presented to the residents of the community by George and Mary Ann Wurts as a place for union worship. Services have been held here for more than ninety years. The frame building, except for an occasional coat of paint and necessary repairs, is today practically the same as when it was built.

Among those who have acted as superintendents of the Sunday school throughout the years are James Biggs, Lewis Collins, John Brammer, Ewing Chinn, L. F. Smith, and Ernest Bonzo.

BURIAL GROUNDS

As there was no hallowed ground in which to lay the bodies of the pioneers who died in the new land, burial places were chosen on the land of the owners and enclosed by a strong fence for protection from prowling animals. As time passed and changes occurred in the ownership of land, fences disappeared from old family plots, and weeds and vines grew rank on graves and headstones. There are many such old burial places in our county.

Such a condition inspired Katherine Atherton Grimes to write the poem "Forgotten Graves," the thought expressed being the first poignant grief, the gradual forgetting, and finally the total neglect.

There are many family burial grounds still in use in the county that are well cared for. Some of these are the Waring cemetery near Lynn, the Warnock cemetery on upper Tygart Creek, the Van Bibber cemetery at the Falls of Little Sandy River, and those at Wurtland, Raceland, and perhaps at other places. In the old McConnell graveyard at Wurtland are graves of soldiers who died at Camp Maggard during the Civil War.

As communities grew churches were built with space about them for burial purposes. There are many of these in the rural communities, some churchyards filled, not only with the families of the old settlers, but with those from other communities. Among these are the graveyards at Brick Union, Mt. Zion, and Siloam. At Oldtown there are many old dates on the gravestones. In that churchyard there is the stone of Lucy Virgin Downs and many members of her family. Here also are buried members of the Deering family, pioneer furnace builders.

In the Collins graveyard on East Fork lie the remains of Andrew and Mary Kane Hood, first pioneers, and not far away in the Shuff graveyard is the grave of Jesse Boone. Since these men were two of those hardy pioneers who helped to organize the county and the county seat, each one should be remembered by a memorial at his burial place.

Other early graveyards in the county are the Anglin, in the eastern part of the county, the Howland on Tygart Creek, and the Laughlin, English, Thomson, and Killen near Springville. The Killen graveyard is within the limits of the old Indian Fort. When a community became a town, a cemetery was laid off usually at, or near, a pioneer burial plot. At Greenup the early settlers were buried on the lowest level of the hill in the rear of the town. As this level became crowded graves were made higher on the hill and now they have almost reached the top. On the left of the roadway is that part allotted to the Negroes, and many of those graves are of those faithful ones who died in the service of their masters.

On Decoration Day in May there can be seen a steady stream of people going to graves to place their flowers. Some visit those lonely, neglected spots on the old farms; some those churchyards that have been mown anew; and others, cemeteries of the towns and cities which are kept in orderly neatness. All have the same purpose in their hearts, to pay respect to those who have passed to the Great Beyond.

Six

SCHOOLS

EARLY EDUCATION

The first teacher in the town of Greenup seems to have been a man named Silas Wooten. He taught in a rude cabin, and it is said his school was attended by pupils from across the river in Ohio as well as those from Greenup.

In 1798 the Legislature of Kentucky passed an act which provided that all existing counties should be granted the proceeds of 8,000 acres of land, with which to purchase land and erect a building for the teaching of academic subjects, to be under the direction of trustees. Greenup County was not organized until 1803, but in 1810 a special act of the legislature was passed to establish an academy in Greenup County. On the plat of Greenup made in 1803 there were four lots, 82, 83, 84, and 85, on Perry Street between Harrison Street and Laurel Alley, two of which were left vacant and the other two marked "Warnick." Doubtless the vacant lots were left for a school building, and in 1815 the trustees purchased two acres on Perry Street and a two-story gray brick building known as the Greenupsburg Academy was erected. Schools supported by private tuition were taught here until 1835.

On record in the clerk's office is a deed which reads, "John C. Kouns and his wife, Elizabeth, to Greenup School Trustees Lot 26 (on Main Street) in 1827 for a Seminary." There is nothing to show that it was ever used as such and it was returned by deed to John C. Kouns July 10, 1854, by George Wurts, E. J. Hockaday and C. M. Wilson as trustees of said Seminary.

In B. F. Kidwell's *History of Education in Greenup County* we learn that a law establishing a system of elementary schools was passed by the Legislature February 16, 1838, whereby towns and communities meeting certain requirements would be aided by a state fund provided for that purpose. Two districts qualified, one being Greenup. It would be interesting to know what other district in the county qualified. It was probably one of the furnace neighborhoods.

In 1843 Greenup County was supervised by three commissioners, Bazil Waring, William Dupuy, and John Culver. This system prevailed until 1879 or 1880, when Charles A. Smith was made superintendent of schools. He was succeeded by "Whig" Clifton, and he, by John B. Norris. Pupils attending school in the late fifties and early sixties probably attended the Academy, where Professor George Ormsby and his wife taught. There were but two rooms then, but about 1875 the lower room was partitioned into two rooms. After the Civil War one of the early teachers was Miss Davidson from Ohio, who boarded in the family of John L. Mackoy. He lived on the corner of Main and Harrison Streets, where the bank and adjoining building now stand. Mrs. Addie Jones, who lived on Main Street, was the next teacher, then Mrs. Charlie Van Bibber, who taught for several years. After the lower room was divided, Mrs. Lola Roe Morton, Miss Annie Davidson, Miss Sallie York, and other Greenup women were teachers.

Professor Kenyon came to Greenup as a teacher about 1874, or perhaps earlier, and taught for five years. He had a great many pupils, many of them from other parts of the county. John B. Norris was both a public and a normal school teacher. His normals were attended by pupils from Boyd and Carter Counties as well as from Greenup County.

The Academy was the only brick school building in the county before 1891. Before that time the school buildings throughout the county were built of logs. In 1931 there were twenty-seven frame and fourteen brick buildings. The first graded school was organized at Greenup in 1875, probably under Professor S. T. Kenyon. The first teacher's certificate was granted in 1873. About 1889 the Academy was changed, with two rooms and an auditorium in the old part, and a hall and two rooms added on the lower side. Later more rooms were built onto the new part of the building.

The first high school commencement was in the spring of 1891. The graduates were Nettie Wilson, J. M. Literal, J. L. McCarty, Dollie Robb, Lizzie Hollingsworth, E. M. Sellards,

Nannie Warnock, Nora Hertel, Janetta Reid, Harriet DeBard, Fannie Warnock, and J. D. Kiser.

After the 1937 flood this school building was razed and the present one erected. A splendid new high school building was erected at Riverton a number of years ago.

Greenup County is now well supplied with schools. Russell, Raceland, Wurtland, McKell, Fullerton and South Portsmouth all have splendid buildings, while throughout the county the buildings are kept in good repair.

PRIVATE SCHOOLS

The first private school was the Greenup Academy, which was started in 1815 and continued as such until 1835.

Charles Kingsberry taught in the Seaton Academy on the Seaton farm back of Greenup in 1840. He was from Boston.

Miss Elizabeth Lyons taught a private school at Lynn, on Tygart Creek, about 1858.

Miss Pollock taught a private school in Greenup in the late 1850's.

When the George Wurts family lived on the John McConnell farm the law office was used as a private school for children of that locality. These children were Matt Davisson and Mary Collins from Ohio, the Brammer and Wurts children of Wurtland, the Stark and Biggs children from Greenup.

Miss Helen A. Seaton taught a private school in Greenup in 1856 and 1857.

Above the Seaton farm in the rear of East Greenup, long known as Academy Hollow, lived a King family in a house which was part log and part frame. Mrs. King taught a private school in one part of the house which was attended by the children of the John Seaton and Jesse Corum families.

PUBLIC SCHOOL COMMISSIONERS AND TEACHERS

COMMISSIONERS

1841-1843 Bazil Waring, William Dupuy and John Culver	1884-1885 F. B. Trussell
	1885-1886 W. H. Clifton
1844-1846 M. Warnock, J. Davidson and Marshall Baker	1886-1890 Charles A. Smith (First Superintendent)
1847-1849 J. Davidson, William Corum and Samuel Seaton	1890-1898 L. R. McCarty
	1898-1906 J. M. Literal
1850-1852 E. J. Honaker	1906-1910 L. F. Thompson
1853-1855 L. D. Ross	1910-1914 J. G. Pritchard
1855-1858 Robert Galbraith	1914-1918 Sophia E. Kitchen
1859-1862 J. Davidson	1918-1925 J. N. Hatfield
1863-1866 Robert Galbraith	1925-1929 R. J. Nickell
1867-1869 F. B. Trussell	1929-1930 Mrs. R. J. Nickell
1870-1871 S. J. Filson	1930-1933 Robert Nickell
1872-1874 S. H. Walcott	1932-1933 Jesse Stuart
1875-1878 J. W. Womack	1933-1938 Fred Maynard
1878-1880 W. H. Clifton	1938-1942 Tong West
1881-1883 J. B. Norris	1942-1950 Fred Maynard

TEACHERS

Miss Annie Davidson, daughter of Jeremiah and Eliza Corum Davidson of Greenup, taught school for forty-nine years. Thirty-seven of these years were in Greenup and elsewhere in the county, beginning in 1875. She taught the remainder of the forty-nine years at other places in Kentucky and in Illinois. She married Dr. Littlejohn of Oconee, Illinois.

Other teachers who gave years of service in Greenup were:

Don Judd, 1 year.........1873	S. E. M. Coulter, 2 years...1881-1883
S. T. Kenyon, 5 years......1874-1879	J. D. Norris, 1 year........1883-1884
Cyrus Eakman, 1 year......1879-1880	J. B. Nash, 1 year.........1884-1885
Park C. Watts, 1 year......1880-1881	Daniel Null, 1 year........1885-1886

TEACHERS WHO GAVE YEARS OF SERVICE IN THE COUNTY

Miss Mary Reed	Miss Alice Jones	Miss Lucy Gray
Miss Agnes Baker	Miss Myrtle Hartley	Mrs. Emma Thomson
Miss Kate Stark	Miss Nina Mitchell	Miss Myra Thomson
Lawrence McCoy	George Clark	Miss Lyde Mytinger
Miss Mary Callon	Miss Lavenia Gray	Miss Lucy Hartley
Miss Effie Ghent	Hugh Curry	John Merrill
L. R. McCarty	Miss Emma Reed	Fillmore Musser
Miss Lucy Sellards	Taylor Warnock	Miss Loue A. Jones
Edward Ghent	Miss Ida Osenton	Miss Susan Davisson
Robert A. E. Leslie	Miss Ida Hodges	H. Green Richards
Miss Sallie Tinsley	Miss Laura Ghent	Miss Emma Warnock
Mrs. Sarah Warden	Henry Powell	Miss Lucy Roe
Miss Nora Stark	Charles A. Smith	Miss Etta Smith
Miss Maude Mitchell	Allen Berry	Miss Louella Hall

EARLY MUSIC TEACHERS OF GREENUP

Mrs. John Ormsby	Miss Mary Elizabeth Seaton
Mrs. George Gibbs	Miss Ratie Van Bibber
Miss Bessie Brugh	

Seven

INTERESTING ITEMS & SOCIAL LIFE

INTERESTING ITEMS

The *Independent* was the first newspaper published in the county, and from the issue of May 25, 1871, which is in the *Greenup News* office, the following notes have been taken:

Professional cards were those of George E. Roe, Edward F. Dulin, Halbert and Biggs, Samuel J. Filson, Jeremiah Davidson, Ireland and Trussell, and Jesse Corum, all attorneys-at-law.

Samuel Ellis, M. D., office and residence on Main Street; John T. Sellards, Physician and Surgeon, Hunnewell, Kentucky; C. M. Brammer, M. D., Physician and Surgeon, Fulton Oil Works; The Kouns House, J. E. Winn, Proprietor; The Kentucky House, John Smutz, Proprietor; Drugs, W. S. Kouns, Druggist and Apothecary, Masonic Hall; Merchants: J. Sydenstricker; Eifort and Hertel, General Store; J. S. McMullan, Hardware Dealer, Elizabeth and Washington Streets. Few people of our county today can recall the names of any of the above residents of Greenup.

The following is a statement of the taxable property of the county according to the assessment for 1871:

214,233 acres of land valued at	$1,719,763
151 town lots valued at	156,541
2,225 horses valued at	156,870
366 mules valued at	34,405
5,360 cattle valued at	81,322
14 stores valued at	76,724
pleasure carriages valued at	3,486
gold and silver valued at	1,190
pianos valued at	3,250
bushels of corn raised valued at	404,938
bushels of wheat raised valued at	31,580
tons of pig metal valued at	25,448
income in U. S. Bonds	1,171

The following is a copy of a letter written in 1868, by Dr. Alfred Spalding of Greenup to his son, George, who was away from home attending school. The doctor wrote: "A very bad accident occurred just below Gallipolis yesterday when the steamer, 'Harry Dean,' blew up and burned, having a large quantity of oil on board. Mr. Robinson Biggs and Captain Norton, of Ashland, were both lost and neither of them have been found yet." (Several months later the body of Mr. Biggs was found and identified by his wife by the socks which she had darned.)

In this letter Dr. Spalding also wrote that "the railroad (Eastern Kentucky Improvement Company) is progressing as well as can be expected in bad weather. The track is completed to the oil well, all of the tunnels are through except the Barney tunnel, and they think the road will be completed in April."

To the above was added by Alfred, a younger son at home, "They have a very fine locomotive. The well at the engine house was a failure."

John B. King, an attorney-at-law, lived at the upper part of the Corum property, later the Colonel Worthington home. His wife taught school in their home, which the Seaton and Corum (Jesse) children attended. Children of the King family were Bruce, Charles, James, and Gertrude. Charles served in the United States Army for many years. Bruce is said to have been a writer, but none of his writings have been located in Greenup County at this time.

Many things for use in the homes were made in early days. These were mostly kitchen utensils, and some things made at Caroline Furnace are heirlooms in homes in that section of the county. One of the things made at this furnace was an iron coffin. There may have been others, but this is the only one known of at this time.

When the Chesapeake and Ohio Railroad bought land from Henry Powell in 1924, bodies were moved from the old Powell Graveyard to other burial places. One of the coffins was made of iron, rusty but whole. It contained the body of Mary Ann Powell Campbell, buried sixty-five years. At the head of the coffin was a movable lid, which a relative pushed aside. Looking through the glass beneath, he said that the body, dressed in black with a white cap about the head, was perfectly preserved.

Greenup County was formed from Mason, and Mason from Bourbon, which was taken from the northern part of Fayette in 1785. Fayette was one of the three counties formed in 1780 from Kentucky County, which was a part of Fincastle County, Virginia. Boyd County (1860), formerly part of Greenup County, was named for Hon. Linn Boyd, a Kentucky representative (1859).

When Boyd County was formed, its population was 6,044 in 1860, and 8,573 in 1870; Ashland's population in 1870 was 1,459, and Catlettsburg's was 1,019. In 1830 the population of Greenupsburg was 204, and in 1870 it was 507; that of the county, in 1830, was 5,852, while in 1870 it was 11,463.

The following copy of a record of the August 1807 term of court shows that the early settlers of the county believed in having good roads.

"The 4th day of May charge was brought on affidavit of Nimrod Canterberry and Edward Gilky against Moses Kibby for not keeping the road in repair leading from Little Sandy Licks to the Greenup Courthouse."

JOHN HOCKADAY, Clerk

William Lowery, foreman of the Jury.
Reuben Rucker, Sheriff.

Note: Little Sandy Licks was situated at Raccoon.

Basil Warnock owned the first automobile in Greenup. Dr. Albert S. Brady owned the second one, which was called "The Red Devil."

An early surveyor of Greenup County was Robert Galbraith While surveyor there in 1848 he made a map of Kentucky which was very interesting.

Old waybills show that the first freight agent for the Chesapeake and Ohio Railroad at Riverton in 1888 was George Gibbs, and the first one at Greenup was O. H. Dickey.

FIRES

There are no records of losses by fire in the early days of the county. In the late 1860's, the Tanner home on lower Front Street in Greenup was entirely destroyed and was never rebuilt. In 1872 Jehu Sydenstricker's general store on Harrison Street burned to the ground. Another building was erected on the site. In 1883 the store of James M. Sowards on the corner of Main and Washington Streets was badly damaged by fire and was restored but was again burned. The Womack brothers bought the damaged store, rebuilt it, and carried on the mercantile business there for almost sixty years.

In 1887 the old mill at the head of Front Street was destroyed by fire. The Seaton homestead on Seaton Avenue burned in the 1890's and valuable furnishings and papers were lost. The brick house on the old Rankins farm burned in the same year. This was located west of Greenup and was built in the early 1800's with bricks burned in the Rankins brick yard on the farm. In 1887 a frame mill owned by Wilson and Sowards on Railroad Street burned and was replaced by the present brick structure.

Between 1870 and 1900 several farmhouses in the county were destroyed. Among them were the Wilson Gammon homestead on Lower Tygart Creek, the William Biggs homestead at Smith Branch, the Matthew R. Warnock, Samson Bredon, Dr. B. F. Bennett, Edward Warnock, and James Taylor homes. The last five homes were located in the Warnock Settlement on upper Tygart. The William Bryson home of red brick at Gray's Branch burned in the early 1880's. It was soon rebuilt. In 1875 the James Martin home above Greenup burned. It was a frame house and was replaced in 1876 by a brick house.

FLOODS

From Collins' *History of Kentucky* the following extracts from the journal of Colonel George Croghan are quoted: "On January 29th, 1751, in company with Christopher Gist and others, we reached the Shawnee town situated on both sides of the Ohio River. There were about forty houses on the south side and about one hundred on the north side, also there was a building about ninety feet long in which the Shawnees held their councils."

Also, records show that on July 23, 1775, Colonel Croghan was here as an agent for the British and in his journal said: "There was a great flood in the river and, although the Ohio banks were high, the water at Shawnee, or Lower Town, was nine feet over the top and all houses on the north side, except three or four, were destroyed."

The following record of the flood crests of the Ohio River in Greenup County for the past 116 years are given by William Myers:

1832—61.5 feet	1910—59.0 feet	1939—57.2 feet
1847—60.6 feet	1913—67.0 feet	1940—60.4 feet
1883—59.4 feet	1927—56.9 feet	1943—59.11 feet
1884—66.8 feet	1933—59.9 feet	1945—63.9 feet
1897—57.9 feet	1936—62.7 feet	1948—64.1 feet
1907—59.8 feet	1937—73.8 feet	

GREENUP COUNTY FIRSTS

The first sheriff was Josiah Davidson, 1804.

The first circuit judge was John Colvin, 1805.

The first circuit clerk was John Hockaday, 1805.

The first tax commissioner was James Howe.

The first jail was built in 1806.

The first courthouse was built on the public square in 1806.

The first court was held in the home of Andrew Hood in 1804.

The Greenup Academy was built in 1815.

The first doctor in the county was Dr. Henry Green.

The first store in the county was owned by Benjamin Chinn.

The first store in Greenupsburg was owned by Robert Daugherty.

The Rev. Robert Lindsay preached the first sermon in Greenupsburg.

The first lawyer was named Fishback.

Benjamin Locke of Ohio built the first courthouse.

Silas Wooten taught the first school in Greenupsburg.

Reason Davis operated the first ferry.

O. S. Timberlake was the first tavern keeper in Greenupsburg.

A man named Robinson was the first tailor in Greenupsburg.

The first jail was built of hewn logs and stood near the present location of the Methodist Church.

The first steamboat, the "New Orleans," passed down the river in 1811.

The first towboat, the "Condor," came in 1835.

The first wooden covered bridge was built across Little Sandy River about 1840.

The first iron bridge was built across Little Sandy in 1884.

The first electric light system was installed in Greenupsburg in 1896 by James Sowards, Sr.

The first telephone system was installed in 1900 by a company of Flemingsburg, Kentucky. The exchange was in the home of Mrs. Mary Sellards of Main Street, with Rose Sellards the operator for many years.

OLD RESIDENTS

Andrew Hood was probably the oldest person to have lived within the present limits of the county. A statement made by his great-granddaughter places his age at one hundred and fifteen years. He is buried in the Collins graveyard on East Fork.

Mary Bonifant (or Bonifil) Gray was born in Maryland and

died on Tygart Creek November 25, 1872, at the age of one hundred and thirteen years, eight months, and eighteen days. She is buried in a Gray graveyard on Gray's Branch.

Nancy Million Stark was born in Stafford County, Virginia, and died at Oldtown at the age of one hundred and six years. She is buried in the Anglin Cemetery near Hopewell.

William Biggs was born at Mt. Sterling in 1800 and came to Greenup County when he was thirteen years old. He died in 1897 at the home of a daughter in Huntington, West Virginia. He is buried in the Brick Union Cemetery at Gray's Branch.

Elizabeth Lyons Stark was born in Virginia in 1802. She died at Riverton, at the home of a daughter, Mrs. Cassie Kouns, July 3, 1894. She is buried in the Kouns burial ground up on a hill.

Ann Elizabeth Lyons Womack was born at Oldtown, October 4, 1835. She was a daughter of Rezin and Elizabeth Lyons, and married William Archer Womack at Oldtown. They were the parents of eleven children, of whom James Watt was the oldest. Mrs. Womack died May 15, 1929, at the age of ninety-four, and is buried in the Oldtown Cemetery.

Mary Claxton Smith was born March 11, 1849, and celebrated her one hundredth birthday at Riverton, March 11, 1949. She was born on Claxton Ridge in Owens County, and came with her husband, Francis Marion Smith, to Greenup County in 1874. They bought a farm on Crane Creek and were the parents of twelve children. Those living are Mrs. Charles Willis, with whom she made her home; Mrs. Lowell Stevens of Siloam; Robert; Mrs. Sally Floyd of Samaria; Mrs. Sam Blevens of Crane Creek; Andrew, James, Joe, and John, of Hopewell; and Reuben of Samaria. Mrs. Smith had one hundred and thirty-two grandchildren, more than two hundred great-grandchildren, and twelve great-great-grandchildren. During her lifetime there were twenty-one United States presidents and four major wars. Mrs. Smith died in 1950.

Matilda Baker Crisp, the daughter of Allen and Lucinda Baker, was born on Hood's Run, December 13, 1851. She married Newton Crisp, son of Joel and Elizabeth Sammons Crisp, of Floyd County, December 10, 1872. She has always lived in the Tygart Valley, making her home now with her daughter, Lucy Crisp Taylor. In 1949 Mrs. Crisp crocheted a cushion for her rocking chair. She celebrated her ninety-eighth birthday December 13, 1949.

Kate Stark Virgin was born at Oldtown October 19, 1852, the daughter of Henry and Adelaide Howe Stark. She married Harvey Virgin and always lived at Oldtown. She began teaching school in the 1870's and was still teaching in the 1890's. Children of the family are Roscoe of Florida, Edward of Ashland, and Nora Meadows of the home place at Oldtown, with whom Mrs. Virgin lived.

James Watt Womack, the oldest son of William Archer and Ann Elizabeth Lyons Womack, was born November 24, 1852. He celebrated his ninety-seventh birthday November 24, 1949.

MYSTERIOUS DISAPPEARANCES

In the 1850's Smith Hitchcock left his home at Mt. Zion to locate a new home for his wife and ten children. He was never heard of afterward.

Cardinal F. Stark was a merchant during the late 1850's and early 1860's. In 1861 he went to Pittsburgh to sell iron. He returned to the landing at Greenup but did not get off the boat. He sent a message to his wife, Elizabeth, to ship the iron to Pittsburgh. Later she received a letter from him in Kansas, saying he was going across the plains. This was the last that was heard from him.

In the middle 1860's George Wurts, a son of Samuel Grandin Wurts, of Wurtland, was sent on a business mission by the Wurts brothers to New Orleans. On his return trip he disappeared from the boat. As he had been in the habit of walking in his sleep, and as his valuables were found intact, it was supposed that he had walked overboard while asleep.

TRAGEDIES

In the early 1880's Harvey Van Bibber was found on Sunday morning lying on Harrison Street. He had committed suicide by shooting himself. He was a bachelor and made his home with his sister, Mrs. Mary Van Bibber McCoy.

In 1887, William H. Mackoy, of Siloam, was killed when a gun he was carrying was accidentally discharged as he was mounting his horse.

In 1889 Mrs. Music, an aged woman of Fullerton, was struck by a Chesapeake and Ohio passenger train as she was crossing the track to go to her home. This was the first fatality of the new railroad in the western section of the county.

A second fatality occurred at Fullerton when Captain Jack McCallister was killed by a passenger train. He was pilot of the ferry and was on his way to the boat when killed. This was in the early 1900's.

In 1892 Eva, young daughter of Elijah and Martha Davenport of Mt. Zion, was burned when a lighted lamp fell from a chandelier in the Mt. Zion Church. She had lighted the lamps for an evening service and was alone when the accident happened. She ran into the churchyard, where her father came to her rescue, but she was so seriously burned that she died the next day.

The account of this hanging was copied from a paper belonging to Mrs. Albert Hale of Wurtland, Kentucky:

Greenupsburg received the name of "Hangtown" because of the hangings which took place in the early days, on a tree near Little Sandy River. The last public hanging took place in June 1852, when the most terrible murder in the annals of Greenup County took place near Argillite. William Brewer and his wife were killed one night by five men. These were soon apprehended, tried, convicted, and three of them were sentenced to be hanged. One of the three hanged himself in the jail cell before the date of the hanging.

Instead of hanging these men on the tree where the hangings originally took place, a scaffold was built on west Main Street near the Little Sandy River. A cart carrying the condemned men, who were sitting on their coffins, passed slowly under the scaffold, the black caps were placed in position, the nooses in the ropes were adjusted, the fife and drum played the death march, the oxen and cart moved on, and the bodies were left hanging in the air.

On the day of this execution Greenupsburg was filled to overflowing with people, women as well as men. They came for miles on horseback, on mules, in wagons, and on foot. The women wore dresses with very full skirts and were dressed in costly attire of that time. Men with great mustaches were present, wearing bleached muslin pleated shirts, blue jean trousers and nail-keg hats.

HEIRLOOMS

Under the title of Early Settlers mention was made of some of the early possessions brought by the pioneers from the old homes to the new. Besides the black iron yard kettles used in washing and in the making of soap, there were large brass and copper ones for the making of apple, pumpkin and wild plum butters. With the spinning wheel came the carder and the hatchel —the last being a square of wood set with iron prongs through which the wool was drawn to free it from any foreign particles.

In 1883, at the home of Jacob Everman, near Hopewell, the sheep had been sheared, the wool cleaned, and the women of the household were carding and spinning it into yarn to be knit into socks, stockings, gloves and hoods for use in the coming winter. Here, too, was a wooden hopper, into which ashes were emptied and water added, and the resulting liquid was used for the making of soap. Doubtless, these same things were done in many rural homes at that time and, perhaps, for many years later.

There are, probably, many treasured heirlooms in families throughout the county, from Virginia, Maryland, and Pennsylvania, and some even from "overseas." In the eastern section of the county descendants of the Mead, Powell, Chinn, Nicholls and Paull Walker families treasure many of these. In the Mead home is a Bible stand on which rested the Bible of Benjamin Mead, who held services for his slaves. In this home also is a split-bottomed chair with which Benjamin and Sophia Brown Mead started housekeeping one hundred and thirteen years ago.

In the Nick Powell home is an ancient gilded mirror and a marble top pedestal table of rosewood. Mary Powell has a dining table used for one hundred years.

Helen Savage has a pair of quaint old vases and a chest of drawers that were in the Nicholls and Paull Walker families. She has, also, a silver knee buckle worn by her grandfather, John Powell Walker, in the days when gentlemen wore small clothes.

Sallie Chinn of Russell has the original deed given to Elizabeth Brown Mead by Charles Buford, original owner of five thousand acres of land in the vicinity of the Mead, Powell and Chinn lands.

Wurts Chinn owns the rock with the name D. Boone cut on it that was found on the Scott farm at Danleyton.

At the Biggs home at Frost are two spinning wheels, a large one for spinning wool and cotton, and a small one for the spinning of flax. Here, also, are a hatchel and candle moulds, early editions of McGuffey's Readers and other books, one bearing the date 1814. Besides an iron and a copper yard kettle is a large salt kettle used at the salt wells.

Mrs. Nina M. Biggs, of Frost, has a pedestal table and a mirror that were in the Stark home at Greenup in 1858. Mrs.

W. A. Biggs, of Greenup, has the mother-of-pearl keys that were removed from the Stark piano when it was badly damaged by the 1913 flood.

In the Hartley home at Oldtown is a cord bed, a spinning wheel and old candlesticks. At the Stark home is a reel and a spinning wheel used by the original Stark family who came to Oldtown in 1816. At Flat Hollow, in the Gammon home, is a brass kettle which is said to be one hundred and fifty years old, also a coffee grinder seventy-five years old.

In the Fullerton home at Fullerton are many valuable heirlooms. One of these is a book entitled *A Practical Discourse Concerning Future Judgement*, written MDCCXXXI (1731) by William Sherlock and dedicated "To the Queen, Her Most Excellent Majesty." It was brought from England by Mary A. Tyrrel, who came to Pennsylvania with an aunt when she was sixteen years old.

In the Fullerton home is a copy of the *Cincinnati Weekly Times* of 1862, containing the death notice of Edward Peatling, who was killed at the Battle of Perryville, during the Civil War. Edward Peatling married Mary A. Tyrrel, who later became the wife of Harvey Fullerton. Here, too, is a small trunk, two hundred years old, that belonged to the Tuke family of England, ancestors of Mrs. Harvey Fullerton. A cedar chest of the Tyrrel family contains a notebook of old dates, one being of 1792. Other valuable possessions are a cherry dining table which has been in use for eighty-five years, a walnut stand with drop leaves and drawers, and a spool bed bought by Harvey Fullerton and his wife when they began housekeeping.

ENTERTAINMENTS OF EARLY DAYS

In the 1860's and 1870's balls were given by the town people in the Masonic building, and later in the long dining room of the Kouns House. In 1880, Joseph Pfaff built a hall on Harrison Street between Main and Perry Streets, especially for the pleasure of the young people. These social affairs were attended not only by the Greenup folk, but by many from other places.

Miss Annie M. Davidson, a teacher of Greenup County, was a very fine elocutionist. In the 1870's and 1880's no public entertainment was complete without a reading by Miss Davidson.

EXHIBITION.

An entertainment will be given by the young

Ladies and Gentlemen

OF

Greenupsburg, Ky.,

AT THE COURT HOUSE,

Thursday and Friday Evenings,

JUNE 4th AND 5th, 1868.

The patronage of the public is earnestly solicited, as the object is to raise funds to repair the Greenupsburg Academy.

PROGRAMME—FIRST EVENING.

MUSIC	String Band
A SONG	Glee Club
RIENZI'S ADDRESS TO THE ROMANS	Master Thos. Ellis
TABLEAU	The Rogue
TABLEAU	Gipsy Queen
DECLINES TO BE PRESIDENT	Master E. Pollock
SONG—"Maid of Athens."	Misses M. Kouns & E. Corum
CHARADE—"No Rose without a Thorn."	
SONG—"The Two Cousins."	Misses E. Ellis & M. Hollingsworth
TABLEAU—"Marriage Scene."	
MUSIC—"Instrumental."	Miss S. Ireland
TABLEAU—"Comic."	The Barber
SONG	Glee Club
TABLEAU	School
MUSIC—Instrumental.	Miss Lu Ireland

FARCE.

"Betsey Baker, or Too Attentive by Half."

Mr. Mouser	R. Shoup
Mr. Crummy	W. J. Sands
Mrs. Mouser	Miss E. Ellis
Betsey Baker,	Miss A Kouns

ADMISSION - - 50 CENTS

Tickets may be obtained at the Drug Stores, Messrs. Robb & Ireland's, Brown & Reed's, Brooks & Pratt's.

Doors Open at 7 ½. Performance to Commence at 8.

PORTSMOUTH TIMES PRINT.

An outstanding entertainment in the early 1890's was a piano concert given by a colored musician, "Blind Tom." His real name was Thomas Greene Bethune and, although born in slavery and blind from birth, he was a world renowned prodigy of the century. He had wonderful ability to remember and reproduce sounds, especially in music. At the close of his concert he demonstrated this ability by reproducing one of Miss Bessie Brugh's own compositions without missing a note, after hearing her play it once.

Miss Bessie Brugh, who taught music to the children of Greenup for many years, always presented her pupils in a musical recital during the week of the County Teachers' Institute in August. This recital was given in the courthouse and was well attended. It became an institution which the public anticipated with great pleasure from year to year.

The Greenup Cornet Band

In the *Greenup Independent* of January 2, 1872, was printed a list of the boys composing the Greenup Cornet Band:

G. W. Callihan, *Leader*	William Hager	Charles Callihan
C. H. Fagins	Frank Myers	Allen Myers
Harvey Van Bibber	Benjamin F. Roe	Isaac McMullan
Sigmund Burkhardt	James McMullan	James Lacock
William Fagins		

In 1885 those who composed the Greenup Cornet Band were:

Thomas Peters	Albert Woodrow	Martin Wilson
Alfred Hager	Grant Mitchell	James Smith
Robert Wilson	Stanley Mitchell	George Winn
Charles Hager	Charles Wilson	

FRATERNAL ORDERS

The Greenup Masonic Lodge was the first organization of the kind in the county, having received its charter in 1827, and in 1829 numbered one hundred and fifty-five members. The first Masonic address was given by Hon. John M. McConnell, prominent citizen and lawyer, one of the earliest representatives and senators of the county. The first Master of the Lodge was Thomas T. Shreve. In 1831 John C. Kouns presented the lodge with a Kouns Bible, which has been in use one hundred and sixteen years.

The Masonic Building was erected at the corner of Main and Harrison Streets in 1865 and was used for the meetings until the past few years. The charter members were John Kouns, John Hockaday, Dr. Henry Green, and Dr. James Van Bibber.

James Watt Womack became a member of the Greenup Lodge in 1876 and has filled every office at different times.

The Greenup Eastern Star was organized in 1895. Charles and Lucy Lilly Sellards Taylor helped to organize the chapter and served as the first Worthy Patron and Worthy Matron. The charter members were Agnes Roe, Nettie Wilson, Nannie Hurn, Fannie Warnock, Sallie Winters, Esther Myers, Jane Dickey, and Mildred Womack Wilson. There are now more than one hundred members.

The Russell Masonic Lodge was organized in 1905 and has a large membership. The Russell Eastern Star was organized in 1910 and has a membership of one hundred and sixty.

The South Portsmouth Lodge was organized in 1930 with thirty-four charter members. Later it became known as the Harrison Fullerton Masonic Lodge and meets at Fullerton. The Fullerton Eastern Star was organized in 1933-34. Mrs. Forest King was the first Worthy Matron and the first Worthy Patron was Turl Brooker. Forest King was the assistant Worthy Patron and Mrs. Turl Brooker was the assistant Worthy Matron.

Russell, Raceland, Greenup, and Fullerton have Odd Fellows Lodges, and Rebeccas. Throughout the county are other organizations, units, and clubs, all of which are of benefit to the people and the county.

Eight

SOLDIERS

REVOLUTIONARY SOLDIERS PENSIONED
IN GREENUP COUNTY

James Applegate was a sergeant in the First Regiment, U. S. Lines. His pension was granted in Greenup County November 11, 1826.

Jeremiah Burns, Sr. (1752), Private in Captain George Lambert's Company, Colonel George Matthew's Regiment in the Virginia Line. Engaged in the battles of Germantown, Monmouth, and Siege of York. Pension allowed in 1818 when he was a resident of Greenup County. His wife also received a land grant for his service in the Revolution. He came to Greenup County with his family and died there October 13, 1824. His descendants are Mrs. Catherine Bateman and Mrs. Caroline Burns Meek of Ashland, and Mrs. Corrine M. Wilson and daughter, Miss Maude Wilson, of Portsmouth, Ohio.

John Chadwick (1750) enlisted 1780 and 1781 as private in North Carolina Line under Captain John Bruce; 1782 commissioned ensign and also orderly sergeant; was in the battle of Guilford Courthouse; and was pensioned in 1832. His widow, Lucinda Chadwick, was given one hundred and sixty acres of land for his service in the Revolution. At the time he entered the service he resided at Shallow Ford of Big Yadkin River in Surry County, North Carolina. After the war he moved to Bourbon County, Kentucky, and in 1800 he moved to Big Sandy, Greenup County, where he lived in 1836.

Thomas Dixon—Service record missing.

Moses Fuqua, Sr.—Captain in Virginia Militia.

Thomas Hackworth—Service record missing.

William Hammon—Service record missing.

John W. Howe was a private in the Virginia Militia. His pension was granted October 18, 1833, at the age of eighty-two years.

John Johnston was a second private in the Connecticut Line. His pension was granted July 21, 1819, and he died August 30, 1824, at the age of eighty years.

James Lawson enlisted in Hampshire County, Virginia, in 1777 in Captain Moses Hutton's Company. In 1782 he served three months in Captain McCarty's Company under Colonel Dark. He applied for his pension in 1833 and it was allowed. He is buried in Greenup County.

Elisha Mayhew was a private and his pension was granted October 13, 1818. He died November 2, 1819.

James Norton—Service record missing.

James Patton was a private in the Pennsylvania Line. His pension was granted November 12, 1822, at the age of eighty-three years.

Thomas Richards—Service record missing. He is buried in the family graveyard on Short Branch.

Charles Riggs was a private in the Maryland line. His pension was granted June 8, 1833. He was seventy-eight years old.

Clayburn Sartin was a private in the Virginia Line. His pension was granted August 9, 1833.

Godfrey Smith was a private in the Virginia Line. His pension was granted June 11, 1820, at the age of fifty-nine years.

Joseph Westlake—Service record missing.

Thomas Waring was an ensign and second lieutenant in Captain Gaskins' Company, Fifth Virginia Regiment. His name appears first in Company Roll, October 28, 1776. He came to Greenup County in 1784 and died there in 1818.

John Young carried dispatches at Valley Forge when he was just a boy. He applied for a pension while a resident of Greenup County.

Reuben Young—Service record missing.

Andrew Zornes was a private in the Pennsylvania Line. His pension was granted January 15, 1823, at the age of seventy seven years.

SOLDIERS OF THE WAR OF 1812
BURIED IN GREENUP COUNTY

George Naylor Davis was a captain in the Regiment of Colonel Isaac Shelby at the Battle of the Thames, under General William Henry Harrison, in the War of 1812. He was born in Cecil County, Maryland, in 1781, and married Harriet Bragg of Lewis County, Kentucky, in 1805. His home was in Greenup County, where he died February 11, 1847. He is buried in the cemetery at the Brick Union Church at Gray's Branch.

Moses M. Fuqua, Jr., was a private in Captain William Huston's Mounted Company from Scioto County, Ohio, in the War of 1812. He was born in Campbell County, Virginia, the son of Moses and Judith Woodson Fuqua, and married Cynthia Ann Collins of Alexandria, Ohio (Portsmouth). They settled on a farm near Tygart Creek not far from Mt. Zion. He died there in 1834 and is buried on the farm where he lived. A stone marks his grave.

Samuel Wilson Gammon was stationed at Limestone (Maysville), Kentucky, while serving in the War of 1812. He was born April 9, 1792, the son of Richard and Mary Wilson Gammon of Virginia, and married Martha Morton Fuqua (1818) in Greenup County. They spent their entire lives at the Gammon home on Tygart Creek, and he is buried in the cemetery at Mt. Zion.

Thomas Lloyd Gray—Service record missing.

Major James Howe fought in the War of 1812. He was at the Battle of New Orleans.

Carter Hailey served in the War of 1812. Service record missing.

John C. Kouns was Major of the First Kentucky Regiment and was on the staff of General Andrew Jackson at the Battle of New Orleans in the War of 1812. He was the son of Jacob Kouns, and married Elizabeth, daughter of Martin Smith of Greenup County. He served several terms in the Greenup County Legislature. He is buried in the Greenup Cemetery.

James Lawson enlisted in 1791 in Captain Robert Loman's Company in Virginia. He served three months with General Arthur St. Clair and was in St. Clair's defeat in the War of 1812. He was the son of Thomas Lawson of Hampshire County, Virginia, and came to Greenup County about 1800. He married (1) Ruth Wilson, (2) Sophia Johnson, (3) Phoebe Metz. James Lawson was born in 1760 and died in Greenup County in 1844. Place of burial is not known.

Basil Waring enlisted in the War of 1812 from August 26 to November 6, 1813, as a private under Captain Gaines. On account of his youth he ran away from home to join an older brother, Francis Waring, who was in the War. He became a colonel of Kentucky Militia, but was often called "General." Basil Waring was born in Mason County, Kentucky, May 11, 1791, and died in Greenup County. He married (1) Sarah Mackoy, (2) Jane A. R. McCall, and (3) Tabitha Mackoy. This information is taken from Tabitha's pension application dated April 15, 1878. Basil Waring died July 31, 1844, and is buried in the Waring Family Cemetery at Lynn, Greenup County.

James Williams, Jr., was a private in William Wilson's Company of Ohio Militia March 3 until August 15, 1814. He was the son of James Williams, Sr., and was born in Pennsylvania in 1778 and died September 8, 1873, in Greenup County. He married Sarah Brower in Adams County, Ohio, 1814. He is buried in Caroline Cemetery at Flat Woods.

CIVIL WAR SOLDIERS

(This list of soldiers was furnished by J. Harve Elam)

Joshua Bailey, born in Greenup County, December 27, 1835, was the son of John and Rachel Fisher Bailey. He served as a private in Company I, Tenth Kentucky Cavalry. He married Nancy Colegrove, daughter of William and Elizabeth Fitspatrick Colegrove, and they had a son, Samuel, of Lynn.

Two brothers of Joshua Bailey, Charles and Thomas, also served in the Civil War, the latter in the Twenty-second Kentucky Regiment.

George M. Baker, born October 13, 1845, in Greenup County, served two years in Company K, Fortieth Kentucky Infantry. He married (1) Mary C. Perkins, and their children were Mary A. and Julian. He married (2) Susan, daughter of Allen and Lucina Hailey Baker, and they were the parents of Faith, Ann, Agnes, George M., James, Allen, Martha, Ellen, and Betsy. Parents of George M. Baker, Sr., were Irving and Marie Koontz Baker. Henry C. Baker, a brother of George M., served in the Civil War, but his record is not given. The Baker home was at Hood's Run.

Abednego Burton served in Company C, Twenty-second Kentucky Infantry. He was born August 9, 1838, in Greenup County, and his parents were Joshua and Mary Patton Burton. He married Margaret Hornbuckle of Ohio. Three brothers,

James, Thomas, and Hezekiah, also served in the Civil War. The home of this Burton family was on Coal Branch.

James W. Burton, born in Greenup County March 18, 1835, served, one year in Company K, Tenth Kentucky Cavalry. He married (1) Sarah Carner, and their children were Wayne and Flora, (2) Helen Richards, daughter of Zachariah and Ruth Wills Richards of Coal Branch. Other members of these families serving in the Civil War were Riley and Richard Richards.

John W. Burton served one year in Company F, Fifty-fourth Kentucky Mounted Infantry. He was born in Greenup County June 19, 1839, the son of James and Mahala Bailey Burton, and married Lucinda, daughter of John S. and Elizabeth Floyd Cook. They were the parents of Lydia, John E., Ulysses G., and James. His father, James Burton, was a member of the Twenty-second Kentucky Infantry, and his brother, Thomas, served in the Fifty-fourth Kentucky Mounted Infantry.

James Carr served in Company C, Twenty-second Kentucky Infantry, enlisting in 1861. He was born in Pennsylvania April 14, 1842, and came from there to Greenup County in 1855. He married Emma Archey and their children were William, Eva, Adam, Mary, Elizabeth, Joseph, and John. Two brothers of James Carr also served in the Civil War in Kentucky Regiments.

George Colegrove, a brother of Mrs. Joshua Bailey, served in the Fourteenth Kentucky Infantry.

Henry Colegrove served in the Civil War in Company B, Twenty-second Kentucky Infantry. He was born in Greenup County, son of Nathan and Sarah Clark Colegrove, and married Miss Rutherford of Ohio in 1865. They were the parents of Scott, Nathan, Perla Richards, Edward, William, Madison, Carrie, and Leona. Three brothers of Henry Colegrove, Samuel, Melvin, and Jesse, also served in the Civil War. The Colegrove family lived at Short Branch.

Henry Diedrich served in Company K, Tenth Kentucky Cavalry. He was born in Hanover, Germany, June 22, 1843, came to Greenup County in 1856, and engaged in farming. He was a son of William and Hannah Diedrich. He married Malinda, daughter of John and Catherine Vogelsong Kaut, in 1864, and they were the parents of Catherine M., John L., Samuel W., Christian, Hannah, and Thomas. Two brothers of Mrs. Diedrich, John C. and George A. Kaut, were also in the Civil War.

Nicholas Dorn served in Company G, Second West Virginia Cavalry. He was born in Pennsylvania December 25, 1842, came to Greenup County in 1871, and engaged in farming. In 1877 he married Helen Moore Wills, daughter of William and Mary Richards Wills. Their children were Minnie Fisher of Ashland, Lindsey, Orin Gould, Mary, and James. Others of these families in the Civil War were William Dorn, Wallace, and John F. Wills.

John Fields served as a corporal in Company B, Forty-fifth Kentucky Mounted Infantry. He was born in Virginia August 16, 1846, and came to Greenup County in 1873. His parents were Jonas and Agnes Gilman Fields, and he married Nancy J. Foster in 1866.

James W. Greenslate enlisted in Company A, Forty-fifth Kentucky Mounted Infantry. He was born in Greenup County August 17, 1845, and married Mary, daughter of Samuel S. and Hannah Smith Meek. She was a granddaughter of Godfrey Smith, who fought in the Revolutionary War in Virginia. Her grandfather Meek was also a soldier in the War of 1812. Children of James W. and Mary Meek Greenslate were Sarah, William, Emma, James, Jr., Silas, Hannah, Thomas, Charles, and Mary.

Captain Alfred Hailey enlisted at Catlettsburg September 27, 1862, in Company D, Thirty-ninth Kentucky Mounted Infantry. He was promoted to lieutenant and was commissioned captain in the same regiment. Alfred Hailey was born in Greenup County May 4, 1834, son of Carter Hailey, who fought in the War of 1812, and Elizabeth Drury Hailey. His wife was Lavina Friend, whom he married in 1856, and they were the parents of William, Mollie, Curtis, Stella, and Andis. Irving, C. C., and James Hailey also served in the Civil War. James H. Drury had four sons who served in the war. He was a relative of Elizabeth Drury Hailey.

George Kaut served in Company K, Fifty-third Kentucky Mounted Infantry. He was born in Greenup County October 22, 1844, the son of John and Catherine Vogelsong Kaut. He married (1) Alice Hunt, and their children were Neva, John A., Benjamin W., William H., and Charles A. His second wife was Martha J. McMeans, and their children were Katherine, Juliet, and Harry.

James C. Lewis enlisted in Company F, Tenth Kentucky Cavalry. He was born in Pike County, Kentucky, April 27, 1839, and his parents were Noah and Nancy Chapman Lewis. Coming to Greenup County in 1871, he engaged in farming, and married Frances Appleton of Mason County. They were the parents of Charles, Ernest, Otto, Myrtle, Minnie, Addie, Norman, Sallie, and Annie. Jacob Lewis, a brother of James C. Lewis, served in the War and died in Andersonville Prison.

John Moran joined Company F, Fifty-fourth Kentucky Mounted Infantry in September 1864 and was made lieutenant. He was born in Dinwiddie County, Virginia, and came to Greenup when a child with his parents, Thomas and Bridget Hart Moran. He married Mahala Wallace of Pine Grove, Ohio, in 1847. She was the daughter of John and Mary Colbert Wallace and her father had served in the Mexican War. John Moran was postmaster at Greenup from 1871 to 1882. The children of this family were Mary E., Malissa J., and John Russell.

James Perry joined Company H, Fifty-sixth Ohio Volunteer Infantry, enlisting in 1861, and served for five years. He was born in Scioto County, Ohio, December 14, 1839, and came to Greenup County in 1876. He married Ruby J. Bennett in Greenup County in 1876, and their children were William, Sarah, Lucinda, James, Luella, and Isabel.

Frederick Victor served in the Eleventh Pennsylvania Reserves as a private and lost an arm in the Battle of the Wilderness. He was born in Virginia August 27, 1836, and came to Greenup County in 1871. He engaged in farming on Smith Branch. In 1870 he married Elizabeth Stewart and their children were Charles, Edward, Sherman, Ella, Lucy, and Mary. Isaac Artis, grandfather of Frederick Victor, was a Revolutionary Soldier.

William Withrow was a corporal in Company G, First Ohio Volunteer Infantry. He was born in Uniontown, Pennsylvania, June 21, 1834, and came to Greenup County in 1862. His parents were Daniel and Sarah Devore Withrow. He married Catherine Bryson, daughter of William B. and Elizabeth Lawson Bryson, and their children were Elizabeth, Sarah F., Jennie B., Lavinia Dugan, Ruby H., William B., and Daniel.

Hiram Ziegler served in Company B, First West Virginia Artillery, as sergeant of the Fourth Detachment. He was born in Greenup County March 1, 1839, and married Emily Gilkerson of Wayne County, West Virginia.

Shadrach Lindsay Mitchell joined Company C, Twenty-second Regiment, Kentucky Infantry, serving as first sergeant, first lieutenant, and quartermaster. At Vicksburg and Port Hudson he was stricken with fever and sent to Greenup to recuperate. Shadrach Lindsay Mitchell was born November 26, 1838, in Monroe County, Ohio, the son of Shadrach and Elizabeth Roseberry Mitchell, who had come from Green County, Pennsylvania, and settled in Lewis County, Kentucky. Shadrach, Jr., was born while his mother was on a visit to her old home in Ohio. In 1858 he came to Greenup, where he later joined the army. His wife was Frances Belle Stark of Greenup, and their children were Maud, Nina, Gertrude, Clarence, Elizabeth, Fay, Goldia, Claud, Vernon, and Chester. (See Mitchell family.)

John James Tanner enlisted in the Confederate Army in 1862, in Company C, Second Battalion Kentucky Mounted Rifles. He became Chief of Escort to Lieutenant George B. Hodge of the Army of the Tennessee. He was born in Greenup County October 3, 1842. When he died he was buried in Greenup County, but later his body was moved to his wife's home at Henderson, Kentucky. (See Tanner family.)

Francis Coburn Robb was commissioned as first lieutenant in the Twenty-second Regiment of Kentucky Volunteer Militia December 2, 1861. Later he was commissioned as adjutant of the Twenty-second Regiment of Kentucky Infantry, July 9, 1863. He was honorably discharged January 20, 1865, at the age of twenty-seven years. Francis Coburn Robb was born in Lewis County, Kentucky, the son of Robert and Sallie Sanders Robb. He married Georgeanna Garland of Lewis County, and they were the parents of five children, Anna, Lutie, Dollie, Samuel, and Francis Trussell.

John H. Willis was a Union soldier in the Civil War. He was in Company E, Fifth Regiment of the West Virginia Volunteer Infantry. He served from 1861 to 1866. His wife was Abigail Slavens of Ohio, and they had eight children: John, William, Edward, Gard F., Elizabeth, Amy, Harvey, and Simeon S. John H. Willis and his wife are buried in the cemetery at the Christian Church, Siloam, Kentucky.

William Jackson Worthington was Captain of Company B of the Twenty-second Kentucky Volunteer Infantry. He was commissioned a major and later lieutenant colonel. He was with General Grant at the siege of Vicksburg and Battle of Cumberland Gap, and was under the command of General Burnside on the Red River Expedition at New Orleans. He was twice married and had seven children. (See Worthington family.)

There were other Civil War soldiers in Greenup County, but those already mentioned were granted pensions while residents of the county, according to records at Frankfort, Kentucky.

Pleasant Timberlake was a Civil War soldier, but the record of his service was not found.

Charles Brooker served in the Civil War and was the last living soldier of that war in Greenup County. He died at the age of ninety-five years.

MUSTER ROLL OF COMPANY "B,"
FOURTH REGIMENT INFANTRY
SPANISH AMERICAN WAR

(This list was furnished by Hon. Joseph B. Bates)

Name	Rank	Enlisted	
George A. Corum	Captain	June 22, 1898—2 yrs.	Greenup, Ky.
Christopher D. Russell	Q. M. Sergeant	June 29, 1898—2 yrs.	Greenup, Ky.
Emery McDowell	Q. M. Sergeant	June 29, 1898	Greenup, Ky.
David Walker	Sergeant	July 2, 1898	Greenup, Ky.
Homer M. Reed	Sergeant	June 24, 1898	Greenup, Ky.
Josiah B. Merrill	Sergeant	June 25, 1898	Greenup, Ky.
Fairfax Dickey	Sergeant	June 25, 1898	Greenup, Ky.
George W. Gibbs	Corporal	June 25, 1898	Greenup, Ky.
Henry H. Phelps	Corporal	June 25, 1898	Greenup, Ky.
Clairborne Fox	Corporal	June 29, 1898	Greenup, Ky.
James H. Campbell	Corporal	June 25, 1898	Greenup, Ky.
George W. Cremeans	Corporal	June 25, 1898	Greenup, Ky.
Benjamin Callihan	Corporal	June 23, 1898	Greenup, Ky.
Grant Purnell	Corporal	June 23, 1898	Greenup, Ky.
George M. Allen	Corporal	June 29, 1898	Greenup, Ky.
William E. Marcum	Artificer	June 23, 1898	Greenup, Ky.
Grant Victor	Cook	June 25, 1898	Greenup, Ky.
Henry H. Prewitt	Musician	June 25, 1898	Greenup, Ky.
Thaddeus Chaffins	Wagoner	July 2, 1898	Greenup, Ky.
Francis M. Arnett	Private	June 27, 1898	Greenup, Ky.
Samuel Alexander	Private	June 23, 1898	Greenup, Ky.
Ervin Blankenship	Private	June 25, 1898	Greenup, Ky.
James A. Boggs	Private	July 2, 1898	Greenup, Ky.
Aaron Brock	Private	July 2, 1898	Greenup, Ky.
Harvey T. Brown	Private	June 25, 1898	Greenup, Ky.
Dan Burchett	Private	July 2, 1898	Greenup, Ky.
Samuel Bush	Private	June 25, 1898	Greenup, Ky.
Marion Combs	Private	June 25, 1898	Greenup, Ky.
Albert S. Davis	Private	July 2, 1898	Greenup, Ky.
Roy W. Degman	Private	June 29, 1898	Greenup, Ky.
William H. Flock	Private	June 25, 1898	Greenup, Ky.
Alexander Fultz	Private	July 2, 1898	Greenup, Ky.
Willis Fultz	Private	June 24, 1898	Greenup, Ky.
Gordan G. Gault	Private	June 29, 1898	Greenup, Ky.
Henry W. Gibbs	Private	June 25, 1898	Greenup, Ky.
James Gibbs	Private	June 23, 1898	Greenup, Ky.
Frank M. Griffin	Private	June 24, 1898	Greenup, Ky.
Henry C. Griffith	Private	June 25, 1898	Greenup, Ky.
John Hale	Private	June 27, 1898	Greenup, Ky.
George A. Hanners	Private	June 25, 1898	Greenup, Ky.
James A. Hanners	Private	June 25, 1898	Greenup, Ky.
William W. Hanners	Private	June 27, 1898	Greenup, Ky.
James O. Harrison	Private	June 24, 1898	Greenup, Ky.
Marion Hicks	Private	July 2, 1898	Greenup, Ky.
Walter P. Hicks	Private	June 22, 1898	Greenup, Ky.

Name	Rank	Enlisted	
William A. Hicks	Private	June 24, 1898	Greenup, Ky.
Martin I. Hitchcock	Private	June 25, 1898	Greenup, Ky.
George Hollingsworth	Private	July 2, 1898	Greenup, Ky.
John Jarles	Private	June 25, 1898	Greenup, Ky.
Benjamin F. Kiff	Private	June 29, 1898	Greenup, Ky.
Peyton B. Kiser	Private	June 25, 1898	Greenup, Ky.
James F. Lee	Private	June 29, 1898	Greenup, Ky.
Samuel Meek	Private	June 25, 1898	Greenup, Ky.
Belford Middleworth	Private	June 29, 1898	Greenup, Ky.
Charles E. Myers	Private	June 25, 1898	Greenup, Ky.
Edward McMeans	Private	June 23, 1898	Greenup, Ky.
Jesse Nichols	Private	May 25, 1898	Greenup, Ky.
Charles A. Norris	Private	May 29, 1898	Greenup, Ky.
John G. Prichard	Private	July 2, 1898	Greenup, Ky.
Wallace B. Reed	Private	June 23, 1898	Greenup, Ky.
James H. Releford	Private	June 25, 1898	Greenup, Ky.
Larkin M. Rice	Private	June 25, 1898	Greenup, Ky.
Wirtz Riley	Private	June 25, 1898	Greenup, Ky.
John O. Royal	Private	June 27, 1898	Greenup, Ky.
George W. Stiltner	Private	June 25, 1898	Greenup, Ky.
Ernest Stockham	Private	June 24, 1898	Greenup, Ky.
James Sullivan	Private	June 25, 1898	Greenup, Ky.
John Urban	Private	June 23, 1898	Greenup, Ky.
John Victor	Private	June 25, 1898	Greenup, Ky.
Andrew W. Welburn	Private	June 24, 1898	Greenup, Ky.

All these men enlisted at Greenup. They were mustered in at Lexington, Kentucky, July 6, 1898, and were mustered out February 12, 1899, at Anniston, Alabama.

Nine

VILLAGES

ARGILLITE

The word "Argil" means a white clay or slate. When breathed upon, it emits a peculiar odor, and Argillite was probably applied to this section of the county by the men who were testing for ore, preparatory to building the furnace, in 1818. This was the first furnace in the county and was built by Richard Deering, and John and David Trimble.

There was a mill built there in 1864 by the Eastern Kentucky Improvement Company. It was three stories high and sawed lumber. Logs were floated down Little Sandy River and drawn up to the mill by steam power. There was a crosstie yard, and telephone poles were made and shipped on the Eastern Kentucky Railroad. The mill was later operated by James and George Hoop as a grist mill. Products of this section were lime and charcoal. A good grade of coal has been mined in this vicinity.

Old families of Argillite were the Davissons, Clarks, Gholsons, and Fortes.

COAL BRANCH

The Coal Branch settlement received its name because of the veins of coal found there. Iron ore was once dug from the hills and charcoal was burned, both being hauled by ox teams. Thomas Richards was the earliest settler. Early history says that he came from Ohio and operated the ferry across Little Sandy in 1810. He first lived in the ferryhouse on Lot 111 and later lived in the hewed log house on Water Street.

Since then the members of the Richards family have lived on Coal Branch. Other settlers were the Burtons, Wills, Fetters, and Patricks.

DANLEYTON

Danleyton on the East Fork of Little Sandy was settled early by farmers. These were the Callihans, Ryes, Berrys, Hoods, Boyds, and Hales, and some of the descendants of these families still live in the neighborhood. The early settlers here found a number of Indian mounds and many relics which led them to believe that it may have been an Indian village.

Some members of the Rye and Berry families became school-teachers and professional men. Edgar Rye went from here to northwest Texas in the 1870's and lived near Fort Griffin. While there he wrote a book, *The Quirt and the Spur*, portraying the life of the cowboys, outlaws, and Indians in the country surrounding the fort.

In this book he tells of Henry Jacobs, who was sheriff there, and of a brother, John Jacobs, who lived near. These men were the sons of Jackson Jacobs (see Jacobs family).

FROST (MT. ZION)

Frost is a comparatively new name for the very old community of Mt. Zion. In 1820 the Mt. Zion Methodist Episcopal Church was organized and built upon the hill, and the community was known by this name until the coming of the Chesapeake and Ohio Railroad in 1889. The old name was still in use for a while, and then the station was changed to Kings. Later the station and a post office were named Frost. The church, however, is still called Mt. Zion.

Frost has always been, and is yet, a community of fertile farms. Two communities have grown up on the old King Farms, Upper and Lower King's Additions. The residents are mostly employed in the steel mill and railway shops across the river in Ohio.

The early settlers of Mt. Zion were Fuquas, Kings, Lawsons, Biggses, Savages, Johnsons, and Thomsons. Descendants of most of these families still own some of the original farms. These settlers were slave owners in the early days of the county, and they took care of their slaves after the Civil War, if the slaves cared to stay with them.

FULLERTON

The site of the village of Fullerton is on a part of the original tract of land owned by Josiah Morton in the early days of the county. Sixty-five years ago there were but four houses within the present limits of Fullerton. Harrison Fullerton later owned some of this land and his house was situated on the river bank. The two-story house in the center of the town was built by a man named Fisher of Portsmouth, and the family of Mrs. Fisher's sister, named Music, lived in it. This house has been owned and occupied by Mrs. Emma Winn Bennett since the early 1890's. There were two log houses on the hill in the rear of the present town.

During the next few years farmers from Tygart Valley and nearby came to Fullerton and built homes. Among them were the Warnock, Meadows, Holbrook, Taylor, and Bennett families. About 1890 Captain George Winn of Greenup established a ferry at Fullerton (see Ferries). With the coming of the Chesapeake and Ohio Railroad about this time, the village grew more rapidly and soon became a thriving community. Riverview, Morton's Addition, and South Shore have been added to the original village of Fullerton.

Clyde King had a brick yard at Fullerton in 1895. This is now known as the Taylor Brick Yard. W. W. Warnock and John Morton kept the first general stores. Dr. Matthew Meadows was the first practicing physician and also had a drug store. Lyman Warnock and John Morton had livery stables. Captain George Davis and John Taylor had a lumberyard.

At one time Coney Island was the name of an amusement place near Fullerton, but it has passed out of existence.

GRAY'S BRANCH

Gray's Branch was named for the Gray family who came from Maryland to Greenup County in 1808. There were so many Lawson families in the community that it was sometimes called the Lawson Settlement. Other pioneer families were Bryson, Reid, Waring, Culver, Morton, and Hill. As time passed these families gave way to Bryan, Walker, Jones, Hall, Johnston, Mackoy, Burns, McClave, Hurst, Ratcliff, Gray, and Kiser.

The church was the center of interest in the community, uniting the people in their religious and social life, as was the custom in early days. Greenup Union Church, the first Presbyterian Church in the county, was located here. The school was always known as Woodland because of its location in a grove of oak and beech trees. Only a few of these trees remain.

Before the coming of the Chesapeake and Ohio Railroad the people of Gray's Branch had to go to Greenup for mail. When the railroad was completed in 1889, a post office was established and named Mackoy for the first postmaster, James B. Mackoy, who kept the office in his general store near the Bryson homestead where he lived. Faris Hill was the first mail carrier. About twenty years later the post office name was changed to Gray's Branch. the same as that of the railroad station. Later postmasters were M. E. Mackoy, Mrs. John Kiser, Mr. Setser, John Kiser, Louis Hill, and Mr. Mercer.

A box car on the siding served as the first depot. The first station agents and telegraph operators were John Bennett from Huntington, West Virginia, and John Rollin Coleman from Greenfield, Virginia. Mr. Coleman was transferred to Greenup and he, with his family, became residents of the county for a number of years.

Only a few of the early families have descendants living there at the present time. Miss Florence Hill, the postmistress, descends from the Hill and Morton families; Mrs. Alberta Kiser Smith lives in the home of her parents, Mr. and Mrs. John Kiser; Mrs. Hattie McClave Sandy's home is on the site of that of her grandfather, John Milton Hill; Mrs. Mattie Hill Merrill lives in the home of her parents, Mr. and Mrs. Amos Hill.

HOPEWELL

Richard Deering, one of the earliest furnace builders in the county, built a forge at Hopewell and later converted it into a furnace.

When the Eastern Kentucky Railroad was extended to Hopewell, a station was built at Hopewell and the Irvin families were the station agents and the postmasters for many years. Besides the Deering and Irvin families, other early settlers were the Curry, Anglin, Norris, and Hannah families. The Anglin cemetery near Hopewell was opened about 1806 and there are many very old graves in it. Probably the oldest person buried there was Nancy Million Stark (mother of Mary Stark Anglin), who lived to be more than one hundred years old.

In early days George Naylor Davis made salt at Hopewell and shipped it down the Little Sandy River to Greenup, where it was stored in a building on lower Water Street.

HUNNEWELL

In early days Hunnewell and Cane Creek were small farming settlements, but with the building of the furnace in 1845, the settlement began to grow as men began digging ore, making and hauling charcoal, and working at the many things required to be done in and about a furnace. The Kentucky Improvement Company started to build a railroad, and in 1865 had extended it as far as Argillite, where there was a furnace. In 1868 this railroad was completed to Hunnewell. This name was given in honor of a Mr. Hunnell, one of the members of the company building the railroad. How the name became changed to Hunnewell no one knows. In 1870 Hunnewell had a population of six hundred, and Cane Creek had about two hundred.

The furnace company operated a general store, a slaughter house, two barber shops, and all businesses necessary for its people. The village was a prosperous place for many years, but when the furnace blew its "last out" in 1886 the furnace days were over in Greenup County. The old furnace methods were losing propositions in competition with the modern methods.

When the Eastern Kentucky Railroad ceased operations, many workers began moving away until Hunnewell has lapsed into its former status as a farming community. In those early days residents of Hunnewell were the Conways, Weavers, Campbells, Gilliams, Elams, Eiforts, and Whittingtons.

LIMEVILLE

Limeville is still known by its original name, although the post office has been known as Tongs for many years. In the 1870's Limeville was a very busy place and had the only post office between Greenup and Portsmouth. The mail was delivered by boat or brought from Wheelersburg, Ohio.

Limeville was so named because of the quantity of lime burned and shipped up and down the river from Pittsburgh to Cincinnati.

The land on which Limeville is located was bought from the Gray family in 1849 by William Tong, who built and operated the first lime kiln. In 1870 John H. Merrill took over the lime business. He also kept a general store and employed Fillmore Musser from Portsmouth, Ohio, as storekeeper.

Old settlers of Limeville were the Grays, Tongs, Youngs, Merrills, Cartwrights, Wests, McNeals, Duvals, and Camerons.

LYNN

This community was first named Liberty. It was settled early in 1800 by farmers from Virginia—the Pratts, Brookses, Pughs, Moseleys, and Joneses. A Christian Church built here was long known as the Liberty Church. This frame church was torn down and a new one built on the same site. This burned and the Liberty Church was of the past.

In 1846 a shoemaking industry was begun here, being promoted probably by people who knew of Lynn, Massachusetts, the largest shoe factory city of the country. The name Lynn came into common use and, when a post office was established here, it was given that name and has remained so since.

During the shoemaking era, tanneries were operated here by the Pratt, Brooks, and Pugh families. When the shoe industry collapsed, the farmers returned to their usual occupations.

Above the Liberty Church was the Waring Settlement. A Methodist Church was organized in 1849 and built on land donated by John Waring. Other families here were the Howlands and Dupuys. Dr. Charles Secrest lived near Liberty Church and practiced over a wide area.

Jean Thomas, author of *The Traipsin' Woman*, tells an interesting story of the Waring community. Her aunt, Nancy Bell, married Basil Waring and lived in the Waring Settlement. An emigrant family going west in a covered wagon had a very sick child who died when the family was near the settlement. They were permitted to bury their child in the Waring private cemetery.

OLDTOWN

Oldtown was settled very early in the 1780's and probably was so named from the fact that traces of an old town were found there. This later proved to have been an Indian town, from the number and kinds of relics uncovered.

Charles Womack had received a grant of land from Virginia, containing several thousand acres, before Greenup County was organized. Settlers who came here in early days were the families of John Howe, Richard Deering, Archer Womack, Barton Stark, Abraham Norris, and the Virgin, Hartley, Kouns, Lyons, and Clifton families.

John Howe was the original owner of the Kendall and Carnahan lands and built a brick house where Dr. Carnahan later built his home. He used some of the material from the Howe house for the foundation of his home.

During the busy furnace days Oldtown was the center of Laurel, Buffalo, and Hunnewell Furnaces and had a large trade with the people from all of them. Cardinal Stark had a store at Oldtown in 1843-44, which later became the Womack and Kouns store. When J. W. Kouns moved to Greenup in the 1880's, it became the Womack store and it is still owned and run by a member of the Womack family, Orin Womack. The Womacks operated a mill and a tannery, ran the store, and had the post office, besides carrying on extensive farming activities.

PALMYRA

Palmyra is one of the oldest settlements in the county. John Young came from Virginia in 1784 and patented land lying along the Little Sandy River. James McCallister married a daughter of John Young, and there have been McCallister families in that vicinity ever since. Seymour Harding built a house in 1824 at Palmyra. He was related to the Young family, and a grandson, Seymour H. Willis, was a resident of Greenup for many years.

The Tanner family came to Palmyra in 1790. They built a two-story brick house, with a basement, which had two stairways, one leading to an upper story for use by the slaves, and the other for the family's use. Mr. Tanner owned many slaves and the house was built by slave labor. The Tanners and the Van Bibbers were related by marriage, John Passmore Tanner having married Rhoda Van Bibber in 1830.

RACELAND

Raceland is a comparatively new town which has grown rapidly. Abraham Buford received a grant of five thousand acres of land from Virginia for his services rendered during the Revolutionary War. This grant extended from below Russell to the Poage lands. There was an early law suit over the lands, which was settled in favor of Buford, who gave the land to his son, Charles. The land was sold by Charles Buford in farm tracts.

Some of the early settlers who bought this land were Joseph Powell, Benjamin Mead, and the Chinn families. Much of the land is still owned by descendants of these people. A house built by Elizabeth, widow of Benjamin Mead, on Pond Run, is still standing, although it is over one hundred years old. A grandson, Benjamin Chinn, sold this land in town lots and named the place Chinnville, which in recent years was changed to Raceland because of a race track constructed there. After a few years the race track passed out of existence, but the name still is used for the village.

RUSSELL

Russell was named for John Russell, who was connected with the early iron industry. In 1870 it was just a village across the Ohio River from Ironton, Ohio. Above Russell was the original Poage land and below it was the Abraham Buford land. These joined near Russell.

Early residents of Russell were employed mostly at Ironton by the Kelly Iron Mills. A ferry was in use there very early. The town was incorporated in 1874, but its growth was slow until the coming of the Chesapeake and Ohio Railroad in 1889. With the building of the railroad shops the town grew by leaps and bounds, overflowing into the surrounding villages of Raceland, Flatwoods, Wurtland, and Worthington.

From 1875 to 1880 the Russell School was on a par with the country schools of the county and did not show much improvement until 1891, when a four-room school building was erected. A census of the schools in 1876 shows that Russell had fifty-six pupils. A teacher there in 1874-75 said there were no sidewalks, and during the winter the streets were a sea of mud. From the status of a country school the schools have reached a high standard now.

Early in 1900 Russell began to have good streets, large business houses, nice homes and churches. Some of the families who have made Russell what it is were the Fosters, Carners, Rameys, Fishers, Callihans, and Richardses.

The following item is from the September 1942 *Russell Times:* "In 1874 Russell was incorporated and a post office was established. In 1888 J. D Foster moved to Russell from Ironton; in 1888 Captain Wayne Carner built a hotel; in 1888 the Chesapeake and Ohio Railroad built a roundhouse; in 1891 a four-room school was built; in 1891 the Young Men's Christian Association was formed; and in 1898 the Odd Fellows were organized."

SHORT BRANCH

Short Branch lies south of Greenup, across Little Sandy, and is so called because it is the land on a very short branch from Little Sandy to Coal Branch. The oldest settler was probably Cyrus Van Bibber, who built his house near the Little Sandy Falls. The old Van Bibber cemetery is on a hill nearby.

Jackson Worthington bought the original Van Bibber home in the late 1870's and the family lived there for many years. This home has been owned by the Prichard and Kitchen families in later years.

Other families living at Short Branch were Thom, Dorans, Colegrove, and McCoy. D. J. McCoy was a lawyer who had an office in Greenup. Of this family, Lawrence went to Bath County and married there. He was the editor of the Owingsville newspaper. Members of the Colegrove and McCoy families are still residents of Short Branch.

SILOAM

Siloam is situated in a wide and fertile farming section of the Ohio River Valley between the village of Limeville on the east and Frost (Mt. Zion) on the west. The Mackoy family from Campbell County, Virginia, were probably the first settlers in this neighborhood, arriving in 1800, and owning nine hundred acres of land. In later years families who came into the neighborhood were Damron, Artis, Albertson, Bahner, Bush, Walker, Johnston, Tanner, Gammon, Lamblin, Williams, Brown, and Little.

The first post office was known as Little, being named for the first postmaster, Captain W. W. Little. The first general store, opened in 1901, was owned and operated by H. Green Richards. The Siloam Christian Church was built on land given by the Mackoy family, as also was the first public school at Siloam. Several generations of the early families are buried in the cemetery around the church. In recent years another church has been built across the road from Siloam Church, with a cemetery surrounding it. The land on which this church stands was originally a part of the John Johnston farm, later owned by the Hardin family.

SMITH BRANCH

The first settler on Smith Branch was Godfrey Smith, a Revolutionary soldier, and the Branch was named for him. He and his wife, Margaret Hoover, were married in Pennsylvania and came down the Ohio River on a flatboat in 1810. He owned much of the land on Smith Branch and sold four hundred acres to William Biggs in 1843. The Crosset and McKee families were other early landowners on Smith Branch.

Farming was the principal occupation in that neighborhood. In the late 1870's Bernard Kuehborth bought timber and operated a saw mill on Smith Branch. Another occupation was charcoal making. This product was hauled to the Ohio River by ox teams and loaded on barges for the Kelly Iron Mills at Ironton.

SOUTH PORTSMOUTH (SPRINGVILLE)

Springville, the original name of the village, came from the fact that numerous springs bubbled forth at the foot of the high hills. The name was changed to South Portsmouth for the convenience of the Chesapeake and Ohio Railroad when it was built through the county. The voting precinct, however, still retains the original name of Springville.

The first settlement within the bounds of the county was made here. This has been claimed to be the first settlement in Kentucky. The real settlement was below the present town, across from the mouth of the Scioto River in Ohio, which in early days was two miles below the present mouth. The inhabitants were French traders and Shawnee Indians and did not remain long. Collins' *History of Kentucky* states that Christopher Gist came to the mouth of the Scioto River and was ferried to the south side of the Ohio River, where he found about forty houses.

The Mounds found below Springville are supposed to have been erected by the Mound Builders before the coming of the Indians.

The early settlers of Springville were the Laughlin, Killen, Thomson, Arnold, McAllister, Lawson, Bagby, Sprinkle, and Zuhars families. The Laughlins, Killens, and McAllisters were river people, being pilots or captains on the boats. A sketch of the Laughlin family is given elsewhere in this book.

From the early days a ferry operated from Springville to Portsmouth. This ferry was maintained until the Grant Bridge was completed in 1922.

Among the early industries at Springville was a tannery built by the father or brother of General U. S. Grant, hence the name of the bridge. The tannery was near the present entrance to the bridge. A foundry was built in 1839 by Coles and Robinson of

Portsmouth; a distillery was operated in 1854 by Joseph Smith, also one by James Bryson; a grain mill was operated by a man named Seifort and another by Matt Miller, who converted his mill into a factory for making paint. It was later sold to the Adams Brothers of Portsmouth, who manufactured explosives. The building burned and a young girl lost her life in the fire.

John Abbott lived on Springville Hill and had a collection of native wild animals in a zoo on the hill. Steps were built up to the top where, in the 1880's, there was a building used for picnics and dancing.

Most of the inhabitants of Springville attended church services at Portsmouth, Mt. Zion, or Siloam. There was a small frame Christian Church on the hill near the center of the village, but the Methodist Church was not built until much later, and the present Christian Church was built more recently.

The first postmaster was Joshua Lawson, who had a store on Front Street.

There are several very old cemeteries lying below the village. The oldest is the Laughlin-Killen cemetery, which is within the limits of the old Indian fortifications, now owned by a descendant, Russell McElhaney. Another is the Thomson-English cemetery.

In the 1870's Colonel Peter Kinney built a home on the flats near the upper end of Springville, where the family spent the summers. This place was known later as the McAllister place.

WURTLAND

Wurtland was the busiest village in the county in the early days and is still a very important place. When the Iron Forge Works was in operation here the place was known as Fulton. Also it was known as the Oil Works because of the fuel made from cannel coal mined in the vicinity. There was a landing here called Old Steam, where boats made regular stops for passengers, mail, and freight. Old Steam Furnace was located about three miles from this landing.

When oil was first made at the Oil Works, the cannel coal was hauled from the mines with ox teams. When Wurts and Ryan began operating the plant they built a tramway up the branch to the mines and used a small engine to draw the cars.

At Wurtland, during the Civil War, there was an army camp named Maggard, and soldiers who died were buried in the McConnell Cemetery.

The name became Wurtland after George and Samuel Wurts sold Laurel Furnace to the Scott family and came to live at Fulton. George Wurts bought the John McConnell home and used Mr. McConnell's law office building for a school for his and other children in the neighborhood (see Private Schools). This home was later occupied by the James D. Biggs family and at present is owned by the John Harris family.

The first church in Wurtland was built by three denominations, Presbyterian, Methodist, and Baptist, and is now known as the Union Church (see Churches).

Benjamin Chinn was one of the first settlers of this section and was the first merchant in the county. John Hamon Chinn was also a merchant, and was succeeded by his son Benjamin. Hamon II was a merchant and his son, Wurts, a descendant of the Samuel Grandin Wurts family, operates a store which is located a short distance from the original Benjamin Chinn store.

GREENUP COUNTY COURTHOUSE
Built 1811-1816. *See p. 21*

Harrison Street in 1885
Greenup, Ky.

GREENUP CORNET BAND. *See p. 91*

GREENUP COUNTY LANDMARKS

ANVIL ROCK

LAUREL FURNACE. *See p. 56*

BRIDGE ACROSS LITTLE SANDY RIVER
Built 1884. *See p 8*

"NEW ORLEANS"
First Steamboat to go
down the Ohio River
See p. 44

Ferryboat "CAPTAIN JOHN"
at Fullerton
See p. 49

Steamboat "FANNIE DUGAN"
Built in Portsmouth 1872
See p. 45

Steamboat "GREYHOUND"
See p. 48

BETHLEHEM CHURCH 1892
See p. 70

GREENUP PRESBYTERIAN 1859
See p. 73

MT. ZION CHURCH 1873
See p. 71

SILOAM CHURCH 1840
See p. 69

JOHN McCONNELL
HOME. *See p. 211*

WILLIAM BRYSON
HOME. *See p. 134*

"SANDY PLAINS"
ROBERT JOHNSON
HOME. *See p. 192*

"GRAVENSTEIN
PLACE"
WILLIAM BIGGS
HOME. *See p. 125*

EMZY DOWNS OSENTON Grave
See p. 157

GEORGE NAYLOR DAVIS
1812 Soldier
See p. 95

JOSIAH MORTON
Revolutionary Soldier
See p. 225

EMZY DOWNS OSENTON. *See p. 233*

DR. RICHARD MORTON
See p. 226

HANNAH BINGHAM MORTON
See p. 226

MARY GRAY.

Born in Prince George's county, Maryland, March 9th, 1739, age next 113 years. Now living in Greenup county, Kentucky 20 miles from Portsmouth O.

HER DESCENDANTS.

First Generation—Children—13.
Second   "   Gr. Children, 65.
Third   "   Gt. Gr. Children, 617.
Fourth   "   Gt. gt. gr. Children, 337.
Fifth   "   Gt. gt. gt. gr. Children, 44.

MARY BONIFANT GRAY
See pp. 84 and 171

THOMAS T. G. WARING
and NANCY MEFFORD WARING
See p. 289

WILLIAM ALEXANDER BIGGS
See p. 127

JAMES WATT WOMACK
See p. 306

Standing: GEORGE NICHOLAS BIGGS, 61 years; JAMES DAVIS BIGGS, 69 years. Seated: THOMAS NAYLOR BIGGS, 75 years; DR. ROMULUS CULVER BIGGS, 65 years; and WILLIAM BIGGS, 77 years. (Photographed in 1907.) *See p. 124*

Ten

FAMILIES

ANGLIN

The Anglin family came from Virginia to Greenup County during its earliest years. Gabriel and John are listed as citizens in the 1811-1812 census. They settled in the southeastern section of the county near the Little Sandy River. When Carter County was formed from Greenup in 1838, the line ran through the Anglin lands, John living in Carter, and Gabriel in Greenup County.

Gabriel Anglin married Mary, daughter of Barton and Nancy Million Stark of Oldtown. They were the parents of James, who was killed in the Civil War; Caroline, who married Charles Spangler and had two children, Iva and Virginia; Virginia, who married (1) Travis Kendall, who was killed in the Civil War, and (2) Dr. Alonzo Carnahan; Talton, who had five children, James, Talton, Jr., Mary, Cora, and Lola.

Lucinda Anglin, sister of Gabriel and John, married Alexander Hannah March 25, 1826. They lived on Little Sandy, above Hopewell.

ATKINSON

Thomas Atkinson, Sr., was born in England. He went to Ireland to engage in the manufacture of cloth. His son, Thomas, came to Washington, Pennsylvania, where he died in 1784. His son, Thomas III, married Mary Ann, daughter of William Craycraft of Uniontown, Pennsylvania. In 1794 and 1795 they sold their lands of six hundred acres and came to what was then a part of Clark County, later Bath County, Kentucky. A deed shows that Thomas Atkinson paid taxes on two hundred acres of land on Flat Creek, Clark County, Kentucky.

Thomas and Mary Ann Atkinson were buried in the Springfield Cemetery, Bath County, his stone bearing the date 1754-1812 and hers 1760-1844. Their son, William Sanford Atkinson, married Lucy Coshow, and they had a son, William Franklin, who married Miranda Donaldson. Their son, John Donaldson Atkinson, married Lucy Donaldson, a cousin, and they were the parents of James Dallas Atkinson. James D. was born in Stanton, Powell County, Kentucky, and attended the University of Kentucky. He was in World War I, serving in the major battles. He was wounded and shell shocked. He married Frances Aileen Halbert, daughter of Judge William C. and Frances Bate Halbert of Lewis County, and came to Greenup County to practice his profession of law. James D. and Frances Halbert Atkinson are the parents of James D., Jr., and Nancy (see Halbert family).

BAGBY

The Bagby family came from England to Virginia before the Revolutionary War. Robert Bagby came from Virginia to Lewis County, Kentucky, about 1800. He had a son, John, who was born in 1819 and married Sarah Thomson of Lewis County. Their children were William, Thomas, Alice Gordon of Huntington, West Virginia, Elizabeth Dunham, and Frances Henry of Springville, Greenup County. William Bagby married Isabella Bruce, daughter of Thomas Bruce, and they moved to Springville in the 1860's. They were the parents of Walter Bagby of Portsmouth, Ohio, Arthur and Malcolm Bagby.

Thomas Bagby, a brother of William, was State Senator from Lewis, Greenup, Carter and Elliot Counties. Walter, son of William and Isabella Bruce Bagby, married Emma Eastham of Boyd County in 1895. He was a carpenter until 1897, when he bought a grocery store in Portsmouth, Ohio.

There is an old cemetery located near the Ohio River on the old Bagby Farm.

BAKER

Humphrey and Ann Harrie Baker came to Greenup County from Virginia in the early 1800's. They came down the Ohio River on a flatboat and settled on Tygart Creek, where they bought eight hundred acres of land, and all of the land, with the exception of one share, has remained in the Baker family to the present time.

There were five sons, Allen (1809), Marshall (1811), Irvine, Robert, and Hiram. Allen married Lucina Hailey and their children were Susan Baker, Julia McGinness, Matilda Crisp, Mary, Alice Meadows, Clarinda McGinness, Lavina Campbell, and one son, George, who married Mollie McGinness. Marshall married (1) Mary Ann Hanks, and they were the parents of Sophia Baker, who married Cyrus Van Bibber. For his second wife Marshall Baker married Mary Carnegy Waring. There were no children. Irvine Baker married Maria Kouns, Hiram married ——————— ——————— and had a son, Dr. Allen Baker, who married Ella Bennett. They had a son, Allen, Jr., who married Loue A. Jones, daughter of Thomas and Letitia Morton Jones of Gray's Branch. They lived on a farm at St. Paul in Lewis County. George Baker married his cousin, Susan Baker, and they were the parents of Faith, Agnes Hartley, Marshall, James, Ella, and Betsey. Marshall married Martha Webb and they were the parents of William, Anna, and Pauline Williams.

Matilda married Newton, son of Joel and Elizabeth Sammons Crisp of Floyd County, Kentucky, and their children were: Newton; Julia McGinness Hall; Robert; Sina Chaffins; George, who married (1) Cora Patton and (2) Opal French; Lucy, who married Ottis Taylor (see Taylor family); and Jonas.

BARNEY

Three brothers, Thomas, Squire, and Benjamin Barney, resided in Greenup County before 1823. They settled on Tygart and Shultz Creeks. Thomas married Barbara Shaffer. He died in 1851 and his wife in 1873. Squire married Rebecca Douglas January 22, 1822. Court records, dated July 29, 1838, mention heirs of Squire Barney, deceased, as being Elizabeth Ann, Martha Ann, Sarah Ann, Benjamin Franklin, and Amy Barney Nichols. Benjamin, the third brother, married Sitha, daughter of James and Jane Greenslate, June 3, 1827.

The children of Benjamin and Sitha Barney were Elizabeth, John R., and Sarah Jane, who married Elisha Long (see Long family).

Thomas and Barbara Barney were the parents of Thomas Marion, Jr., who married Sarah Dortch; Jacob, who married Rachel Nichols in 1840; Amy, who married Joseph Nichols in 1845; Leonard, who married Susan Dortch; Henry, who married Rebecca Dortch; Naomi, who married Henry Ribble in 1840;

Mary, who married Frank, son of David and Elizabeth Bush Artis; Lizzie, who married Mr. Meeks; and James, who married Isabel Young and lived near Siloam. Their children were Viola, who married James Ratcliff; Peter, who married Mary Ratcliff; Fred; Taylor, who married Addie Lamblin; and Ida.

Thomas Marion Barney, Jr., (1823-1915) and his wife, Sarah Dortch (1828-1890), were both born in Greenup County and married there in 1848. They went to Ennis, Texas, in the 1870's. He died in Ennis and she in Crisp, Texas. Their children were Frank, who died in Ironton, Ohio; Charles William, who married Sarah Ann, daughter of Parker and Nancy Walker Ratcliff of Greenup County, who had also moved to Texas; Nora, who married William Smartwood; Lydia, who married Alex Blackwell; Isaac Wesley, who married Cornelia Perry; Sally, who married Charles Winterrowd; Haden, who married Ida Williams; and Lola Louise, who married William Lowe and resides in Santa Barbara, California.

Charles William Barney (1853-1948) and his wife, Sarah Ann Ratcliff (1855-1934), were married in Greenup County in 1874 and went to Ennis, Texas, with his parents. Their children were Burley Seward, who married Alice Brewer; William Moore, a bachelor; Minnie, who married William Edmonston; Etta May, who married Jackson Turner; Roby, who married Bessie Medford; Thomas Marion, who married Willie Lowe; and George Harrison, who married Kathryn Mae Wilson. All these Barney children were born in Texas.

George Harrison Barney (1888) and his wife, Kathryn Mae Wilson, born in 1910 at Telico, Texas, make their home at Ennis, where Mr. Barney has been postmaster for a number of years. They are the parents of George H., Jr., who married Muriel Willis; Kathryn Virginia, who married Noll Sewell; and Robert Owen, who married Maxine Barnes.

BARTLEY

John Bartley came to Greenup County about the time it was formed. He was one of the first jailers. At the February term of court in 1813, Joshua Bartley was appointed jailer "in the room of" John Bartley. Joshua Bartley lived on Harrison Street where the Patton Hotel was kept for many years. He served but a short time as jailer, for, in the record of May term of court 1813, "John and James Bartley, as administrators of his estate, entered into bond with Jesse Boone and Benjamin Chinn." Oba Timberlake was appointed jailer at this term of court, "in the room of Joshua Bartley, deceased."

The Bartleys moved to the Fulton Oil Works (Wurtland) and James married Cassandra Wilcoxon Nicholls. Children of this family were Fleta Pickens, John, Cassandra Jones, and Mary McCormick. Her son, James McCormick, Jr., married Mary, daughter of William Corum and his wife, Edith Passmore Corum, of Greenup.

BATES

HORACE BATES

Horace Watson Bates was born at Hanover, Plymouth County, Massachusetts. He married Fannie Goodwin, who was born at Plymouth, Massachusetts. Mr. Bates came from Boston to Riverton in 1868, to take over the general management and vice presidency of the Eastern Kentucky Railroad. He made his home at Riverton until his death in 1901. Mr. and Mrs. Bates were the parents of a daughter, Alice, born at Plymouth, Massachusetts, in 1864, and a son, Sturgis Goodwin, born at Cincinnati, Ohio, in 1866.

Alice Bates married Joseph Kouns Pollock of Greenup in 1902, and they went to Cincinnati to make their home. She is recently deceased. Sturgis married Sally Russell Biggs, daughter of James and Alice Wurts Biggs, of Wurtland, in 1899. They have a son, Sturgis, who was born at Riverton in 1907. He is married and lives at Atlanta, Georgia. They have two children, Sturgis III and Alice.

After the death of Mr. Horace Bates, the son, Sturgis, succeeded his father with the Eastern Kentucky Railroad in the same capacity, until it was abandoned in 1928. After that, Mr. and Mrs. Sturgis Bates went to Ashland, Kentucky, to make their home.

JOSEPH BENGAL BATES

Joseph Bengal Bates was born in 1893, the son of Jesse and Hannah Caudill Bates, of Knott County, Kentucky. He received his early education at Hindman School and was graduated from Richmond Normal and Teachers College at Richmond, Kentucky. He taught school and for three years conducted a Normal School at Greenup. In 1921 he was elected county clerk and served four terms—sixteen years. In 1934 he was elected congressman from the district and he is still serving in that office. He is a member of the Masonic Lodge of Greenup.

Mr. Bates married Virginia, the daughter of Larkin Monroe Rice and Annie Laurie Myers Rice of Wurtland. Their children are Joseph R. Rice and Rebecca, who married Shannon Vinson.

BELL

The Bell and Mefford families were residents of Mason County, Kentucky, when Maysville was established as a town in 1787. One of the six men appointed to lay off the town of one hundred acres was George Mefford. A sister of George Mefford, Sarah, married Carter Bell, and their children were John; Jesse; Elizabeth, who married a cousin named Mefford; Phoebe, who married Mr. Outten of Mason County; Nancy, who married Basil A. Waring of Tygart; and Lydia, who lived with the Dr. Samuel Ellis family of Greenup. Basil A. and Nancy Mefford Waring lived in Tygart Valley all their married life.

George William Bell married Katherine Smith and they were the parents of Dr. George Bell and Jean Bell Thomas of Ashland. Dr. George Bell is a writer and lecturer. Jean Bell Thomas, known as the "Traipsin' Woman," is the originator of the "Mountain Folk Song Festival," and the "McGuffey School" at Ashland. Her stories of mountain life have been published in leading magazines and some of her books are *The Traipsin' Woman, Devil's Ditties, Ballad Making*, and *The Singin' Gatherin'*.

BENNETT

Among the family names connected with the early history of both northern Kentucky and southern Ohio is that of the Bennett family. Thaddeus Bennett was a Revolutionary soldier and served with the New York Militia in 1777. He married Eunice Bentley and, with his wife and seven children, he left New York about 1818 on a raft which he had built at Olean, New York, and floated down the Allegheny and Ohio Rivers, landing near the mouth of the Little Scioto River in Ohio. They located near Stockdale in Scioto County, and later moved to the present site of Harrisonville. Two more children were born in Ohio, making a family of nine in all. A widowed daughter, Sallie Bennett Fenton, with four small children, came with the family from New York, and one of her daughters, Elizabeth, later married Jefferson Kendall, a son of William and Rachel Brown Kendall, of Scioto County.

Joseph Bennett, born in New York in 1794, was the seventh child of Thaddeus and Eunice Bentley Bennett, and married a widow named Elizabeth Mills Bennett. They lived in a log house at the settlement he later laid out as a village in 1837 and called Harrisonville for his friend, William Henry Harrison. Here their eight children were born, Thaddeus, William Parmoley, Benjamin Franklin, Jane, Elizabeth, Susan, Sarah, and Lovina. The three sons came to Greenup County and settled on Tygart Creek as farmers and millers. Joseph Bennett was a soldier in the War of 1812, and died at the home of his son in Greenup County, but was buried in the cemetery at Harrisonville, Ohio.

Thaddeus, the eldest child of Joseph Bennett, was known as Colonel Bennett and was active in the operation of the charcoal furnaces in both Ohio and northeastern Kentucky. He married Lucinda Howell and they were the parents of Joseph, Lucy, Louise, Elizabeth, Ella, Henry Clay, and Thomas. Lucy married David Alexander Bryson, Jr. (see Bryson family); Ella Bennett married (1) Dr. Allen Baker of Tygart and had one son, Allen; (2) John David Keister, and their children were Rella Barton, the wife of Nile King (see King family), Frank Bennett Keister, and Clay; Louisa married George W. Gammon as his first wife; Elizabeth married Wilson Greenslate (see Greenslate family); Clay married Elizabeth, daughter of Mordecai Walker; Joseph died young; and Thomas married Nancy Booten. The children of Thomas Bennett were Franklin, Clay, Mary, Lucinda, and Lyde. Franklin married Emma Bennett Winn, his cousin; Clay married Emma Secrest, his cousin; Mary married Leonard Powell; Lucinda married Charles Bruce of St. Paul; and Lyde died when young.

William Parmoley, the second son of Joseph Bennett, ran a grist mill at what is known as Bennett's Mills on Tygart Creek. He married Abigail Bonser of Scioto County, Ohio, and their children were Thaddeus, John, Samuel, Hannah, Ruby, Abigail, and Ellen. William Parmoley Bennett died in 1886 and was buried in the cemetery at Bennett's Mills.

Benjamin Franklin, the third son of Joseph Bennett, was born in Harrisonville, Ohio, and grew to manhood there. He married Sarah Ann Snodgrass in Scioto County, Ohio, in 1849 and moved to Tygart Valley near the Globe Iron Furnace. Here he built a flour mill and made the first flour in Greenup County. He studied law and was admitted to the bar in 1866. He opened an office in Greenup and built a fine brick house on the hill in the rear of the town, in the late 1870's. Benjamin Franklin Bennett was a sergeant in the Fifty-sixth Ohio Infantry during the Civil War, road commissioner in Greenup County for four years, a delegate to the State Constitutional Convention in 1890, and representative from his district to the General Assembly. The name Bennett has played a prominent part in the political life of Greenup County for many years.

The children of Benjamin Franklin Bennett were Joseph Bentley (see his sketch following), Mary Hannah, Lucinda, Isabel, Emma, and Sarah Ann. Mary Hannah married John Merrill (see Merrill family); Lucinda married Thomas Smith; Isabel married William Secrest and they were the parents of Emma Secrest, who married Clay Bennett; Emma married (1) Captain George Winn and (2) Franklin Bennett; Sarah Ann married Mr. Taylor of Indiana.

JOSEPH BENTLEY BENNETT

Joseph Bentley Bennett was born in Greenup County, the son of Benjamin Franklin Bennett. He studied law and practiced in Greenup for many years. He was elected county judge, county attorney, and later served eight years as congressman from his district. After his term of office was over he returned to Greenup and practiced law again.

Mr. Bennett married Anna, daughter of Charles Mytinger, of Greenup, and they were the parents of nine children: Arthur, Charles Bentley, Frances, Katherine, Emmabel, Julia, Mary, Sallie, and Joseph, Jr. Arthur married Esther Morton of Greenup and they lived in Washington, D. C.; Charles Bentley married Lucille Wilson, daughter of Robert E. L. Wilson, and they live in Greenup. The daughters married and make their homes elsewhere.

BIGGS

The Biggs family is of Scotch-Irish descent, being one of those families of Scotland to take up arms to defend the Presbyterian form of church government. They were persecuted and fled to Ireland. There were three brothers who came from Ireland and settled at or near Brownsville, Pennsylvania, in the middle of the eighteenth century.

Captain John Biggs was an Indian fighter and settled near Zanesville, Ohio. He was killed in 1773 near Wheeling along with Lieutenant Ashley. General Jack Biggs settled on the Miami River near Cincinnati and he also was in the Indian wars. William Biggs of Virginia was with General George Rogers Clark at Fort Jefferson in 1780. *The History of the Valley of Virginia*, by Samuel Kercheval, mentions one General Benjamin Biggs who was stationed at Fort Laurens in 1773, when it was attacked by Indians and fourteen men were killed.

Andrew Biggs, a son of William and Elizabeth Biggs, was born in 1769. He married Judith Robertson of Bryan Station in 1795. They lived in Mt. Sterling, Kentucky, and their children were Sallie (1796), Elizabeth (1798), William (1800), and Robinson or Robertson (1802). Judith Robertson Biggs died at Mt. Sterling in 1804. Andrew Biggs remarried and in 1813 he came to Greenupsburg, where he kept a store and a tavern on Washington Street. Sometime later he moved to a farm on Smith Branch, where he died in 1827, and where he is buried.

William Biggs, born in 1800, was thirteen years old when his father moved to Greenupsburg from Mt. Sterling. When but a boy he carried the mail from the Big Sandy River to the western boundary of the county on horseback. William Ely, who wrote the book, *The Big Sandy Valley*, speaks very highly of William Biggs as the captain of a boat that plied the Big Sandy River, and says that Mr. Biggs was twenty-one years old at that time.

In 1827 William Biggs married Lucy Blakemore, daughter of George Naylor and Harriet Bragg Davis, pioneer residents of the county. Mr. Biggs became a man of affairs; he owned slaves, he had a wood yard and a landing where the river boats stopped for fuel, and he loaded flatboats with produce for New Orleans. He was a shrewd trader, and became the owner of several fine farms in Greenup County, as well as land in the states of Missouri and Arkansas.

Mr. Biggs was interested in many enterprises. In 1854 he bought a hotel in Portsmouth, Ohio, and it became known as the Biggs House. In 1870 an addition was built to it, but in 1871 it was destroyed by fire. In 1872 it was rebuilt, and when finished there was a formal opening with a grand ball which was attended by almost one thousand people. Mr. Biggs was presented with an inscribed gold-headed cane, which is now in the possession of his great-grandson, William M. Biggs, of Frost, Kentucky. Among other enterprises, he was a partner with John Means and Samuel Cole of Ashland, Kentucky, and John Peebles and Benjamin Gaylord of Portsmouth, in 1864, in the purchase of the Lexington and Big Sandy Railroad, and also the Ashland Coal and Iron Railroad some time later.

William and Lucy Davis Biggs were the parents of twelve children. These were Andrew, William and Robinson (twins), Thomas Naylor, Susan, James Davis, George Nicholas, Dr. Romulus Culver Biggs, Lucy, Samuel Green, Lola Lloyd, and Ann Eliza.

Of this large family separate sketches are given of those who were best known in Greenup County.

Andrew, the eldest son, married Maria, daughter of Major John C. Kouns, and they moved to Louisville, Kentucky. Their children were Elizabeth Craveson, Mary Musselman, William, Susan Tabler, and Nancy Stallings. Living in Louisville now are two daughters of the Craveson family, Mary Louise Graff and Susan Craveson.

George Nicholas Biggs, the sixth son of William and Lucy Davis Biggs, married Jane Elizabeth Bryson, daughter of William and Elizabeth Lawson Bryson of Gray's Branch. Mr. and Mrs. Biggs lived in the Bryson homestead until 1881, when they moved to Huntington, West Virginia, where he became a successful merchant. Their children were Samuel Green, James Davis, and Elizabeth Bryson Watts.

Ann Eliza, the eldest daughter of William and Lucy Davis Biggs, married James Hockaday and their children were Irvin and Lucy, who married Cyrus D. Van Bibber (see Van Bibber family). They lived in Huntington, West Virginia.

Dr. Romulus Culver Biggs, the seventh son, married Emma Brown of Wheelersburg, Ohio. There were no children. He practiced his profession in Greenup and Ashland. Dr. and Mrs. Biggs are buried at Wheelersburg.

Lucy, the second daughter, married Dr. Andrew Beardsley, of Huntington, West Virginia. They had two daughters, Lola, who married Elliot Northcott, an attorney; and Willie, who married Frederick McDonald of Huntington.

Samuel Green Biggs, the eighth son, married Agnes Peyton of Ripley, Greenbrier County, West Virginia, and they made their home in that county. They had three children, Lucy, Charles, and Agnes.

Lola Lloyd, the third daughter, married Judge William Thompson of Huntington. She died when a young woman, leaving a daughter, Lucy.

Two other children of William and Lucy Davis Biggs, Robinson and Susan, died while young.

Mr. and Mrs. Biggs are buried in the cemetery at the Brick Union Church at Gray's Branch. The Biggs family were always staunch supporters of that church as long as it was in existence, and members of the family served in various offices of the church.

Robinson Mills Biggs, born in 1802, a brother of William Biggs, Sr., married Ann, daughter of John Culver of Gray's Branch, and they were residents of Greenup County until 1860, when Boyd County was formed. They were the parents of three children, Robinson Mills, who died when a young man, Jane Young, and Elizabeth O'Ferrel. The two daughters were residents of Ashland. Like his brother, William, Robinson was engaged in many enterprises, among them the building of Mt. Savage Furnace. He was a passenger on the steamboat "Daisy Dean" when the boilers exploded and seven men were drowned. Among them were Mr. Biggs and Captain Norton, a prominent man of Ironton, Ohio.

Elizabeth Biggs, a sister of William and Robinson Biggs, married John Rice of Virginia and was the grandmother of Miss Dora Seaton of Greenup.

WILLIAM BIGGS, JR.

William Biggs, Jr., married Rebecca Ann, daughter of Benjamin and Ann Wurts King of Laurel Furnace, and they began their married life at his father's farm three miles below Greenup. In 1866, when their son, Maurice, was two years old, they went to Mt. Zion to make their home on the farm where Mr. Biggs's brother, Thomas Naylor, had lived. Mr. and Mrs. Biggs lived there for many years and he became a highly respected farmer in that section of the county. This farm has been owned and operated by members of the Biggs family for a hundred years or more. The home was known as "Gravenstein Place," named for the large orchard of Gravenstein apples on the farm.

The children of this family were Dr. Robinson Mills Biggs, Maurice King Biggs, Anna Wurts, Lucy Davis, Sarah Grandin, Helen Rebecca, and Winifrede. Dr. Robinson Mills Biggs died unmarried; Maurice King Biggs married Nina Aura Mitchell (see following sketch); Anna Wurts died unmarried; Lucy Davis married Joseph Randolph Damron of Siloam and they lived in Huntington, West Virginia; Sarah Grandin married James Bullock of Louisville, Kentucky; Helen Rebecca died unmarried; Winifrede married Dudley Irvin Smith of Huntington, and they went to California, where she and her son still reside.

Late in life Mr. Biggs retired from farming and he, with Mrs. Biggs, went to Huntington to live. They are buried in Woodland Cemetery at Ironton, Ohio. Their son, Maurice King Biggs, assumed the management of the farm when his father retired, and he carried it on until his death in 1937. Since that time his wife, Mrs. Nina Biggs, continues to make her home there and manages the farm.

MAURICE KING BIGGS

Maurice King Biggs was born at the William Biggs homestead below Greenup in 1864 and went with his parents when he was two years old to the Biggs farm at Mt. Zion (Frost), known since as the William Biggs, Jr., home. He married Nina Aura Mitchell of Greenup, and they lived on his father's farm. Their children were Susan, William Mitchell, Maude Frances, Rebecca Damron, and Maurice King, Jr.

Susan married William Merrill and they were the parents of four children, of whom only one survives, Marianna, wife of Franklin Meadows of Fullerton.

William Mitchell Biggs married (1) Irma Gammon of Siloam, and they had a son, William Maurice, who married Mabel Phillips of Sunshine, and they live in Greenup; (2) Martha Morton of Fullerton, and their children are Taylor Lindsay, who married Judith Lawson of Frost, and Helen, wife of Theodore Ray of Glasgow, Kentucky.

Maude Frances married Andrew Wayne King and their children are Andrew Wayne, Jr., (Drew), Don, and Nina Lou. All three served in World War II. Andrew (Drew) served in the Pacific area, Don in the African-European area, and Nina Lou was a member of the Woman's Army Corps, stationed in Florida. Andrew, Jr., married Olive Fannin of Tygart; they have four children, and live in Roanoke, Virginia; Don married Mary Lou Hart of Kings, and lives in Chillicothe, Ohio; and Nina Lou married Morton Ware of Portsmouth.

Rebecca Damron Biggs married (1) George Gammon of Siloam and (2) Frederick Forsythe of Lexington. They live in Greenup.

Maurice King Biggs, Jr., married Sylvia Mowery of Fullerton and they live at Lockland, Ohio. They have one son, Jerry.

Thomas Naylor Biggs

Thomas Naylor Biggs married Ellenor Humphreys of Carter County, Kentucky, and they went to Mt. Zion to make their home on the farm his father, William Biggs, Sr., had bought from Pleasant Savage. Thomas built, and for ten years lived in, the house on this farm which has since been occupied by the William Biggs, Jr., family. Five of his ten children were born in this house. Later he moved to the farm which had been his father's home, three miles below Greenup on the river. This farm had been in the Biggs family since before 1839. Members of the family still own some of this land on Smith Branch. The home was called Oak Lane and here Mr. and Mrs. Biggs reared their family of eight children, two having died in infancy.

Their children were William Alexander, John Humphreys, Ellen Humphreys, Lydia Connor, Thomas Naylor, Jr., Dr. James Davis, Romulus Culver, and Royina. William Alexander married Maud Mitchell (see following sketch); John Humphreys, a lumberman in West Virginia, married his first cousin, Mary (Mollie) Rucker, and their children were Lucy, Eston, Lahoma, Maxine, and Mabel; Ellen Humphreys married John Taylor Lawson (see his sketch under Lawson family); Lydia Connor married John Thompson Womack (see his sketch under Womack family); Thomas Naylor, Jr., married Mary DeBard of Greenup and they had three sons, Dr. Alfred of Chicago, Naylor of Tiffin, Ohio, and Seaton, deceased; Dr. James Davis practiced his profession in Williamson, West Virginia, and married Adelaide, daughter of Major Burchett; Romulus Culver studied law, but died when still a young man; Royina married James Taylor, the son of Butler Taylor of Greenup (see Taylor family).

William Alexander Biggs

William Alexander Biggs, born in 1860 on the farm at Mt. Zion (since known as the William Biggs, Jr., farm) was the eldest son of Thomas Naylor and Ellen Humphreys Biggs. He was six years of age when his parents moved from Mt. Zion to a farm on Smith Branch.

In 1887 Mr. Biggs married Maud Ella, daughter of Shadrach and Frances Stark Mitchell of Greenup. They lived on a farm near his father until 1893, when they moved to Greenup, where he went into the hardware business with his brother-in-law, John Taylor Lawson. After a number of years he withdrew from that business and went into the cross tie business with Robert E. L. Wilson.

The children of William Alexander Biggs are Irene, Frances, Thomas Carlisle (Carl), Ellenor, William, and George Nicholas. Irene married James McCoy of Greenup, and their children are James of Anderson, South Carolina; Frances, wife of Emmett Moore, of Ashland; William of Logan, West Virginia; and Biggs, who married Harriet Hoffman of Greenup. William and Biggs served in the European Theater during World War II.

Frances Biggs married Walter Boyer of Silver Grove, Kentucky, and they live at Riverton. They have no children.

Thomas Carlisle (Carl) Biggs served in France during World War I and was on a ship in the Mediterranean that was bombed in World War II. He was unmarried and was employed on merchant vessels that traveled over the globe.

Ellenor and William Biggs are deceased. William married Talitha Blackburn of West Virginia, and they have two children, William, whose plane went down in the Pacific in World War II, and Barbara of Columbus, Ohio.

George Nicholas Biggs married Martha Diehlman of Mischewaukee, Indiana, where he is a merchant. They have one son.

William Alexander Biggs still owns a part of the land which was bought by his grandfather, William Biggs, Sr., in 1843, and which was inherited by him from his father, Thomas Naylor Biggs. Mr. Biggs was baptized in the Greenup Union Presbyterian Church July 11, 1869, and was closely associated with the church as long as it continued. He was an elder when it passed out of existence in September 1930.

James Davis Biggs

James Davis Biggs, the fourth son of William and Lucy Davis Biggs, married Alice, daughter of George Wurts, and they lived on the Wurts farm in the home built by John M. McConnell. Later Mr. Biggs became the owner of this farm, and lived there all his married life.

He was a staunch supporter of the Greenup Union Presbyterian Church, which he attended faithfully for fifty years. The church records refer to him as ruling elder as early as 1863 and frequent reference is made to him as moderator and as a delegate to the annual meetings of Presbytery.

Mr. and Mrs. Biggs had two daughters, Mary Wurts and Sallie Russell. Mary Wurts married Harry Renick of Ashland, where they made their home. Their children are Alice and Elizabeth. Sallie Russell married Sturgis Bates of Riverton, where they lived until Mr. Bates retired and they went to live in Ashland. They have one son, Sturgis, Jr. (see Bates family).

BINGHAM

James C. Bingham was born in Athens County, Ohio, and in 1867 he married Alida R. Gray of Ulster County, New York. The family came to Russell in 1877, where Mr. Bingham was engaged in the florist business. He had served in the Union Army for the duration of the Civil War. Mr. and Mrs. Bingham were the parents of eight children, Robert H., Walter T., Evelyn, James, Charles, Stella, Mabel, and Rachel.

Robert Bingham married Sophia Chinn of Pond Run; Walter married Mary Callon of Greenup; Evelyn married Charles Hager of Greenup; James married Ida Swearingin of Russell; Stella married Thomas Rogers, Mabel married Robert Rogers, Charles married Margaret Lambert, all of these at Russell; and Rachel married D. S. Newland of Buffalo, West Virginia. A number of these families now live in Ironton, Ohio.

BOOTON

Franklin and Mary Cannon Booton came from Virginia to Greenup County. They settled first on Shultz Creek. Later they bought the Samuel W. Gammon farm on Tygart Creek, where they lived many years, and then moved to Kansas in 1884. The family sold the old Gammon farm to John Metz and Mary Gammon Lawson.

Franklin and Mary Cannon Booton were the parents of Sarah Frances, Nancy, Reuben, Joseph, Belle, William, Maude, Elta, and Elvin. Sarah Frances married Lafayette Foster of Tygart, and their children were Minnie, wife of William Glover (see Glover family); Arthur of Portsmouth, Ohio; Dora, wife of George Laidley of Scioto County, Ohio; Kathryn, wife of Karl King, who moved to Oklahoma; Lewis and Oscar, both of whom went to Kansas and married there.

Nancy married Thomas, son of Colonel Thaddeus Bennett of Tygart (see Bennett family). After Thomas Bennett died his widow married George Tanner of Siloam (see Tanner family).

BRADEN

There were families of this name in the county in its early days, as observed in old records. A marriage license was issued in 1827 to James Braden and Mary Smith.

The family history began with Sampson Breeding, who owned a farm in southwestern Virginia, near what is now Gate City. In 1849 he got the "Gold Rush Fever" and left his farm to go to California. He came to Greenup County to visit a relative, Basil Bright, who had come from Virginia and settled on Tygart.

Sampson Breeding had married Lucy, a daughter of Thomas Biggs of Virginia. While visiting the Bright family, she started on horseback to the home of William Biggs of Smith Branch. While fording a creek, she was thrown into the water and, as a result, she took a severe cold from which she did not recover. Sampson Breeding remained on Tygart Creek. The name gradually changed to the present form, Braden.

Children of the Braden family were Wesley, Isouria, John, Elizabeth, and Sarah Jane. Wesley married Cassandra, daughter of Eli and Rachel Duzan Cooper of Upper Tygart Valley; Isouria married Albert Abdon and their children were Henry, Inez, Eva, Ethel, and Gladys; Elizabeth married Matthew Warnock (see Warnock family); Sarah Jane married Francis M. Warnock (see Warnock family). Other members of the family were James, who married Frankie Fullerton of Fullerton, whose children were Eva Killen and Omar; Herbert, who married Inez Abdon of Tygart Valley, and who is a merchant in Greenup; Horace Braden, who married Laura Boyles and lives on Upper Tygart Creek.

James Braden, who married Frankie Fullerton, was the son of Wesley and Cassandra Cooper Braden.

BRAGG

Thomas Bragg was born in Culpeper County, Virginia, in 1754. He was a captain in the Virginia Regiment commanded by Christopher Greenup, who was later Governor of Kentucky. On September 20, 1781, he married Lucy Blakemore of Kentucky. They had a daughter, Harriet, born 1787, in South Carolina. At Vanceburg, Kentucky, Harriet Bragg married George Naylor Davis, who was born in Maryland in 1781.

George Naylor and Harriet Bragg Davis came to Greenup to live. He served in the War of 1812. He was active in the early affairs of the county, serving as justice, and in 1840-41 he served as sheriff.

Other children of the Bragg family who settled in Greenup County were Armistead Churchill Bragg, who married Susan Morton of Gray's Branch in 1812, and John Blakemore Bragg, who married Lucinda Crump in 1817.

BRAMMER

Joshua Brammer was probably the first of the name to come to Greenup County. The family came from Ohio and settled below the Fulton Oil Works (now Wurtland). The children were John, Joseph, and a daughter, Susan.

John married Polly Knap in 1825. Joseph married Nancy, a daughter of Rev. John Lee of Virginia. Susan married Daniel Davisson and settled near Oldtown. They had a son Matthew whose children were Lilly and Susan. John Brammer, seventy-eight years old, of Wurtland, gives the following family history: "Barzell Brammer married Sarah Artripp and they were the parents of Laura, John, and Alice, none of whom married."

C. M. Brammer was a practicing physician at Wurtland in the late 1860's and in the 1880's.

The Brammer family was connected with the John L. Collins family by marriage. Joseph Brammer and John L. Collins purchased the James Martin farm, and other land below Wurtland adjoining the Wurts farm. Mr. Collins died and the land was divided.

Mahala Brammer married John Hiatt in 1830.

BROOKS

Edward Brooks married Amanda, daughter of John and Eliza Bellow Pratt, March 7, 1840, and lived on Tygart Creek near Lynn, or Liberty. They were the parents of John E., Thomas, William Fletcher (Sank), Edward, Jr., Samuel, and Martha.

John E. Brooks married Alice Bruce of Vanceburg and they moved to Parsons, Kansas. Thomas Brooks married while he lived on Tygart Creek. He bought property on Perry Street in Greenup from Joseph Pollock and lived there when he was associated with his cousin, Benjamin F. Pratt, in the Pratt and Brooks General Store, in the 1860's and 1870's. Thomas Brooks moved to Kansas, where his wife died and he married a second time. William Fletcher (Sank) Brooks married Lucy, daughter of Adolphus L. and Henrietta Powell Reid. They went to Parsons, Kansas, where she died. Edward, Jr., and Samuel Brooks went to Kansas before they were married. Martha Brooks, the only daughter of Edward and Amanda Pratt Brooks, married Charles Callihan (see Callihan family).

Edward Brooks, Sr., died at his home on Tygart Creek and his wife, Amanda Pratt Brooks, went to live with her sons in Kansas, where she later died.

BROWN

Benjamin Franklin Brown

Benjamin Franklin Brown was the son of John Brown, Jr., of Scioto County, Ohio, and Charity Johnson Brown of Mason County, Kentucky. He was born in 1827, married Susan Calvin, and located in Greenup. He began keeping store in the building at the corner of Main and Washington Streets, which was built by Blake and Hall in 1856. Later Adolphus Reid entered this business with Mr. Brown, but withdrew and opened a general store on the corner of Main and Harrison Streets, where he was assisted by his sons, Charles and Morris.

Benjamin Franklin and Susan Calvin Brown were the parents of Mary, who married Robert Robb; Anna, who married Charles Schmutz; and Sallie, who married Thomas Ogg and went to California. The only children of these families were those of Robert and Mary Brown Robb. Of these, Lyda and Frank went to California, and Nellie married and lived in Cincinnati.

Eliza Brown, a sister of Benjamin Franklin Brown, married John F. Day April 2, 1835. She was born February 1, 1816. They occupied the cottage on Main Street which was the Brown home for many years. This property was made into a two-story house by Butler Taylor, who later owned it. John F. and Eliza Brown Day had a daughter, Eliza Ann, who married Charles Thompson Kehoe November 27, 1854, and their daughter, Carrie, married Dr. Joseph S. Rardin of Portsmouth, Ohio. Their daughter, Helen Lansing Rardin Yates, is a resident of Roanoke, Virginia.

John Brown, Jr., was the son of John Brown, Sr., a Revolutionary soldier who rendered service in the company of Captain Israel Moore in 1782 in Pennsylvania. He was born in Chester County, Pennsylvania, and married Hannah ———— at West Whiteland, Pennsylvania, about 1786. They had three children:

Rachel, born 1788, who married General William Kendall; Eliza, born in 1790, who married Governor Robert Lucas of Ohio; and John, Jr., born December 9, 1793, who married Charity Johnson.

John Brown, Sr., was the son of Adley Brown, also a Revolutionary soldier of Pennsylvania.

JOHN BROWN

John Brown (1835-1924) married Nancy Montgomery (1842-1922) and lived in Magoffin County, Kentucky. About 1860 they came to Greenup County and settled on Little Sandy, where he worked on the Womack land. Some time later the Brown family moved to Coal Branch and then to a farm on Tygart Creek. They spent the greater part of their married life in the county and reared a large family, all of whom have moved from the county except their eldest son, William, age ninety-one, who lives with a son, Clarence, at Gray's Branch. Another son, Walter, who married Polly, daughter of James and Lucy Jane Ratcliff Hurst, lives in Greenup, where he is a contracting carpenter.

James Brown, age eighty-nine, the second son of John and Nancy Brown, moved to Scioto County, where he was a farmer for many years. His daughter, Mrs. Cora Russell, lives in Portsmouth.

Two daughters of John and Nancy Brown, Lydia, who married James Reason (Polk) Craycraft, and Maude, who married Garfield Craycraft (see Craycraft family), also moved to Scioto County and live at Wheelersburg.

Late in life Mr. and Mrs. Brown went to Portsmouth to make their home and spent the remainder of their lives there. They are buried in the Wheelersburg Cemetery.

BRYAN

This family lived at Gray's Branch in the 1850's, and perhaps earlier. They were farmer folk. Mrs. Nancy Bryan was a member of the Greenup Union Presbyterian Church in 1858. James and Parthenia Bryan lived on the farm, but in the 1870's James Bryan was elected county judge and the family moved to the brick house below Little Sandy River. Their children were William, Maggie, Emma, and Jennie. William married Martha Morton and had four children, James, Frank, Mary, and William; Maggie married William Rock of Charleston, West Virginia; Emma married Edward Winn of Greenup and the family later moved to Texas; Jennie married Clarence Lacock of Greenup, and they lived in the brick home where the Bryan family lived many years.

BRYSON

John Brison, or Bryson, was a first lieutenant in a Pennsylvania Regiment of the Revolutionary War. His commission was dated April 11, 1777, and his name appears on the list of Pennsylvania officers appointed by a Council of Safety pursuant to a resolution of Congress dated September 16, 1776. He was a prisoner of war on Long Island in 1778. (Record given in Evans' *History of Scioto County*.)

John Bryson was an ancestor of William Bryson, who married Elizabeth Forman Lawson, daughter of John and Catherine Taylor Lawson, pioneers of Gray's Branch. Both families came from Virginia. The children of William and Elizabeth Lawson Bryson were William, who went to California and married there; James, who married and went to Missouri; Catherine, who married William Withrow; Jane, who married George Nicholas Biggs; and John Lawson Bryson, who married (1) Mary Frances Gammon in 1855. Their children were James, Elizabeth, who married Mason Burns, Ellis, who married Ellen Maria Burns, and Mary Frances, who married Robert Burns. John Lawson Bryson married (2) Harriet Gammon in 1872, a sister of his first wife. They had one daughter, Lyda, who married (1) George Justice and they moved to Oklahoma. He died and she married (2) Calvin Pitman.

William and Katherine Bryson Withrow were the parents of Elizabeth Hilliard, Ruby, wife of Morton Warnock, Lavenia Dugan, and Jennie, the wife of Albert Middaugh. They had two sons, William and Daniel Withrow.

BRYSON FAMILY OF SCHULTZ CREEK

William Bryson was born in Donegal County, Ireland, about 1770. He married Jane Bones of Donegal County and their son, David Alexander, was born in 1795. He married Hulda Cowper, who was born in Edinburgh, Scotland. They migrated to Dunsfort, Washington County, Pennsylvania. Richard Cowper Bryson, the eldest child, was born in 1818 at Dunsfort, as was Margaret Cooney Bryson, who was born in 1820.

About this time David Alexander and Hulda Cowper Bryson moved to Lewis County, Kentucky, and the rest of their sixteen children were born in Lewis County. Abraham Huston Bryson, the third child, was born in 1822. He married Martha Dortch of Schultz Creek, Greenup County, and they always lived there. Another son, Andrew Jackson Bryson, married Frances Dortch and they lived on Schultz Creek also.

David Alexander Bryson, Jr., married Louella, daughter of Colonel Thaddeus and Lucinda Howell Bennett, of Fairview, Greenup County. Mary Jane Bryson married William H. Vaughters, of Scioto County, Ohio. Other members of the Bryson family moved to Ohio and Illinois.

Abraham Huston Bryson's son, James, married Nancy McCallister of Springville, and they were the parents of Arthur R., a lawyer, and Dr. A. J. Bryson, both of Ashland; Huston, who lived at the homestead; and Nellie Fields. Children of David Alexander and Lucy Bennett Bryson were Louisa, Louella, and Joseph. Louisa married Caleb Hitchcock of Mt. Zion; Louella married Jura Fullerton, son of Harrison and Mary Jane Cadot Fullerton, of Fullerton, and they moved to Ohio; Joseph married (1) Sallie McCallister of Springville, and (2) Minnie Robeson of Kansas.

Listed in the early marriages of Greenup County:

Abraham Bryson married Martha Dorch July 7, 1846.

Hannah Bryson married Ephraim James August 14, 1821.

Jane Bryson married Solomon Van Bibber January 3, 1826. Permit of the bride's father, William Bryson.

John Bryson married Susan Stewart March 10, 1821. Permit of the bride's father, Charles Stewart.

Priscilla Bryson married George Rice May 6, 1816. Permit of the bride's father, F. Bryson.

Rutha Bryson married John Davis November 21, 1826.

BURNS

Denny and Sarah Jane Burns came to Greenup County from Mercer Bottom near Charleston, West Virginia, about 1880. They made their home at Gray's Branch, where Mr. Burns was a farmer. In this family there were six sons and four daughters: Theodore, Walter, Mason Garrett, John, Robert, William (Dock), Minerva, Sarah, Mary, and Ella.

Walter married and lived in West Virginia.

Mason Garrett was born in Ohio County, West Virginia, in 1850. He married Elizabeth, the eldest daughter of John Lawson

Bryson, and they lived on a farm at Gray's Branch for many years. Late in life they moved to Oklahoma, where Mr. Burns died and Mrs. Burns still lives at the age of ninety-two. They had no children but shared the comforts of their home with several orphan children, one of them being Maggie Timberlake (see Timberlake family).

John Burns married Laura Wade and their children were Walter Clay (Pete), Denny, Charles, Margaret, Carrie, Minnie, and Myrtle. Of this family Denny married Miss Moore; Carrie married Leonard Berkley; Walter Clay (Pete) married Maude Swearingen and their children are Minnie, wife of George Preston, Clay, and Georgia, wife of Denny Van Hoose. They make their home in Wheelersburg, Ohio.

Robert Burns married Mary Frances, the second daughter of John Lawson Bryson. They also went to Oklahoma, where Mr. and Mrs. Burns have died and their two daughters, Bessie and Elizabeth, have married and still live.

William (Dock) Burns married Mary Kinney, daughter of James and Nancy Kinney Walker of Siloam and they moved to California; Minerva married George Artis and moved to California; Sarah married James Madison McClave (see McClave family); Mary married John McNeal (see McNeal family); and Ella married Ellis Bryson (see Bryson family).

Mr. and Mrs. Denny Burns are both buried in Siloam Cemetery and the inscriptions read: Denny Burns, born 1809, died 1881; Sarah Jane Burns, born 1819, died 1900.

BURTON

The Burton family was among the earliest settlers of Coal Branch. Two brothers, Joshua and James, are the first of the name known in the county. Joshua married Mary Patton and they were the parents of James W. (1835), Abednego (1838), Thomas, and Hezekiah. James W. married (1) Mary Carner and their children were Wayne and Flora, wife of Winfield Warnock. This family has always lived on Coal Branch and some of them still reside there. James Burton married (2) Helen Wills Richards of Coal Branch. Abednego married Margaret Hornbuckle of Ohio.

James Burton, the brother of Joshua, married Mahala Bailey and they were the parents of John W. (1839) and Thomas. John W. married Lucinda, daughter of John S. and Elizabeth Floyd Cook. Their children were Lydia Nichols of Tygart Valley and

John E., who married Jane Cook. They were the parents of John, Thomas, Artissa Marlow, and Cynthia Ann, who never married. Of this family, Thomas married Mary Adam and had a large family: James, John, Thomas, Jr., Edward, Everett, Laura Bays of Little Sandy, Perla, wife of Butler Virgin of Oldtown, and Lilly, who married (1) Mr. Harvey and (2) T. P. Davis.

Everett Burton married Martha Blaine of Portsmouth. Their children were Helen, a well-known teacher in Greenup County for several years, and in the Portsmouth Schools for the past six years; and Olive French of Texas.

BUSH

John and Amanda Howe Bush came to the Siloam neighborhood about 1880 and bought a part of the original Mackoy land from the Albertson family. They spent the rest of their lives there and reared a large family. The children were David, Lizzie, Henry, Mary, Ella, Isaac, Robert, Hiram (Treat), and William.

David married (1) Tillie Miller and had a son, Clarence; (2) Jennie Moran and they moved to Ashland. Lizzie (1853-1940) married Mr. Lapool and had no children. Henry married Jennie Lee (1858-1941), a descendant of the Lee family of Virginia. Their children were Ethel, who married Lytle Morgan; William, who married May Allen of Wakefield, Ohio, and their children are Allene McGary, George, and Carroll, who is deceased. Mary married Edward Ghent.

Ella Bush married William Burtram and their children were Ruth, Oswald, Denver, Willard, Maurice, Edith, Pearl, Chester, Ronald and Donald (twins), Marie, Mildred, and Lulu. Marie married James Woods of Portsmouth and they live in Dayton; Lulu married Frank Millar of Scioto County and they live in Portsmouth; Mildred (deceased) married Mr. Brehmer of Portsmouth; Edith married Arthur Barr; and Ruth married Mr. Owery.

Isaac Bush married Lizzie Miller, sister of Tillie Miller, (1) wife of David Bush. They descended from the Stockham family of Scioto County. Robert Bush (1871-1942) married Susie, daughter of John and Eliza Hitchcock Tooley, and they lived on his father's farm. Their children are Beulah Rosenbaum and Helen Howland. Mrs. Bush lives in South Shore. Hiram (Treat) Bush married Anna Angel and their children were Gladys, Virginia, Lena, Mildred, Clifford, Forest, and Raymond. William

Bush married (1) Maggie Logan, (2) Samantha, daughter of John Davis.

The Bush family were always active members of Siloam Church, and a number of them are buried in the cemetery there. The inscriptions on Mr. and Mrs. Bush's stones read: "John B. Bush, born January 14, 1831, died April 8, 1916, and Amanda Bush, born May 10, 1832, died January 1, 1901."

CALLIHAN

The Callihan family settled at Palmyra about 1830. Among the early marriage licenses recorded is one issued to William Callihan and Nancy Davisson February 23, 1830, upon the written permit of the bride's father, Andy Davisson. These names have been connected with Palmyra, Argillite, and other places along the Little Sandy River.

Charles Callihan lived at Three Mile (Plum Grove). He married Elizabeth Swearengin and their children were John, Clem, Charles, Jr., Florence Dortch, Nancy Smith, Sarah Artis, and Effie Dysard. John Callihan married Samantha Patton and their children were Clara Henry, Jennie McGuire, Elizabeth Smith, William, John, and Joseph.

Clem Callihan married Emma Burkhardt and their children were Mary Galford, Samuel, Leslie, Eugene, George, Pauline Ruark, Sigmund, Edna Anderson, and Louise Paynter. Samuel married Esther Smith; Eugene married Irene Weeks; George married Sophia Dowdy; and Sigmund married Alice M. Shepherd.

Horatio Callihan married India Pratt and their children were George, Charles, and Christopher. George married Lavinia Morton of Tygart. He was a farmer and while stacking hay he was fatally injured by falling on the prongs of a pitchfork. Charles Callihan was also a farmer living below Greenup. He married Martha Brooks of Lynn. Christopher never married.

Robert Callihan married Rhoda Puthoff and was proprietor of the Andes House on Main Street in the 1870's.

The sons of Charles and Martha Brooks Callihan have long been residents of Greenup. William married Ruth Winkler of Wheelersburg, Ohio; George married a niece of Ruth Winkler, Elsie Duduit, also of Wheelersburg; Vernon married Agnes Doran; and Alfred married Emma, daughter of James and Lois Tanner Rankins. There was another son, Clarence.

Gabriel Callihan was another of the name who lived at Palmyra in the early days.

CALLON

Samuel Callon came from Mason County, Kentucky, to Greenup County in company with Dr. Allen Baker about 1850. He married Sarah Ann Stepter of Tygart Valley and they had quite a large family when they moved to Greenup in 1879. They were the parents of eight sons: Carlisle, Leonidas, Allen, Nathaniel, Samuel, William, Walter, and Albert; also one daughter, Mary, who married Walter T. Bingham of Russell, later of Ironton, Ohio. Walter T. and Mary Callon Bingham were the parents of William of Columbus, Ohio; Edith; Samuel of Ashland; Dorothy Burdette of Ironton; and Lois Hill of Butler, Pennsylvania.

Carlisle H. Callon married Sarah Tumbleson of Tygart; Nathaniel married Anna Warnock of Greenup and they moved to California; Walter married Matilda Byrne of Greenup. Carlisle H. and Sarah Tumbleson Callon had three sons, Rhodes, Dent, and Roe Paynter.

CARNAHAN

The Carnahan family is of Scotch-Irish descent. They came from Ireland to Pennsylvania at a very early date. Dr. James and Delilah Hopkins Carnahan came to Kentucky and settled in what was at that time Greenup County. They had seven sons, of whom one, Alonzo, was born in Greenup County in 1841. He studied medicine and took a course at the Johns Hopkins Hospital at Baltimore, Maryland.

Dr. Carnahan located at Oldtown, where he married Virginia Anglin Kendall. He built a house on the site of the old brick homestead of James Howe, using brick from the old house for the cellar and foundation of the new. He was, also, a farmer and one of the earliest tobacco growers in the county.

Dr. and Virginia Kendall Carnahan were the parents of five daughters, Mary D., Lenore, Caroline, Virginia and Jessie. Mary D. married Walter Orin Womack of Oldtown, where they made their home. Their children are Carl, Virginia Ann, Eloise and Richard Glenn (Dick). Lenore married Dr. E. E. Raike of Riverton. They went to Kansas, where Dr. Raike was located for many years. They have a daughter, Anna Carnahan Clark, of Iowa City, Iowa. Caroline married Dr. Henry Morris, of Lawrence County, Kentucky, who located in Greenup. They had no children but reared Earl Nickell, now of Huntington, and Ella Marie Cates of Riverton, a nephew and a niece of Dr. Morris. Virginia married Charles Stuart and they live at the old Carnahan farm. Jessie married Harry C. Steil of Ashland. Their children are Robert, Edwin, Carnahan, and Maxie Dean.

CARTWRIGHT

Cyrus Cartwright came to Limeville to work at the Greenup Lime Works. He was born at Hanging Rock, Lawrence County, Ohio, in 1844. His parents died when he was a small boy and he was reared by an aunt and uncle, Mr. and Mrs. Joseph Eicher, who had seventeen children of their own. Mr. Cartwright served for three years in the Civil War and spent six months in Libby Prison.

After William W. Tong's death in 1879, Mr. Cartwright operated the Lime Works for several years and then he opened a general store near his home at what is now known as Tongs Post Office. He carried on this merchandise business until his death in 1915. His store was located on the side of the road in front of the J. W. West home and later he moved it in the lane beside his own home, which was built in 1888.

Mr. and Mrs. Cartwright had two children, Maurice Edmund, and Emma Brown (Brownie). Maurice Edmund started to work as a telegraph operator for the Chesapeake and Ohio Railroad when he was seventeen years of age. He was a prominent official of the Baltimore and Ohio Railroad in Wheeling, West Virginia, at the time of his death in 1945. Emma Brown Cartwright married H. Green Richards (see his sketch under Richards family).

Mr. and Mrs. Cartwright are both buried in the Mt. Zion Cemetery. Mary J. Cartwright 1837-1917
Cyrus Cartwright 1844-1915

CHINN

John and Sophia Brown Chinn came from Virginia to Greenup County about 1812 and settled in the eastern part of the county on the Ohio River. They came about the same time as the Mead and Powell families, who settled in the same section of the county. John Chinn was a farmer and soon acquired considerable land in the neighborhood, later called Chinnville. John and Sophia

Brown Chinn were the parents of Benjamin F., John Hamon, Thomas, and Mollie Burtenshaw.

Benjamin F. Chinn married Maria Jane Bradshaw in 1864, and they were the parents of eleven children: Ella Mackabee, Sophia Bingham, Orville D., Effie Crump, Jane Foster, Benjamin F., Jr., Minnie, Lucy Leach, Walter, Bertha Williams, and Sallie.

John Hamon Chinn married Sophia Mead and their children were Benjamin and John Hamon, Jr. John Hamon Chinn was a merchant near what is now Wurtland. He married MaryWurts and their son, Wurts, operates a general merchandise store which is within a mile of the original Benjamin Chinn store, said to have been the first store between the mouth of the Big Sandy and the Scioto Rivers. Grandin Wurts Chinn, a son of Wurts Chinn, is associated with his father in the general merchandising business.

CLANCY

The Clancy family lived west of where Russell now stands. The family was allied with the Mead and Powell families of that section. George Perry Clancy married Nancy Arnold and, in 1833, he bought land from the Hollingsworth family. Dr. Hollingsworth is buried in the William Paull graveyard on the hill near Riverview above Russell.

George, a son of George Perry and Nancy Arnold Clancy, married Emmoline Mead, and a daughter, Elizabeth, married Ellis M. Powell. Members of the Clancy family moved west.

This is one of the Pond Run families.

CLIFTON

The Clifton family were early settlers at Oldtown. Daniel S. Clifton married Elizabeth Jane Howe, daughter of James Howe and granddaughter of John Howe, the pioneer who came from Virginia to Greenup County. The children of Daniel S. Clifton were James, Daniel, John, and William H. (Whig). Daniel and Whig were teachers in the county schools and the latter was school commissioner of the county in 1883-1884.

Whig Clifton married Sarah, daughter of Charles Russell of Argillite, who operated the grain and lumber mill there for seventeen years. They were the parents of Georgia, who married Mr. Callihan and moved to Louisiana, John, Paul, Chester,

Edward, Hargis, and Charles. Edward and Charles went west, and several of the others went to Louisiana.

Daniel Clifton married Mercy Hogan. Their children were Paul, Ernest, James, Maud, May, and Elizabeth. The old Clifton home is still standing at Oldtown, but there are no members of the family living in the county as far as can be learned.

COLE

Alfred E. Cole was a son of Allaniah Cole, whose father, Ephraim Cole, was born in Maryland. Ephraim Cole was a Revolutionary War soldier and served for three years in Colonel Lee's Regiment of Maryland troops. Alfred E. Cole was elected Circuit Judge of the Ninth District in 1882 and served until 1893. The Cole family was also interested in the Citizens' Banks of Maysville and Greenup.

William Throop Cole was born in 1869 at Flemingsburg, Kentucky. He was a son of Alfred E. and Abigail Throop Cole. The family moved to Maysville where William received his early education. He completed his education at Vanderbilt University and entered the law office of his father, and brother, Allan. He was a member of the Kentucky House of Representatives in 1890-91. In 1895 he came to Greenup to practice his profession and in 1896 was appointed to fill the unexpired term of County Judge J. B. Bennett, who had been elected to Congress. He was the first commonwealth attorney of the new Twentieth Judicial District of Kentucky.

In 1896 Mr. Cole married Jeannette (Nettie), daughter of Adolphus L. and Atlanta Martin Reid, of Greenup. Their children were Abigail, Alfred E., Josephine, Herbert, Jeannette, Helen Elizabeth, Mary Louise, Vivian O., and Dorothy. Abigail died in girlhood; Josephine married Dr. G. R. Wilder of Bishopville, South Carolina; Herbert is located in West Virginia; Jeannette is the wife of Samuel G. Leslie of Greenup; Helen E. married Jack R. Phipps, Mary L. married Everett Wells, and Vivian O. married Robert Woods, all of Ashland; Dorothy is the wife of Edward Bruce of Atlanta, Ga.

COLEGROVE

Nathan Colegrove married Sally Clark in 1839. Their son, Henry Colegrove, was born at Pennsylvania Furnace in 1840.

He married Mary Elizabeth Rutherford of Ohio in 1864. They were the parents of nine children: Scott, Nathan, Pearl, Edward, William, Luella, Madison, Carrie, and Leona.

Scott married Annie Thom of Short Branch; Pearl married Zachariah Richards; Edward married Lola Richards; Carrie married Eugene Richards; Leona married Arthur Foster of Mt. Zion. William was accidentally killed in the oil fields of California in 1900. Henry and Marie Rutherford Colegrove were residents of Short Branch, and a number of their children married and settled there.

COLLINS

The Collins family was of Irish descent and came from Virginia to Ohio. James Collins married Henrietta Davidson of Haverhill, Ohio. They came to Greenup County and settled on a farm on Little Sandy River. The children of this family were Nathaniel, Elizabeth, Henrietta, Margaret, Annie, John, Thomas, and a younger daughter, who went west.

In February 1871 Nathaniel Collins married Lydia Dougherty, daughter of the Dougherty family who had come from the Shenandoah Valley of Virginia. The young couple lived at Raccoon Furnace for a while and then moved to the farm back of Greenup, later owned by the Brugh family. Here four of the Collins children were born. They moved to a farm in W Hollow and five more children were born there, making nine in all. The children of this family were Sibbie, William, Henrietta, Nathaniel, Alice, Mary, Caroline, James, and Amelia. Sibbie is the wife of Samuel Huffman and lives in Russell; William married Juliet Hockaday of Greenup; Henrietta married Stanley Mitchell; Nathaniel married Ollie Willis and lives in Ashland; Alice married George Rigrish of Tygart Valley; Mary married Birch Hunt of Tygart and they live in New Boston; Caroline married Warren Brown of Cincinnati and they went to Texas; James married Sallie, daughter of Colonel William Worthington; and Amelia is a nurse, residing in Portsmouth.

There were several other Collins families who settled in Greenup County who had come from Pennsylvania. Some of them were related and others not. John C. Collins owned a large farm below Wurtland from 1847 to 1877. The sons of this family were Jacob, John, and Lewis. John married Rebecca Davidson of Ohio and they were the parents of Lucy and May, both of whom died in young womanhood. John Collins was sheriff of the county from 1898 to 1901 and town treasurer for many years. He was called "Uncle John" by his friends and neighbors.

Jacob Collins lived on the Collins farm above Greenup for many years. His daughter married Dr. Franz in Russell.

Lewis Collins married Teresa Clark of Greenup. They were the parents of Frank and Martha. Martha married Ralph, son of Dr. M. S. and Florence Hunt Leslie. They have a daughter, Lois.

COOPER

Eli Cooper came to Tygart Valley from Mason County, Kentucky, in 1824, and made his home with the Pogue family. He married Rachel, daughter of Peter Duzan, whose family had come from Mason County a short time before and settled at Grassy. Peter Duzan carried the mail on horseback from Grassy to the nearest post office, which may have been Greenupsburg.

Three of Eli Cooper's children were John, Fletcher, and Ransom. John married Mary Huffman of Tygart Valley; Fletcher married Louisa Moore; and Ransom married Harriet Elanor Pogue, daughter of General Robert and Jane Hopkins Pogue. They lived on the original Pogue land on Upper Tygart, and Coopersville became quite an important place in the valley. Ransom Cooper operated a lumber mill, a cooper shop, and a general store, also farming much of the land. The children of this family were Minnie, Eula, Annie, Jennie, Mollie Faris and John Poage (twins), Ewing, and Frank.

Minnie married Edward (Ted) Duncan and lives at Kehoe, where she has kept a general store and been the postmistress for many years. Her home and the store are located on the original Pogue land. The Duncan children are Hattie, Doris, Eula, Ewing, Winnie, Della, and Ransom.

Eula Lee Cooper married Clayton Stephenson and lives in Cleveland, Ohio; Annie married Orville D. Chinn (see Chinn family); Jennie married Ezra Smith and lives in Russell; Mollie Faris married John Ellis Taylor (see Taylor family); John Pogue married Carrie Duncan and lives on the original home site. They are the parents of thirteen children: Raleigh R., Ethel Queen, Anna Lee Arthurs, Hazel Wallace, Mary, Sallie Booth, Norma, Dolores Lawson, Gladys Hunt, Frank E., Kenneth, Douglas, and Eunice Riffe.

Ewing Cooper married Mary Duncan, twin sister of John Pogue Cooper's wife, Carrie Duncan; Frank married Irene Elhoff of New Boston. Both Ewing and Frank are merchants and have been prominent citizens in the city of New Boston, Ohio, for more than thirty years.

CORUM

Jesse Corum was the first of the Corum name to be found in the early records of the county. His sons were William and Jesse; his daughters were Margaret Stewart, Eliza Ann Davidson, Rebecca Heisler, and Amanda Raison. William (Billy) Corum married Edith J. Passmore. He succeeded John Hockaday as county clerk, with his son, George, as his deputy. George became clerk when his father retired from the office. The Hockaday and Corum families held the office of county clerk for about eighty-five years.

George Corum married Lena Taft; Mary married James McCormick; and the youngest daughter, Sallie, went west many years ago. The Corum home was in the rear of Riverton and was bought in the early 1880's by Colonel William Worthington, who lived there for many years. This property is now owned and occupied by members of the J. W. Crawford family.

Jesse Corum also lived on the Corum land below the William Corum home. His house burned and the Bennett brick home now stands on the site. There are no descendants of the Jesse Corum family in the county now. Mr. Corum died in the 1870's and his widow married C. W. Mytinger about 1882. The Corum children were Maude, Laura, Kate, Lily, and Ernest.

CRAWFORD

John Crawford (1833) married Nancy Jane Morrison and came from Philadelphia, Pennsylvania, to West Union, Adams County, Ohio. Later he came to Riverton as wharfmaster for the Eastern Kentucky Railroad. The children were William Noble, George, Eliza Belle, John Walker, Mary Frances, Anna Mae, Bertha Lee, and Chester Hubert.

William Noble became a telegraph operator. He married Maggie Stella Walker and they had one son, William Noble, Jr. Eliza Belle married John W. Smith (see Elmer Smith family). John Walker Crawford (1870) married Daisy Ziare Ridenour

(1872) in 1897. He was a telegraph operator for the Chesapeake and Ohio Railroad for many years. He bought as their home the large brick house back of Riverton, which was built by William Corum and later occupied by the Colonel Worthington family. Mrs. Crawford and their son, John Walker, Jr., still live there. Mr. Crawford was fondly called "Brick Top" by his friends because of his red hair.

CRAYCRAFT

CRAYCRAFT FAMILY IN PENNSYLVANIA

The name Craycraft has been spelled in Pennsylvania as Craycraft, Cracraft, and Creacraft. Joseph Craycraft was born in Lincolnshire, England, and came to Frederick County, Maryland, about 1720. There were six sons, three of whom, Joseph, Charles, and William, remained in Pennsylvania. The other three went west, one to Ohio, one to what is now West Virginia, and the third to Limestone, Mason County, Kentucky.

A daughter of one William Craycraft, Mary Ann, married Thomas Atkinson, son of Thomas Atkinson of Washington County, Pennsylvania (see Atkinson family). Joseph Craycraft, Jr., had a son, Dr. Charles Craycraft, who lived in Washington County, Pennsylvania, and served in the Revolutionary War. He was taken prisoner and held some time by the British. His wife was Ellen, daughter of Thomas Atkinson, and he died in Pennsylvania in 1824. The children of this family were three sons, all having the original family names, Joseph, Charles, and William.

CRAYCRAFT FAMILY ON TYGART CREEK

There were Craycrafts living in Greenup County as early as 1804, when Elizabeth Craycraft made a deed to John Craycraft. In 1829 Elizabeth is listed as the heir of Thomas Dillon and the wife of Captain Charles Craycraft. In 1809 Charles Craycraft married Sarah, daughter of Reuben Stevenson, and in 1846 Ann, daughter of Charles Craycraft, married William Warnock (see Warnock family).

Reuben Craycraft, born in 1846, son of Charles and Rachel Craycraft, married Barbary Ann (1843-1893), daughter of James Greenslate, and lived at the Globe on Tygart Creek, where they reared a large family. The eldest son, James Reason (Polk), married Lydia Brown and lived in Greenup County until about

1900, when they moved to Scioto County, Ohio, where his widow still lives; a daughter, Sarah Eliza, married William Long (see Long family); and a younger son, Garfield, married Maude Brown, sister of Lydia, and they live at Wheelersburg.

One Elizabeth Craycraft married Dr. James M. Moore of Belfast, County Downs, Ireland, and in 1872 settled in Ironton, Ohio, where he was a physician until his death in 1894. They had one son, William Robert Moore.

The early marriage records show the following Craycraft marriages:

Ann Craycraft and William Price, February 18, 1836.

Elizabeth Craycraft and John Price, Sr., December 12, 1835.

John Craycraft and Charlotte Griffa, April 19, 1843.

Malinda Craycraft and William U. Buncks, August 28, 1836.

Hugh Craycraft

Greenup County Court Records of 1811 show that Hugh Craycraft bought land on Tygart Creek from the Coleman heirs for two dollars per acre. This was a part of the land included in the treasury warrant dated 1783 (see Land Grants). Hugh Craycraft may have been the father of James Matison Craycraft, who also lived on Tygart Creek.

James Matison Craycraft (1809) and Thursy Stewart (1816) were married in Greenup County December 11, 1837, and made their home on a large farm on lower Tygart Creek. The children of this family were Sarah, who married John R. Barney; Lyde, who married Tom Gammon; Sue, who married Peter Reeves; and four sons, James Hugh, William, Robert, and Joshua.

In 1869 James Matison Craycraft and all his family, some of whom were married and had children, went to Missouri and settled near Lee's Summit. The parents are buried there; Mr. Craycraft died in 1873 and his wife in 1888.

One son of this family, James Hugh Craycraft (1841) was married to Harriet Elizabeth Christman in Greenup County by the Rev. J. M. Farmer, in 1866. A teacher in the county, she was the daughter of Charles Humphries and Elizabeth Glover Christman, who lived on a farm on Tygart Creek. The James Hugh Craycraft family had a son, Roy, who was two years old when they left Greenup County, and three daughters who were born in Missouri. One daughter, Annie, returned to Greenup County for a visit in 1898. She met and married her distant cousin, Charles Glover (see Glover family). They lived in Fullerton, where their daughter, Elizabeth, was born. She is now a resident of Kansas City, where her aunt, Mrs. Hattie Spake, daughter of James Hugh Craycraft, also resides. Mrs. Spake has in her possession a church hymnal which her mother, Harriet Elizabeth Christman Craycraft, carried when she attended church at Mt. Zion before they went to Missouri. Mrs. Spake furnished the material for this sketch.

CRAYNON

Hugh H. Craynon, Jr., son of Hugh, Sr., and Mary Anna Gibbons Craynon, who were natives of Donegal County, Ireland, was born on the banks of the Brandywine, Wilmington, Delaware, September 8, 1850.

When he was quite young, during the covered wagon days, the family, like many others, journeyed westward, going as far as Wisconsin, where they remained for a time, probably one or two years.

They returned to Greenup County, Kentucky, stopping at Uhlen's Branch, where a furnace was located, and where they were living in 1865.

Later they moved to the then flourishing furnace town of Hunnewell, Kentucky, where the forefathers of so many families of this tristate area, including Greenup, Ashland, Huntington, etc., lived at one time.

In 1871 Hugh Craynon, Jr., began work with the then very new Eastern Kentucky Railroad Company, which was at that time under the management of Mr. Sturgis G. Bates, Sr., who came here from Boston, Massachusetts.

In 1874 he was married to Miss Catherine Noonan, daughter of Mr. and Mrs. Timothy Noonan, residents of Hunnewell, but natives of County Cork, Ireland. After their marriage they moved to Ashland, Kentucky, where they lived until 1879, when they returned to Hunnewell, and he again began work with the Eastern Kentucky Railroad as an engineer, a position he held until his retirement in 1929. They were the parents of five children: John Noonan Craynon, Thomas Timothy Craynon, Anna Loretta Craynon, Mary Ellen Craynon Hutton and Elizabeth Catherine Craynon Morton.

The Craynons moved to Riverton, Kentucky, about 1886, where they continued to make their home. Mr. Craynon passed away in 1932 at the age of eighty-one, and after a period of fifty years with the Eastern Kentucky Railroad Company.

CURRY

The Curry family is of Scotch-Irish descent and came from Virginia to Kentucky. Harry and Nancy Shields Curry were the parents of four sons who came to Greenup County and settled in and around Hopewell in the early days of the county. They were Henry Sloan, James, Hugh, and Robert. Many of their descendants still live at Hopewell and in other parts of the county.

Henry Sloan Curry married a widow, Nancy Cummings Anglin, whose family came from Virginia and settled near Hopewell. The children of this family were Henry Sloan, Jr., Adrian, Lafayette, Jane, Nancy, Mary Ann, and Robert Nixon. Adrian married Carrie Huffman; Lafayette married (1) Kate Shears, and (2) Carrie Curry; Jane married Alex Irwin; Nancy married Charles Norris (see Norris family); Mary Ann died young; Robert Nixon married Jane Lowe and settled in Texas.

Henry Sloan Curry, Jr. (1847), the eldest son, married Emma, daughter of George and Piety Hackworth Dixon Arthur Riffe (see Riffe family). Their children are Leona, Gertrude, Annie, Irene, Charles, Hattie, Harry, Mary J., Luella, Fern, and Doris. Leona married Dr. Frank Brady, lives in Florida, and has four sons; Gertrude married Ward Womack and they lived at Oldtown fifty years before making their home in Florida (see Womack family); Annie married Barr Irwin, lives in Ashland, and has four sons and one daughter; Irene married Green Hartley (see Hartley family); Charles married Maude Coyle and lived in Owensboro, Kentucky; Hattie married Samuel Warnock and lives in New Boston, Ohio (see Warnock family); Harry married Lucy Lawson, daughter of John Taylor Lawson, and has one son, George H., who lives in Greenup; Mary Jane married William A. Adams of Argillite, lives in New Boston, Ohio, and has six children; Luella married William Ireland Myers and lives in Greenup; Fern married Charles Floyd, lives in New Boston, Ohio, and has three children; Doris married Clyde Earwood.

James Curry, the second son of Harry and Nancy Shields Curry, married (1) Samantha (Lucinda) Eastham in 1837, and (2) Sarah Bradshaw. The children of the first marriage were Amanda, Mirian, and Alice; those of the second marriage were John, James, Henry, William, Mary, Nancy, and Laura. Amanda married Henry Jackson; Mirian married Moses Womack of Carter County; Alice married Jeff Sparks; Nancy married Mann Montgomery; Laura married John Bush; Henry married Anna

V. Stark and went west; William married Emma Riffe, daughter of Orville D. (Bud) and Arminta Curry Riffe.

Hugh Curry, the third son, married Margaret Bellew and their children were Nancy, Arminta, Talton (Tay), Henry, Hugh, and Ellen. Nancy married William Henry Riffe, and Arminta married Orville D. (Bud) Riffe (see Riffe family); Talton (Tay) married Lucy Willis; Hugh never married. He was a teacher in various colleges both in the North and the South. and was known as Professor Hugh Curry. He died at the age of ninety-seven at the home of a grandniece, Hazel Hill, in Ashland. His sister, Ellen, married (1) Hickman Floyd, and (2) Mr. Day.

Robert Curry, the fourth son, married Mary Miles and went west, some of his family living in Arizona and some in other western states.

DAMRON

Solomon King Damron (1826) brought his family from Pike County, Kentucky, to Greenup County in April, 1871. He bought the John L. Mackoy farm at Siloam and there three generations of the Damron family have lived. Mr. Damron was a good farmer and the family was a prominent one in the Siloam neighborhood for many years.

Mr. Damron married Martha Ann Layne (1833) in Pike County in 1851. The children of this family were Mary, Belle, Annie, James, Joseph Randolph, Robert O., and Richard (Dick). Mary married William L. Davidson of St. Paul, Minnesota, in 1877; Belle married C. J. Henderson of Gallipolis, Ohio, in 1879. He was a river man and was killed in a steamboat explosion. Annie married Caleb Dusenbury of Huntington, West Virginia, in 1892, and they had two children, Burmah and Martha; James was a merchant in Catlettsburg, where he married (1) Emma Clinefelter in 1881, (2) Edith Beltlin of Cincinnati; Joseph Randolph married Lucy Davis Biggs, daughter of William and Rebecca King Biggs of Mt. Zion, and they made their home in Huntington, West Virginia; Richard (Dick) married Neola Peters of Montgomery, West Virginia, where they live.

Robert O. (1866) married Mollie Gordon (1871-1939) of Tygart in 1892. He remained on his father's farm and, after the death of his father, he took complete charge of the farm. His children were Paul, Kate, Lucy, William, Harry, and Raymond, all of whom grew up at Siloam. Paul never married and lives in Portsmouth; Kate married Howard B. Campbell of Sommersville,

West Virginia, and their children are Joan Damron, Mary Elizabeth, and James; Lucy married William Caldwell and lives near Waverly, Ohio, and their children are Robert, Mrs. June Anderson of Columbus, William, and Raymond; Dr. William Damron, a dentist in North Manchester, Indiana, married Florence Nagel of Sciotoville, Ohio, and they have three children, Rebecca, James Robert, and Mary Nagel; Raymond married Bonnie Deavers of Birmingham, Alabama, lives in Miami, Florida, and their children are Donald and Linda; Harry is married and lives in Webster Springs, West Virginia.

Burmah Dusenbury married Dolories ——— of Atlanta, Georgia, and their daughter, Jean, is the wife of a doctor in Nashville, Tennessee. Martha Dusenbury married Ben Lubin of Huntington, where they make their home.

DAVENPORT

Elijah P. Davenport came to Greenup County from Amelia County, Virginia, in the late 1860's. He was a widower with two sons, Thomas and Leslie. He taught school at Mt. Zion for some time and married Martha, daughter of John Fuqua, and granddaughter of Moses, Jr., and Cynthia Collins Fuqua.

Mr. and Mrs. Davenport were the parents of Alvin Terry, Anthony Preston (Tone), Eva, Gertrude, Dora, Elijah (Tide), Lennis, and Belle. Terry married Nancy Boynton of Haverhill, Ohio. She also was a descendant of Moses Fuqua, Jr. Their son, Boynton Davenport, is a dentist in Portsmouth. Anthony Preston married Lola Tooley of Mt. Zion and they have two children, Mildred and Anthony, Jr. They live in Scioto County and Mr. Davenport was an employee of the Norfolk and Western Railroad before his death. In 1892 Eva was so badly burned while lighting the lamps for evening service at Mt. Zion Church that she died; Gertrude married Orville Smith of Scioto County; Dora married Frederick Rigrish of Lower Tygart Valley; Elijah (Tide) married Jennie Schultz of Lucasville, Ohio, and they had a son, Charles. Elijah was killed in a motorcycle accident near Portsmouth, where they lived. Mrs. Davenport lives in Lucasville. Lennis and Belle both died in young girlhood.

The two sons of Elijah P. Davenport by his first marriage lived in Virginia. Leslie was a doctor and Thomas a lawyer.

The Davenport family lived at Mt. Zion for many years. Mr. Davenport died in 1894.

DAVIDSON

Jeremiah Davidson was the son of John and Margaret Armstrong Davidson, who came down the Ohio River on a flatboat from Redstone, Pennsylvania, to Burlington, Ohio, in 1801. When a young man, Jeremiah came to Greenup County to practice law, and was very active in the early events of the county.

He married Ann Eliza Corum and their children were Theodore, Charles, Henry, Annie, and Edward. Henry Davidson married (1) Nancy Deering of Hopewell and they had a son, William. He married (2) Frances Ware, the daughter of Asbury and Sarah Fuqua Ware, and their son was Samuel. The daughter, Annie, was a teacher for many years in the Greenup County schools, and in Illinois, where she married Dr. Littlejohn. They made their home in Oconee, Illinois. Edward never married and died at Greenup.

The eldest son of the Davidson family, Theodore, decided in 1861 to study medicine. Dr. Samuel Ellis offered him the use of his medical library, office, and advice, all free of charge. He spent three years studying here, and in 1864 he matriculated at the Cincinnati College of Medicine and Surgery. When he returned to Greenup he thought that Liberty was a good place to open an office, but had no means of transportation. A good friend came to his aid again when Judge John Seaton gave him the use of one of his saddle horses free of charge, and he began his practice at Liberty. After a few years he moved to Quincy in Lewis County, and later located permanently in Portsmouth, Ohio. Here he was city physician in 1877 and also physician to the Board of Health. While filling this office his watchfulness prevented an epidemic of small-pox in Portsmouth while it was raging in other cities. He served as president of the Hempstead Memorial Academy of Medicine and held the position of president of the United States Examining Board of Surgeons.

Dr. Davidson married Anna Eliza, daughter of Asbury and Sarah Fuqua Ware of Mt. Zion. She was the sister of the wife of his brother, Henry Davidson. They were the parents of seven children: Samuel Ellis, William H., Carrie Eunice, Reed Miller, Asbury Ware, Theodore Frelinghusen, and Herbert. William Henry conducted the Davidson Business College in Ironton, Ohio, for many years. Reed Miller Davidson was a newspaper man in Ashland until, in 1919, he went to Egypt, Palestine, and

Albania to do Red Cross work. Later he had charge of the Near East Relief in Cairo, Egypt, until 1940, when his health failed and he returned to the United States and died soon afterwards.

DAVIS

Captain George W. Davis came from the Big Sandy Valley in early 1900 to take charge of the ferry that operated between Fullerton and East Portsmouth. George Winn, the owner of the ferry, "B. F. Bennett," had died. Captain Davis married (1) Josephine Hager of Johnson County, Kentucky, and she died leaving one son, John. He married (2) Virginia Porter, and their children were Glenn, Robert, George, Ernest, and Harry. As his third wife, he married Kate, daughter of Captain Jack McAllister of Springville.

Captain John Davis was married and had a family of five children when they came from South Point, Ohio, to live at Fullerton. The children were Hager, who married Kate, daughter of George D. and Emma Bennett Winn; Hazel, who married James Hannah; Olive, who married Robert Brown, a grandson of Captain Samuel Brown of the Springville Ferry; Doris, who married Robert, son of Taylor and Margaret Rucker Johnson of Mt. Zion; and Paul, who lives at home.

Glenn, the second son of Captain George W. Davis, married Laura Pugh. He was killed at Coney Island by a drunken man. Ernest married (1) Ruth Bennett, and (2) Helen Boggs of Greenup. He was accidentally shot while hunting in Lewis County in 1948.

George Naylor Davis

In the Brick Union Church yard at Gray's Branch is a stone erected to the memory of George Naylor Davis, a soldier in the War of 1812. He was in the regiment of Colonel Isaac Shelby, under the command of General William Henry Harrison at the Battle of the Thames.

George Naylor Davis, born in 1781 in Cecil County, Maryland, was the son of Nicholas and Rebecca Ward Davis. He married Harriet Bragg in 1805 in Lewis County, Kentucky, and they came to live in Greenup County. Harriet Bragg was the daughter of Thomas and Lucy Blakemore Bragg, who had come from Virginia to Lewis County. Her father was a captain in the Virginia Regiment of Colonel Christopher Greenup in the Revolutionary War.

Among the eleven children of George Naylor and Harriet Bragg Davis were Lucy Blakemore, who married William Biggs, Sr., and Eliza Boone, who married Dr. Alfred DeBard. They were the parents of Dr. Alfred DeBard, Jr., of Greenup (see his sketch under DeBard family).

George Naylor Davis was active in the early affairs of the county, being a justice of the court for many years, and sheriff in 1840-1841, with his son, James Ward Davis, as his deputy. He died in 1847.

Prominent in early public affairs of Greenup County were the brothers of Rebecca Ward Davis, mother of George Naylor Davis. James Ward was deputy sheriff in 1810-1811; Thomas Ward, in 1812-1813; and William Ward, in 1819-1822. James Ward was high sheriff in 1825-1826-1827.

DeBARD

Two brothers named DeBard came from France and settled at or near Jamestown, Virginia, about 1750 or 1760. One of the brothers had two sons, Ephraim and Jesse, and both of these served in the Revolutionary War. They were in the Battle of Brandywine.

Ephraim DeBard married Mary Blackwell Lawrence of Virginia in 1799 and came to Clark County, Kentucky. They had ten children, one of whom, James, born in 1800, married Eliza Lewis Davis in 1829 and lived in Carter County, Kentucky. One of their seven children, Alfred Davis DeBard, was born in Carter County in 1833, and became a doctor as his father was. He studied his profession in Louisville and began his practice in Ashland, Kentucky. He came from there to Greenup in 1857 to attend the patients of Dr. Alfred Spalding, who had suffered a broken leg. Dr. DeBard remained as a partner of Dr. Spalding. He met Miss Helen Augusta Seaton and they were married in 1859. He established a practice for himself, lived, and had his office on upper Front Street.

Dr. DeBard was a physical examiner of draftees during the Civil War and also of applicants for pensions after the war. He bought in Cincinnati, and brought to Greenup County, the first forceps used for extracting teeth. These forceps are the prized heirlooms of a granddaughter in Tennessee. He operated a drug store in Greenup for several years.

Dr. Alfred and Helen Seaton DeBard were charter members of the Presbyterian Church, organized in Greenup in 1859. He was an active member of the Masonic Lodge of Greenup and a Knight Templar of the Maysville Commandery. He retired late in life but continued living in Greenup until his death in 1912.

The children of the DeBard family were Alfred, Mary, Helen, Carrie Belle, Harriet Davis, Margaret, and Eunice. Alfred went to Kansas when a young man, married there, and had seven children. Later in life he went to California, where he died in 1943. Mary married Thomas Naylor Biggs, Jr. (see Thomas Naylor Biggs family). Helen married (1) Scott Clifton of Greenup, (2) James Burns of Ashland, and they were the parents of three children. Harriet Davis, a nurse in the Ancon Hospital during World War I, is now retired and lives in New York. Margaret married Samuel Wurts Peters of Greenup and moved to Knoxville, Tennessee, where Mr. Peters died and where Margaret still lives. A daughter, Margaret Peters, married Wayne Womack of Greenup and they live in Louisville, Kentucky. Eunice married William Butler Taylor of Greenup (see Taylor family). Carrie Belle died when a child.

DEERING

Richard Deering was one of the first furnace men to come to Greenup County. He bought a farm west of Hopewell in the vicinity of what was Pactolus near the little Sandy River, and engaged in salt boiling. He was above the average of his day for enterprise and investigation and was something of a mechanic. He noticed iron ore in his fields and on the hillsides and thought he might do some smelting, as in his old home in Pennsylvania.

In 1815 he constructed a crude cupola and charged it with a small quantity of iron stone. The result proved so satisfactory that he engaged four or five moulders to run his iron into hollow ware. The success of this crude attempt induced him in 1818 to form a partnership with David and John Trimble for the erection of Argillite Furnace, the first iron plant to be established in Greenup County. It was located six miles southwest of Greenupsburg, on the left bank of the Little Sandy River. In 1824 Richard Deering built a forge at Hopewell and converted it into a furnace in 1832.

Richard Deering's children were John, William, and Martha. John married Sally Rains in 1822; William married Nancy

Hannah in 1827; and Martha married Elisha Mayhew in 1827. William's children may have been Nancy, who married Henry Davidson of Greenup; Mary, who married William Warnock; and Martha, who married Jacob Everman of Hopewell. Members of the early Deering family are buried in the Oldtown Churchyard.

John Deering, a brother of Richard, made the blast cylinder and the water wheel of the Argillite Furnace. He seems to have moved to Lawrence County, Ohio, and lived at Hecla Furnace, where he and his wife, Ruhamah Davis Deering, are buried. A small village near Hecla is still known as Deering, named for this family. They intermarried with the Gholson family in Lawrence County and Mrs. Doris Deering Gholson Rapalee of Portsmouth, Ohio, is a descendant of the John Deering family.

It has always been said by the folks of the Hopewell section of Greenup County that William Deering invented a mowing machine and brought it down to Argillite, about six miles away. It has been told also that the Deerings wrote to some Chicago relatives asking them to come to look at the machine, and they did so. This was in 1832-34. The machine proved too heavy for use, but about the same time, in Illinois, near Chicago, a mowing machine was invented by a William Deering, who may have been a relative of the local Deering family. The people of Greenup County like to think the mowing machine idea was born here.

DORAN

Nicholas Doran was born in Pennsylvania in 1842. His parents were James and Mary Dotson Doran. He came to Greenup County in 1871. He married Helen Moore Wills of Coal Branch in 1877. They were the parents of Lindsay, Minnie, Orin Gould, Agnes, James, Olive E., and Edith. Lindsay died in infancy; Minnie married J. E. Fisher of Ashland; Orin Gould married Estella Richards of Short Branch; Agnes married Vernon Callihan of Greenup; James married Susan Terrill; Olive E. married C. S. Bennett of Dayton, Ohio; and Edith married Philip J. Leslie of Greenup.

Orin Gould and Estella Richards Doran were the parents of Weldon C., Richard N., Orin Gould, Jr., and Helen. Weldon married Beulah Goode; Richard N. married Louise McKee; Orin Gould, Jr., married Mary Elizabeth Byrnes; and Helen married Mark Roberts. They live in Philadelphia, Pennsylvania.

Children of Vernon and Agnes Doran Callihan are Dorothy McCubbin and Betty Bertram. Philip J. and Edith Doran Leslie are the parents of James Robert and Mary Alice.

DOWDY

John Henry Dowdy, born in Gallia County, Ohio, was the son of Wyatt and Martha Dowdy, who came to Kentucky in 1879. He married Nancy Jane Smith in Lawrence County and came to Greenup County in the early 1890's. He first settled on Tygart Creek, then moved to Fullerton, where he was employed at the Taylor Brick Yard. Later he was employed by the Norfolk and Western Railroad Yards, and while working there he was injured so seriously that he was retired.

Mr. and Mrs. Dowdy were the parents of eleven children, nine of whom are living. Among these are Carroll, a teacher in the county for several years and now a resident of Cincinnati, Ohio, and Fred, who taught school in Greenup County and then entered the ministry. He now lives in Pine Gap, Arkansas. Other children of the family are Mrs. Sophia Callahan, William Dowdy, Mrs. Annie Smith, Mrs. Hazel Stewart, and Ellis Dowdy, all of Fullerton; Mrs. Marie Tomlin of Niles, Ohio; and Mrs. Mildred Scott of Portsmouth. Mr. Dowdy had one hundred and eleven grandchildren and great-grandchildren.

DOWNS

John Downs was probably the first person of the name to settle in Greenup County. He married Lucy Virgin, daughter of Jeremiah and Lucy Dickinson Virgin, in Cincinnati. The marriage license was issued in 1800 by General St. Clair, who was governor of the Northwest Territory at that time. John and Lucy Virgin Downs came to Oldtown about 1807 and lived there until her death in 1847. They were the parents of Emzy, Sarah, Jeremiah, and Nellie.

Emzy Downs married Emanuel Osenton of Oldtown (see Osenton family). She is buried in the cemetery at the Oldtown Methodist Church beside her mother, Lucy Virgin Downs, and a marker has been erected at both graves. The inscription on Lucy Virgin Downs's marker states she was born in 1769 and died in 1847, the first white child born of American parents west of the Allegheny Mountains.

Henry Downs came from central Kentucky to Oldtown and married Polly Ann Lyons. Their children were David and Henry. David married Louise, daughter of Henry and Adelaide Stark, of Oldtown, and they were the parents of Bertis, of West Virginia, and Addie, a well-known teacher in the Greenup County schools for many years. She has now retired.

The other son, Henry Downs, married Nancy Kouns Gibbs, a widow with two children, Emma and Sallie. Emma married Scott Warnock (see Warnock family), and Sallie married Elexius Riffe (see Riffe family). They were the parents of Julia Scott, Amanda, Blanche, and William.

Other members of the Downs family listed in Greenup County Court Records were Thomas G. Downs, who married Matilda Davis in 1826, and James Downs, who married Polly Ann Virgin in 1844.

DUPUY

The following information comes from the book, *The Huguenot, Bartholomew Dupuy and His Descendants*, by the Rev. B. N. Dupuy (Presbyterian). A copy of this book was loaned to the authors by a descendant of Bartholomew Dupuy, Paul Hicks Dupuy, of Portsmouth. Also Mrs. Inez Mosely Dupuy of Lynn gave interesting material on the Dupuy family.

Bartholomew Dupuy was born in 1652 in the province of Languedoc, France. He enlisted in the army when he was eighteen and was a soldier for fourteen years. He was a lieutenant in the king's household (Louis XIV). In 1684 he retired from the army, bought a chateau and vineyard in Velours, and married Countess Susanna Lavillon.

Persecution of the Huguenots broke out afresh, and as Bartholomew Dupuy was yet in the king's favor, he was given a chance to abjure Protestantism. He and his wife refused to become Catholics, but the king gave him a paper granting him protection until December, 1685. He began carrying out his plans to leave France by selling his property. Dressing himself as one of the king's guardsmen and his wife as a page, and carrying the paper signed by the king, after eighteen days they reached the frontier and escaped into Germany.

Bartholomew and Susanna lived fourteen years in Germany and in 1699 went to England. King William offered free passage to America to the Huguenots, and four shiploads came to Virginia.

Bartholomew and his family came on the fourth ship. It is probable that their four children were born during the first fifteen years after the escape from France. These were Peter, John James, Martha, and Philippa.

Other French families who came to Virginia at this time (1700) were the Chastains, Levilains, Lefevres and Gueriants. They were settled at Manikin (or Monacan) Town, in King William Parish, near Richmond on the James River. Each of the two hundred families was given one hundred and thirty-three acres of land. Bartholomew died in Manikin Town in 1743.

Peter, the eldest son of Bartholomew and Susanna Lavillon Dupuy, married Judith Lefevre in 1722. John James married Susan Levilain; Martha married ――― Chastain, and Philippa married John Levilain in 1730.

(In *Woodsons and Their Connections*, as well as in Harper's *Colonial Men and Times*, and other genealogical records there are many variations of the name Le Villian.)

The Dupuys of Greenup County are descended from Bartholomew's eldest son Peter, who married Judith Lefevre. The fourth son of Peter and Judith Lefevre Dupuy was named Peter. He married Elizabeth Malone and their eldest son was named William. He served as captain in the Revolutionary War, moved from Pittsylvania County, Virginia, to land known as "The French Grant," near Wheelersburg, Ohio, and from there to Springville (South Portsmouth), Kentucky, where he died. His first wife was Elizabeth Fuqua and his second, Peggy Littlejohn.

The Greenup Dupuys are descended from William and Elizabeth Fuqua Dupuy. Their eldest son, Moses Fuqua Dupuy, was born in 1799 and died in 1889. In 1818, he married Phebe Stephenson. Albert Gallatin, the fourth son of Moses and Phebe Stephenson Dupuy, was born in 1829. In 1862 he married Ann B. Lee. They had six children, Agnes Mary, Samuel Edward, Rosswell, William, Ernest Richard and Bessie.

Agnes Mary Dupuy married William J. Stevens of Titusville, Pennsylvania, where they lived. Samuel Edward married Anna Belle Athey and moved to Colorado. Rosswell married Virginia B. Hardman and lived on Tygart. He was killed in 1945, when a car struck him near his home. His wife died of heart failure a week later. William married Gertrude Humphreys. She died in 1946, and he is living in California. Ernest Richard married Beulah Jayne, and Bessie is deceased.

Of the descendants of William Fuqua Dupuy, the best known to residents of the county were the Rosswell Dupuy family. The children of this family were Raymond, who went to Texas; Essie Marie (deceased); Clifford Hardman, who married Sally Roberts; Virgil (deceased); Rosamund, who married Niles Greenslate and resides at Russell; Kenneth (deceased); Mary Agnes, who married William Miller; and Mildred, who married Herman Webb.

Ernest Dupuy, the fifth son, and Beulah Jayne Dupuy live on Tygart. Their children are William Jayne, who married Josephine Jeffers; Ernestine, who married V. B. Howland; Richard, who married Mary Inez Moseley; and Robert, who married Mondalia Boggs. All of this family, except William Jayne, who resides in Ohio, live on the Dupuy home lands.

Jesse, the fifth son of Peter and Elizabeth Malone, married Ann Stewart and settled on Tygart Creek. They were members of the Christian Church at Siloam and are buried in the churchyard there. A son, John M., married Ann Blair. Children of the family were Louisa, who married George Reeg and had a son, Arthur; Wesley, who married Mary Conroy and had a daughter, Henrietta, a teacher in the Portsmouth High School. Another son was Thomas J., who married Sarah Hicks. Their son, Paul Hicks Dupuy, married Dorothy Wright. They are the parents of Paul H., Jr., Mary Martha, James W., and Richard E. These descendants of Bartholomew Dupuy live in Portsmouth, Ohio.

ELAM

The Elam family came from Scott County, Virginia, to Boyd County, Kentucky. In Boyd County, a son, Harve, married Chrisanne Davis of Carter County, and during the Civil War moved to Hunnewell in Greenup County, where he acquired a great deal of land. Two children of the family were Cora and James Harve. Cora married Dr. Jay Carter and they lived in Greenup several years, where Dr. Carter practiced his profession. They had no children but reared an adopted daughter, Irene, wife of Forrest McKee of Ashland. James Harve Elam married Helen, daughter of Albert and Mollie Winters McCoy of Greenup. They are the parents of James Harve, Jr., and Davis, and live in East Greenup. Mr. Elam has been sheriff of the county and master commissioner.

FANNIN

The Fannin family emigrated from Virginia to Lawrence County, Kentucky. Isaac Newton Fannin was a circuit rider of the Big Sandy Valley. He married (1) a Miss Chaffin, and (2) Mary Stuart, of the "Jeb" Stuart family. Their son, Isaac Newton Fannin, Jr., came to Greenup County in 1890 as a student minister of the West Virginia Conference, and from 1890 to 1893 he served the Mt. Zion Circuit, which included the new church of Bethlehem near Rocky. His father, Isaac Newton Fannin, Sr., came to Greenup County during those years to administer the rites of baptism to converts. After being ordained, the Rev. Fannin married Flora Leese of West Virginia.

James Alfred Fannin, another son of Isaac Newton Fannin, Sr., of Lawrence County, came to Greenup County in the late 1890's. He married Laura Ellen Elkins of Lawrence County and lived on Tygart Creek. They were the parents of Flora Ensor of Tygart; Beulah, wife of Robert Lawson (see John Lawson family); Olive, wife of Andrew King (see Maurice Biggs family); Minnie Virgin of Oldtown; and Clyde of the U. S. Army.

Probably the first of the Fannin name in Greenup County was John D. Fannin, who came from Lawrence County in the 1880's. He was the son of Lewis and Elizabeth Riffe Fannin and married Elizabeth Lakin in Lawrence County. They settled on a farm at Beechy on Tygart Creek in Greenup County. Later they moved to Plum Fork, then to the Globe on Tygart, and later to a farm near Limeville. The children of this family were Emery (deceased), Mrs. Ida Fout of Portsmouth, Clem of Baltimore, Maryland, and Ella of Portsmouth, who married Herchel McClave (see McClave family).

William Jefferson Fannin (Bud), a relative of John D. Fannin, married Mary Queen of Lawrence County, and moved to Greenup County. He lived on the farm at Beechy, where John D. Fannin had lived. They were the parents of four sons: Garrett, Fred, D. R., and Beckham. Garrett married Reba Blankenship and lived at the Beechy farm; Fred married Hyla Roberson and lives at the mouth of Tygart near Fullerton; D. R. married Nellie Foster.

FISHER

Jacob Fisher, the first of the family that came to Greenup County, was born in 1802 in Pennsylvania. He came to Amanda

Furnace, in the eastern part of the county, with fifty cents, and went to work for the company cutting wood for charcoal. By his thrift and energy he had become the owner of seven farms at the time of his death. He was married twice, his first wife being Miss Sutton. They were the parents of George, Joseph, Maria, Haney, Addie Thompson, and Eliza who never married. There were no children by the second marriage.

George Fisher married Elizabeth Lambert of Lawrence County, Ohio, and their children were Jacob, Joseph, and James. Jacob married Amanda Bartley McCormick and they were the parents of three sons: Joseph, James, and Jacob. Joseph married Mary Mourier; James married Evelyn Ramey; and Jacob married Shirley Steele.

Jacob, son of George and Elizabeth Lambert Fisher, was prominent in all public affairs of the county. He was sheriff from 1930 to 1934 and was elected judge in 1938. The family have been residents of Russell for many years.

Other members of the Fisher family were Lucy, wife of Judge Lewis Edmonson Nicholls of Wurtland; Annie, who married John Paull Jones, manager of Amanda Furnace; Matilda, who never married; and Della, who married (1) Samuel G. Nicholls and (2) Alfred May.

FOSTER

John B. Foster was born in Pennsylvania and came to Scioto County, Ohio, where he married Catherine Culp in 1807. By a former marriage, he had a daughter, Jane, who married Truman Greenfield Waring in 1834 (see Waring family). John B. and Catherine Culp Foster settled on a farm in Tygart Valley. They were the parents of three sons, Isaac, Cornelius, and Lafayette.

Isaac went to Missouri and Cornelius also spent some years in the West. Later he was an itinerant Methodist preacher. He died unmarried and is buried in Mt. Zion Cemetery. Lafayette married Sarah, daughter of Franklin and Sarah Cannon Booton, and they were the parents of Minnie, wife of William Glover (see Glover family); Arthur of Portsmouth; Dora, wife of George Laidley of Scioto County; Kathryn, wife of Karl B. King (see King family); Lewis, and Oscar of Kansas.

George and Dora Foster Laidley are the parents of Edna, Winifred, and Oscar.

FRYE

Adam Frye and his wife came from Augusta, Kentucky, to Greenup in the late 1870's. Mr. Frye was a tinner and had his shop on Main Street for many years. Their children were Charles and Nellie. Charles, a telegraph operator for the Chesapeake and Ohio Railroad, married Minnie Kilgore of East Greenup, and they moved to Covington, Kentucky; Nellie married Roy Mitchell.

Mr. Frye married, as his second wife, Mollie Raike of Riverton, who had been a teacher in the rural and Greenup City graded schools. Their daughter, Kate, married Drexel Dunn of Wurtland.

FULLERTON

James and Hannah Smith Fullerton came from Virginia and located at Jackson, Ohio. They had two sons, Harvey and Harrison, who came to Greenup County. They settled in the western end of the county and the village of Fullerton was named for them.

Harvey Fullerton married, at Jackson, Mary Tyrrell Peatling, who was born in London, England, and had come with her aunt to Brighton, Pennsylvania. There she married Mr. Edward Peatling and they came to Jackson, Ohio, where they were living when he was killed in the Civil War, leaving her with three sons. After her marriage to Harvey Fullerton they bought a farm at Brown Cave near Schultz Creek in Greenup County. Late in life they moved to the village of Fullerton.

The three Peatling sons were John, William, and George Lincoln. John married Amanda Hunt, daughter of Simpson and Ann Bradshaw Hunt, and they went to Abilene, Kansas, where he still lives; William married Pet Dortch, daughter of William Dortch, and went to Oklahoma; George Lincoln went to Missouri and married there.

The children of Harvey and Mary Peatling Fullerton were Frankie, Lyde, James, Mary A., Carrie, Elmer E. (Dock), and Lillian M. Frankie married James Braden of Tygart Valley and they went to live in Florida; Lyde married Dennis (Denny) Warnock of Greenup and she still resides there; James married Myrtle Rogers of Sciotoville, Ohio, and they moved to Kansas; Mary A. lives in Fullerton in the old home; Carrie married Edward Moore of Tygart Valley; Lillian married Forest King of King's Addition (see King family); and Elmer E. (Dock), a prominent attorney in Greenup, married Pansy, daughter of William J. Rardin, and their son, Dr. Hobart Rardin Fullerton, lives in Cincinnati, Ohio.

Harrison Fullerton married Mary Jane Cadot, daughter of Lemuel and Catherine Baccus Cadot, a French family, in Scioto County, Ohio. Harrison Fullerton's house was situated on the river bank in the village of Fullerton. They were the parents of Jura, who married Louella Bryson, daughter of Lucy and David A. Bryson; and Nancy, who married Henry Holly. Jura and Louella Bryson Fullerton had a son, Jura Cadot Fullerton, whose daughter, Ellenora Houser, lives in Troy, Ohio.

FUQUA

Captain Moses Fuqua, born 1738, son of William Fuqua of Lunenburg County, Virginia, was a descendant of the French Huguenot, Guilliame Fouquet of Henrico County, Virginia. He served in the Revolutionary War. In 1759 he married Judith, daughter of Obadiah and Constance Watkins Woodson. She was a descendant of Dr. John Woodson, who came with Governor Dinwiddie to Jamestown, Virginia, in 1619.

The records of Greenup County show that some time between 1797 and 1800 Captain Fuqua bought a tract of land of more than thirteen hundred acres along the Ohio River between Mt. Zion and Tygart Creek, brought his large family and many slaves from Campbell County, Virginia, and settled there. Judith Woodson Fuqua never came to Kentucky, as she died before they left Virginia. Moses Fuqua died about 1814. His will dated 1808, with a codicil dated 1811, is recorded in Greenup County Court Records.

The children of this family were Obadiah (1760), Sally (1762), William (1764), Nancy (1766), Samuel (1769), David (1771), Lavinia (1775), Elizabeth (1776), Moses, Jr., (1778), and Mary (Polly) (1780). Not all of these came to Kentucky. Obadiah married Mary Morton, daughter of Captain John Morton of Prince Edward County, Virginia, in 1785, and settled on the Kanawha River in Virginia; Sally married Benjamin Cook of Franklin County, Virginia, and while they never came to Kentucky, their daughter, Nancy, came as the wife of Thomas B. King (see King family).

William Fuqua married Sarah Morton in 1789 and their children were William, Jr., who married in 1823 Lydia, daughter of Thomas T. G. Waring, and went to Missouri; Martha M. (1798), who was married to Samuel Wilson Gammon in 1818 by Thomas B. King (see Gammon family); Mary M. (1802), who married Rival D. Jones of Tygart Valley in 1821; and Richard (1804), who married Mary Hollyday Waring in 1831.

Nancy Fuqua married Josiah Morton in 1790 (see Morton family); Samuel married Polly Armistead in Charlotte County, Virginia, in 1797, and probably remained in Virginia; Lavinia married John Mackoy in Campbell County, Virginia, in 1795 (see Mackoy family); Elizabeth married William Dupuy in Campbell County, Virginia, (see Dupuy family); Moses, Jr., married Cynthia Ann, daughter of John and Elizabeth Collins, who had come from Virginia to Alexandria, Ohio (Portsmouth); Mary (Polly) married Jeremiah Ward in 1803.

Moses Fuqua, Jr., was a large land owner and prominent in the early affairs of the county, serving as sheriff in 1813. He served in the War of 1812 (see 1812 soldiers). His home was near Mt. Zion and his son, John Fuqua, lived in the homestead in later years; also Taylor and Catherine Thomson King lived there for some time. She was the granddaughter of Moses Fuqua, Jr., her parents being Anthony and Mary Fuqua Thomson. This house burned in 1900 while occupied by Nathaniel T. and Lulu Morton King. Moses Fuqua, Jr., died in 1834 and is buried, with several other members of his family, on land which was a part of his farm.

In his will, Moses Fuqua, Jr., left his farm to his son, John, with the condition "that he help his mother, Cynthia Collins Fuqua, raise the young daughters, Catherine, Martha, Cynthia Jane, Marie, and Louise." John Mackoy and Benjamin S. Rankins were executors of the will, with Thomas B. King, Karnes Laughlin, and John Brown as witnesses.

The daughters of Moses Fuqua, Jr., were noted for their beauty both in Greenup County and across the river in Portsmouth. Mary married Anthony Thomson (see Thomson family); Sarah married Asbury Ware (see Ware family); Catherine married Anderson Thomson (see Thomson family); Martha married Stephen Smith; Cynthia Jane married James Morton (see Morton family); Lavinia married Benjamin Rankins; Louise married Julius B. Higley; John Fuqua married Lydia Stephenson in 1813, and their daughter, Martha, married Elijah P. Davenport (see Davenport family).

The following marriage licenses are found in the clerk's office at Greenup:

Elizabeth Fuqua and John Stewart, December 21, 1831.

Nancy Fuqua and Reuben Chapman, July 28, 1809.

Polly Fuqua and Beaver Kimber Barton, July 19, 1813.

GAMMON

Much of the following material was obtained from the Rev. William Jefferson Gammon of Montreat, North Carolina, formerly a resident of Missouri.

The name Gammon is of English origin. Samuel Wilson Gammon, born in Virginia in 1792, was the son of Richard Dozier and Mary Wilson Gammon, who came to Greenup County about 1800. Mary was the daughter of Samuel Wilson of Berkeley County, Virginia, and Richard Dozier is said to have come from Norfolk County, Virginia, where, in 1685, John Gammon had received a grant of land from the English King.

On coming to Greenup County the family bought a large tract of land on Tygart Creek which extended along Schultz Creek for a long distance. The children of Richard Dozier and Mary Wilson Gammon were Samuel Wilson (1792), William (1794), John S. (1797), Joshua Smith (1799), Martha (1801), Josiah (1803), and Robert (1806). In 1818 Samuel Wilson married Martha Morton, daughter of William and Sallie Morton Fuqua; William never married; John S. married (1) Hannah Berry, (2) Mrs. Mary King, and Martha Ann, daughter by the first marriage, married Clay Morton (see Morton family); Joshua Smith married Harriet Stewart in 1839; Josiah married Clarinda Stewart in 1835; Robert married Lucinda Anderson in 1831. Both Josiah and Robert went to Lee County, Iowa. Later Josiah went to Clark County, Missouri.

Samuel Wilson Gammon, the eldest son, served in the War of 1812 (see Soldiers of 1812). His children were Richard Dozier (1819-1839); William (1820), who went to Missouri; John W. (1823); Sarah (1825); Mary (1826), who never married; Martha (1828); Lovina (1836); and Samuel Wilson (1839). John W. married Elizabeth Warner and they were the parents of James William (Billy) and Mary Hannah. James William (Billy) married

Hattie Belle, daughter of George Wilson and Alethia Tanner Gammon, and their children were Helen, Orin, Clarence, and Margaret; Mary Hannah married John Metz Lawson (see Lawson family). Sarah Gammon married John Taylor Lawson (see Lawson family); Martha Gammon married Captain William S. Smith, known as "Bush" Smith, in Carter County, and they went to Jackson County, Missouri; Lovina M. married George W. Warner, brother of Elizabeth Warner, who married John W. Gammon, and they moved to Sumner County, Kansas; Samuel Wilson, the youngest son of Samuel Wilson Gammon, Sr., went to Missouri with his brother, William, married Louise Fleming Worthington, and their son is Rev. William Jefferson Gammon, who married Pauline Christler Hodges.

The children of Joshua Smith, the fourth son of Richard Dozier Gammon, were Mary Frances, first wife of John Lawson Bryson (see Bryson family); George Wilson, who married Alethia, daughter of John P. and Rhoda Van Bibber Tanner; Ann Price, who married George A. Bollenger and moved to Missouri; Joshua Madison, who married Louisa, daughter of Milton and Ruth Lawson Kendall of Scioto County, Ohio; Thomas Jefferson, who went to Missouri; and Harriet (Hattie), the second wife of John Lawson Bryson (see Bryson family).

George Wilson and Alethia Tanner Gammon had a large family of children: Hattie Belle, who married James William (Billy) Gammon; Elettie Helen, who never married and lived all her life in the old home; Lydia Frances, who married Alfred Simpson; Ottis Van, who married Lulu May Lawson; Hester, who married Joseph Lane, son of John Smith of Siloam, and whose son, Hoytt, lives in Portsmouth; Mary Maud, who married Isaac E. Smith; Stella Lois, who married Charles Cox and lives in Portsmouth.

Joshua Madison and Louisa Kendall Gammon bought a farm at Siloam from Mrs. Lavinia Dugan Ware. Here they reared their nine children and spent the rest of their lives. Nellie Ruth married Mode F. Mackoy (see Mackoy family); Milton Smith and Lola May went to Oklahoma and married there; Elbert married Julia Sheward of Sciotoville, Ohio, and they were the parents of Charles Madison, Thomas Milton, Mabel Harriet and Bertha Louise Dadosky, both of Portsmouth; Olive married Charles Aeh of Scioto County, and they had a son, Raymond; George Madison married Rebecca D., daughter of Maurice and Nina Mitchell Biggs of Mt. Zion; Irma Alice married William M. Biggs (see Maurice Biggs family), and their son, William M., Jr., lives in Greenup; two daughters, Clara and Lilly, died in young girlhood.

GAMMON LETTERS

Extracts from letters written by members of the Gammon family to relatives who live in Iowa.

Letter written by Joshua S. Gammon of Greenup County to his brother, Robert, who lives at Franklin Center, Lee County, Iowa.

December 5, 1850.

Dear Brothers and Sisters:

We are all well at present and hope these lines will find you all enjoying the same blessings. Our friends are all well. Martha Gammon is married to William Smith, son of John Smith, and Sarah Gammon is married to Taylor Lawson. Mary and Margaret Brown are married to John and Isaac Shoemaker. When you write give us a history of the friends and country and I will do the same.

JOSHUA S. GAMMON

Letter from Samuel W. Gammon to brothers, Robert and Josiah Gammon, living in Lee County, Iowa. (They had moved to Iowa in 1838.)

June 20, 1841.

Dear Brothers:

I received your letter bearing date of March 23, 1841, on the 14th instant and am thankful to hear you are all well and satisfied with the country. We are all enjoying the same blessings with the exception of our father. He is very feeble and has had one or two very bad attacks since I wrote to Josiah last season. Indeed we did not expect him to live but a short time. He is better at this time.

You speak of money being scarce and hard times. The same disorder rages here. Produce is cheap—corn is worth from twelve and one-half to twenty-five cents per bushel and bacon from three and one-half to four cents per pound. Wheat is fifty cents per bushel. All speak of having a very cold spring. We have had the same here, just planted our corn in April, and there came a cold wet spell. When it cleared off the ground baked so hard that the corn could not get through it. We had to plant over which made us late. Since that time it has been so dry that it looks like we should raise but very little.

You mention of getting a letter from Romulus E. Culver stating that E. Brooks becomes paymaster to you instead of Hardwick. I have seen Brooks and he states he expects to pay balance to you. If you will take leather at a low price it shall be ready by the last of October or sooner, if you will let him know when you will take it.

There has been nothing take place in the neighborhood worth relating since I wrote to Josiah except the death of cousin Robert Brown which took place last winter. He was attacked with a violent cold, it settled on his lungs and took him off in a few days. The people in the county are generally healthy at this time so far as I have been informed and I believe that I have heard from all parts of it.

Our candidates to represent us in the next legislature are amongst us every few days promising what they will do if we will send them to Frankfort. I will name some of them: Jeff Evans, Nehemiah Cravens, R. M. Biggs, Robert Smith, and John T. Woodson, all genuine Whigs. There is no big treasury candidate out yet, but I expect there will be one come out in the heel of the evening.

I have got none of the seed of Mrs. Bryson's big potatoes yet.

No more at present only all friends wish to be remembered to you and family and to Josiah and family and all inquiring friends.

SAMUEL V. GAMMON

N. B. There have been fine showers of rain here since I commenced writing.

GIBBS

Mr. and Mrs. George Gibbs lived at Riverton for many years. They came from Wareham, Massachusetts, at the time the Eastern Kentucky Railroad was built, and he served as civil engineer for the company as long as it required an engineer. He also did surveying out in the country for the farmers.

Mrs. Gibbs's maiden name was Elizabeth Hodge, and she was from Plymouth, Massachusetts. Being a very fine musician, she gave music lessons to some of the young folks of Riverton and Greenup. There were four children in the family, Laura, George, Jr., Bessie, and Charlotte.

When Mr. Gibbs's services were no longer needed with the railroad, the family moved to Cincinnati, Ohio.

GLOVER

John Glover came from London, England, to Maryland and settled near Ellicott's Mills in Frederick County. His children were Joshua, Samuel, and Sarah. Samuel married Elizabeth Barnes of Cecil County, Maryland, and through every generation of the Glover family until the present time there has been a Samuel Glover and an Elizabeth Barnes.

Samuel Glover and family emigrated to Mason County, Kentucky, in 1795 and settled on a farm near Mays Lick. They had thirteen children: John, named for the grandfather, Ezekiel, Elijah, Johnsa, Nathaniel, Joshua, Sarah, Samuel Barnes, Asa, Anna, Margaret, Azel, and Elizabeth Barnes. Twelve of these lived to manhood and womanhood, and most of them to old age. Seven lived and died in Portsmouth, Ohio, or in the vicinity of Portsmouth.

Elijah, the third son of Samuel Glover, the emigrant from Maryland, was born in 1782 and was in his fourteenth year when they came to Kentucky. In 1800 he married Catherine Jones, the daughter of Griffith Jones, who with his family had also come from Maryland and settled on a farm in Mason County about five miles from the Glover farm. After their marriage they came to Ohio and settled at Alexandria, where two of their children, Samuel and John, were born. In 1804 they moved to Portsmouth, where seven more of their children were born: Ezekiel, William, Nathan, Elijah Barnes, Samuel Griffith, Elizabeth Barnes, and Anna Maria. Elijah Glover, Sr., was an important man in the early affairs of Scioto County, and some of his descendants still live there.

Samuel Griffith Glover is important because he is the one who came to Greenup County. He was born in 1813 and after his marriage to Sarah Fuqua of Greenup County, he lived on a farm on Tygart Creek. They were the parents of two sons, Johnsa, born in 1837, and Samuel H., born in 1845. Samuel Griffith Glover, like his father, Elijah, was a quick-tempered man and, in 1846, in an argument with another, he was struck and killed.

Johnsa Glover was known as Dr. Glover, being both a doctor and a Methodist preacher. He married Mrs. Sarah Bancroft Lawrence of Massachusetts, and they had one son, William Madison, who married Minnie Foster, the daughter of Frances Booton and Lafayette Foster of Tygart Creek. They were the parents of two sons, William Raymond of Ohio, and John C. of the U. S. Army.

Samuel H. Glover was born in 1845 and married Maria, the daughter of Richard and Martha Garrett Morton, who lived at the mouth of Tygart Creek. Their children were William M., Virginia, Charles, Ethel, Robert, Samuel, and Olive. Samuel H. Glover was a farmer and a stock dealer living a few miles up Tygart. About 1890 he was gored by a steer and died of blood poisoning. Mrs. Glover continued to live on the farm for some years, but later, she and her daughters went to Sedalia, Missouri, where her son, Charles, was living.

170

William M. married Ella King Walker (see King family); Virginia married (1) Mr. Hovey, (2) William McVey, and lived at Fresno, California; Charles married Anna Craycraft of Missouri; Ethel married William Pollock in Missouri, and now she lives with her daughter, Virginia, the wife of Leon Burkey, at Hallsville, Missouri; Olive married Earl Garvey of Siloam, and she died leaving a daughter, Jean, who married Charles Flaig and lives in Portsmouth; Robert married Marie Bradbury and they had nine children; Samuel married Maude Gooch. He was killed when his team of horses ran away coming down Morton Hill. Three Samuel Glovers, each of a different generation, met tragic deaths.

The children of Robert and Marie Bradbury Glover are Louise, who married Carl Ackley and lives in Portsmouth; Isabel, who married George Nelson and lives in Arlington, Virginia; Jean, who married Jack Holton and lives in Miami, Florida; Eleanor, who married Ralph Lamblin and lives in Miami, Florida; Robert, who lives in Eureka, California; Thelma, who married Lieutenant Robert C. Brown of the U. S. Army; Gayle, who married Jack Setzer and lives in Hickory, North Carolina; Edith, who married Richard Burdette and lives at Waverly, Ohio; and Claude, who lives at home.

GOBLE

Abraham Goble was a resident of Greenup County before 1811. In 1838, when Carter County was separated from Greenup, this family became automatically residents of the new county. Marriage licenses were issued to Sarah Goble and John Hartley in 1811; to Jemima Goble and Amos Kibby; to James Goble and Belle Williams; and to John Goble and Flora Pirrung, all of Greenup County.

GRAY

The Gray family emigrated to Maryland from England at a very early date. Thomas Lloyd Gray was born in Prince George County, Maryland, in 1755. In 1781 he married Mary Bonifant, who was born in the same county April 7, 1764. In 1803 the Gray family moved to Washington County, Pennsylvania, and from there came down the Ohio River on a flatboat to Greenup County about 1808.

Thomas Lloyd Gray had taken the oath of allegiance in Prince Georges County, Maryland, in 1779, and served in the Revolutionary Army from Virginia. For his services he received a two hundred acre land warrant (old Kentucky records and deeds).

The children of the Gray family were John Lloyd, Elizabeth (Betsy), Elias, James, Letitia, Anary, and others. John Lloyd, born in Prince Georges County, Maryland, married Elizabeth Osborn in Greenup County; Elizabeth (1790), also born in Maryland, married Jacob Smith in Washington County, Pennsylvania, and they came to Greenup County with the Gray family, settling on Tygart Creek at Liberty; Elias married Joanna Richards and lived on Tygart Creek; James was the ancestor of the Gray family of Ironton, Ohio.

About 1818 John Lloyd Gray bought a tract of eight thousand acres along the Ohio River and extending far back into the hills, including the present village of Limeville. He had a wood yard at Gray's Landing, from which he supplied the boats with wood for fuel and loaded flatboats with wood for New Orleans.

William Lloyd, a son of John Lloyd and Elizabeth Osborn Gray, was born near Limeville in 1825. He married Caroline Elizabeth Lyons of Oldtown in 1849 and their children were Alice, Mary, Cassandra (Cassie), Lavina, Lucy, Rose, and John. Alice married John Moore and lived in Portsmouth; Mary married James Reynolds of Greenup County; Cassandra married William White and lived in Portsmouth; Lavina, Lucy, and John went with their parents to Idaho; Rose married (1) Lucius Mickle of Gray's Branch, and their son, Everett, lives in Parkersburg, West Virginia; (2) Ernest White, who lived in Portsmouth.

John and Alice Gray Moore were the parents of Olive, wife of Robert G. Harris, who lives in Pasadena, California; Pearl, who lives in the West; Maude, who taught in the Portsmouth schools and is the author of textbooks which were widely used. She, with her two sisters, Myrtle and Garnet Hull, live in Birmingham, Alabama.

Elias and Joanna Richards Gray were the parents of William (1839), who married Hannah Menach and lived on Tygart Creek. Their eight children were Frank Marion (see his sketch following); William Bonifant, who lives in Michigan; Emma, who married William McCormick; Fannie, who married John Morton (see his sketch under Morton family); Ella, who married Dudley

Morton (see Morton family); Arabella (Kitty), who married John Taylor (see Taylor family); Gertrude, who married John Nichols; Elizabeth, who married (1) John Ramey and (2) Mr. Reed, and lives in Michigan; Henry, who lived in Portsmouth; Alice, who married (1) Alfred Adkins and (2) Monroe Stevens.

Elizabeth, daughter of Thomas Lloyd and Mary Bonifant Gray, who married Jacob Smith, lived near Liberty and had a family of two sons and eight daughters. Their daughter, Cynthia, married James Littlejohn, and they were the parents of Smith of Ironton, Mary and Manlius of Wheelersburg. Elizabeth Smith Gray died at the home of a daughter, Mrs. Serot, at Jackson, Ohio, in 1880, at the age of ninety. Jacob Smith was born at Redstone, Pennsylvania, the son of Godfrey Smith, a Revolutionary soldier, who died in Greenup County.

The Littlejohn family of Grayson, Carter County, Kentucky, were descendants of James and Cynthia Gray Littlejohn. The members of the family were John, Julia, and Matilda Littlejohn Dobbins of Maysville, Kentucky.

FRANK MARION GRAY

Frank Marion Gray, son of William and Hannah Menach Gray, was born on Tygart Creek April 11, 1864. He married Nellie, daughter of Henry Clay and Martha Gammon Morton, in 1886, and their children were Kellen, Lena, Wade, and Myrtle. Kellen married Sadie Smith; Lena married Hubert Adams and has two daughters, Geneva, wife of Floyd Timberlake, and Bernice, wife of Delbert Bostick; Wade married Lula Hannah; and Myrtle married Edward Fansler and lived in Scioto County.

Mr. Gray spent most of his life at Fullerton. He served as County Road Commissioner for four years, and had a grocery store in partnership with his brother-in-law, John Morton, for a number of years. Later he opened a store of his own at Happy Corners. He died December 3, 1940, and Mrs. Gray died August 1, 1928.

GREENSLATE

The first of this name in Greenup County was John Greenslate. According to family tradition, he was born in York, England, came to North Carolina, and was a soldier in the Revolutionary War.

Children mentioned as heirs of John Greenslate in court records of 1832 are George, James, John, Silas, Jane, and Cynthia (or Sitha) with her husband, Benjamin Barney (see Barney family).

George Greenslate married Cynthia Ann Jones in 1834 and their children were Wilson and George William. Wilson kept a store at the mouth of Coal Branch and was also one of the operators of the first lime kilns at Limeville. Elizabeth Greenslate Simon of West Portsmouth is the daughter of George William Greenslate.

James, the second son, married Jane Bradshaw. The court records of 1847 mention the heirs of James Greenslate as Jane, his wife, Mary, Jane, Elizabeth, Neomy, Barbary Ann, Calamity, and James, Jr. Elizabeth married Thomas McKee (see McKee family); Barbary Ann married Reuben Craycraft (see Craycraft family).

Descendants of the Greenslates were the family of James Greenslate, Jr., and those of Wilson and Elizabeth Bennett Greenslate, all living on Tygart. The James Greenslate family bought the Dr. Moore farm and made their home there.

Children of James Greenslate were Willie, wife of Robert Warnock; Sallie, wife of Harvey McAllister; Emma, wife of Francis Warnock; Silas, who married Imogene Howland; Charles, who married Miss Bramblett; Belle, wife of Morris Waring, who lives in Norfolk, Virginia; Sam, who married (1) Miss Bennett and (2) Miss Church.

The children of Wilson Greenslate were Walter, who married Lulu, daughter of James Warnock; Thad; Carl, who married Lorena Richards; Laura, wife of Robert Bruce of Lewis County; and Lutie, deceased.

Greenslate marriages other than those mentioned:

Abigail Greenslate and James Osburn, December 25, 1812.

Helen Greenslate and Tom Baggs, July 2, 1836.

Lucinda Greenslate and Benjamin Dunnaway, September 17, 1821.

Martha Greenslate and Asa E. Oliver, July 5, 1826.

Mary Greenslate and James Meek, October 24, 1817.

Silas Greenslate and Elizabeth Jones, September 3, 1835.

Silas Greenslate and Malinda Burton, January 11, 1836.

HAGER

George Hager was born in Hagerstown, Maryland, and married Miranda Hinton of Hinton, West Virginia. From West Virginia the family came to Greenup in the 1850's. Their children were Julia, William, George, James, Alfred and Charles.

Julia married John Hollingsworth of Greenup, and they were the parents of Edward, James, George, and Elizabeth, who married Joseph Scott; her daughter, Lima, is the wife of Taylor King (see King family).

George Hager married Amanda Sanders of Greenup and they went to Huntington, West Virginia.

James Hager was a clerk in Dr. A. G. Sellards' drug store in Greenup in the 1880's. About 1895 he went to Portsmouth as a pharmacist in the drug store of Daniel Spry. Some years later he established his own drug store in Portsmouth. He married Maude Jennings, of Portsmouth, and she has in her home the old-fashioned clock of the early Hager family. Mr. Hager continued in the drug store business until his death in 1943.

Charles Hager was a telegraph operator in the employ of the Eastern Kentucky Railroad at Riverton in the 1880's. He went to Russell as an operator for the Chesapeake and Ohio Railroad. There he married Evelyn Bingham and they were the parents of Claud of Tennessee, James and Charles of Ashland.

HAILEY

John Hailey settled on Lot No. 3 in the French Grant, Scioto County, Ohio, about 1800. He married Rachel Fleshman and their children were Richard, Carter, Lucinda, Andrew, William, and Julia. Carter married Elizabeth Drury of Burlington, Ohio; Lucinda married Mr. Jones, who built a cotton factory and a grist mill on Front Street in Greenupsburg; Andrew went south to the Red River country; and Julia married Anthony Smith and lived at the homestead.

Carter Hailey, a soldier of the War of 1812, and his wife, Elizabeth Drury, probably lived in Greenup County, as their son, Alfred Carter Hailey, was born there in 1834. He served in the Civil War (see Civil War soldiers). In 1856 he married Lavina Friend and they were the parents of William, Mollie, Curtis, Stella, and Andis. Alfred Carter Hailey was a cabinet maker by trade. John Hailey, another son of Carter Hailey, married

Elizabeth Mead of Ohio and came to Greenup County. They settled at Alcorn. The children of this family were Mary Artis, Ardena Gilbert of Cincinnati, Flora Griffith, George of St. Petersburg, Florida, and Julia, who married Leander Patton of Greenup (see Patton family).

In 1844 Lucina Hailey married Allen Baker. (Old marriage license.)

HALBERT

George T. Halbert was a son of Daniel and Rachel Thomas Halbert. He was born and reared in Lewis County. He served in the Mexican War. He studied and practiced law in Lewis County and in the late 1860's came to Greenup, where he practiced his profession for many years. He married Matilda Truitt in Lewis County and they were the parents of Marshall, Roberta, Irene, George, Jr., and Lucy. Mr. Halbert built a fine brick home at the corner of Front and Hickory.

Shortly after moving into the new home Marshall was instantly killed when a gun he was carrying was accidentally discharged. Mrs. Halbert died soon afterward. Mr. Halbert married Jane Pratt of Greenup and in a few years the family removed to their old home at Vanceburg, where Mr. Halbert resumed his law practice.

Roberta married Dr. Albert Erb and they went to Buffalo, New York. Irene married Dr. Lewis Dunn of Paris, Kentucky, and located at New Paris, Ohio, where he was a practicing surgeon for many years. They were the parents of two sons, Marshall and Halbert. The Dunn family moved to Minneapolis, where Dr. Dunn continued to practice his profession until his death. Marshall is a resident of Westport, Connecticut. Halbert is located in Washington, D. C., and is Chief of National Statistics of Health Service.

George, Jr., went to Minneapolis, where he was engaged in the real estate business. He married and died in that city. Lucy went to New York City to study painting during World War I, but became a nurse, returned to Minneapolis, married William Sternke, and died there.

JUDGE WILLIAM C. HALBERT

Isaac and Elizabeth O'Daniel Halbert were of Scotch-Irish descent and came from England to Fairfax, Virginia, before the Revolutionary War. From Fairfax County the family moved to Culpeper County. Isaac served as a private from Culpeper County, in a Virginia regiment. In 1785, the family came overland to Pittsburgh and down the Ohio River to Limestone (Maysville), Kentucky. From Limestone the family went to Boonesborough Station, where they remained three years, then bought a large tract of land in Bourbon County, Kentucky, which was surveyed by Daniel Boone (on file in Land Office at Frankfort).

In 1799, Isaac Halbert bought land in Lewis County, at that time a part of Mason County, and moved to it in 1801, where he built the third house in Lewis County. Several children had been born before the family moved to Lewis County. Six sons served in the War of 1812. Two of these were Daniel and Stephen, the latter serving under Isaac Shelby at the Battle of the Thames.

In 1813, Stephen Halbert married Mary Cottingham and a son, William Cottingham, was born in 1817 in Lewis County. William Cottingham Halbert was sheriff of the county, studied law, was admitted to the bar in 1856, was county attorney, and was elected state senator 1866-1870.

William C. Halbert was born in Lewis County in 1850. He was a son of William Cottingham and Lavinia (Halbert) Halbert. William C. studied law with his father, was admitted to the bar in 1874, was elected county attorney, served two terms in the legislature, and was elected circuit judge in 1912. He served until his death in 1931. Although he was born and reared in Lewis County, because of his long tenure of office as circuit judge, he became well known and highly esteemed by residents of Greenup County and should have a place in its history. He married Frances Bate of Newport, Kentucky, and they were the parents of three sons: Russell, William Carter, Jr., and John, and a daughter, Frances, who is the wife of James D. Atkinson, a prominent attorney of Greenup. They have two children, James D., Jr., and Nancy Halbert.

HAMOR

Abraham Hamor, born in 1814 in Northumberland County, Pennsylvania, worked on the canals, a common means of transportation in those days. He came to Greenup County about 1835 and stayed for a short time before he went West. About twenty years later he returned to the county and bought a farm at

Flat Woods. He worked at the furnaces and was assistant manager of Bellefonte Furnace when John Russell was the manager, later becoming manager himself.

In 1856, at the age of forty-two, he married Julia, the twenty-one-year-old daughter of Henry and Jane Anderson Williams. Their children were Jane, Margaret, Henry, Martha and Mary (twins), Sarah, Elizabeth, and Abraham. Jane married George Robinson and lived in Greenup; Margaret married John Bradbury of Adams County, Ohio; Martha married George Norman and lived in Ironton, where her daughter, Mary Norman Fisher, now lives; Abraham married Rose Collins and lives in Flat Woods. The other children never married and the only surviving daughters, Elizabeth and Mary, live in Ironton.

HANNAH

The Hannah family came from Virginia to Greenup County in the early 1800's. They settled in the bend of Little Sandy, above Hopewell. In 1812 a marriage license was issued to John Hannah and Susan Barklow. In 1826 Alexander Hannah married Lucinda, daughter of John Anglin, who lived in the same section. Other members of this family were George Washington (Wash) and Robert.

Gabriel Hannah was an early settler at Palmyra, on Little Sandy. A daughter, Nancy, married Charles Norris in 1822, and Sallie married William Deering in 1827. The Norrises lived on Little Sandy near Oldtown and the Deerings at Hopewell.

Charles Hannah, of the Alexander Hannah family, moved to Tygart near Bennett's Mill. Two of his sons were James and William. James married Matilda Robinnette and they were the parents of Charles G., Walter, James, Clyde, Lula, Belva, and Carrie. The James Hannah family moved to Fullerton in the 1890's. Charles G. married Sophia Prichard of Greenup and moved to Portsmouth; Walter married Nola Neal of Fullerton; James married Hazel Davis of Fullerton and they have two sons, Byron and Walter of Fullerton; Lula married (1) Wade Gray and (2) Russell Paynter and lives in West Virginia; Belva and Carrie died in young womanhood; Clyde married Agnes Mantle of Portsmouth.

William Hannah remained on Tygart. He married Emma McCallister of the Springville family. Their children were Sherman, James, Charles, Blaine, Gertrude Keene, Etta

Thompson, and Tempa Triplett. Blaine Hannah married Martha Hatfield and their children are Pearl and Les.

Sherman married Anna Seitz of Cincinnati and lived on Tygart for several years. Two of their children, born on Tygart, were Katherine Bailey and Emma Zeek. James married Annie Cross of Springville; Charles married Effie Nichols. They live on Schultz Creek. Their children were Raymond; Taft; Robert; Delbert; Russell; Ernest; Earl, who was killed in an automobile accident; and two daughters, Freda Collins and Gladys Bryson.

Harold Hannah was the son of Sherman Hannah by his first wife.

HARTLEY

The name Hartley is of English origin. Thomas Hartley, the first one known of that name, was born in 1760 in Berkeley County, Virginia. He was a soldier of the Revolutionary War, enlisting in Virginia and serving from the beginning to the close of the war, seven years. He married Elizabeth Williams in Virginia and they moved to Nicholas County, Kentucky, in 1794. In 1806 he was drowned in the Licking River. Mrs. Hartley continued to live in Nicholas County until her death in 1816. The children of this family were John, Mordecai, Mary, Phoebe. and William, born in Berkeley County, Virginia; Margaret, Hannah, Daniel, and James, born in Kentucky.

John Hartley, the eldest son, came to Greenup County and married Sally, daughter of Abraham Goble, in 1811. They were the parents of thirteen children: Mary, Emily, Perry, Abraham Goble, Hannah, Elizabeth, Jennette, John, Jacintha, William S., James D., Green V., and Miles.

Mary Elizabeth (Polly) Hartley, the eldest daughter, married Andrew Jackson Sellards in 1830 (see Sellards family).

Abraham Goble Hartley married (1) Elizabeth Hartley, his cousin, of Nicholas County, Kentucky, and (2) America Wheeler of Argillite. Their children were Charles, who went to Oklahoma, Evelyn, who went to the state of Washington; William, who went to New Mexico; and Lilly, of Gray's Branch.

William S. Hartley was born at Oldtown in 1828. He married Elizabeth Wills and their children were Green, Bennett, Olive Lewis, Sally, and Myrtle Virgin. Green married Irene Curry of Hopewell; Bennett married Agnes Baker of Tygart Valley; Sally married Ernest Lewis.

James D. Hartley, born at Oldtown in 1831, married Mary A., daughter of Thomas and Polly Richards, in 1858. Their children were Amos G., Elva E., James R., Effie A., Lucy L., and Ephraim (called Thomas). Amos G. married Nina Stark of Oldtown and their children were Watt Sellards, Lucy Rae of Buffalo, New York; James, who served in World War I and is located at Fort Leavenworth, Kansas; Horace of Detroit; and Edith, who is a nurse at Cherokee, North Carolina. Elva E. married John W. Kiser and their daughter, Alberta, who married William S. Smith, lives at their home at Gray's Branch, where she has a general store. Effie A. married George W. Ensor of Oldtown and their children were Halstead and Edward of Alabama, George and Emmons of Fullerton, Charles of West Virginia, and Nelle Nippert of Raceland. Lucy L. married Simeon Fitch and their adopted daughter, Mrs. Mabel Patterson, lives in their home at Gray's Branch. James R. married Iowa Ensor and their daughter, Daisy Atkins, lives in Alabama. Ephraim H. (or Thomas) married Effie Webb.

Green V., son of John Hartley, was a soldier of the Civil War and was taken ill in the South. He died at a hospital in New Orleans.

Daniel, son of Thomas and Elizabeth Williams Hartley, was born in 1801 and married Sally Howell in 1826.

Members of the Hartley family have emigrated to Indiana, Illinois, Kansas, Oklahoma, Washington, and other western states.

HEISLER

Edwin Heisler and Rebecca Corum were married in 1846. They lived on the corner of Main and Laurel Streets, the old Corum home, for many years. The children of this family were Martha, Amanda, George, Benjamin, Edward, and Josephine. Martha married Joseph Pugh of Greenup and they moved to Vanceburg, Kentucky.

Mr. Heisler was a furniture dealer and an undertaker of Greenup for many years. The business was located at the corner of Perry and Laurel Streets.

HILL

John Piersall Bartley Hill came to Greenup County when he was twenty-two years old and made his home with the family of Darius B. Reid at Gray's Branch. He was born in Fayette

County, Pennsylvania, in 1807, the son of Joseph and ———
Bartley Hill of Red Stone Fort, Pennsylvania. His wife was
Ruby Seeley, born in 1815 in Washington County, Pennsylvania,
the daughter of Samuel and Lucy Graves Seeley of Whitehall,
Washington County, New York. The Seeley family lived in the
French Grant, Scioto County, Ohio, and it was at their home
the young couple were married in 1835. After living five years
on a farm in Lewis County, near the present site of Quincy, they
moved to Greenup County and bought the Romulus Culver farm
near Gray's Branch. Their family of ten children grew up there.

Mr. Hill was active in the Greenup Union Presbyterian
Church and was one of the ruling elders for many years. Both
he and his wife, some of his children, and grandchildren, are
buried in the cemetery at that church.

The children of this family were John Milton; Amos Seeley;
Electa, the second wife of Smith Herbert; Joseph; James Lawrence
and William Wallace (twins); Samuel Seeley; Ruby, the first
wife of Smith Herbert; Aaron Fuller, who married Susie Herbert;
and Clark Bayless.

John Milton Hill married (1) Harriet Mickle, who died in
1884, leaving a family of seven children. The children were
Florence D., who died in infancy; Mary Louella, wife of Claude
McClave (see McClave family); William Bartley; Flora Belle,
wife of Myrt E. Mackoy (see Mackoy family); Louis Milton,
who married Jennie Jones, daughter of Morton and Dora McNeal
Jones; James Clarence; Bayless; and Ruby Lottie. John Milton
Hill married (2) Ellen Payne in 1889.

Amos Seeley Hill married Sarah Elizabeth Smith in 1864.
She was the daughter of Charles Moorman and Mary Ann
Ratcliff Smith. Their children were Annie L., who married
Lemard Van Bibber (see Van Bibber family); Mary, who married
George Betts of Adams County, Ohio, and had a daughter,
Elizabeth; Louverna Mae, who married (1) John Bennett of
Huntington, West Virginia, and (2) the Rev. Edward T. Waring
(see Waring family); Faris, who died when a young man; Mattie,
who married Josiah Bennett Merrill (see Merrill family).

Ruby, daughter of John P. B. and Ruby Seeley Hill, became
the first wife of Smith Herbert and they had a son, Elmer. After
her death the son was reared by his aunt, Electa Hill, who later
became the second wife of Smith Herbert, and they lived in the
Hill homestead.

The children of John and Louverna Hill Bennett are Lelia Martin, Doris Lester, Selden Hill, Kathleen Gregory, Lillian Smith, Helen Flannerty, and Carrie Sewell. Members of this family have always lived in the South—Georgia, Florida, and Texas.

The children of Louis Milton and Jennie Jones Hill are Florence, Ralph, Earl, Edith Sommers, Ruth, Garnet Mauk, Charles, and Rose Evelyn Jenkins. Louis Hill makes his home at Haverhill, Ohio. Mrs. Hill is deceased.

HITCHCOCK

Caleb Hitchcock came from Connecticut soon after 1800 and settled at the mouth of Munn's Run in Scioto County, Ohio. Here he owned most of the land where New Boston now stands. Jesse Hitchcock may have been the brother of Caleb. Evans' *History of Scioto County* states that Jesse and Caleb Hitchcock were prominent in the organization of Wayne Township in Scioto County. Lydia, daughter of Jesse Hitchcock, married, in 1812, Gabriel Feurt, who was an early settler of Scioto County.

Some members of the Hitchcock family came to Kentucky and settled on Tygart Creek near Mt. Zion. A marriage license was issued in Greenup County on March 7, 1808, to W. Caleb Hitchcock and Susanna Furgus, upon the written permit of the bride's father, Jonathan Furgus. Their son, Smith F., was born in 1809.

Smith F. Hitchcock married Rebecca Stockham in 1833 and they were the parents of John Jefferson (1834), Maria (1836), Hannah (1840), Susanna Lawson (1841), James (1844), Smith, Jr., (1845), Lavinia (1847), Eliza Tooley (1850), Joseph S. and Caleb Bennett, twins (1853).

Caleb Bennett Hitchcock married Louisa, daughter of David Alexander and Lucy Bennett Bryson. Their children were Jura Bryson, Robert Lee, Joseph Gaylord, Corinne Slater, and Elta Gambill.

HOCKADAY

The Hockaday family moved from Virginia to Clark County, Kentucky. Isaac Hockaday and his son, John, came to Greenup County very early, probably about the time of the organization of the county, in 1803. Isaac Hockaday was clerk of the county when the first court of sessions was organized. He may have returned to Clark County, as there is no further record of him in Greenup County. John Hockaday became clerk, with his nephew, Irvine, as his deputy. John and Margaret Donathan Hockaday bought the farm above Greenup from Jesse Boone. Mrs. Juliet Collins has the original deed from Jesse Boone to John Hockaday given in 1807, and another in 1817. Jesse Boone was probably the first settler of the land and it has been in the possession of the Hockaday family ever since that early time. Two homes on this land have been destroyed by fire. John and Margaret Hockaday are buried in the cemetery on the farm.

John Hockaday's son, Edwin, lived on this land and farmed it, and he owned the storehouse located in the rear of the farm on the river. The Eastern Kentucky Railroad at Riverton was on the land belonging to the Hockadays. Edwin Hockaday's children were George, who married Minnie Kouns, daughter of William Smith and Caroline Van Bibber Kouns; James, who married Ann Eliza Biggs, daughter of William and Lucy Davis Biggs; Edwin, who married Rebecca Seaton, daughter of John and Mary E. Rice Seaton; Martha, who married Jefferson McCommas of Virginia; Eugene, who married Frances Lake and lived in Mississippi.

George and Minnie Kouns Hockaday's children were May, who married Morris, son of Adolphus and Henrietta Reid; Carrie, who married Ezekiel Shackelford of Mt. Sterling, Kentucky; Walter, who married Julia Dorsey; Edwin, Jr., who married Mary Anderson; and Juliet, who married William Collins, son of Nathaniel and Lydia Daugherty Collins.

James and Ann Eliza Biggs Hockaday had two children: Irvine, who married Minta Weddington of Pikeville, Kentucky; and Lucy, who married Cyrus Van Bibber, son of Charles and Caroline Van Bibber. They lived in Huntington, West Virginia.

HODGES

Harvey L. Hodges came from Virginia to Greenup County in the early 1860's. In 1864 he married Martha Smith, daughter of Charles Moorman and Mary Ann Ratcliff Smith. The children of this family were Ida, Jessie, and Etta. Mr. Hodges was a plasterer by trade and the family lived at the upper end of Elizabeth Street.

Miss Ida Hodges was a teacher in the Greenup County schools for several years, but her health failed and she died while still a young woman. Jessie married Joseph Praither, son of Thomas Praither, a farmer on Hayport Road near Wheelersburg, Ohio, and they made their home on his father's farm. Their children were Thomas L.; Martha H. of Huntington, West Virginia; Joseph; and Louise, who married Howard Riggs of Wheelersburg. They became residents of Greenup, where he is the mayor. Etta, or Tet, as she was known to her friends, married Edward Salsman, a telegraph operator for the Chesapeake and Ohio Railroad at Greenup, and later they moved to Cincinnati. Tet Hodges gathered news for the Greenup newspaper and was a clever writer, having a natural talent for writing in either a serious or a humorous style. She also wrote poetry.

HOFFMAN

Two brothers, John and Jacob Hoffman, came from Cincinnati to Greenup County about 1870. They first lived at Hunnewell and later came to live at Greenup. John was a butcher by trade and Jacob was a teamster. Both being economical, they accumulated a great deal of property.

John Hoffman married Caroline Eberwine of Indiana and they were the parents of John, George, and Charles. John studied medicine in Cincinnati and married Mary Elizabeth, daughter of Summerfield and Elizabeth Stark Reed. They located in Champaign County, Illinois, where he practiced his profession. Charles also studied medicine, and he located in Danville, Illinois. George is a pharmacist in Champaign. Both Charles and George married in Illinois. Dr. John and Mary Elizabeth Reed Hoffman were the parents of Dr. John Neal Hoffman of Canton, Ohio; Caroline Lynn Grostephan, of Temple City, California; Margaret Grunewald of Pasadena, California; and Elizabeth Stark Carlton of Florida. Mrs. Mary Reed Hoffman makes her home in California.

Jacob Hoffman married Katherine Roth of Cincinnati, and their children were Samuel, who married Sibbie Collins and made his home in Russell; William; Carrie; Lizzie; John, who married Harriet Sweagler; Edward, who married Harriet Duncan of Webbville; and Kate, who married Howard Trent, a Methodist minister. Children of Edward and Harriet Duncan Hoffman of Greenup are Virginia Taylor, Lewis, Jack, and Harriet McCoy.

HOLBROOK

John Holbrook, the first of the name known to have settled in Kentucky, came from North Carolina to Owen County, and from there to Greenup County about 1840. He married Betsy

Guilkey and they lived on a farm on upper Tygart Creek. Their children were Colby; Edward, who married Sallie Ann Battman; Grace, who married Charles Stewart and lived at Kehoe; Nancy, who married Charles Worthington and lived at Liberty; Manlius, who married Miss Alexander; and Mary Ann (Molly), who married James Franklin Taylor (see Taylor family).

Colby Holbrook married Mary Jane Huffman and they made their home on Tygart Creek. Their children were Nancy, Belle, David, John, Olive, Maude, Virgil, Lula, Charles, and Hetty.

Nancy married Henry Clay Thomas and their children were Virgie, Essie, and Bruce. The two last named are deceased. Miss Virgie Thomas lives in Portsmouth, and is retired. Belle married William Traylor and their children were Essie Tingler, Ollie Deisel, Wayne, Virgil, Cecil, Jonie Johnson and John (twins), Agnes Heather, and Othis. David married Alma Warnock and they had a son, Robert. John married (1) Catherine Warnock, (2) Rose Young. His children were Forest, Margaret Page, Clotine Wells, and Catherine. Olive married Charles Jacobs and they had a son, Colby. Maude married Benjamin F. Bennett and they had a son, Frank. Virgil married Minnie Kotcamp and had two daughters, Nellie Mae Derck and Edna Huffman. Lula married Dr. Matthew Meadows (see Meadows family). Charles married Elizabeth Warnock and had two children, Lloyd and Dana. Hetty married Clarence Carter and had two children, Irene Kase and Clarence, Jr., who has become an internationally known artist. The subject material for several of his famous pictures has been found in Greenup County. Among them are "Winter Hills," "Let Us Give Thanks," and "Jane Reed and Dora Hunt," which are the best known.

HOLLINGSWORTH

The Hollingsworth family came to Greenup County in the 1820's and were established citizens in the eastern section of the county in the 1830's. John Hollingsworth obtained a "Certificate of Slavery" in 1830. He was a justice of the peace in the late 1820's and 1830's, and was a representative to the State Legislature from 1834 to 1835. In 1834 he bought a tract of land from Poage and Company, which lay above the present town of Russell. In 1837 he bought a tract from Charles Buford, part of the original Buford Grant.

In 1837 John Hollingsworth sold land to George Clancy, and Edward Hollingsworth sold land at the Fulton Oil Works to

George Wurts. A farm below the "Works" was sold to James Martin, who had come from Virginia in 1850.

In 1845 Edward Hollingsworth married Elizabeth Ann, daughter of John C. and Elizabeth Smith Kouns. They lived at the Kouns homestead at the head of Elizabeth Street and were the parents of John Hollingsworth, who married Julia, daughter of George and Miranda Hinton Hager, and of Mary, who married William Sands, a brilliant but erratic young lawyer.

John and Julia Hager Hollingsworth were the parents of Edward, George, James, and Elizabeth Scott. William and Mary Hollingsworth Sands were the parents of three daughters, Betty, Madge, and Nell.

Dr. Hollingsworth, of this family, is buried in the William Paull Cemetery on the hill near Riverview, above Russell.

HOOD

(A part of the following sketch was taken from a record made by Anthony G. Clark, in 1847, and the remainder was given by Mrs. Albert Hales of East Fork, August 8, 1948.)

Andrew and Mary Kane Hood came from Virginia and settled in what is now Greenup County. He is said to have been the first man to live within its limits. He had fought in the French and Indian War and drew a pension for his services. He was active in the organization of the county and town and in all its early affairs. It is said that he was one hundred and fifteen years of age when he died. In the Collins Cemetery on East Fork, he lies buried, along with his wife and some of the members of his family. It is said also that Jesse Boone died at the home of Matilda Hood Davison on East Fork, and is buried in the Shuff cemetery nearby.

Andrew and Mary Kane Hood were the parents of fourteen children, one of whom, Andrew, Jr., born in 1810, has been confused with his father, Andrew, in the matter of age. Another child, Maria, married John Collins in 1833, and their child, Helen, married George Kidd in 1870. Inez, the daughter of George and Helen Collins Kidd, married Albert Hales, who was born in Birmingham, England. He was a Christian minister, and after their marriage they went to Liverpool, England, where he served a church on Beaumont Street. Their home was on Upper Parliament Street. When World War I began, Mrs. Hales came to the United States and Mr. Hales continued his work in Liverpool until later. After he came to the United States he went to West Liberty, where he served a church for three years, and then went to Jackson, Kentucky. Mrs. Hales now lives on a small farm on East Fork.

George Kidd was in William H. Sower's company, Regiment of Kentucky Volunteers, for three years and was discharged July 17, 1865.

HORN

The first record of the Horn family in the county is that of the marriage of one Martha Horn, daughter of Frederick Horn, to Thomas Mosely, April 14, 1834.

In 1848 Jonathan Horn (1823-1859) married Eliza Ann Smith (1825-1905), daughter of William Woodson Smith and his wife Polly Ward (see Martin Smith family). The relationship of Jonathan Horn and Frederick Horn is not known. Jonathan Horn lived on a farm near the Bend of Tygart Creek and Mt. Zion. Here three children were born: William, John, and Ada Elizabeth.

In 1873 Ada Elizabeth Horn (1853-1938) married Thomas Lawson (1843-1918), grandson of William Lawson, who owned much of the land on which Portsmouth is located. Thomas Lawson had a store at Middleport, Ohio, where the family lived a number of years. Their four children born there were Earl, Ernest, Marie, and Maude Eliza. Marie died when a child. Later the family moved to Portsmouth, where Mr. and Mrs. Lawson spent the remainder of their lives.

In 1906 Maude Eliza Lawson married Asa B. Dawson in Portsmouth and they made their home in Michigan. Their children are Charles of Jackson, and Betsy, wife of Mark Stevens, of Grosse Pointe Farms, Detroit.

HOWE

James Howe, the son of John and Mary Howe, was born in Montgomery County, Virginia, in 1774. His father was a soldier in the Revolutionary War, and James, when a boy, carried dispatches for the army. Later he was a major in the War of 1812 at the Battle of New Orleans. (see James Gilruth letters).

James Howe married Martha Hood, a sister of Andrew Hood, an early pioneer of Greenup County. They lived above Greenupsburg on Town Branch, near the Hood family, and later moved to Oldtown, where they built a brick house, said to be the first brick house in the county. Their home was known as "Willow

Grove" and was later owned by the Dr. Carnahan family. James Howe donated the ground for the log church which stood at Oldtown for many years. The present Methodist church is located on this site. James Howe died in 1845 and is probably buried in the Oldtown churchyard.

The children of the Howe family were Elizabeth Ann (Betsy), John, George, Mary J., Matilda, Rebecca, Adelaide, Martha Ann, and James Andrew. Betsy married Daniel Clifton (see Clifton family); John married Sarah Dickerson; George married Sarah Fannin; Mary J. married John Montgomery; Matilda married William Hood; Rebecca married James William Warnock, (see Warnock family); Adelaide married Henry Stark (see Stark family); Martha Ann married William Hunt; and James Andrew married a widow, Malvina Cameron Craycraft.

The children of James Andrew and Malvina Craycraft Howe were Lucina, Anna, Alexander, Walker, Simon, and Dolly. Dolly, who is a great granddaughter of the Revolutionary soldier, James Howe, married Albert Ratcliff and lives on Tygart Creek (see Ratcliff family).

HOWLAND

Charles Howland came to Greenup County from Virginia and brought many slaves with him. He bought a large tract of land on Brushy Creek of Tygart and, as Kentucky was still a part of Virginia, he had to pay that state for his land. The original Howland house is said to be still standing and is more than one hundred and sixty years old. In 1867 Joseph Akers built a stave mill on the Howland land. Later the Hale family bought some of the original tract, but much of it is still owned by descendants of the Howland family.

Benjamin, a son of Charles Howland, married Priscilla Stevenson in 1821 and they were the parents of George and Ursula. George married Ann Warnock and they were the parents of Clyde, Edward L., Sallie, Ella, Priscilla, Edna, Steve, Gene and Imogene (twins), and Sophia. Of these children, Clyde married Dora Johnson of Carter County and their children are Virginia, Benjamin, and Edith, wife of Clarence Miller. Edward L. married Ida Waring and their children are Louise Veach, Lucy Dunn, Jessie Victor, and Horace. Sallie married James Dupuy. Ella never married and is deceased. Priscilla never married. Edna died as a child. Steve never married. He was county clerk and died in office. Gene married (1) Jennie Waring and their child was

Anna Virginia; (2) Bertha Hardman. Imogene married Silas (Cuddy) Greenslate; and Sophia married Burriss (Bud) Hale.

Clyde and Dora Johnson Howland live in one of the original Howland homes. It had been a two-room log house with a half-story above, and George Howland made it into a modern home by adding two rooms and a sunroom with a porch across the front. The log house was weatherboarded on the outside and nicely finished on the inside. Since it was built on a hillside, there is a basement of several rooms.

Gene Howland also lives on a part of the original land.

Ursula, the daughter of Benjamin and Priscilla Stevenson Howland, married George Roe of Tygart. They moved to Greenup where Mr. Roe practiced law (see Roe family).

HUNT

The Hunt family came from England to Virginia and, about 1817, they came to Kentucky to work at the iron furnaces. Reuben Hunt, the first of the name in Greenup County, was born in Virginia in 1794, and he settled on Schultz Creek, where he died in 1841. His four sons were Carlisle, Simpson, Harrison, and Ambrose.

Carlisle married Miss Warnock of Tygart Valley and they lived on a farm on Tygart Creek near what is now The Globe. Their children were Reuben; Cynthia, wife of Alfred Spalding Timmonds; Sallie Warnock; Allen; Jack; and Patty, wife of Dr. Moore of Ironton, Ohio. Reuben married his cousin, Rebecca, daughter of Simpson Hunt. They were the parents of six sons: William, Wesley, Thomas, Simpson, Carlisle, who married Minnie Moore, and James.

Simpson Hunt married Ann Bradshaw and they were the parents of Thomas O.; Elvira, wife of Pheene Allen; Cinda, wife of John Alley; Emma Dillon; John; Simpson; Milford; Amanda, wife of John Tuke Peatling, who went to Kansas; and Harriet Warnock. Thomas O. married Ezzadora, daughter of George and Sarah Mildred Coleman McClave of Enterprise, and their children were Edward, Abe, Gertrude, wife of John Collins; Lona, wife of Sherman Fillmore; Thaddeus; Birch; Thomas; and Anna, wife of Wesley Monahan. Birch married (1) Millie Rigrish and has a son, Lionel, (2) Mary Collins of Greenup, and they live in New Boston. Edward married Sarah Elizabeth Kelly and lives in Portsmouth.

Harrison Hunt married Sarah Craycraft and their children were Hannah, Sada, Ella, Jennie, Taylor, Scott, George, and William. Hannah married Owen Hockley and has two sons, Jack and Frank; Sada married James Arthur and their sons are John and George; Ella married Ambrose Crump and their children are Frank and Mollie; Jennie married James Smith and their children are Arthur, Hattie, Stanley, McKinley, and Sadie; Taylor married Lou Nippert of Schultz Creek and their children are Theodore of West Virginia, Lena Fannin of Scioto County, Harry, Oscar, Dora, and Sally Nippert; Scott married Buena Major and their children are Walter, Mattie, Clyde, Kate, Clara, and William A.; George married Ann Shoffer and their children are George and Lona; William married Sallie Colter of Lynn and their children are Dr. A. P. and Leslie. Dr. Hunt, a physician and surgeon, practiced for ten years in Fullerton and has practiced in Portsmouth for a number of years. In 1913 he married Bertha Frizzell, principal of the Lewis County, Kentucky, High School. They had two sons, Russell and Raymond, both dying in childhood. Leslie Hunt married Myrtle Tipton of Portsmouth, where they reside. He is a retired patrolman.

Ambrose Hunt, the fourth son of Reuben Hunt, lived on Little Sandy River near Oldtown. He had no children.

IRELAND

William C. Ireland and his wife, Pamela Robb Ireland, came from Lewis County to Greenup in the late 1840's. He was a lawyer, representing the district in the legislature from 1859 to 1863, and was a judge of Greenup County.

The Ireland family lived on the southeast corner of Main and Harrison Streets. Judge Ireland owned what has been known as the Pfaff corner, which belonged to Joseph Pfaff, the tailor, in 1867. Later the Irelands moved to Ashland, where the Judge continued the practice of law.

The children of the Ireland family were Lutie, Sallie, and Samuel. Lutie married John Hampton, a lawyer, who was converted by the evangelist, George O. Barnes, and he became a successful minister of the Methodist Church. (Hampton City, near Catlettsburg, was named for the family of which the Rev. John Hampton was a member.) Sallie Ireland married a Mr. Norton of Ashland. He was a member of the Norton family so actively connected with the iron industry in Ashland. Nothing is known of the son, Samuel Ireland, but he may have gone to Texas.

JACOBS
JACKSON JACOBS

Jackson Jacobs and Jane, daughter of Charles Russell, were married in Greenup County in 1842. They lived on the southeast corner of Main and Washington Streets in a very large frame house, painted tan and brown. This house was razed by James M. Sowards, who built the present house and office on this site. For many years this has been owned and occupied by Dr. Henry Morris and wife.

Mr. and Mrs. Jacobs were the parents of Henry, Martha, John, and Thomas. Martha married James Stark of Oldtown, and the rest of the family went to Texas to live in the early 1880's. James and Martha Jacobs Stark had two children, Henry and Nina. Henry married and lived in Ceredo, West Virginia; Nina married Herbert, son of William W. and Mary Deering Warnock of Greenup and Hopewell, and they went to Ashland to make their home.

WILLIAM JACOBS

William Jacobs settled near Wurtland, where he bought a large farm. The children of the family were John, Harrison, Henry and Fannie Smith. John married Miss Rouse and they were the parents of Mary J. Stewart, Belle Hunt, Charles, Efford, Samuel, James, Aera, Edward, Earl, and Harry.

The children of Harrison Jacobs were Arizona, Tay, Sylvania, and Wilford. The children of Henry Jacobs were Lydia Caldwell, Aaron, Mazie, Enola, William, and Hamilton.

Other members of the Jacobs family were Shelton, Caroline, Fred, and Ella. Shelton married Ann Eliza, daughter of John Nicholls, in 1837 (old marriage records).

JOHNSON

Robert Johnson was born in Patterson Valley, Hampshire County, Virginia, in 1824, the eldest of the twelve children of Joshua and Nancy Sheets Johnson. He came to Greenup County about 1846, and in 1850 he married Sarah Catherine Lawson, born in 1828, the daughter of John and Catherine Taylor Lawson, who lived in the Lawson Settlement near Gray's Branch (see

Lawson family). Their children were William, Nancy Sheets, Clara Virginia, Robert Taylor Lee, and two who died in childhood.

Mr. Johnson began farming on rented land, but in 1858 he bought land of his own and added to this from time to time until he owned one thousand acres between Siloam and Mt. Zion neighborhoods. In 1869 he bought and moved to the home which had been built by his brother-in-law, Hollyday Waring. He called this "Sandy Plains," and here he and Mrs. Johnson spent the remainder of their lives. Mr. Johnson was a citizen noted for his integrity, his fair dealing, and his generosity; he served as a member of the Mt. Zion school board, and as one of the county commissioners in the 1880's.

The eldest son, William, died at the age of twenty-one; Nancy Sheets married Volney Thomson of Springville (see Thomson family); Clara Virginia married John Newton Horr of Portsmouth, where she still resides, and their son, Robert Johnson Horr, a graduate of West Point, now lives in New Jersey; Robert Taylor Lee married (1) Margaret Rucker of Carter County and (2) Orpha Gerding of Fullerton. He lived on his father's land all his life. The two children of the first marriage were May, who married Victor E. Bevens and lives in Pikeville, Kentucky; and Robert Johnson III, who married Doris Davis of Fullerton. Robert III is the only member of the Johnson family who owns and lives on the original land which belonged to Robert Johnson, Sr.

Robert and Catherine Lawson Johnson are buried in the Mt. Zion Cemetery.

JOHNSTON

JOHN JOHNSTON

Among the families who migrated from Ohio to the Siloam neighborhood was that of John Johnston, coming from South Point, Lawrence County, Ohio. Mr. Johnston spent his early life on the Ohio River steamboats in the capacity of clerk and pilot. He turned his attention to farming before leaving Lawrence County, and in the expansive river bottom farms at Siloam he saw fine possibilities of stock raising. In 1872 he purchased the Marsh farm of four hundred and fifty acres and farmed here extensively for twenty years. In 1892 he retired and returned to his native state. He purchased a home at Ironton, Ohio, but a few years later he moved to Wheelersburg, Ohio, where he died in 1898. Mrs. Johnston died there also in 1907. Both are buried in Woodland Cemetery at Ironton, Ohio.

John Johnston was born in Lawrence County, Ohio, in 1821, the son of William and Elizabeth McCoy Johnston. In 1845 he married Caroline C., daughter of John Brisco and Eliza Robinson Ricketts, who had come to Lawrence County from Front Royal, Virginia, in 1830, when Caroline was four years old. Their oldest son, James, married Annie E. Veazey of Lawrence County, and lived on his father's farm until about 1890, when he moved to Ashland, where he went into business with the Poage Brothers. The six children of James Johnston were Anneca, a retired government clerk of Washington, D. C.; Elizabeth, wife of James V. Adams of Lynchburg, Virginia; Anna (deceased), wife of Everett A. Colson, who for five years was Financial Advisor to the Emperor of Ethiopia; Isabelle (deceased), a teacher in the Ironton schools for thirty-five years; Austin Lee, an electrical engineer on the Island of Guam; and Edwin Scott, an internal revenue agent in Milwaukee, Wisconsin. Austin Lee married Irene Lindsay of Cincinnati, and Edwin Scott married Margaret Overman of Waverly, Ohio.

The older daughter of John Johnston was Lydia A., who married Millard Fillmore Drury of Illinois in 1884, and at the present writing she is the only survivor of John Johnston's children. She is in her hundredth year and lives at Diamond, Missouri, with her only child, Mrs. Albert Matthews, and her grandsons, Robert and Dan Matthews.

The younger daughter, Ella Jane, married James Bryson Mackoy (see Mackoy family); the second son, John Brisco Johnston, married Hannah Lawson Mackoy (see his sketch following); Charles Wesley, the youngest son of the family, died at the age of thirty-two and was unmarried.

JOHN BRISCO JOHNSTON

John Brisco Johnston, the second son of John and Caroline Ricketts Johnston, was born near South Point, Lawrence County, Ohio, in 1860. At the age of twelve years he came with his parents to live on the farm at Siloam. He was educated in the public schools and attended college both at Delaware and Lebanon, Ohio. After his marriage, he lived on the Adolphus Reid farm at Gray's Branch until 1892, when his father retired. At this time he moved to Siloam and assumed the management of the home

193

place, later becoming the owner of the larger part of it. Here he farmed and raised stock extensively for eighteen years.

He married Hannah Lawson Mackoy, daughter of Henry Clay and Samantha Timmonds Mackoy of Siloam. She was educated at the Young Ladies' Seminary in Portsmouth and at the Girls School in Vanceburg. Mrs. Johnston died at Siloam October 25, 1907. Mr. Johnston sold his farm in 1910 and engaged in the milling business at Waverly, Ohio, where he died in 1915. Both are buried in Greenlawn Cemetery at Portsmouth, Ohio.

There were eight children in this family, three having died in childhood. Edith M. is a retired teacher of the Portsmouth High School, now living in Portsmouth and Alexandria, Virginia; Edna E. (widow of Conrad M. Strong) lives at "Clarens," her historic estate, near Alexandria, Virginia; Carroll M. is deceased; Vevay Grace is deceased; and Mayme Virginia is Ohio University Supervising Critic in the Athens High School in Athens, Ohio.

JONES

JOHN JONES

The John Jones family lived near Maloneton about 1850. Mr. Jones, who was a farmer, owned a large tract of land on Tygart Creek, and it extended from Culpeper and Enterprise to the Ohio River, near Limeville.

John Jones married Sitha Greenslate Barney (1810-1908), widow of Benjamin Franklin Barney (see Barney family). She lived to be almost one hundred years old and is buried in the Fairview Cemetery. The children of this marriage were William and George Henry Jones.

In 1863 George Henry Jones (1839-1912) married Ann Eliza, daughter of Charles and Elizabeth Glover Christman, who was a teacher at the Globe School. They had five sons: Robert Mason Bierly (deceased), Edward Curtis, Samuel McTracy (deceased), George of Cincinnati, and Charles Teate of Fayetteville, Ohio.

Edward Curtis Jones married Eliza Bates of Boyd County, and lives in Ashland. (Mrs. Jones is now deceased.) Their children were Gerald Thompson Jones and Olive, wife of the attorney, Thomas Burchett, both living in Ashland. Mrs. Burchett is active in various organizations and holds important offices in both the National and State Societies of the Daughters of the American Revolution. Mr. Jones was associated with the old Ashland Coal and Iron Company (later the American Rolling

194

Mill Company), and has recently retired from the presidency of the Home and Savings Building Association after being connected with the company fifty-one years. He is still actively engaged in the real estate business.

The first lime kilns near Limeville were built on the Jones land near the river and were operated by George Henry Jones and his double first cousin, Wilson Greenslate. The Jones family sold their land to George Roe of Greenup County and Landon Stockton of Kenton County, Kentucky, and became residents of Boyd County some years ago.

THOMAS W. JONES

Thomas Wylie Jones (1831) married Letitia, daughter of Hezekiah and Hannah Burton Morton, in 1853. They lived on a farm which was a part of the original Morton Land near Gray's Branch.

Children of this family were Morton H. (1855), Louisiana (1865), Maude Hannah, and Letitia, who died as a small child. Louisiana, or "Miss Loue" as she was better known, was one of the best known teachers of the county for many years. In 1899 she married Allen Baker, and they lived on a farm at St. Paul, in Lewis County, Kentucky. She died there in 1924 and is buried in Brick Union Cemetery.

Morton H. Jones married Dora, daughter of Thomas and Jane Montgomery McNeal, who lived near Rocky. Mr. Jones was a blacksmith and had a shop along the road near his home on land which had been a part of the Morton farm. In later years the family moved to Springville. The children of the family were Jennie Bell, who married Louis Hill (see Hill family); Lewis, who married Ada Burlingame and lives in Covington, Kentucky; May, who married David Thomson; Lola, who married Benjamin Hanners; Kate, who married Charles Craycraft. The last three live at South Portsmouth. Other children, Josie Maude, Frances Cleveland, and Elizabeth, are deceased.

Maude Hannah Jones married Lee Hancock and lived for a time in Birmingham, Alabama.

KELLY

In the late 1870's Joshua Kelly of Ironton, Ohio, bought the Laurel Furnace land from Robert and Thomas Scott and made it into a stock farm. Mrs. Kelly was an invalid and she, with their young daughter, remained in Greenup. After a few years Mrs. Kelly died and Mr. Kelly married Nora Stark of Oldtown. She was a very successful school teacher of Greenup and of southern Kentucky.

Joshua and Nora Stark Kelly were the parents of Sarah Maud Willis of Ashland, Nora Stark Kelly, a teacher of Louisville, and Joshua Kelly, Jr., (deceased). Mrs. Nora Stark Kelly died and Mr. Kelly married, as his third wife, Elizabeth, daughter of William A. and Ann Lyons Womack of Oldtown.

KENDALL

1421-1501	The Kendall line of ancestry begins with John and Margaret Kendall, whose sons were John, Thomas, William, Henry, and George.
1441-1520	Henry and Edith—sons were Francis, Richard, Thomas, John, and William.
1480-1561	Francis and Mary—sons James, Jeremiah, Bartholomew, Edwin, John, and Thomas.
1504-1578	James and Elizabeth Miles—sons William, Samuel, Henry, John, James, and Thomas.
1527-1601	William and Sarah Brayme—sons John, William, Thomas, James, Samuel, and Henry.
1548-1628	John and Mary Miles—sons William, Thomas, Edwin, Henry, Miles, and John.
1575-1655	William and (1) Mary Leigh (Lee), (2) Elizabeth Arlington; sons of Mary Leigh were John, William, and Thomas. A son of Elizabeth Arlington was John (the kinsman).
1599-1688	William Kendall, who made his first trip to Jamestown, Virginia, when he was eighteen years old, married (1) widow Carrington (no issue); (2) Susan Baker, and had two children, Mary, who married Hancock Lee, emigrant, and William. He married (3) widow Matthews and died in 1686, a few weeks before a son was born, and Mrs. Kendall named him William Kendall.

NOTE: This line of ancestry is taken from the *Kendall Book of Ancestry* loaned by Vernon V. Kendall.

The Kendall family can probably trace their ancestry farther back than any other family in this section. Authentic records of the family begin in 1248 in West Moreland County, England. Members of the family came to America and settled in Massachusetts and Virginia. The Kendall family of Greenup County have descended from the Virginia branch through John Kendall (1617-1679), who married Susanna Savage, June 4, 1667, who also lived at Jamestown, coming there at the same time as the

Kendall family, being a kinsman. Members of this branch emigrated to Kentucky during the period from 1760 to 1825.

Captain George Kendall was a member of the first council in Jamestown (1607), he and Captain John Smith working together for the good of the colony. Captain George was killed and was buried with military honors in the Jamestown churchyard, with the Reverend Robert Hunt, the first preacher at Jamestown, in charge.

Thomas, a son of John and Susanna Savage Kendall, married Elizabeth Ann (Mary) Washington in 1692. Their son, William (1695), married Sarah Payne (Mason) in 1716, and a son, William, married Jemima Kirk May 10, 1738. A twin of William (Samuel, 1749-1821) married Mary Smith in 1780. She was born in 1750 and died in 1800.

William Kendall, who was born in 1695, had a son, James, (1719) who married Julia Travis in 1741. Their son, Jesse (1742), married Jane Allen in 1764. They had six sons. A son, Travis, married Nellie Jewell October 9, 1818 (Nelson County, Virginia, record). Allen Kendall's son, James P., married Sarah Humphrey. The. Rev. Allen Kendall was born in 1804 and died in 1873. He married Elizabeth Brown (1809-1890). They moved from Tazewell County, Virginia, to Morgan County, Kentucky, in 1832, and from there to Texas, in 1858. They were the parents of Travis Collard Kendall, who was born in Morgan County in 1840 and was killed in the Civil War in 1864. He married Mary Virginia, daughter of Gabriel and Mary Stark Anglin of Hopewell, Kentucky. They were the parents of Travis Texas Kendall, who was born in 1862 and died in 1928. He married Daisy, daughter of Allen T. and Lucy Osenton Womack of Oldtown. They were the parents of Travis W. (1888), Owen C. (1891), Vernon V. (1896), Lucy, Daisy Irwin, and Allen Wickliffe Kendall.

Travis W. married Dorothy Dempsey and they have two children, Dorothy and Joe. Owen C. married Elizabeth Van Bibber. They have a son, Robert. Vernon V. married Mary Dean Norris. Their children were Lucille and Charles, who was killed at Okinawa in World War II.

NOTE: William Kendall, a merchant of Jamestown, Virginia, made his first trip there when he was eighteen years old. Mary Kendall, born 1760, married William Stark.

KIDWELL

Benjamin Franklin Kidwell was born in 1878, the son of Ezra and Eliza Haines Kidwell. He was educated in Bracken

County, Kentucky, and taught school in that county and in Mason County. Coming to Greenup County, he was principal of the Russell schools, and under his supervision these reached a high standard.

In 1903 he married Louise Courtney and they were the parents of two children. His wife died, and he married Maud B. Mason. They are the parents of five children. After retiring from the Russell Schools he became superintendent of the Catlettsburg schools; but for several years he has been a resident of East Greenup, having retired from school work.

KING

Thomas B. King married Nancy, daughter of Benjamin and Sallie Fuqua Cook of Prince Edward County, Virginia, and came to Greenup County about 1812. In the county clerk's office is a deed dated October 16, 1812, which reads "Benjamin Cook to Thomas B. King and Nancy Cook land beginning at the first large gut above the mouth of Tygart."

The following interesting item is taken from Evans' *History of Scioto County:* "May 21, 1821, a sermon was preached by Dan Young at the home of Thomas B. King, on the death of Benjamin Mead, who died April 19, 1821." Benjamin Mead was the father of Armistead Mead, an early resident of the county.

Thomas B. and Nancy Cook King were the parents of Benjamin F. King and a daughter, who was drowned while escaping from a sinking steamboat on the Ohio River. Benjamin F. King was a lifetime resident of the home farm near the mouth of Tygart Creek. He married Nancy, daughter of John and Lavinia Fuqua Mackoy (see Mackoy family). They were the parents of John T., Benjamin F., Jr., Zachary Taylor, James M., Maria, Nora, and Virginia (Jennie).

John T. King married Lydia, daughter of John and Rhoda Van Bibber Tanner, of Palmyra. He was a farmer and stock dealer, and lived on a part of the King land, where he built a large brick house about 1880. In 1883 and 1884 he was a member of the legislature. The children of this family were Ella, Clyde, Erie, John Van Bibber, Nile, Forest, James Floyd, Paris, and Persia. Ella married (1) William Walker (see Walker family); (2) William M. Glover, and they had a son, Harry, who went to Colorado. Clyde married Sallie Moore of Mt. Zion in 1885 and they lived on the home farm for a time but later moved to Scioto

County. Their children are John T. of Chicago; Edith Moore, wife of Ora R. McClure of Wheelersburg, Ohio; James Albro, deceased; Clyda Newhouse, of Mowyrstown, Ohio; Earl O.; and Marie K. Kok of Baltimore, Maryland.

Erie King married James Hogan of Massachusetts; John Van Bibber married Mary Ellen, daughter of George W. and Lavina M. Glover Warner of Kansas; Nile married Rella Keister of Tygart and they were the parents of two sons, Leslie and Baker; Forest married Lillian, daughter of Harvey and Mary Tyrrell Fullerton, and lives in the homestead built by his father; James Floyd died unmarried; Paris married (1) Lena Hill and had two daughters, Helen and Margaret; (2) Belle Thomas and lives in Portsmouth; Persia died when a small child.

Benjamin F. King, Jr., married Brunette Elliot of Lewis County, and they were the parents of Bruce of Lexington, Kentucky; Nancy, who married Harry Horr of Portsmouth, later moving to California; Benjamin, who married Fannie Gerding of Fullerton and lives in Portsmouth; William and Edward, both of whom went to California; Karl, who married Katherine, daughter of Lafayette and Sarah Booton Foster, moved to Oklahoma, and has two daughters, Brunette and Lelia; Lena Maria, who died unmarried; Mabel, who married Clyde McNeal (see McNeal family).

Zachary Taylor King married Sarah Catherine, daughter of Anthony and Sarah Thomas Thomson, and they were the parents of Nathaniel Thomson and Harry. Nathaniel married Lulu, daughter of Richard and Lavina Reed Morton, and their children were Andrew Wayne, who married Maude Biggs (see Maurice Biggs family); Myrtle Etherly of King's Addition; Taylor of North Carolina; Homer of Cincinnati; Agnes Dorton of Paintsville, Kentucky; Katherine Williams and Gladys Richardson, both of Hillsboro, Ohio; and Freda Dorton of Langley, Kentucky. Harry, the second son, married Bessie Gerding of Fullerton, and they were the parents of Louise Andrews of Cleveland; and Fred, who died when a boy. They make their home in Portsmouth.

James M. King married Octavia Elliott of Lewis County and they lived in the Benjamin King homestead. They had no children but reared a foster daughter, Helen Ferree, who married Carl Morton (see Morton family).

Maria King married John Musser of Portsmouth. Their daughter, Nancy, married John Kinney and they had three sons,

Wesley, Clifford, and Arthur. Wesley lives in Portsmouth, Clifford in Oklahoma, and Arthur is deceased.

Nora King married Thomas Thompson and they lived in Scioto County. Their children were Owen, William, Walter, Paul, Katherine (Kitty), Della, and Lena. Katherine (Kitty) married John Chick of Portsmouth, where she resides. Their children are Marjorie, Helen Miller of Ashland, and Lucile Coombs of Detroit.

Virginia (Jennie), the youngest child of Benjamin F. and Nancy Mackoy King, married Nathaniel Thomson of Springville (see Thomson family).

KINNER

Five Kinner brothers, sons of Lafayette Kinner, came from Lawrence County, Kentucky, to Greenup at different times. Elwood came in 1889, to clerk in the store of B. F. Brown. When Mr. Brown died, Elwood Kinner and Stanley Tibbetts bought the business and later built a store on South Main Street. Stanley Tibbetts died and Fred and John Kinner came to clerk in the store. Later Burgess and Kouns Kinner opened a grocery store on Elizabeth Street.

Elwood Kinner married Fannie, daughter of Matthew and Elizabeth Breedin Warnock, and they were the parents of a son, Matthew Warnock, who married Mabel, daughter of Ward and Gertrude Curry Womack of Oldtown. He was employed as a government inspector, with headquarters at Huntington, West Virginia, and is now deceased.

Fred Kinner married Clara and Kouns married Edith, daughters of Matthew Scott and Emma Gibbs Warnock. Fred and Clara Warnock Kinner were the parents of Maxwell D. of Charleston, West Virginia; John D. of Ashland, Kentucky; Fred, Jr., and Earl W. of West Liberty, Kentucky, where Mrs. Kinner has lived since the death of her husband. Children of Kouns and Edith Warnock Kinner were Jack, who lives in Atlanta, Georgia; Scott, who lives on the Kinner farm in Lawrence County; and Helen, who married J. W. Johnson of Washington, D. C.

Burgess Kinner married Nancy, daughter of Alex and Dove Curry Irwin of Hopewell, Kentucky. Their children are Elizabeth, wife of Russell Davis of Lexington, Kentucky; Irwin, who married Mary Frances Lawson; James A., who married Eunice English; and Paul L., who married Thelma Crum. The sons live in Greenup.

Caroline married Davis Elam of Greenup and lives in Louisville, Kentucky.

John D. Kinner married Lona, daughter of Butler and Lydia Clifton Taylor of Greenup. Their children are Robert, David B., and Elwood, all of Greenup. John D. Kinner is deceased.

KINSLER

Christian Kinsler, a German who kept a small store on Perry Street, lived with his family in a cottage next to the store until 1879. At that time he built the brick house across the street from the grade school and moved into it. The children of the family were Eliza, Sarah, and John.

KOUNS

Jacob Kouns was the first person of the name to settle in Greenup County. He came from Pennsylvania in 1792 and was an important man in the early affairs of the county. The very early court records state that he was one of the three men appointed to let out and superintend the building of a temporary courthouse on the public square, July 7, 1806. One of the earliest marriage recorded in the new county of Greenup was that of Sally Kouns to Jacob Neal, September 16, 1804, on the permit of the bride's father, Jacob Kouns. A son, John C. Kouns, was married in 1818 to Elizabeth Smith, daughter of Martin and Nancy Price Smith.

John C. Kouns built the Kouns House in 1827 and the original part of the building is still used by descendants of the Kouns family. A recent survey of old buildings in Greenup shows that those built by Major John C. Kouns were built so substantially that they are still among the best buildings of the town. The Kouns homestead at the head of Elizabeth Street—later the home of the Hollingsworth and Sands families for many years—now owned by Edward Hoffman, is still one of the handsomest and most substantial residences in the town. Another residence built by John C. Kouns is that of the Owen Kendall family at the corner of Front and Hickory Streets. Archer Womack bought this property from the Kouns family, and members of his family owned it until the past few years, when it was sold to the Kendall family. It is still a most livable house. John C. Kouns gave the land on which the Methodist Episcopal Church was built in

1845, so he probably was interested in the construction of this building.

John C. Kouns was a major in the First Kentucky Regiment in the War of 1812 and was with Andrew Jackson at New Orleans. He served several terms in the state legislature.

The children of John C. and Elizabeth Smith Kouns were Dr. William Smith Kouns, Elizabeth, Sarah A., Nancy, and Maria. Dr. William Smith Kouns married Caroline Van Bibber October 21, 1841, and they lived in Greenup where he was a druggist for many years; Elizabeth married John Hollingsworth (see Hollingsworth family); Sarah A. married Joseph Pollock (see Pollock family); Nancy married John Winn (see Winn family): and Maria married Andrew Biggs (see Biggs family).

The children of Dr. William Smith Kouns were Minnie, Ann, Maria, Elizabeth, and William. Minnie married George Hockaday (see Hockaday family); Maria married Jehu P. Sydenstricker and they moved to Tennessee; Elizabeth married John Ball and they lived in Georgia; and William married Fannie Roberts and kept the Kouns drug store until his death.

KUEHBORTH

Bernard Kuehborth came to Greenup County and bought the timber on the hills near Coal and Smith Branches about 1860, or a few years later. He had saw mills on both of these branches and he brought a number of German families to live there and to work at his mills. Several of the Coal Branch German families were Heineman, Harris, George, and others. Mr. Kuehborth married a lady from Portsmouth, Ohio, and their children were Alice, Albert, and Emma. He built the house, on Main Street in Greenup, which J. W. Kouns (Billy) bought from him and later sold to John T. Womack. A daughter of Mr. Womack, Anna Laura Myers, lives in this house now.

Mrs. Kuehborth died, and Mr. Kuehborth took his children to the King home near Greenup to be cared for. In 1874 he was a member of the town board of Greenup. No one knows what has become of this family, but there are some descendants of the German families which Mr. Kuehborth brought to Coal Branch still living in that vicinity.

LACOCK

Another family, allied to the Pratt and Brooks families, was that of Benjamin Franklin Lacock of Greenup. Mr. Lacock married Sarah, daughter of John and Eliza Bellow Pratt of Liberty. The children of the Lacock family were Frank, Clarence, Ina Jones, James, Daniel, Cassius, and Bird.

Clarence Lacock married Jennie, daughter of James and Parthenia Bryan, and lived in the Bryan homestead. Mr. Lacock was clerk on the steamboat "Fannie Dugan" and later was clerk on the Greenup Wharfboat.

The Lacock family moved to Huntington about 1900.

LAUGHLIN

William and Mary Laughlin were early residents of Spring-ville. Their children were Matthew, William, Alexander, and Robert, who married Judith Fuqua in 1830. The Killen family descended from the Laughlin family. In 1832 William J. Killen, a steamboat captain from New Orleans, married Judith Laughlin, and they were the parents of Virginia K. Redden of Lewis County, Robert, William J., Ida McElheny of Springville, and Lucy Egner of Portsmouth, Ohio. Children of William and Ida Killen McElheny were Baxter, Russell, and Harry. Charles (Cap) Killen married (1) Eva Braden and (2) Gertrude Walker. Children of Harvey and Virginia Killen Redden were Eugene and Bertha. Russell McElheny married Nettie, daughter of David and Nettie Lawson Miller of Springville.

The Laughlin and Killen cemetery is located within the limits of the old Indian Village below Springville. The oldest stone gives the date of birth 1762.

LAWSON

Thomas Lawson was born and reared in England. He married Hannah Farley and came to America, settling at York, Pennsylvania, about 1718.

A son, Thomas, born 1718, was a soldier in the Revolutionary War, serving in the Fourth Pennsylvania Regiment from 1777 to 1779. Sometime before 1780 he bought a tract of land in Hampshire County, Virginia, and sent his sons with his slaves to settle there. Later he moved the family to Virginia. Thomas Lawson, and his wife, Hannah, are buried at Fort Ashby, Virginia.

There were twelve or more children in the Lawson family. Some of these married and remained in Virginia, while six of them came to Greenup County, Kentucky. William (1761), the second son, who disliked the institution of slavery, settled in Scioto County, Ohio. He married Susannah Earson and is the ancestor of the Portsmouth Lawsons.

Of those Lawsons who came to Greenup County, some settled along the Ohio River opposite Munn's Run in Ohio, and the others settled on Tygart Creek. Anna (1769) married Samuel Walker in Kentucky, and their son, James, lived on a farm near Siloam (see his sketch under Walker family); Hannah (1775) married a Mr. McQuillen and had a daughter, Hannah; Margaret (1777) married E. Burton and they were the parents of Joshua, and Hannah, who married Hezekiah Morton (see his sketch under Morton family); Thomas (1779) married Barbara Earson.

James Lawson (1760), eldest son of Thomas Lawson of Virginia, served in the Revolutionary War from Hampshire County, Virginia, and was in the War of 1812 after he came to Kentucky. He married (1) Ruth Wilson, (2) Sophia Johnson, and (3) Phoebe Metz of Adams County, Ohio. He lived on a farm a few miles below Greenup. His will, dated 1841, in Greenup County Court records, mentions the following children: Thomas, William, Charity, Mary (Polly), Nancy, Patience, Iley, John, Lucy, and Jane. Charity married John Bartley; Mary (Polly) married Edward Boyd; Nancy married Elijah Dunn; Patience married William Smith; Iley married Joseph Hill, brother of John P. B. Hill, and she died in California in 1912, being one hundred and five years of age; John married Lucy Palmer; Lucy married Dr. Nathaniel K. Moxley, a well-known physician of Ironton, Ohio; and Jane married Edward Metz.

John Lawson (1781), youngest son of Thomas Lawson, married (1) Susannah Blue in 1800. She was the daughter of Uriah and Susannah Williams Blue of Hampshire County, Virginia. She died in 1806, leaving a daughter, Hannah, who married Moses Mackoy in Greenup County (see Mackoy family). In 1808 John Lawson married (2) Catherine, daughter of John and Elizabeth Foreman Taylor of Hampshire County, Virginia, and soon they moved to Greenup County, Kentucky, where they settled on a farm near the Anvil Rock. Children of the second marriage were Elizabeth Foreman (1809), who married William Bryson (see his sketch under Bryson family); Maryann (1812), who married Romulus Culver, and whose children were John, and Ann Biggs; Rebecca Jane (1815), who married Hollyday Waring (see Waring family); Thomas, who married Ann Tanner; Sarah Catherine (1824), who married Robert Johnson (see his sketch under Johnson family); John Taylor Lawson (1818), who married Sarah Gammon, daughter of Samuel and Martha Morton Fuqua Gammon, and lived on a farm joining the William Biggs farm about three miles below Greenup. Their children were Thomas, who married Nancy Rogers; Martha Elizabeth, who married Dr. Andrew Watson Sellards (see Sellards family); Catherine, who died when a young lady; and John Taylor, Jr. (see his sketch following).

All of these Lawsons lived along the river about six miles below Greenup and within a few miles of each other. There were so many of this family that the section, later known as Brick Union, was called the Lawson Settlement.

John Taylor Lawson, Jr.

John Taylor Lawson, born October 22, 1857, was the son of John Taylor Lawson, Sr., and his wife, Sarah Gammon Lawson. He was born and reared on the Lawson farm near Gray's Branch. He was educated at the Ashland Academy, Ashland, Kentucky. In 1884 he married Ella H., daughter of Thomas Naylor and Ellen Humphreys Biggs, and they lived on the Lawson farm with his mother until 1891, when they moved to Greenup, where Mr. Lawson went into the hardware business on Harrison Street. In 1893 his brother-in-law, William A. Biggs, joined him in this business. Later Mr. Biggs withdrew from the firm and Mr. Lawson moved the store to its present location on Main Street, where his son, Biggs Lawson, continues the business.

John Taylor and Ella Biggs Lawson were the parents of seven children: Katharine, Lucy Margaret, Mary Ellen, William Jacob, James Biggs, Robert Johnson, and Winifred. Katharine married William Bowen Gallaher, Jr., of Waynesboro, Virginia, and they have a son, William Bowen Gallaher III; Lucy Margaret married George Henry Curry, and they have a son, George Henry, Jr., of Greenup; Mary Ellen married Frank Wallace Myers of Greenup, and their children are Wallace, Ellen, Katharine, and Winifred; William Jacob died at the age of twelve years; James Biggs married Irene Pearl Diedrich and their children are Mary Emily, John Taylor, and Lucy; Robert Johnson died at the age of eighteen years; Winifred Paynter married Van Dyke Pollock of Greenup, and both are deceased (see Pollock family).

Ella Biggs Lawson died December 23, 1904. Later Mr. Lawson married, as his second wife, Mary Johnson, daughter ot Colonel John Johnson of Keyser, West Virginia. On September 3, 1929, Mr. Lawson was struck by an automobile in front of his home and instantly killed. He had been a member of the Greenup Union Presbyterian Church since 1872 and was a trustee of the church when it was sold to the Christian Church congregation in 1919.

JOHN LAWSON

John and Hannah Lawson were early settlers in the Bend of Tygart Creek. A son, Thomas, married Susan Hitchcock of Mt. Zion and their children were Martha Tibbs, Rebecca Grose Davis, Smith Hitchcock, Caleb, Robert, William F., and Samuel, who married (1) Ida Sturgill and had one son, Homer; (2) Effie Shiver; (3) Mrs. Ida Fetters. Smith H. lived unmarried at the homestead; Martha Tibbs, Rebecca G. Davis, and Caleb moved to Ohio; William F. married Ella Rye of Danleyton, and they were the parents of Raymond, Robert, and Ray. Raymond married Ada Wilson of Scioto County, Ohio; Robert married Beulah Fannin of Tygart; and Ray died early in life.

Hannah McQuillen Lawson was born in 1800 and lived to be ninety-seven years old.

JACOB LAWSON

Jacob Lawson married Elizabeth, daughter of Joshua and Hannah Van Bibber Rawlings and settled in the Bend of Tygart Creek. The two Lawson families owned nearly all the land in the Bend. Children of this family were Joshua, John M., Charles, George, James, and Addy. Joshua married Mary Thomson of Springville, and their children were Reuben, Nettie and Anna.

John M. married Mary H., daughter of John and Elizabeth Warner Gammon of Tygart, and they lived many years in the old home of Samuel Gammon on Tygart. They were the parents of Elmer, Denver, Etta, Grace, Howard, and Merle. Elmer married Elizabeth, daughter of Charles Smith of Tygart Valley, and lives at Sciotoville; Etta married Charles McNeal (see McNeal family); Grace married William Harper of Siloam and lives in Vanceburg; Howard lives in Wheelersburg; Denver and Merle never married and live in Sciotoville.

Charles, the third son of Jacob Lawson, went to Colorado and married there. James and Addy, the two younger children, never married.

LESLIE

William Robert Leslie came to New York City from Scotland with his brother, John. They became separated there and never saw each other again. William Robert went to Pennsylvania, where he married Elizabeth Buchanan and later moved to Augusta County, Virginia, where four children were born. William Robert Leslie was a soldier in the Revolutionary War. He came to Pike County, Kentucky, with his son, Robert, in 1802, and there he died.

Robert Leslie was born in Augusta County, Virginia, in 1763. He married Elizabeth Compton and they moved to Pike County, Kentucky, in 1802. He died in 1822. Robert and Elizabeth Compton Leslie were the parents of fifteen children, of whom Martin, the youngest son, was born in Pike County in 1807. He married Sarah Auxier Mayo in 1845 and they were the parents of Martin Samuel, born in 1852, and Robert Allen English, born in 1854. Martin S. studied medicine and came to Greenup in 1882 to practice his profession. He married Florence Hunt, of Fayette County, Kentucky, and their children are Ralph, who married Mattie Collins; Samuel, who married Jeannette, daughter of William and Jeannette Reid Cole; Philip, who married Edith Dorn; and Dr. Robert G., who is a practicing dentist in Ashland, Kentucky.

Robert Allen English Leslie was a teacher in the Greenup County schools in the 1870's. He married Mary Frances Womack of Oldtown. They lived most of their married life in the Big Sandy Valley and in Virginia. Their children were June, May, Robert, Guy Womack, and Ruth Cleveland. The last named lives in Washington, D. C. Robert A. E. and Mary Womack Leslie died in Burkesville, Virginia, in 1926 and 1943, respectively, and they are buried in Riverview Cemetery at Greenup.

LITTLE

Captain William Wallace Little

Captain Little became a resident of Greenup County in 1882, when he traded a ferryboat, which he owned, to Captain Sam Brown for a two-hundred-acre farm at Siloam, and became a farmer. He was the first postmaster at Siloam and the post office was named for him. It was known as Little until about 1901, when the name was changed to Siloam.

Born in Lewis County, Kentucky, in 1825, the eldest of thirteen children, William Little came with his parents to live at Manchester, Ohio, when a small boy. His education was meager because he went to work as a cabin boy on the steamboats at an early age. By his energy and force of character he rose to the position of pilot and master and became known as Captain Little. He was the owner of six boats and no less than three of the ferryboats which operated between Portsmouth and Springville. The boats he owned were "The Pike," "Boskirk," "Vida," "Gaylord," "Brilliant," and "Eldorado."

In 1855 he came to live in Portsmouth, where he was prominently identified with civic affairs and the First Presbyterian Church. He operated a coal business along with his steamboats until he moved to his farm.

Captain Little was married to Mary A. J. Timmonds of Adams County, Ohio, in 1854. She died in 1855 and he married, as his second wife, her sister, Harriet Amanda Timmonds. They were the daughters of John Wesley and Mary Woodworth Timmonds and the granddaughters of Richard Woodworth, a Revolutionary soldier. Captain Little had seven children by his second marriage. The eldest, William H., born 1857, married Ida Davis, daughter of Captain Jacob and Rosanna Smith Davis of Sciotoville. He died in 1888 leaving the widow and one daughter Genevieve, who is the wife of Norman Apel of Portsmouth. The only surviving child of Captain Little, Mary J., lived with her parents at Siloam until the death of her father in 1897, after which she and her mother moved to Portsmouth.

LONG

The Long family came to Greenup County from Virginia in the early days. A son, Elisha, married Sarah Jane, daughter of Benjamin and Sitha Greenslate Barney. They made their home on Gray's Branch, where they lived on top of a high hill. This location seemed ideal for growing peaches and Mr. Long was well known for the fine peaches from his orchard.

There were nine children in the family: Elizabeth, Lucinda, Cynthia, John, William, Sarah, Amanda, Elisha, and Ella. Elizabeth married John Reynolds; Lucinda married John Michael; Cynthia married Benjamin Artrip; John never married; Sarah married John Rollins; Amanda married William Earwood; Elisha married Emma Diggins; Ella married Walter Linckous and is now living with her daughter, Mrs. Burke, in Sciotoville; and William married Sarah Eliza, daughter of Reuben and Barbary Ann Greenslate Craycraft. His widow is still a resident of Gray's Branch, making her home with a niece, Mrs. Chinn. She has two sons, William Mason, of Gray's Branch, and Charles Roy, of Washington Court House, Ohio.

The children of William and Amanda Long Earwood are Lou Callihan, Cora McCormick, Ellis, Butler, Clyde, and Zona, who married Harry Chinn and lives at Gray's Branch.

LYONS

Hezekiah Lyons was born October 1, 1776, in Washington County, Pennsylvania. He was the son of Samuel Lyons, whose father was Daniel Lyons, both of whom came to Kentucky in 1776, with the Virgins and other families (Ref. *Collins' History of Kentucky*). Samuel and Daniel Lyons were in the Revolutionary War and were paid off at Fort Pitt, Pennsylvania. Hezekiah Lyons fought in the War of 1812 with Mad Anthony Wayne against Tecumseh at the Battle of Fallen Timber in 1792. He was married to Cassandra Virgin, born in 1783, daughter of Reason Virgin, and they became residents of Greenup.

Among the fourteen children of Hezekiah and Cassandra Virgin Lyons were Reason (Rezin), who was born in 1803 and died in 1842; Greenup, born and died in 1807; Hezekiah, Jr., born in 1811; Mary Susan, born in 1816; Eli; Washington; and Remembrance. Rezin Lyons married Elizabeth Pugh and lived at Oldtown. Hezekiah, Jr., went to Missouri and he has many descendants there. He is buried at Edina, Missouri. Mary Susan married John Lionbarger and they lived in Portsmouth.

The children of Rezin and Elizabeth Pugh Lyons were Caroline, who married William Lloyd Gray (see Gray family); Ann, who married William Archer Womack (see Womack family); Cassandra (Cassie), who married John W. Kouns (see Kouns family); Mary Kerin, who married Samuel Griffith Jones; Carilla and Rezin Virgin, deceased.

McCLAVE

George McClave was born in Dublin, Ireland, probably about 1800. He came first to Baltimore, Maryland, and from there he went to Portsmouth. In 1821 he married Sarah Mildred Coleman in Greenup County. She was descended from the Madison family of Virginia, the same as that of President James Madison. Her parents came from Culpeper County, Virginia, to Greenup County and lived on a farm near the covered bridge over Tygart Creek at Enterprise. After the daughter's marriage the Coleman family returned to Virginia and left the farm and one woman slave to the young couple. The children of this family were William, George Washington, James Madison, Claudius, Roy, Ellen, Alice Nora, and Ezzadora.

William went to Carter County, where he married Sarah Underwood and they had a family of twelve children. George Washington McClave went to visit his brother, William, and there he met and married Jennie Burchett. They lived at Gray's Branch on a farm. Their children are Cora, wife of Ewell Strother in Portsmouth; Mayme (deceased), wife of Jack Hartberger of Roanoke, Virginia; Gladys of Huntington, West Virginia; Susie, wife of Frank Deterla, who lives in Portsmouth; Ellen, wife of Walter Berges of Stamford, Connecticut; Leroy, who married Bess Reinohl and lives in Sciotoville; James Lemuel, who married Mae Sparks and lives in Portsmouth.

James Madison McClave married (1) Sarah Burns, daughter of Denny and Sarah Burns of Rocky, and their son, Herchel, married Ella Fannin; (2) Julia Byrne and they had a daughter, Bernice. The family lived in Russell after Mr. McClave's second marriage. Herchel and Ella Fannin McClave had three children: Irene (deceased), Irma, and James. Herchel is deceased and Mrs. McClave lives in Portsmouth.

Claudius McClave married Louella Hill, eldest daughter of Milton and Harriet Mickle Hill of Gray's Branch, and their children are Ethel Belle (deceased), Sarah Mildred, Clotine (see Pollock family), Ruby May (see Warnock family), Hattie Hill, Alice, and Arthur Bayless. Sarah Mildred married John Covert and lives at Fullerton; Hattie married Clark Sandy and lives at Gray's Branch; Alice married W. K. Rea and lives in Scioto County; Arthur Bayless married Golda Adkins and lives at Covington, Kentucky.

Roy, the youngest son of George and Sarah Coleman McClave, died when a child. Ellen, the youngest daughter, was a teacher in the county. She married Samuel McChesney and they lived at Mt. Joy, Ohio. Alice McClave married Riley Hall and they lived on a farm at Gray's Branch. Their children were John;

210

Louella, wife of Edward Lamblin of Siloam; Ida, wife of Mr. Alexander, who went to California; and Luther, who married Mary Middaugh and lives at Wheelersburg. Ezzadora McClave was the first wife of Thomas O. Hunt (see Hunt family).

George McClave, known as "Squire," was a carpenter and made some of the first washboards used in the county. He is buried in the Fairview Cemetery and Mrs. McClave is buried in the Brick Union Cemetery.

McCONNELL

John M. McConnell was born in 1791 in western Pennsylvania and was of Scotch-Irish descent. He was apprenticed to a tailor, and when his term of service was over at the age of twenty-one, he received a horse, a suit of clothes, and a sum of money from his employer. In 1813 he rode the horse to Portsmouth, Ohio, crossed the Ohio River, and came to Greenupsburg. He taught school, studied law, and practiced in Greenup County. In 1819 he married Lucy Ward Lewis, widow of Charles N. Lewis, who had come from Albemarle County, Virginia.

Mr. McConnell bought a tract of land four miles above Greenup and laid off four acres for his house and grounds. From the roadway to the house he planted an avenue of trees which were ruthlessly destroyed by a later owner. He also built a law office near the house, which was used in later years as a private school.

Mr. McConnell was a successful lawyer and was state senator from 1826 to 1830. In 1834, not long after he had finished his beautiful home, he died at the age of forty-three. He left his widow, a son, Charles, and several daughters. Charles was a lawyer and a judge of northeastern Kentucky. John McConnell had taken a young man named James M. Rice into his family to study law. He became a prominent lawyer, and when he married he named his oldest son John McConnell Rice. Years later, in the 1880's, the names McConnell and Rice were united when Ida, daughter of the Hon. John Rice, and the granddaughter of James M. Rice, became the wife of James H. McConnell, son of Charles L. McConnell, and grandson of John M. McConnell.

The McConnell farm became the property of George Wurts and later of James Davis Biggs. It is now the property of the Harris family of Wurtland, and both house and law office are still in good condition (see picture).

McKEE

John and Elizabeth Reed McKee came from Tober Moor, in Londonderry County, Ireland, to Canada, in 1840. The McKees were of Scotch-Irish descent. From Canada they came to Pittsburgh, where Mr. McKee was a merchant. Losing their property by fire, the family came to Greenup County and settled on Smith Branch when their son, Thomas, was seventeen years old. He married Elizabeth Greenslate in 1855. One daughter, Mary, had married John Crosset in Pennsylvania. Esther, another daughter, married Manasseh Galligher.

Thomas and Elizabeth Greenslate McKee lived on Tygart Creek until 1874, when they moved to Riverton. They were the parents of William, Miller, Mary, David, Edward, Annie, and Nettie. William was born in 1858 and began working for the Eastern Kentucky Railroad in 1875 in several capacities. He became conductor in 1883, which position he retained until 1898, when he was made chief clerk and auditor. He continued with the Eastern Kentucky Railroad until it was abandoned in 1928. William McKee married Mary Ellen Webb of Webbville, Kentucky, and they were the parents of Russell, Forest, Louise Dorn, Loraine, Loretta Widly, and Elizabeth Parkhill, the last two mentioned living in the state of Washington.

Miller McKee made his home in Huntington, West Virginia; David lived in Missouri; and Edward lived in Colorado; Nettie married a Mr. Hensley of West Virginia.

McMULLAN

James McMullan, born in 1793 in Dover, Delaware, married in 1815 Tryphena Smith, born in 1795. Their children were Susan Marie, James Smith, Francis, Tryphena, John, and David Smith.

James McMullan inherited slaves, but he was opposed to buying and selling them. His convictions were so strong that when he had a debt which the price of one slave would have paid, he sold his plantation instead of a slave to pay it. He then freed all his slaves and was left, as he thought, a poor man. With his family, he joined a covered wagon train which was leaving for western Pennsylvania. They remained near Pittsburgh for a few years and came to Greenup County about 1844.

The family brought with them letters of transfer from the Presbyterian Church of Kittanning, Pennsylvania, while the

212

daughter, Susan Marie, who had married Jesse D. Wilson in Pennsylvania in 1840, brought her letter of transfer from the First Presbyterian Church in Allegheny, Pennsylvania. They presented these letters to the Greenup Union Presbyterian Church at Gray's Branch in March of 1844. (Ref. Greenup Union Church Record, p. 8).

James Smith McMullan married Susan Mears in 1846 and lived on the corner of Washington and Perry Streets in Greenup. Their children were Tryphena Smith, Susan Mears, James (Bud) (1850), Isaac, Belle, Sadie, William (Billy), David, and Henry. James (Bud) married Anna, daughter of Adolphus L. and Henrietta Powell Reid of Gray's Branch. She died soon after her marriage and is buried in the Greenup Union Cemetery. Sadie married James Tate, a Presbyterian minister. Billy was drowned at Riverton while swimming in the Ohio River. The McMullan family moved to Cleveland, Ohio.

Tryphena, daughter of James and Tryphena Smith McMullan, married William Hard, of Haverhill, Ohio, in 1845. They had two children, Mary Cook Hard, who married Henry Bertrand Boynton of Haverhill, and a son, Charles Ellsworth Hard. The family moved to Portsmouth, where Charles E. Hard became prominent as a lawyer, postmaster, and editor of the *Portsmouth Blade;* also he was active in both state and national politics, at one time being secretary to Warren G. Harding, while he was President of the United States.

John McMullan, another son of James and Tryphena Smith McMullan, married Ann Thomas and their children were James (1847) and John G. (1849). There may have been other children.

McMULLEN

William Henry McMullen was born in Staunton, Virginia, in 1860. He was a son of Henry and Frances Taylor McMullen. His father was a soldier in the Confederate Army and was killed before the birth of his son, who, from the age of three, was reared by his grandparents, David and Sarah Taylor.

When he was nineteen years old he came to Springville, Greenup County, and married Anna Eliza Zuhars. They made their home there and five children were born, two dying when young. The others were Luella Barton of Beattyville, William J. of Portsmouth, and Sydney of South Shore.

William J. married Maude McWilliams of Portsmouth and they are the parents of a son, William. Sydney married Nelle May of South Portsmouth, and they are the parents of Sydney Annelle. Luella Barton never married and is a well-known resident of Beattyville (see Zuhars family).

McNEAL

Thomas McNeal came from Pennsylvania to Greenup County before the Civil War. He married Jane Montgomery and they lived on a farm near Rocky, which land had been a part of that originally owned by the Gray family. Here they reared their children: Josephine, Dora, Mary, John, Joseph, and William.

Josephine married David Brant of Lucasville, Ohio, and their only child, Elizabeth, married Mode F. Mackoy (see Mackoy family); Dora married Morton Jones (see Jones family); Mary married Andrew Simmons and they went to Kansas to live; Joseph married Louella Dortch of Tygart and they went to Abilene, Kansas, where their three children still live; William, the youngest son, married (1) Anna Weaver and they had two sons, Thomas and Ellis; (2) Mrs. Ella Walker Weaver.

John McNeal, one of the older sons, married Mary, daughter of Denny and Sarah Jane Burns of Gray's Branch, and they lived on a farm near Rocky. Their children were Clyde, Charles, Mace, Flora, Edith, and Grace. Clyde married Mabel, daughter of Benjamin King of Mt. Zion, and they went to Oklahoma; Charles married Etta, daughter of John and Mary H. Gammon Lawson of Mt. Zion; Edith married Dee Garvey of Siloam and they have two daughters, Katherine and Wilma. All of the children of John and Mary Burns McNeal are deceased except Mrs. Garvey. She resides in Portsmouth since Mr. Garvey's death.

Thomas and Jane Montgomery McNeal are both buried in the Siloam Cemetery. The inscriptions on their stones read:

Thomas McNeal, born June 18, 1820, died August 14, 1899.

Elizabeth Jane McNeal, born February 1, 1827, died January 27, 1896.

MACKOY

The Mackoy family came from Scotland to Virginia about 1700. They settled in King William County and later went to Campbell County. In 1800 two brothers came to Kentucky. James, a miller, settled near Dover in Mason County, where he had a grist mill, and John, a farmer, settled on a farm ten miles below Greenupsburg on the Ohio River, where he resided until his death in 1843. He owned a number of slaves and more than nine hundred acres of land, which he divided among his ten children, and his descendants owned part of that land for more than one hundred and twenty-five years. He was one of the founders of the Siloam Church and the ground on which the church and cemetery are located was a part of his farm. Five generations of the Mackoy family are buried in that cemetery.

John Mackoy (1772) married in 1795 Lavinia Fuqua (1775), daughter of Captain Moses and Judith Woodson Fuqua, of Campbell County, Virginia. The children of this family were Judith, James, Moses Fuqua, John, Sarah, Obadiah Fuqua, Martha, Nancy, Thomas, and Lavinia. Judith (1815) married Nathaniel Morton; James married Judith Morton; Moses Fuqua (see his sketch following); John located in Covington, Kentucky, in 1829, where he married Elizabeth Hardia and where his son, William Hardia, and his grandson, Harry Brent Mackoy, have been prominent attorneys; Sarah married General Basil Waring (see Waring family); Obadiah Fuqua was married three times (see his sketch following); Martha married the Rev. Nehemiah Cravens and is buried in Mt. Zion Cemetery; Nancy married Benjamin King (see King family); Thomas never married; Lavinia married James Savage in 1838 (see Savage family).

OBADIAH FUQUA MACKOY

Obadiah Fuqua Mackoy owned several farms in the vicinity of Siloam and was active in the affairs of the county. Late in life he sold the last of his farms to Josiah Merrill and moved to Jackson County, Missouri.

Obadiah F. Mackoy married (1) Judith Knight of Mason County, Kentucky, (2) Malvina Waring Powell, daughter of Clement O. Waring, and (3) Cassandra Chinn King, widow of Thomas B. King, in 1841. The children of the first marriage were two daughters. Mary, who married Thomas Watkins of Portsmouth in 1850, had a daughter, Judith Elizabeth, wife of Mathias Wall. The second daughter, Judith, married (1) Alfred Chinn of Greenup County and they went to Missouri. After he was killed in the Civil War, she returned with her three children to her father's home near Siloam. Later she went to Illinois, where she married (2) Mr. Devereau, an Englishman. Mabel Chinn and

Hazel Chinn Soeder, descendants of Judith and Alfred Chinn, live in Alameda, California.

Children of Obadiah and Malvina Waring Powell Mackoy were Sarah, Ella Waring, Clement O., and Malvina W. Children of the third marriage with Cassandra Chinn King were John and Richard. Nothing is known of these children after the family went to Missouri.

Moses Fuqua Mackoy

Moses Fuqua Mackoy (1800), born on the Kanawha River in Virginia while his parents were en route to Kentucky, married Hannah Lawson (1803) in 1824. She was born in Hampshire County, Virginia, the daughter of John and Susannah Blue Lawson. Moses Mackoy was a farmer and also a student of Alexander Campbell's teachings. For more than twenty years he was a minister of the Christian Church at Siloam, at the country churches on Tygart Creek, and in Portsmouth. His home, called "Elmbank," was later inherited by his daughter, Mrs. Lavinia Dugan Ware, who sold it to Madison and Louise Kendall Gammon when she went to live with her son in Huntington, West Virginia.

The children of Moses F. and Hannah Lawson Mackoy were John Lawson, Lavinia, Henry Clay, and Moses, Jr.

John L. (1830) married in 1851 Mary E., daughter of John and Eliza Pratt, and their children were Mary Lavinia, Amanda, John Pratt, Samuel Walter, and Maggie. The family lived on a farm at Siloam until the 1870's, when it was sold to Solomon K. Damron and the family moved to Greenup. The eldest daughter, Mary Lavinia, married Charles Reid (see Reid family), and they, with her father's family, moved to Ennis, Texas, in 1876. Amanda Mackoy married Dr. McCall and their son, Randall, is a resident of Ennis at the present time. He married Lena Virginia Mulfinger and their son, Robert Alfred, is a physician in Augusta, Georgia. Maggie married James Kirkpatrick and lives in Waco, Texas. She has two daughters, Fay Miller of Dallas, Texas, and Virginia LeBow of Waco, Texas.

Lavinia Mackoy married (1) Thomas Dugan, a prominent banker and business man of Portsmouth, and their children were Fannie and James. Fannie married James Adams of Portsmouth and they had two sons, William Dugan and Earl; James married Lizzie Gore of Gray's Branch and they lived on a farm at Siloam. They sold this property to the Tanner family about 1886 and moved to Huntington, West Virginia, where they reared a fine family of ten children: Lavinia, Thomas, Walter, Mathias Wall, Fannie, Charlotte, Pearl, Alice, Irvin, and Elizabeth. Two sons, Mathias and Irvin, are active business men of that city at the present time. Lavinia Mackoy married (2) Elias Ware.

Henry Clay Mackoy (see his sketch following).

Moses Mackoy, Jr., married Augusta Sheward of Sciotoville, Ohio, in 1862, and lived on a farm at Siloam until the late 1870's, when they moved to Milford, Texas. The children of this family were Edwin, James Dugan, and Arthur. Edwin Mackoy's widow, two sons, Lynn and James, and a daughter, Mrs. Frances Cooper, still live in Milford. Another daughter, Mrs. Emma E. Tuley, lives in Dallas, Texas.

HENRY CLAY MACKOY

Except for a few years spent as a bank clerk in Portsmouth, Henry Clay Mackoy (1834) spent his entire life on the land where his grandfather settled at Siloam. In 1853 he married, in Portsmouth, Samantha Ellender Timmonds (1834), daughter of John Wesley and Mary Woodworth Timmonds. Mr. Mackoy was a successful farmer, and the hospitality of his home, "Maplegrove," was widely known. Itinerant preachers of the Christian Church were especially welcome.

Six of their ten children lived to maturity. William Henry (1856) married (1) Cora, daughter of Captain Jacob and Rosanna Smith Davis of Sciotoville, Ohio, and (2) Mary Isabella, daughter of Captain Alexander and Melinda Smith Bruce of St. Paul, Lewis County, Kentucky. Two sons by the first marriage are Dr. Frank W. Mackoy of Milwaukee, Wisconsin, and Dr. Morris Davis Mackoy of Ann Arbor, Michigan; a daughter, Willie Bruce Mackoy, by the second marriage, died in 1943. At the early age of thirty-one, William Henry Mackoy lost his life by the accidental discharge of his gun, carried for hunting.

James Bryson Mackoy (1858) married Ella J. Johnston of Siloam (see Johnston family). They established their home at Gray's Branch on the William Bryson farm, where they lived for fifteen years. In connection with the farm he operated the only country store in the community and also kept the post office. In 1896 he moved to a farm at Wheelersburg, Ohio, and in 1918 to Portsmouth, where his two daughters, Mabel Lee and Caroline, reside. He retained his membership in Siloam Church, where he was an elder for more than forty years, being the fourth generation of the family to serve as an official of that church.

Hannah Lawson Mackoy (1861) married John Brisco Johnston (see his sketch under Johnston family).

Mode F. Mackoy (1865) married (1) Nellie M., daughter of Madison and Louisa Kendall Gammon, and (2) Elizabeth, daughter of David and Josephine McNeal Brant of Lucasville, Ohio. A daughter by the first marriage, Bessie Louise, wife of Charles W. King, deceased, resides in Irvington, New Jersey, and a son, Harry Brant, of the second marriage, lives in Huntington, West Virginia. He married Grace Ketter of Wheelersburg. Mode F. Mackoy was a farmer at Siloam during most of his life, but spent his later years in Wheelersburg, Ohio.

Myrt Elmo Mackoy married Flora Belle, daughter of Milton and Harriet Mickle Hill of Gray's Branch. They lived on the William Bryson farm for ten years and then moved to Wheelersburg. Their children are Harriet Lavinia, wife of Barnett F. Brightwell of Wheelersburg; James Carlisle of Orlando, Florida; Marjorie Elmo, wife of William E. Ranshahaus of Columbus, Ohio; and Helen Virginia, wife of Oscar Craycraft of Wheelersburg.

Ella May, the youngest child of Henry Clay Mackoy, married Henry Floyd Ruggles of Lewis County, Kentucky, and they lived on her father's farm. The Chesapeake and Ohio Railroad bought a part of the farm for the bridge and later Mrs. Ruggles sold the remainder. She was the last of the Mackoy family to leave the land where John Mackoy settled in 1800. Mr. and Mrs. Ruggles live in Louisville, Kentucky, and have a son, Ronald Henry, of Chicago.

MARTIN

James Martin was born in Virginia in 1810 and married Janetta White of Virginia in 1833. The family came to Greenup County and bought a farm on the Ohio River above Greenup in 1853. He built a frame house which burned in 1875 and in 1876 he built a brick house which is still in good repair.

The children of this family were Atlanta, George, and Leander. Atlanta married Adolphus Reid and they were the parents of Nannie Powell, Herbert, Jeanette Cole, Emma, Julia, and Homer. Leander Powell married Emma White, a cousin, and they had no children.

The Martin Negroes of East Greenup are descendants of the James Martin family's slaves.

218

MEAD

The Mead family is descended from Richard and Joane Mead of Nursely, Buckinghamshire, England, through their second son, the Rev. Matthew Mead, who was born in 1629 and died October 16, 1699. The Rev. Matthew Mead married and had fifteen children, among them Nathaniel, Richard, and William.

William Mead had several children: John, William, Samuel, Pleasant, and Sarah, who came to America and settled in Bucks County, Pennsylvania. John married Mary Abrell, March 2, 1726, and had two (perhaps more children) sons, Robert and William, the latter born October 10, 1727. John, William, and Samuel (brothers) moved from Bucks County, Pennsylvania, to Loudon County (then a part of Fairfax County, Virginia) in 1746. From there John went to Bedford County, Virginia, where he died in 1754. He was buried in the Mead family graveyard near New London, Bedford County. In 1754, letters of administration were granted to his son, William.

William Mead, who was born October 10, 1727, and died December 30, 1805, married in 1750 (1) Ann Haile (1734-1769) and (2) Martha Cowles Stith. Among the thirteen children of William Mead were Nicholas (1752), Elizabeth (1764), Stith (1767), and Priscilla (1775). Stith Mead married Prudence Watkins Blakely of Henrico County, Virginia, and was a prominent minister in the Methodist Episcopal Church. Priscilla married Benjamin Sims, poet and author.

Robert, son of John and Mary Abrell Mead, married Hannah Rhodes and they were the parents of Benjamin, Robert, Rhodes, Moses, William, Samuel, Eli, Kitta, Eda, and Matilda. In December 1795 Robert Mead conveyed to Benjamin, his eldest son, one hundred thirty-nine and one-half acres of land in Bedford County, Virginia. In September 1811 Benjamin and Elizabeth Brown Mead sold the land and started west with their family. Elizabeth was a daughter of Daniel Brown of Bedford County, Virginia, and married Benjamin Mead December 29, 1796. They crossed the Big Sandy and came down the Ohio into Greenup County in 1812. Benjamin Mead died April 19, 1821, and was buried in a family graveyard which was "set aside by Joseph Powell for the use of any neighbor who wished to be buried there." The village of Worthington has grown up around this burial ground.

Benjamin and Elizabeth Brown Mead settled on land owned by Joseph Powell, who had come to the county in 1799. After the death of Benjamin, Elizabeth bought land near the present site of Raceland. Benjamin and Elizabeth were the parents of Cynthia, Lucy Wilt, Albert Gallatin, Henry Armistead, Sophia, John L., Matilda Dickerson, William R., and Benjamin F. Cynthia married Charles Stewart; Lucy Wilt married Samuel Powell; Sophia married John Hamon Chinn; Matilda D. married James Nicholls, a captain in the Civil War; William R. married Chloe Adams; and Benjamin F. married Mary Ann, daughter of Lott Pratt.

Henry Armistead and Elizabeth Powell Mead were the parents of Mary Ann, who married John Russell of Ashland; Naomi, who married James Foster; Emoline, who married George Perry Clancy; Sarah Belle, who married Dr. Lewis Prichard; Lucy Elizabeth, who married Charles Hampton; Charles Powell, who married Lida H. Hoople; Henry Armistead, Jr., who married Emma Jane Fisher; and Helen, who married (1) Benjamin Young and (2) Dr. John Morgan White of Ironton, Ohio.

The children of Henry Armistead, Jr., and Emma Jane Fisher Mead were Russell Fisher, George Henry, Mary Elizabeth, and Lucy Ethyl. Russell F. married Nell M. Chambers and they were the parents of Russell F., Jr., and Helen Holt; George Henry married Byrd I. Wood and had no children; Mary Elizabeth married James G. Richards and had a son, James Armistead; Lucy Ethyl never married.

Connections of the Mead family are Browns, Tolers, Prichards, Keysers, Kellys, Trumbos, Austins, and Powells.

MEADOWS

The Meadows family were early residents of Tygart Valley. Abraham Meadows married Lilly Nevers in 1825. He and his son, Benjamin Franklin Meadows, were prominent farmers of Tygart Valley and the latter was elected representative from the district in the late 1870's.

Benjamin Franklin Meadows married America Warnock and they were the parents of Ella, who married (1) James Scott of Hopewell, and (2) Butler Taylor of Greenup (see his sketch under Taylor family); Dr. Matthew Warnock Meadows of Fullerton, who married Lulu M. Holbrook of Tygart; Margaret, who married Clark Warnock (see William Howe Warnock family); John, who went to Kansas; Emma Webb; Irvine; and Edward, who married Nellie Warnock and had a daughter, Olive (see Warnock family).

The children of Dr. Matthew and Lulu Holbrook Meadows are Frank, who married Mariana Merrill, and Herman and Russell, both of Morehead.

MEANS

The Means family has been identified with the eastern section of Greenup County (Boyd County) since 1855. John, Thomas, Jr., Hugh, and William Means were the sons of Thomas Williamson and Sarah Ellison Means of Adams County, Ohio. They were the grandsons of Colonel John Means, who came to Adams County, Ohio, from Spartanburg, South Carolina, in 1819, bringing all of his slaves. He freed the slaves as soon as he arrived.

John Means, the best known member of the family in Greenup County, was born September 21, 1829, at West Union, Adams County, Ohio. In 1851 he was bookkeeper and manager of Buena Vista Furnace; in 1855 he moved to Catlettsburg, Kentucky; and in 1857 he moved to Ashland, where he lived until his death.

John Means became a charter member of the Portsmouth, Big Sandy, and Pomeroy Packet Company—known as the "White Collar Line"—in 1856. In the same year he was a director of the Kentucky Iron, Coal, and Manufacturing Company of Ashland, and also one of the founders of the Bank of Ashland, where he was trustee and councilman for thirty years. He was one of the organizers of the Lexington and Big Sandy Railroad, later known as the Ashland Coal and Iron Railway Company, and was a director of the Norton Iron Works of Ashland. In 1872 he was treasurer of the last named company. The Means family were residents of Greenup County until 1860, when they and many other families of the northeastern section of the county found themselves citizens of the new county of Boyd.

John Means married (1) Harriet Perkins of Marietta, Ohio, and their children were Thomas Hildreth, Harold, Ellison Cooke, Elizabeth Seaton, Lillian Maynard, and Rosalie Bullard. He married (2) Mary Peck Seaton of Greenup.

MERRILL

Josiah and Asa Merrill came from New Hampshire in company with John and Dan Young, the Preston family, and others. They traveled overland by wagon to the Allegheny River and came down the Ohio River on flatboats. They settled at Concord, now Wheelersburg, Ohio.

Josiah Merrill married Margaret H. Pixley and they spent their lives at Wheelersburg. Josiah, Jr., married Sophia Hayward at Wheelersburg and moved to a farm in Kentucky, below Limeville. Adjoining the Merrill farm was one owned by either Dan or John Young, both of whom had been very prominent in the affairs of both Greenup and Scioto Counties.

Josiah, Jr., and Sophia Hayward Merrill were the parents of John Hayward, Ira Preston, Julia, Horace of Washington State, Grant of Oregon, William Sherman, May, Minerva, Smith of Michigan, and Josiah Gage of California. John Hayward married Mary Hannah, daughter of Franklin and Sarah Snodgrass Bennett, of Bennett's Mills. Their children were Josiah Bennett, William Horace, and Annie.

Josiah Bennett (or Joe, as he was known) married Mattie, daughter of Amos and Elizabeth Smith Hill of Gray's Branch, and they are the parents of Joseph B., Bernice M., Charles, Mary Elizabeth, and Annabel. Joseph B. married Elizabeth Betts of Ohio; Bernice M. married Bert Elam of Russell; Charles married Lucille Spratt; Mary Elizabeth married Joseph D. Wilson; Annabel married Albert F. Merce.

William Horace, second son of John Hayward Merrill, married Susan, daughter of Maurice K. and Nina Mitchell Biggs, of Mt. Zion. They were the parents of four children, of whom Maribel Nina, and William, Jr., died when children. A daughter, Mariana, married Frank Meadows of Fullerton.

Annie Merrill, daughter of John Hayward Merrill, married William G. Sharkey and lived in Bluefield, West Virginia, for a few years. Later they came to Russell, where they were living when Mr. Sharkey died.

MILLER

John Miller was an Englishman and married Nancy More of Scotland. They emigrated to Canada, where a son, Matthew, was born. From Canada they moved to Clinton County, Pennsylvania, where seven children were born.

Matthew and a brother, David, went to Gallipolis to operate a grain mill. There he married Emma Bush of Gallipolis and three daughters were born to them: Veva Saunders, Nellie W., and Urania. The family moved to Springville in the 1880's, where they operated a grain mill, later changing it to a paint mill. At Springville two sons, Edgar L. and Russell, were born.

Later David Miller joined his brother in the milling business at Springville. He married Nettie, daughter of Joshua and Sarah Thomson Lawson, and their children are Nettie, wife of Russell McElheny, Elizabeth Edgington, Reuben L., and Garnet, wife of Dr. E. W. Potter of Russell.

Mr. Matthew Miller gave up the milling business to take a position as manager of a company formed by Overturf, Kendall, and Kanouse, of Portsmouth, and James Miller, of Boston, to open up a lead mine in Owen County, Kentucky.

MITCHELL

Shadrach Mitchell (1797) was a son of Shadrach (1760) and Margaret Rinehart Mitchell of Green County, Pennsylvania. He married Elizabeth (1799), a daughter of Matthias (1772), and Sarah Hughes Roseberry (1779) of Green County, in 1817. They came to Kentucky in the early 1830's and settled on a farm near Concord, in Lewis County. They were the parents of eleven children, nine of them boys. The family lived on the farm until the older children married and left home. Selling his farm, Shadrach moved to Concord, where he kept a river tavern and the wharf boat during the 1850's.

In 1858, Sarah Mitchell Stallcup, a widowed daughter, came to Greenup with the three youngest boys, David Sellers, Shadrach Lindsay, and Marling. They kept a store on Main Street for several years. When the Civil War started David had married, Shadrach joined the army, and Sarah Stallcup, with Marling, went to Illinois, where there were relatives. Marling remained in Illinois and became a successful merchant in Mt. Carmel. He was married twice but had no children.

David Sellers Mitchell continued to keep the store in Greenup. He had married Sophia Chillison of Greenup and their children were Grant, Stanley, and Roy. Grant married Maud Cavey of Indiana and they were the parents of Marling of Portsmouth and Robert of Washington, D. C. Stanley married Retta Collins of Greenup and had three children, Roland, and Ruth and Rosamond (twins). Stanley was accidentally killed while in the service of the Chesapeake and Ohio Railroad. Roy married Nellie Frye of Greenup and their children were Leta and Henry Wolford.

The family moved to Ohio. Henry was accidentally killed while handling a rifle.

Shadrach Lindsay Mitchell was with the Army in the Vicksburg campaign and was stricken with malaria at Port Hudson. He was sent to Greenup to recuperate in 1863. He resigned from the Army, and later married Frances Belle Stark of Greenup. Their children were Maud Ella, Nina Aura, Gertrude, Clarence Lindsay, Elizabeth May, Fannie Fay, Goldia, Claud M., Vernon S., and Chester A. Maud Ella married William Alexander Biggs (see his sketch under Biggs family) and lives in Greenup; Nina Aura married Maurice King Biggs (see his sketch under Biggs family) of Mt. Zion; Gertrude married John G. Hughes of Ashland; Clarence Lindsay married Lillian Abel of Brooklyn, New York; Elizabeth married Frederic A. Baker of Orange, New Jersey; Goldia married Robert Barton Hager and lives in New York; Claud M. married Zella Barton of Catlettsburg and lives in Charleston, West Virginia; Vernon S. married Pauline Boynton in Fairfax, South Dakota, and lived at Norfolk, Nebraska, where he died; Chester A. married Kathleen Topping of Charleston, West Virginia, and lived in South Dakota, where he died. He is buried in Ashland.

MORTON

Jonathan Morton

Jonathan Morton and his wife, Letitia, came from Prince Edward County, Virginia, in the earliest days of the county, and settled on a large tract of land below Gray's Branch. He was prominent in the early court affairs of the county, being one of the first justices. From early court records, it is known that he was a faithful attendant at court sessions.

In 1812 a marriage license was issued to Armistead Churchill Bragg and Susan Morton. The same year Jonathan Morton made a deed to Armistead C. Bragg. The relationship of Susan to Jonathan Morton is uncertain.

The children of Jonathan Morton were Quinn, who married Angeline Jane Blankenship in 1842; Martha (Patsy), wife of William Palmer; and Hezekiah, who married Hannah Burton in 1827.

Hezekiah and Hannah Burton Morton lived at the homestead, which was one of the largest brick houses in the county. The bricks were made on the farm. On the second floor was a large ballroom for dancing, with its small adjoining dressing rooms for the accommodation of the guests. A large yard surrounded the house, with shade trees and beautiful flowers. The Mortons were fond of horses and had a race track on their farm at one time.

The children of Hezekiah Morton were Letitia, wife of Thomas Wylie Jones (see his sketch under Jones family); William L.; Margaret Burton, wife of Charles A. Joplin; Ann W.; Mary M. E.; and Hezekiah, Jr. Several of the children went to California to live, among them Miss Ann. She returned to Greenup County, however, and, with Mrs. Joplin, lived in the Morton home many y ars. At their death this fine old home passed out of the Morton family.

JOSIAH MORTON

The Morton family claim English origin and descend from prominent English noblemen, among them Count Robert Morton, who is said to have been a half brother of William the Conqueror. Thomas Morton, probably the first of the name in America, settled in Virginia, where he lived at Morton Hall, Prince Edward County. Here a son, John Morton, was born in 1730. John married Mary Anderson and they had a family of seven sons. He was a captain of the Prince Edward Militia, and his seven sons were in his company.

In his will, John Morton names among his children a son, Josiah, born in 1763, who also served in the Revolution at the Battle of Guilford Courthouse and at the Siege of Yorktown. In 1790 Josiah Morton married Nancy, daughter of Moses and Judith Woodson Fuqua, in Campbell County, Virginia. They came to Greenup County about 1800 and owned a large tract of land which extended from the west bank of Tygart Creek to Stoner Hill. He died in 1838 and was buried on his own land above what is now South Shore.

The children of Josiah and Nancy Morton were Richard Woodson; Nathaniel, who married Judith, daughter of John and Lavinia Fuqua Mackoy, in 1815; Judith, who married James Mackoy in 1820; and Martha Anderson (1806-1865), who married James Ruffner (1807-1868) in 1832, and lived at Kanawha Court House, Virginia, now Charleston, West Virginia. Their daughter, Anestine Woodson, married William H. Hogeman, a lawyer of New York City, and they had a daughter, Martha Morton Hogeman Knight, who is a resident of Charleston at the present time.

Richard Woodson Morton was among the early students of Ohio University at Athens, Ohio, where he met and married Hannah, daughter of Alvin Bingham, who was a prominent man in the early days of Athens County. Richard Morton became a doctor and practiced both in Greenup County and Portsmouth, Ohio, where he was popularly known as "Doctor Dick." The children of this family were James, Richard Bingham, George, Henry Clay, Nancy, wife of Charles P. McCoy, Elizabeth Higley, and Judith.

In 1842 James Morton married (1) Cynthia Jane, daughter of Moses, Jr., and Cynthia Collins Fuqua, and their children were Alvin; James, Jr.; Addie Warnock (see Warnock family); Martha Bryan (see Bryan family); Lavinia, who married (1) George Callihan (see Callihan family), (2) Clay Wade. Nancy, another daughter, married (1) William Fagan and had two sons, Alfred, who resides in Portsmouth, and Earl, who died at the age of twenty-six, while his parents lived in Pittsburgh; (2) Charles Nickell (see Nickell family). James Morton married (2) Penelope Hinton and their children were Maynard, Dudley, John R. (see his sketch following), and Jane, wife of Warren Griffin.

Alvin Morton married Lola Pratt Roe and lived in Greenup. Their children were Agnes Webb, Esther Bennett (see Bennett family), Juliet, wife of Frank Adams of Chicago, Rebecca Sowards (see Sowards family), and Alvin, Jr.

James Morton, Jr., married (1) Ella Brown and their children were Oliver and Orin, (2) Priscilla (Puss) Waring, and their children were Garnet McKee, Margaret Hockaday (see Hockaday family), and Elwood of Riverton.

Maynard Morton, son of James Morton, married Helen Childs of Pittsburgh, where they lived for some time before coming to Fullerton. Their children were Nellie, who married Henry Bush and whose son, Maynard, lives in Greenup; Nancy Sayre; Martha, wife of William Biggs (see Maurice Biggs family); Clay (deceased); and Veo of Fullerton.

Dudley Morton, brother of Maynard Morton, married (1) Ella, daughter of William and Hannah Menach Gray, and they were the parents of Fannie Bell Virgin, Earl, Claude, Gertrude Ragan, Gladys, and Lavinia. Dudley Morton married (2) Sophia Day Phillips and their children are Virginia, June, Pansy, and Dudley.

Richard Bingham Morton, second son of Dr. Richard Morton, married (1) Martha Ann Garrett, who was a niece of Kitty Scott, mother of Mrs. Marshall Field I. Their children were Katherine (Kit) Warnock (see Warnock family), Virginia Smith (see Martin Smith family), and Maria Glover (see Glover family). Richard B. Morton married (2) Lavinia Reed of Virginia and their daughter, Lula May, married Nathaniel T. King (see King family).

Henry Clay Morton lived near the present location of the Morton Funeral Home. He married Martha Ann, daughter of John and Hannah Berry Gammon. They were the parents of Julia Bartlett, who married James Warren Warnock; Mary Nancy, who married Samuel Price Warnock; and Martha, who married Laken Samuel Warnock (see Warnock family); Nellie, who married Frank Marion Gray (see his sketch under Gray family); and Sarah Hannah, who married Moses K. Ratcliff.

Josiah and Nancy Fuqua Morton were charter members, and Josiah was an elder, of the First Presbyterian Church, organized in Portsmouth, May 24, 1817. He was also one of the three men who organized the Greenup Union Presbyterian Church at Gray's Branch in 1829.

John R. Morton

John, son of James and Penelope Hinton Morton, born at Load on Tygart Creek, March 16, 1876, was a lifelong resident of the county. In 1896 he married Fannie, daughter of William and Hannah Menach Gray, and they have a son, Carl. They made their home on a farm near the Lewis County line for a number of years and later moved to Fullerton, where he engaged in the grocery business which he conducted until 1930.

Mr. Morton always took an active part in the affairs of Fullerton and was especially interested in the improvement of the Portsmouth-Greenup Highway and the construction of a good road up the Tygart Valley. He was a member of the Masonic Lodge and the Methodist Church in Fullerton.

In 1915 Mr. Morton and his son, Carl, engaged in the undertaking business and, since his father's death in 1946, Carl has continued in this business.

Carl Morton married Miss Helen Ferree, daughter of Edward Ferree of California, and their children are Richard, Dorothy, Wayne, and Robert. Wayne married Judith Johnson and lives in Fullerton. He is associated with his father in the undertaking business.

Mrs. John R. Morton and her son, Carl, both live on a part of the original tract of Morton land.

MUNN

Captain James Munn served in the Revolutionary War in Pennsylvania and was with Washington at the Battle of Trenton. Captain Munn came from Pennsylvania to Kentucky in 1795 and from there he went to the town of Alexandria, at the mouth of the Scioto River. Later he moved up a creek, which now bears his name, Munn's Run.

Children of the Munn family were James, William, David C., John, Solomon, Nancy, Margaret (Patty), Eleanor (Nell), Polly, and Hannah. James married Felissa Oliver; William married Joanna Hitchcock; Nancy married David McDonald; Margaret married John Oliver; and Eleanor married John Groniger. (Extracts from Evans' *History of Scioto County*.)

The third son of Captain James Munn, Dr. David C. Munn, was a practicing physician at Limeville in the middle of the last century. He was born in 1818 and died in 1867. His wife, Amanda, was born in 1827 and died in 1901. They and four of their children, Essie F., Samuel D., Flora C., and Eudora, are buried in the cemetery at Siloam Church.

The Dr. Munn home was an old-fashioned two-story frame house that stood upon the rise across the highway from the present church at Limeville. This was a very old house in the 1870's. The John Merrill family built a new house on the site of the Munn house in later years. The Merrill home on this location burned some years ago.

MYERS

Allen Myers

The Myers family came originally from Holland by way of France and England to America and settled in Virginia. Allen Myers came from Greenbrier County, Virginia, to Greenup very early, as he built the Myers house on Front Street before 1820. He married India Pratt Callihan, the widow of Horatio Callihan and the mother of three sons, George, Charles, and Christopher Horatio (Kit) Callihan. Allen and India Callihan Myers were the parents of Frank, Allen, Jr., and Alfred. Frank married Libby

Weaver of Hunnewell and they moved to Winchester, Kentucky, later to Texas. Allen, Jr., married Mary Tumbleson of Tygart Valley and their children were Frank, William, Helen, and Mary Allen. Allen Myers, Jr., was accidentally killed in the Myers Lumber Mill on Front Street. His widow married his brother, Alfred, and their children were Alfred (Fred), Timothy, David, and Lauretta. The last two children own and occupy the Myers homestead which has always been in the family. David has a workshop in the building that was built by Allen Myers, Sr., as a blacksmith shop. He was also a cabinet maker, and furniture of his making is in the Myers home. Timothy Myers married Maude Nichols and they have two children, Bonn and Helen.

India Pratt Callihan Myers had a brother, George Pratt, and a sister. (See George Pratt under Pratt family.)

JOHN MYERS

John and Isabel Rogers White Myers came to Greenup from Pennsylvania in 1836. Mr. Myers was interested in the growth of Greenup, and in 1894 he wrote of the town as it was in the early days. Much of that material is incorporated in this history. He was a carpenter and constructed many of the buildings of the town. The Presbyterian Church was one of them, built in 1859-60. He operated the grist and lumber mill at the head of Front Street on Town Branch. Mr. Myers was an active Methodist and was one of the first trustees of the Methodist Episcopal Church, the first church to be built in the town of Greenup, in 1845.

John and Isabel White Myers were the parents of Thomas, John, Laura, and Hannah. Thomas married Lutie, the daughter of Robert and Sallie Sanders Robb, of Lewis County; Laura married Augustus McConahay, of Ohio; Hannah married Benjamin Pratt of the Pratt and Brooks store on Washington Street. Mr. Pratt built the house on Main Street that was the Joseph Bennett home for many years and later was bought for the Methodist parsonage. The Benjamin Pratt family moved to Cincinnati in the 1880's.

For his second wife Mr. Myers married Mrs. Mary Dulin Dickey, a widow with two sons, Charles and Ollie. By this second marriage he had a daughter, Esther.

Children of Thomas and Lutie Robb Myers were Daisy, who married William Wilson of Greenup; Belle, who married Mr. Burdsal of Ohio; Nell; William Ireland, who married Luella, daughter of Henry and Emma Riffe Curry of Hopewell; and Bertie, who married Edward Davidson of Ohio. They had no children but had an adopted daughter who married Clarence Wilkerson, of Van Wert, Ohio.

MYTINGER

Charles W. Mytinger married Josephine Cole of Maysville, Kentucky. Mrs. Mytinger died and Mr. Mytinger came to Greenup County in 1878 with his four daughters, Kate, Lyde, Annie, and Emma. They lived first at Oldtown, where Mr. Mytinger taught school.

The family moved to Greenup in the early 1880's. Lyde and Annie taught school in the county, and Lyde later became a teacher in the Columbus, Ohio, schools, where she remained for many years. She was also an artist and her pictures of local scenes hang in many of the Greenup homes.

Annie Mytinger married Joseph Bentley Bennett (see his sketch under Bennett family). They were the parents of Frances Geyer, Kate Hill, Arthur, Charles Bentley, Emmabel Stephenson, Julia McWhorter, Mary Shaw, Sallie Jacobs, and Joseph B. (see Bennett family).

Three of the Mytinger daughters remained unmarried.

NICHOLLS

John and Cassandra Wilcoxon Nicholls came from Virginia to Greenup County about 1800. They settled below the mouth of Little Sandy River. An uncle of Mrs. Nicholls, Lewis Wilcoxon, settled above the mouth of Little Sandy. The children of the Nicholls family were John, Patty, Nicholas, James Edmonson, Mary, Cassandra, and Alfred. Patty married Benjamin Chinn (see Chinn family), and Cassandra married James Bartley (see Bartley family).

James Edmonson (1791) was a captain in the Mexican War. He married Matilda Dickinson, daughter of Benjamin Mead. They were the parents of Helen Marr, John Henry, Lewis Benjamin, and Orlando.

Helen Marr Nicholls (1831) married George Paull Walker. Their children were Jennie Scott, who married Joseph Savage (see Savage family); William, who married Lillie Wurts; and George Paull, Jr., who married Lucy Wurts.

John Henry Nicholls (1833) married Nancy Henrietta Swearingen. They moved to Missouri in 1881 and in 1883 to South Dakota. Their children were Alfred L., Eugene, Ida, Owen J., James Edmonson, Clement Russell, and Matilda D. Alfred L. married Lulu Grace Campbell; Eugene married Flora Shaw; Ida married William G. Blair; Owen J. married Eliza Graves; James Edmonson married Hattie Massie; Clement Russell married Martha Frame; and Matilda D. married Sherm McLain. A son of Alfred L., Burdett Campbell Nicholls, is a lieutenant in the United States Army, stationed at Fort Knox, Kentucky.

Lewis Benjamin Nicholls (1836) married Ann Eliza Wurts. Their children were Matilda Dickinson, Lewis Edmonson, Lillie May, Jessie Beauregard, Amanda Bartley, and Samuel Grandin. Matilda Dickinson married Henry Ernest, son of Luke Powell (see Powell family); Judge Lewis Edmonson married (1) Lucy Fisher and (2) Sallie Howell; Lillie May married William Smith; Jessie Beauregard married David Smith; Amanda Bartley married John Long; Samuel Grandin married Della Fisher.

Orlando (1840) married Henrietta Eastham in 1862 and died soon after his marriage. They had a son, Orlando, born in 1863.

Judge Lewis Edmonson and his first wife, Lucy Fisher Nicholls were the parents of George Edmonson, who married Eunice Warnock. They have a daughter, Maxine Elizabeth. Judge Nicholls married (2) Sallie Howell of Frankfort, Kentucky, and they were the parents of Lewis Howell of East Greenup.

NICKELL

Joseph Nickell and Amy, daughter of Thomas Marion and Barbara Schaffer Barney, were married in Greenup County in 1845 and lived on Tygart Creek near Lynn, where Mr. Nickell was a blacksmith. The children of this family were Charles, Joseph, Jr., Thomas, Helen, James, Reuben, Mary, Sarah, and Edward.

Charles married (1) Julia Maupin and lived in Beattyville. They were the parents of four children. Of these, Effie married Sandford Williams and moved to New Boston, Ohio, and Lucy married Walter Craycraft of Beattyville. Charles married (2) Nancy Morton Fagan, a widow.

Joseph, Jr., married Elizabeth Ellen Shearn and lived in Springville. They were the parents of Hattie and Mary (twins),

Robert J., and Thomas E. Hattie married Samuel Davis of Springville and went to New Boston to live. Their children are Selma Johnson, who is District Supervisor of the United States Census Bureau in Portsmouth; Hazel, who is a teacher in Los Angeles, California; Robert S., of Battle Creek, Michigan; Gladys, an attorney, who is city solicitor of New Boston and assistant attorney general of Ohio; Jean Schlencar, the youngest child, who lives in Du Quesne, Pennsylvania.

Robert J. Nickell was a prominent teacher and superintendent of Greenup County Schools. He married Lutie Patton of Greenup. Thomas E. Nickell is a prominent lawyer of Greenup. He married Nellie Lybrook of Flat Hollow and they have one son.

Of the other children of Joseph and Amy Barney Nickell, Helen married Thomas Gallagher; James married Sarah Young; Reuben married Abigail Bennett of The Globe, where they lived; Sarah married John Warnock of Tygart Creek, and moved to Portsmouth (see Warnock family); Edward married Nellie Clary of Flat Hollow and their children are Henry and Nellie Pollard of Sunshine.

NORRIS

Abraham and Mary Deane Norris came from Virginia to Greenup County and settled on Little Sandy near Oldtown. Children of the family were Charles, Gallihu, Betty, Love, Eliza, Dean Sanders, Hannah, Ellen Barber, and Bertie. Charles was a teacher for many years. He married Nancy, a daughter of Henry and Nancy Curry of Hopewell, where they lived. Betty married Mr. Hannah. Bertie married Henry Irwin of Hopewell and moved to Grayson. Most of the Norris children married and lived near Oldtown.

Charles and Nancy Curry Norris were the parents of Laura, Henry, Clifford, Emmett, Iona Jane, and Mary Deane. Of these, Laura married (1) Robert Scott of Hopewell and (2) John Harris of Wurtland; Henry married Ellen Colley; Clifford is deceased; Emmett married Myrtle Spence of Hopewell; and Mary Deane married Vernon Kendall of Oldtown (see Kendall family). Emmett and Myrtle Spence Norris were the parents of Naomi Deane, Chlotine, Malcolm, Nancy, Emmett, Jr., Charles William, and Avenelle.

Naomi Deane married Jesse, son of Mitchell and Martha Hilton Stuart of W Hollow (see Stuart family); Chlotine married Russell Zachem of Ashland; Malcolm married Clara Blevins of

Ashland and was lost in the submarine "Gudgeon" in World War II; Nancy married George H., son of Harry and Lucy Lawson Curry of Greenup (see Curry family); Emmett, Jr., is deceased; Avenelle married Robert, son of George and Elsie Duduit Callihan (see Callihan family); and Charles William, unmarried, lives in the parental home.

OSENTON

Samuel Osenton came to Greenup County about 1816. He was born at Cliffe, Kent County, England, in 1783, being one of five children of Henry and Hannah Evrett Osenton. Samuel served an apprenticeship of seven years to learn the carpenter trade, and was an expert cabinet maker. He married Charlot Webb, and their son, James, was born in 1812. The wife died when James was three years of age.

Samuel wanted to come to America, but the ship's company refused to allow his child to accompany him. He constructed an elaborate tool chest in which to bring his nine hundred pounds of carpenter's tools with him. It was made with a false bottom, in which compartment he concealed James, and they arrived safely in New York in 1815. From there they went to Philadelphia, where they spent one year and where he sold three hundred pounds of his tools. The rest he brought across Pennsylvania, through Pittsburgh, and down the Ohio River, to Greenupsburg.

James was boarded with various families and educated in Greenupsburg schools until 1819, when his father married Emzy Downs, daughter of John and Lucy Virgin Downs, and they bought a farm at Oldtown. The children of the second marriage were Lucy Jane, Sarah Ann, Henry Kelly, John Thomas, Samuel, George Nicholas Duke of Cambridge, and Joseph, who died when a child.

Some years later the Samuel Osenton family moved to Olive Hill, in Carter County, where they kept a hotel and public house. Here they acquired much land and many slaves. In 1856 Samuel Osenton died and his body was brought back to Oldtown for burial.

James Osenton's formal education ended when his father moved to Oldtown. He worked for his father on the farm, but while still a youngster he began to drive a team for himself, hauling ore for the furnaces at Hunnewell and Argillite. He dug ore at night so that he could haul all day. With his savings he bought a farm of six hundred and ninety-one acres at Pactolus.

In 1853 he married (1) Maria Sophia Goble and they had a daughter, Martha. After the death of his wife he married (2) Elizabeth Apple and they had a family of six children. James Osenton died on Christmas Day, 1893.

Lucy Jane Osenton (1821) married Allen Womack and her father gave her four women slaves "in consideration of natural love and affection." She spent her whole life at Oldtown, where Mr. Womack was a farmer (see Womack family).

Sarah Ann Osenton (1824) married Judge Joseph H. Strother in 1843. They lived in Carter County and had a large family.

Henry Kelly Osenton married Sciotha McAlester and they had eleven children. Mr. Harold B. Tyree of Detroit, Michigan, to whom the authors are indebted for this sketch, descends from this branch of the family.

John Thomas (1828) married Katherine Cameron of Limeville, and their children were William E. A. and Mary Bell, both of whom died in infancy; Ida Mae (1860), who was a teacher in the county and married James Watt Womack; John Thomas, Jr. (1862), who married Arminta Atkins and whose daughter, Mabel Osenton Stennett, was reared by Mr. and Mrs. James Watt Womack after the death of her parents, and is now a resident of Greenup; George E. (1864), who married Verda Cox; Samuel T. (1866), who never married and lives near Wheelersburg on the farm where his parents lived.

Samuel Osenton (1834) married Sallie Scott and died at Grayson in Carter County in 1878. The children were Robert, who married Annie Lape, Henry Kelly, and Jennie Scott. The two latter live in Cincinnati.

George Nicholas Duke of Cambridge (1842), born at Oldtown, was well educated for that time and a fine violinist. He attended the public schools of Greenup and also Owingsville Academy. While employed by Dr. A. J. Landsdowne at the Carter County Salt Works, he met Daisy Landsdowne. They were married at the Biggs House in Portsmouth in 1861, and lived in Grayson. Later they moved to Ashland and finally to the Landsdowne farm in Carter County.

PATTERSON

Samuel Patterson was born in Londonderry, Ireland. He married Amanda Peters of Ironton, Ohio, and they came to Greenup County, where they lived on a farm at Fulton Forge

(Wurtland). Samuel Patterson was a Methodist preacher as well as a farmer.

The children of this family were Margaret, Alice, Annie, Rebecca, Josephine, Alberta, Sarah, and George.

Margaret married Henry A. Williams (see his sketch under Williams family); Alice married Samuel Livingston of Ironton and their children were Margaret, Samuel, and Hugh; the Livingston family moved to Washington, D. C., where Margaret married and still resides; Samuel and Hugh live in Cleveland, Ohio.

Annie, the third daughter of Samuel Patterson, married William McCall of Sciotoville, Ohio, and their children were William Patterson (killed in World War I), Amanda Fay, George, Louise, Frank, and Marie. Amanda Fay married Mr. Delaney and lives in Washington, D. C.; George married Edith, daughter of Warren and Julia K. Zuhars, and is deceased; Louise married Carl Smith of Portsmouth, and is deceased; Frank is deceased; Marie married Harry LeMaster of Portsmouth and lives in Wheelersburg, where Mr. LeMaster died.

Rebecca, the fourth daughter, married Alonzo Callihan and lived in Ashland; Josephine married Arthur Williams (see Williams family); Alberta married Frank Grimsley and went to California, where she and her two daughters live; Sarah never married; George, the only son of the Patterson family, married Lona Callihan, and their children are Blakely, Stanley, Carl, Alice LeMaster, Nancy Shepherd, and Georgie Price.

PATTON

William Patton came to Greenup County from Floyd County, Kentucky, and settled at Alcorn. He married Anna Archey and they were the parents of David, Leander, and Samantha, who married John Callihan (see Callihan family). David married (1) Pearl Bailey and (2) Georgia Womack. Leander married Julia Hailey of Alcorn and they lived in Greenup. Their children were Lutie, who married Robert Nickell; Una, who married Earl True of Ashland; Lula, who married Forest Neal and had a son, Forest Lee, who was a lieutenant in the army on Okinawa; and a daughter, Clara, who is unmarried.

PAYNTER

Hon. Thomas H. Paynter was born in Lewis County, Kentucky, studied law in Vanceburg, and came to Greenup to practice his profession in 1880. He was a Democrat and became so active in the party that he was elected state senator, and later United States senator. When his term of office expired he became judge of the court of appeals and lived in Frankfort. All these positions he filled with ability and honor.

He married Elizabeth, daughter of Joseph and Sarah Kouns Pollock of Greenup, and they had two children. Winifred married Morton Yonts and lived in Louisville; the son, Pollock Paynter, lived in Frankfort.

PFAFF

Joseph Pfaff and his wife came to Greenup in the late 1850's. He was a tailor and his wife worked with him at that trade. They bought Lot No. 59 on Main and Perry Streets from William C. Ireland, and here the Pfaff family lived.

Children of Joseph Pfaff were Christian, Mary, and Caroline. Christian graduated from the Portsmouth Business College and was a bookkeeper at Pine Grove Furnace in Ohio until the furnace passed out of existence. None of the children were married. All of them have died and are buried in a private mausoleum in Woodland Cemetery at Ironton, Ohio. Caroline Pfaff was the last of the family to pass away.

POGUE or POAGE

This name has been spelled both ways by the families. Robert Pogue bought land on Tygart Creek. Those who settled in northeastern Greenup County used the Poage spelling. Old court records read, "John *Poage*, sheriff in 1820-22 and Thomas H. *Poage* in 1833-35." These were of the northeastern part of the county. Also, John Poage was a justice in 1813. Colonel Annie Poage, a prominent member of the Daughters of the American Revolution in Ashland, was the daughter of Hugh Calvin and Sarah Davenport Poage. Hugh Calvin Poage was born at the Poage Settlement.

The Poage family were Scotch-Irish. Colonel George Poage was a Revolutionary War soldier. Two other members of the family were James H. and Thomas H. William, later county judge of Boyd County, was the second child born in Ashland (Ashland Poage being the first). The two ways of spelling the name may have arisen from the fact that General John Pogue or Poage married Ann Pogue, a relative.

POGUE

This Pogue family was among the early settlers of Augusta County, Virginia, who came to this country in 1740 from Great Britain and proved their importation at their own expense in order to be entitled to public lands. The head of this family was Robert Pogue, and his wife was Elizabeth. They had nine children, all of whom were born before the family came to America. One son, William, came to Kentucky.

William Pogue, born in Ireland in 1735, married Ann Kennedy Wilson in Virginia and their children were Elizabeth, Robert, Joseph, Martha, Mary, Ann, and Amaziah. This family joined Colonel Richard Callaway's train and came to Kentucky in 1775, stopping for six months at Boonesborough. The daughter, Elizabeth, was eleven years old when they came to Kentucky. In February of 1776 the family removed to Harrodsburg, being the second to arrive there, the Boone family being the first. Here the daughter, Ann, was born April 20, 1777, and she is said to have been the fourth white child born in Kentucky (Collins' *History of Kentucky*). Ann married her relative, General John Pogue, and came to Greenup County in 1802. She died there in 1847.

General Robert Pogue, son of William Pogue, married Jane Hopkins, daughter of Captain John Hopkins, a Revolutionary soldier of Rockingham County, Virginia. General Pogue was an Indian fighter and was with General Wayne's Army at the Battle of Fallen Timber in Ohio in 1794. He lived at Mays Lick in Mason County. In 1820 he bought eighty thousand acres of land on Tygart Creek and its tributaries, Three Prong, Brushy, Buffalo, Smith, and Grassy Creeks. This land extended into what is now Carter County and included Carter Caves. He paid thirteen thousand dollars for it. General Pogue deeded this land to his son, William Lindsay Pogue (1794), who sold it in small tracts to the early settlers. The first tract was sold to Peter Duzan in 1824. This was a three thousand acre tract, near the mouth of Buffalo Creek. In 1824, Eli Cooper, who had come from Orangeburg, Mason County, married Rachel, daughter of Peter Duzan, and acquired a two hundred acre tract at what is now Kehoe.

William Lindsay Pogue (or Poage) patented many acres of land in the northeastern part of Greenup County, adjoining the Charles Buford patent. He built Amanda Furnace and named it for his daughter, who was the wife of John Paull Jones. In 1826 he formed a company with William Paull, George Paull Walker, and others, to build Bellefonte Furnace. A large brick house was built on the Ohio River bank for the use of the furnace manager and his family. It had folding doors and an underground passage, where the supplies for furnace use were stored. It has been said that Confederate soldiers were cared for in this underground passage during the Civil War.

Of the William Lindsay Pogue family, Ann married Samuel Garrison and they lived in the extreme western part of the county, now the village of Garrison; John Pogue married Sarah Ann Moore; Eliza married Mr. Gartrell; Harriet Elanor married Ranson W. Cooper (see Cooper family). The Pogue home is still standing below Ashland and is owned by Dr. Kyle J. Kinkead, a surgeon in Birmingham, Alabama, who descends from the Poage or Pogue family. Much of the Poage land has been sold to the American Rolling Mill Company; other parts of it are included in the Bellefonte Subdivision and also in the property of the Ashland Country Club.

The Pogue family was the oldest of the families who settled in Greenup County and who found themselves citizens of the new county, when Boyd was separated from Greenup.

Collins' *History of Kentucky* states that the first buckets, churns, tubs, and noggins used in Kentucky were made at Boonesborough in 1775 by William Pogue. At Harrodsburg he made the first plow and the first loom. Ann, his wife, brought the first spinning wheel to Kentucky and made linen from the lint of nettles and linsey cloth from nettle lint and buffalo wool. She also made the first butter that was made at Harrodsburg. The Pogue family brought the first hogs, chickens, and ducks to Kentucky. William Pogue was killed by the Indians near Harrodsburg in 1778.

POLLOCK

Joseph Pollock was born in Washington County, Pennsylvania in 1812. He was a son of John and Ann Donohue Pollock, who were of Scotch-Irish descent. They migrated to Greenup about 1843 and Mr. Pollock became a merchant there. The earliest post office was located in his store. After the Civil War he sold his store and entered the banking business, which he continued until 1885. That same year he was one of the members who organized the Presbyterian Church in Greenup.

Joseph Pollock married Sarah, daughter of John C. and Elizabeth Smith Kouns, and they had two sons and a daughter, John Edward, Joseph, and Elizabeth. John Edward received his education in the Greenup schools, and for seven years he was clerk in the Eastern Kentucky Railroad office at Riverton. He became a partner with Milt Stevens in the hardware business in 1877 and continued in that until 1893, when he helped to organize the Farmers and Merchants Bank. In 1904 the name of the bank was changed to First National Bank. Mr. Pollock was connected with this institution until his death.

John Edward Pollock married Laura Williams Van Dyke in 1883 and they were the parents of Augustus Van Dyke and Louise. Augustus Van Dyke was also connected with the First National Bank. He married (1) Clotine McClave, daughter of Claude and Ella Hill McClave of Edgington, and they had a son, Joseph; he married (2) Winifred Paynter Lawson, daughter of John Taylor and Ella Biggs Lawson. Both are deceased. Miss Louise Pollock resides in Ashland.

The second son of Joseph and Ann Donohue Pollock, Joseph, Jr., married Alice Bates, the daughter of Horace and Fannie Goodwin Bates of Riverton. He was employed in the office of the Eastern Kentucky Railroad for some years and later moved to Cincinnati, Ohio, where they made their home. Mr. and Mrs. Pollock are deceased.

Elizabeth, the third child of Joseph and Sarah Kouns Pollock, married Thomas H. Paynter, a young lawyer (see Paynter family).

POWELL

Two Powell brothers emigrated from Scotland to the United States. One settled in Virginia and the other in New Jersey. According to an affidavit made by Daniel Boone and Simon Kenton, in the fall of 1799 Joseph Powell, born about 1762, and his wife, Nancy, came to Greenup County. He may have had a brother, Stephen, who came also.

The children of Joseph and Nancy Powell were Vincent, Abel, Benjamin, Stephen, Elizabeth, Catherine, and Samuel. Abel married (1) Lucy ———— and (2) Frances Twiman; Stephen (1797) married Margaret, daughter of Mordecai Williams; Elizabeth married Andrew Powell; Catherine married Zachariah Riggs; and Samuel married (1) Lucy Wiet Mead, daughter of Benjamin Mead, and (2) Angeline Hyden.

Vincent (1788), the eldest son of Joseph Powell, married Mary (Polly) Kelly of Union Landing, Scioto County, Ohio, in 1813. He owned eleven hundred acres of land along the Ohio River situated below the present town of Russell, where the yards of the Chesapeake and Ohio Railroad are now located. The children of this family were John D. (1814), Charles Kelly (1818), Mary Ann (1820), Luke (1821), Henrietta (1824), Elizabeth (1828), and Lucy (1829). John D. died at the age of seventeen; Charles Kelly married Elizabeth Ann Ellington and went to Missouri; Mary Ann married George W. Campbell; Luke married Sallie Sweetland; Henrietta married Adolphus L. Reid (see Reid family); Elizabeth married Henry Armistead Mead; Lucy never married.

Benjamin Powell, the third son of Joseph Powell, married Nancy, daughter of the Reverend John Young, and their children were John Milligan, James, Joseph, and America. John Milligan (1822) married Dorothy Trix, who was born in Germany in 1831. They made their home in Greenup and their children were Ellis, who died unmarried; George L., who died when a small boy; Harriet Esther, who married John Hartman of Wheelersburg, Ohio; James Alvin, who married Emma M. Weber; Benjamin, who married Nannie M., daughter of Adolphus L. Reid and his second wife, Atlanta Martin; Allie Hope, who married Robert E. L. Wilson, and whose daughter, Lucille, married Charles Bentley Bennett (see Bennett family); Nora Belle, who was the second wife of John Hartman.

PRATT

John Pratt

The first record of John Pratt in the county is that of his marriage to Eliza Bellow February 20, 1822. They lived on Tygart Creek at Liberty and their children were William Fletcher, John, James, Samuel, Cassius (Cash), and another son whose name is not known. There were six daughters in the family, three of whom were Amanda, Mary and Sarah. The names of the other three are not known.

William Fletcher married Eliza ———— and had a son, Benjamin F., who married Hannah, daughter of John and Isabel White Myers. John Pratt moved to Columbus, Ohio, and had one daughter. Nothing is known of the two brothers, James and Samuel. Cassius (Cash) Pratt never married. Amanda married Edward Brooks (see Brooks family); Mary married John Lawson Mackoy (see Mackoy family); Sarah married Benjamin Franklin Lacock (see Lacock family).

Court records in the Clerk's office show that in 1864 Benjamin F. Pratt bought a lot and building on Washington Street from George F. Hertel, and that in 1865 Benjamin F. Pratt and Thomas Brooks bought the adjoining lot and building on Washington Street from Benjamin Smith. The buildings were razed and the present building was erected and occupied for a number of years by the Pratt and Brooks General Store. In the late 1870's the Brooks family moved to Kansas and the Pratt family moved to Cincinnati, where Benjamin F. and his son, Edward, went into the commission business.

LOTT PRATT

In 1827 L. H. (Lott) Pratt bought from John Young land lying on the Little Sandy River and Indian Run in the eastern part of the county. Court records show that in May 1844 the estate of Lott Pratt was settled with Nelson Pratt, his son, as administrator. In 1848 Nelson Pratt bought a house and lot on Main Street in Greenupsburg from John Winn and lived there for a time. This house was later the home of the White family.

Nelson Pratt married Eliza, daughter of Joshua Gilmore, June 15, 1842. The family moved to a farm near Argillite before 1855. The children were Sam, John, James, Lott, Mary Jane, and Ellen. Sam lived at Argillite, where he was a farmer, and had seven children. John married Miss Lavender and their children were John, Charles, and Nora. The children of James Pratt were Lott, James, Alvin, Hatha, and Lida. They moved to Hanging Rock, Ohio. Lott, son of Nelson, never married and died in 1884 at Webster, Ohio. Mary Jane Pratt was the second wife of George Halbert (see Halbert family). Ellen Pratt (1855-1940) married James J. Taylor (see John Taylor family).

L. H. (Lott) Pratt had a daughter, Mary Ann, who married Benjamin Franklin Mead August 11, 1841 (see Mead family).

Other children of L. H. (Lott) Pratt may have been George W., Indiana (India) (see Callihan and Allen Myers families), America, and another daughter whose name is not known. George W. Pratt married Eliza ———— and lived on Perry Street in Greenup. The children of this family were Julia Godman of Wheelersburg, Ohio, Sophronia Bierly, India Vincel, Charles, Sallie, and Mary. America Pratt married William H. Ravencraft in 1843. The daughter whose name is not known married a Mr. Vincent and lived in Portsmouth. There were three daughters in the Vincent family: Florence Holmes of Cincinnati, Nellie Sweeney of East Greenup, and Henrietta, who was adopted by the Draper family of Portsmouth after her mother's death.

PRICHARD

William Prichard emigrated from Russell County, Virginia, to Greenup County, Kentucky, in 1811. His wife's name was Dorcus Glover (or Lunsford). After the death of William Prichard, Dorcus married Solomon White in Greenup County and died at the home of her son, James, in Boyd County, Kentucky. William and Dorcus Prichard were the parents of three sons, James, John, and Lewis, also a daughter, Elizabeth.

James married Elizabeth Stewart. Their children were George W. (1821), William Allen (1823), James (1825), Wylie (1827), Lewis (1829), Martha (1832), John Wesley (1834), Kenas Farrow (1836), Charles (1838), Noah (1840), Jerome T. (1842).

Of this family, George W. married Olivia Bolt and moved to Carter County; William Allen married Samantha Jones, studied to be a doctor and practiced medicine in Carter County; James died young; Wylie married Elizabeth Bolt and lived in Carter County; Lewis married Joanna Ross and moved to Indiana; Martha married Crisley P. Banfield; John Wesley married (1) Sarah Jane Mobley and (2) Susan Hulett. A son of the first marriage was John Gurney Prichard, who married Herteline Moore and lived in Greenup County. He was superintendent of schools from 1910-1914. Kenas F. Prichard married Amelia Stewart. He was a lawyer and was the first state senator of Boyd County.

Lewis (1800) was the third son of William and Dorcus Prichard. He was born in Russell County, Virginia, and came to Greenup County with his parents when he was eleven years old. He married Lucy Toler and they were the parents of twelve children. These were William, Joseph, Lewis, James, Robert H., Columbus C., Richard, Andrew Jackson, Lucinda Faulkner, Sarah Vaughn, Mary Ann (unmarried), and another who died young.

William (1827) married Caroline Newman in 1853 and they were the parents of six children; Andrew Jackson (1828) married Nancy Jane Burgess and they were the parents of six children;

Joseph married Caroline Compton and moved to Richardson County, Nebraska, at the close of the Civil War; Lewis (1839) began the study of medicine at the University of Michigan in 1865, received his degree and began practicing at Grayson, Kentucky in 1867. In 1868, he married Sarah Belle, daughter of Henry Armistead and Elizabeth Powell Mead, in Greenup County. Children of Lewis and Sarah Belle Mead Prichard were Henry Lewis (1868), Frederick Charles (1871), and Armistead Mead (1875).

In 1889, the Prichard family moved to Charleston, West Virginia, where Dr. Prichard had widespread interests.

James Prichard (1841) married Henrietta Smith of West Virginia in 1870 and lived at Prichard, West Virginia. They had no children. Robert H. (1844) married Mary Elizabeth Campbell at the home of her uncle, Henry Armistead Mead, in Greenup County, in 1873.

The Prichard families have been connected with Greenup, Carter, Lawrence, and Boyd Counties since coming to Kentucky in 1811.

PUGH

The Pugh family is of Welsh descent, tracing their ancestry back to Owen Glendower, the last independent Prince of Wales. In the 1600's three younger sons of a Squire Pugh emigrated to Virginia. Some of the family emigrated from there to North Carolina and from there to Louisiana, where the history of this branch is told in the *Plantation Parade*, by Harnett Kane.

James and Mary Kerin Fitzpatrick Pugh came from Albemarle County, Virginia, in 1816 and settled at Lynn on Tygart Creek. He built and operated tanneries there to supply the shoe industry, a promising one at the time. When the project failed, many of those engaged in it turned to farming. James Pugh bought a farm on Coal Branch, where he and his wife lived the rest of their lives. They were the parents of Samuel B., Sarah, Cassandra, James, Jr., and Elizabeth.

Samuel B. Pugh married Mary Ann Jones and became a merchant in Vanceburg. They reared a large family. Sarah married Andrew Womack of Carter County and they lived in that county. Cassandra married John Bradford and they had a son, Henry. They lived in Vanceburg. James, Jr., married Cinderella Pugh, his cousin, and they lived on the home farm. Their children were Elijah, Moses, James, and Viola. Elizabeth Pugh married

(1) Rezin Lyons (see Lyons family), (2) Cardinal Fush Stark (see Stark family).

RANKINS

Alexander and Elizabeth Saunders Rankins came from Mason County to Greenup, when the county was yet very new. The Rankins family had been very active in the early affairs of Mason County. They located on a farm lying on the bank of the Ohio River, just west of Little Sandy River. This farm is still spoken of as the Rankins farm, although it has changed owners many times since the days of that family.

Alexander and Elizabeth Saunders Rankins were the parents of Susan, Louise, Cornelia, Fannie, James, Richard, and Alexander, Jr. Susan married George Mefford, who came from Mason County, and their children were Nathan and Sarah. Louise married James P. Winters (see Winters family). Cornelia married Benjamin Ferguson and their son, William, lives in Greenup. Fannie married Thomas Carr, who operated the ferry in the 1870's, and later moved from Greenup. James married Lois Tanner, of Palmyra, and always lived in Greenup. Their children were Emmett, who went south; Kate, who went west; Nellie Jacobs; and Emma Callihan. Richard and Alexander, Jr., were never married.

When Mrs. Elizabeth Saunders Rankins died, Mr. Rankins married Mrs. Ferguson, a widow, whose children were Benjamin, John, and a daughter, who married a Mr. Ewing. In the Ewing family were Harry and Carrie. When their parents died they were reared by the Rankins family.

The old marriage records state that Benjamin Rankins and Lavinia, daughter of Moses Fuqua, were married in 1826. Benjamin may have been a brother of Alexander Rankins.

RARDIN

William J. A. Rardin was born in Pendleton County, Kentucky, in 1848, the son of Mr. and Mrs. L. J. Rardin. His father was drafted into service during the Civil War and William begged to be allowed to go in his father's place. He worked on the farm felling trees and making ties and staves, but was always hoping for further educational opportunities. Later his hopes were realized when he attended a normal school and received a certificate. He taught in the Pendleton and Campbell County,

Kentucky, schools, and meanwhile studied law. When he was twenty-six years old he was admitted to the bar at Falmouth, Kentucky. He married Miss Fannie Eads, of Pendleton County, and in 1881 the family moved to Greenup. He bought the press and fixtures of the Greenup *Gazette*, of which he was editor for many years.

Judge William Rardin was an active Republican and he was elected to represent the party in the Kentucky Legislature. He also practiced his profession, and served as county attorney for two terms and then was elected county judge. He had a record for being one of the best county judges who ever served in that capacity. He was a loyal member of the Christian Church, having been converted when still a youth. He died at his home in Greenup in 1911.

Judge and Mrs. Rardin were the parents of Mrs. Imogene Hockley, Mrs. Nano Bagby, Mrs. Pansy Fullerton, and Mrs. Willie Davenport of Covington, Kentucky. Mrs. Fullerton, who has always resided in Greenup, has a son, Hobart, who is a practicing physician in Cincinnati, Ohio.

RATCLIFF

The Ratcliff family emigrated from England to Virginia and from there they came to Greenup County, where they settled on Tygart Creek in the early 1800's. Samuel Ratcliff married (1) Emma, daughter of Peter Duzan of Upper Tygart Valley. Their children were John T., Parker, James, Betsy, Emma Amanda, and Melvina. Of these children, Parker (1827) married Nancy Ellen Walker (1835) of Siloam in 1854, and went to Ennis, Texas, in the 1870's. Their children were Maggie, who married Thomas Holcomb; Sarah, who married Charles W. Barney (see Barney family); Etta, who married Mr. Campbell; John and George, who lived at Matador, Texas. James Ratcliff married Cordelia Burtram and their children were Wesley, Samuel, Rebecca Gordon, Allen, Lizzie Abbott, Emma Webb, and Tabitha Updyke. Betsy Ratcliff married Mr. Underwood, Emma Amanda married William Warnock, and Melvina married Redmond Burtram.

Samuel Ratcliff married (2) Mary Bryson and their children were Thompson, Isaac, Ham, and Rebecca Brown. Thompson married Nancy Lyons and they lived on Mt. Ebo. Their children were James, John, Charles, Mary, Sarah, Martha, Minnie,

Maud, and Isaac. James married Malvina Barney, John married Lizzie Barney, Charles married Mollie Huffman, Mary married Peter Barney, Sarah married Walker Jackson, Martha married William Flanagan, Minnie married John Lewis, and Maud married George Gordon.

Wesley, son of James and Malvina Barney Ratcliff, married Eliza Matthews and their children were Alice Howe; Hiram, who married Nannie Lamblin; Peter; Albert; Emma Hammond; Sarah Ann Davis; and Ada Rhoden. Albert Ratcliff married Dolly Howe and they live on Tygart Creek.

Samuel Ratcliff married (3) the Widow Coleman of Lower Tygart Valley. He was high sheriff of the county in 1848 and 1849.

Another Ratcliff family was that of Charles and Polly Kouns Ratcliff who lived on Gray's Branch. Their children were Lucy Jane, wife of James Hurst; Mina, wife of Allen Fleming; William, who married Lida Hurst; and James, who married Belle, daughter of Mordecai Walker. William and James went to California.

REED

Summerfield Reed was born in Maysville, Kentucky, in 1837. He was a son of John Craig and Emily Black Reed, who had come from Virginia to Mason County, Kentucky. He studied law in Maysville and finished the course in New York City. He then came to Greenup to practice his profession but did not pursue it very long. Being a very fine penman, he did a great deal of this work for public officials and in the clerk's office while William Corum was county clerk.

In 1862 he married Elizabeth Stark and their children were Dudley, John Craig, Mary Elizabeth, Emily Black, and Daisy. John Craig joined the Army and later entered the Navy, serving on the ship "New York" in the Spanish American War. Mary Elizabeth married Dr. John, son of John and Caroline Eberhardt Hoffman of Greenup (see Hoffman family). Emily Black married William Sparks and they have always lived in Russell. Their children are Elizabeth Williams and Caroline McMillan of Russell, Daisy Arthurs of Fort Thomas, Kentucky, and Jeannette Nichols of Lexington, Kentucky.

Daisy, the third daughter of Summerfield and Elizabeth Stark Reed, was a nurse in World War I and died in Los Angeles, where she is buried in the National Cemetery.

REID

Adolphus L. Reid was the son of Darius and Ann Muir Reid, who came from Virginia and settled on a farm in Greenup County near Gray's Branch. Their son was reared on this farm and lived there with his family. He married (1) Henrietta Powell of Pond Run neighborhood and their children were Charles, Lucy, Anna, Morris, and Edward.

Charles married Mary Lavinia, daughter of John L. and Mary Pratt Mackoy, and they moved to Texas, where her father had gone to live in the 1870's; Lucy married William (Sank) Brooks of Tygart Valley and they went to Kansas; Anna married James, McMullan of Greenup; Morris married May, daughter of George and Minnie Kouns Hockaday, and they lived at Grayson; Edward married a Miss Ward of Charleston, West Virginia.

Henrietta Powell Reid died November 27, 1864, while they lived on the farm at Gray's Branch and she is buried in the Brick Union Cemetery.

Adolphus (known as A. L.) Reid married (2) Atlanta, daughter of James and Janetta White Martin of the Martin farm above Greenup. They were the parents of Nannie, Jeannette, Herbert, Emma, Julia, and Homer (Dick). Nannie married Benjamin Powell of Greenup and they moved to South Carolina; Jeannette married William Cole of Maysville, who had come to Greenup to practice his law profession; Herbert married Dolly Robb of Greenup; Emma and Julia married and went west.

Mr. Reid came to Greenup from the farm in the late 1870's and entered the mercantile business with B. F. Brown on the corner of Main and Washington Streets. He withdrew from this firm in the 1880's and opened a general store on the corner of Main and Harrison Streets. Here his sons, Charles and Morris, were active in the business with him. Mr. Reid was sheriff from 1862 to 1864 and later served as county judge.

RICHARDS

Thomas Richards was a captain in the Mexican War. He came to Greenup County from Cincinnati, Ohio, and operated a ferry in 1810, across the Little Sandy River. His wife was named Polly and they had a family of ten children. Of these Zachariah married Ruth Wills and settled on Coal Branch. They were the parents of ten children; James, Riley, Nathan, Zimri (Dick), Zachariah,

Jr., Mary Hartley (see Hartley family), Irene, Helen Burton, Kate, and Sarah R., wife of Jack Worthington.

James married Mary Gardner and they were the parents of Nancy Alexander, Helen Wakefield, Lena Morris, Ulysses, Henry Green (see his sketch following), and Byron of Washington, D. C. Nathan married Caroline Hannah and their children were Gertrude Fetters, Gene, Lola Colegrove, Lillian Covert, Winifred Terry, and Grace Adkins, Zimri (Dick) married Sarah Worthington of Greenup and they were the parents of Arthur, Alva, and Maude.

Zachariah, Jr., married Perla Colegrove and their children were Stella, Lorena McKenna of Washington, D. C., Henry, and Ross, who was killed in World War I. Stella married Orin G. Doran and they are the parents of W. C., Richard M., who married Louise McKee of Greenup, Orin G., Jr., and Helen, who married Mark Roberts and lives in Philadelphia, Pennsylvania.

Irene married William Hawkins and their children were David, Harry, Alfred, and Frank. Kate married Albert Wakefield and their children were Edna and Byron.

HENRY GREEN RICHARDS

Henry Green Richards, son of James and Mary Gardner Richards, was born September 19, 1862, on Coal Branch. He was a teacher in the county schools from 1880 to 1901. In 1898 he married Emma Brown (Brownie), daughter of Cyrus and Mary Jane Cartwright of Tongs.

In 1901 Mr. and Mrs. Richards moved to the Siloam neighborhood, where they lived near the railroad station. Here he opened a general store which he continued to operate for thirty years. The post office was located in his store and he served as postmaster.

Mr. and Mrs. Richards were active members of the Siloam Christian Church and he served as the superintendent of the Sunday school for a number of years. The children of this family are Ralph, Harold, Genevieve, and James.

Mr. Richards died in 1931 and was buried in the Siloam Cemetery. Mrs. Richards has made her home at Riverton since his death.

RIFFE

Coonrod and Emzy Hatfield Riffe settled on the Big Sandy River near Blaine in Lawrence County. Their children were

George, Elexius, Gordon, Jeff, Jerry, Gabriel, Phoebe, and John. Of these children three came to Greenup County: George, Elexius, and Gordon. Gordon was a Baptist preacher at Lost Creek. He married Rematha Smith and their children were Monroe, Victoria Huffman, Millie Ann Spence, Sarah, Armintha, and Maurice.

George Riffe (1829) married in 1850 a widow, Piety Hackworth Dixon Arthur, daughter of William and Unity Dixon, who had come to Boyd County from Campbell County, Virginia. The children of this family were Ann Virginia, Emma, Perry, Helen Florena (died in infancy), Elexius, Charles, and William Henry. George and Piety Riffe moved to Laurel Furnace, where he was a collier as long as the furnace was in operation. Late in life they made their home with their daughter, Emma Curry, at Hopewell, and died there within five days of each other. Ann Virginia (1852) married Sonny Clark and lived at Oldtown; Emma (1854) married Henry Sloan Curry of Hopewell (see Curry family); Perry (1856) married Sarah Virgin and went to Alabama; Elexius (1862) married Sallie Gibbs and lived at Hurricane, West Virginia; Charles (1864) married Amanda Downs; William Henry (1866) married Parthena Hicks of Hunnewell.

Elexius Riffe, second son of Coonrod Riffe, married Judith Arthur in 1840 and their children were William H., Orville D. (Bud), James, Elexius, Jr., Piety, Lucretia, and Molly. William H. married Nancy Curry, daughter of Hugh and Margaret Bellew Curry and their children were Thomas C., Arthur, Thames D., Willard, Hugh, Milford, Cloyd, Talmage, Carrie, and Nila. Thomas C. married Virginia Ramey and has a son, Vernal, who lives in New Boston, where he has served several years as the town mayor; Arthur married (1) Lucretia Garrett and (2) Margaret Sullivan; Thames D. married Bertha Howard of Garrison; Willard married Minnie Fritz; Hugh married Mary Cooper; Milford married Elizabeth Cooper; Cloyd married Della Cooper; Talmage married (1) Minnie Lyles, (2) Ada Fisher, has a son, Talmadge, and lives in Portsmouth; Carrie married James Jones; Nila married G. E. Sullivan and lives in Garrison, Kentucky.

Orville D. (Bud) Riffe married Arminta Curry, a sister of Nancy, the wife of William H. Riffe. Their children were Edward, who lives on East Fork in Boyd County; Laura, who married Bud Montgomery and settled on Lost Creek; Kitty, who married

(1) Luke Bellew, (2) Thomas Kouns; Orville, Jr., who married Nannie Penix and lives on Crane Creek near Hopewell; Emma, who married William Curry (see Curry family) and lives on Crane Creek near Hopewell; Beulah, who married Isaiah Riffe.

James Riffe married (1) Ellen Mead and (2) Miss Wireman; Elexius, Jr., never married; Piety married David Hamilton; Lucretia married Thomas Chinn (see Chinn family); Molly married Henry Mead (see Mead family).

ROBB

Robert Robb, Sr., and his wife (1) Sallie Sanders Robb, were residents of Lewis County, Kentucky, and their children were Francis Coburn (Cobe), Robert, Jr., Jennie, and Lutie. The Robb family came to Greenup some time before the Civil War and lived there many years.

Francis (Cobe) Robb married Georgiana Garland of Lewis County and they were the parents of Anna, Lutie, Dollie, Samuel, and Francis Trussell. Anna married Ellis Hurn and they were the parents of Garland, Donald, and Georgiana of Ironton, Ohio Lutie married John Sowards and they had a son, James, who is now judge of the Ninth District. Dollie married Herbert Reid and they had no children. Samuel married Florence Smith, sister of Bertis Smith of Greenup, and they had one child, Anna Louise. She married (1) Melville Danner and they had a son, William Robb Danner. Mr. Danner died and she later married (2) Larkin E. Covert. They reside in Portsmouth.

Samuel and Francis Trussell Robb were long time employees of the Ohio Power Company in Portsmouth. Francis Trussell is deceased and Samuel is retired. Samuel has in his possession his father's commission as a lieutenant and adjutant in the Civil War and his honorable discharge, dated January 27, 1865. He also has his own honorable discharge and that of his brother, Francis Trussell, from service in the Spanish American War, dated February 24, 1899.

Robert Robb, Jr., married Mary, daughter of Frank and Susan Calvin Brown of Greenup; Jennie married Robert Barr of Maysville; and Lutie married Thomas Myers of Greenup.

Robert Robb, Sr., married (2) Eliza Stratton of Greenup.

Joseph Robb, a half brother of Robert Robb, Sr., married Lucy Morgan of Maysville. He was a newspaper man and edited the *Grayson News* for many years. They had a daughter, Anna, who married Mr. Salyers.

Pamela Robb, sister of Joseph Robb, and a half sister of Robert Robb, Sr., married William C. Ireland and they resided on Main and Harrison Streets, where the bank is now located. Later this home was occupied by John and Mary Pratt Mackoy, who went to Texas. Judge Ireland also owned the property at the corner of Main and Harrison Streets, which he sold to Joseph Pfaff in 1867, and it was there that Mr. Pfaff had a tailor shop. Judge and Pamela Robb Ireland moved to Ashland to make their home. They were the parents of three children: Lutie Hampton, Sallie Norton, and Samuel.

ROBERSON

Kenas Roberson, born in 1860 in Wise County, Virginia, was the son of Adams and Eliza Branham Roberson. He grew to manhood there and taught school for thirty-two years in Wise, Pike, and Greenup Counties. Kenas Roberson married (1) Evelyn Fulton and they were the parents of Samuel Monroe of South Shore, Wilburn of Virginia, and Mrs. Delphia Alley of Lexington, Kentucky. He married (2) America Childers, of Pikeville, Kentucky, and their children were Mrs. Hila Fannin and Ora, of South Shore; Mrs. Goldie Meenach of South Portsmouth; Mrs. Dixie Keen and Clinton of Middletown, Ohio.

Kenas Roberson was a farmer in Greenup County after he retired from teaching.

Samuel Monroe Roberson was born and reared in Wise County, Virginia, where he taught school for four years. The Roberson family moved to Wurtland in 1905, and here Samuel Monroe bought the store of Alva Cochran, which he sold to Theodore Franz in 1909. From Wurtland the family moved to Fullerton, where Mr. Roberson operated a store for several years. Later he built the present large brick building at South Shore, where he has been in the merchandising business since that time. He has been a merchant of Greenup County for forty-five years.

Samuel Monroe Roberson married Ida Belcher and they are the parents of Pearl Setser of Cincinnati; Beatrice, the wife of Cisco Alexander of South Shore; Violet, wife of Harold McCann of Portsmouth; James and Myrtle, deceased.

A brother of Kenas Roberson, J. P. Roberson, is a resident of Worthington, Kentucky.

ROE

The Roe family came from Virginia to Greenup County and settled on Tygart Creek. Two sons, George and Robert, came to Greenup. George opened a tailor shop and studied law on the side. He later began to practice law and became prominent in his profession. He married Ursula, daughter of Benjamin and Priscilla Stevenson Howland, of Tygart Valley. The children of this family were Mary Doty of Cincinnati, Benjamin (Bud), Nancy Wilson, and Alice, who never married.

Benjamin (Bud) married Agnes Barklow of Portsmouth, Ohio. He was far advanced in his chosen profession of law and had built a nice home when he was stricken with a fever and died in early manhood.

Robert Roe was a carpenter. He married twice, his first wife being Lydia Bradford of Lynn, and his second being her sister, Eliza. There were three daughters, Lola, Lucy, and Nannie. Lola married Alvin Morton (see Morton family).

Lucy Roe married Frank Beaty of Ironton and they moved to Paducah, Kentucky, where he was engaged in river work until his death. Since that time Mrs. Beaty has made her home with her daughter, Mrs. Maude Waldman, of Nashville, Tennessee.

Nannie Roe married Charles Bishop and they lived in Greenup. Their children were Robert, who died when a young man, and Billy, who is married and lives in Ashland.

ROLLINS or RAWLINGS

The Rollins or Rawlings family was among the early settlers (about 1800) near what is now Wurtland. They were farmers and owned slaves, and descendants of those slaves are still living at Wurtland.

Among the old marriage records is that of Joshua Rollins and Hannah Van Bibber, who were married in 1816; Samuel Rawlings and Harriet Powell, who were married in 1830; Jacob Lawson and Elizabeth Rawlings, daughter of Joshua Rawlings, who were married in 1838.

A Negress, whose father and mother were born before the Civil War, said that her father was named Rollins and her mother Manda Biggs. They lived at Wurtland.

RUCKER

The Rucker family was in the county before its organization. Reuben Rucker was sheriff in 1806-1809 and Ambrose Rucker was deputy. Marriage licenses were issued to Ephraim Rucker and Polly Deatly, Reuben Rucker and Mary J. Rucker (cousins), Anny Rucker and George Willis, and to Peggy Rucker and James Kite, all in 1808. The parents were Milton and Anna Rucker.

The Rucker family became residents of Carter County in 1838.

RUSSELL

John Russell was born in Pennsylvania and came to Greenup County from Virginia in the middle 1840's. He was on his way to join the California Gold Rush when he received word at Kansas City, from a member of the Means family, to come to work for them. Returning to Greenup, he went to work at Amanda Furnace and did his work so well that he was offered a partnership in the Bellefont Furnace. The company became known as the Means and Russell Iron Works.

In 1857 Mr. Russell married Ann, daughter of Henry A. Mead. As the years passed he prospered in his many undertakings and acquired a great deal of property. The important town of Russell is named for him.

The given name of John has been handed down through the Russell family of Ashland for many years.

SAVAGE

The Savage family came from Virginia to Greenup County early in 1800. In early marriage records of the county appear the names of Jane Savage and Woodrow Smith, married in 1819; also of Ann Savage and Pleasant Norton, married in 1822.

Joseph Savage married Virginia Walker, daughter of George Paull and Helen Marr Nichols Walker, and they lived at Wurtland. James Savage married Lavinia Fuqua Mackoy, daughter of John and Lavinia Fuqua Mackoy. They came into possession of a farm which had been a part of the Moses Fuqua tract at Mt. Zion. Pleasant Savage, probably a son, owned the farm and he sold it to William Biggs, Sr., in 1848.

In 1772 John Savage and Charles Smith received a military grant of more than twenty-eight thousand acres of land from the State of Virginia. This was located in the extreme northeastern section of Kentucky, embracing the present town of Catlettsburg. The heirs who inherited this land sold it, and, after much litigation, Alexander Catlett received a deed under the John Savage grant and settled there.

SCHMUTZ

John Schmutz came from Germany to Portsmouth, Ohio. From there he and his wife came to Greenup and bought the land on Perry Street adjoining the Pollock land. (It may have been a part of the Pollock land.) They made their home here, which is near the Little Sandy River, and had two daughters, Eliza and Joanna. Mrs. Schmutz died and John Schmutz married Caroline Schmidt of Portsmouth, Ohio, who had come from Germany also. They were the parents of Charles, Elizabeth (who died in young womanhood), and Mary. Mr. Schmutz kept a tavern at the corner of Washington and Elizabeth Streets. He bought the brick home on Main Street and Cedar Alley from Dr. Samuel Ellis, and the family lived there many years.

Eliza married John Mock of Boyd County and some of the family live in Ashland; Joanna married John Hellinger, of Buffalo, New York; Charles married Anna Brown, daughter of Frank and Susan Calvin Brown, of Main Street, Greenup. Miss Mary Schmutz lives in Ashland with her relatives of the Mock family.

SCOTT

Captain Thomas A. Scott was one of the earliest settlers in what was Greenup County, now Carter. He owned a great deal of land between Greenupsburg and Grayson and built the first brick house within the present limits of Carter County.

A son, Robert, moved from Carter County to Ironton, Ohio, and became connected with Mt. Vernon Furnace in Lawrence County. He bought Laurel Furnace in Greenup County in the 1860's. His son, Thomas, was made resident manager, and members of the Scott family were frequent visitors there and at Oldtown and Greenup. Other members of the family besides Thomas were Fannie, Nannie, Jennie, Nora, Rozzie and Harry.

Fannie married a Mr. Spears. They lived in Greenup and a daughter, Kitty, attended the Greenup Academy. Nannie, while on a visit to Chicago, met Marshall Field, a young man engaged in the mercantile business there. He visited the Scott home and he and Nannie became engaged to be married. On the eve of the wedding a tragedy occurred in the home, when Jennie was fatally burned by the explosion of an oil lamp from a chandelier. The wedding was postponed for a time.

Marshall and Nannie Scott Field lived in grand style in Chicago, and many tales came to the old home of lavish entertainments in the Field home. They had two children, Marshall,

Jr., and Ethel. Ethel married Lord Beatty of England. Marshall, Jr., married Albertine Huck of Chicago and went to England, living on an estate adjoining that of Lord and Lady Beatty. Marshall and Albertine Huck Field had a son, Marshall III.

Nannie Scott Field, while traveling abroad, died at Nice, France. Her son, Marshall, Jr., died in New York in 1906. Marshall Field, Sr., died in 1905. Marshall Field III and IV are living in Chicago. Marshall IV is actively connected with the *Sun* and *Times* Company in Chicago.

The Scott family moved from Ironton after selling Laurel Furnace to the Kelly family of Ironton.

SEATON

Samuel Seaton, born in Amherst, New Hampshire, son of John and Elizabeth Kendall Seaton, married Hannah Eddy and they came to Greenup about 1815. He founded the school which was known as Seaton Academy. When his father, John Seaton, died in Amherst, his mother, Elizabeth Kendall Seaton, came to Greenup to live with her son, Samuel. Several years after coming to Greenup Mr. Seaton built a brick house on Water Street and kept a dry goods store in the front room. In 1838 he built New Hampshire Furnace in the western part of the county. Later he bought a farm lying on Little Sandy River in the rear of town, and also another farm in the rear of East Greenup, which has always been the home of the John Seaton family.

Samuel and Hannah Eddy Seaton were the parents of Samuel, Jr., John, Rebecca, and Mary. Samuel, Jr., went to Texas in the 1870's. John married Mary Elizabeth, daughter of Jehu and Elizabeth Biggs Rice, and they were the parents of Elizabeth Secrest of central Kentucky; Rebecca, wife of Edwin Hockaday, who moved to Missouri; William Biggs and Edward Everett of Ashland; Mollie; Dora; and Samuel III. William Biggs Seaton married Isabella Means and they were the parents of Hilda Peebles, Isabella Humphreys, and John Means of Ashland, and Kendall of Bellefonte. Kendall married Grace Mary Watson and their children are Mary Isabel Holt of Versailles, Kentucky, and Nancy Raim of Chicago, Illinois. Edward Everett Seaton married Rebecca Todd of New York and they make their home in Ashland. Miss Dora Seaton lives on the home farm, but not in the original house, which burned some years ago.

Rebecca Seaton, the eldest daughter of Samuel and Hannah Eddy Seaton, married Dr. Alfred Spalding of Amherst, New Hampshire (see Dr. Alfred Spalding family).

DR. AMBROSE SEATON

Dr. Ambrose and Mary Rand Seaton came from Boston, Massachusetts, to Maysville, where he practiced medicine and was partner in a drug store. They were born in Amherst, New Hampshire. A daughter, Helen Augusta, was born in Boston but grew up in Maysville and came to Greenup to teach a select school in 1857. There she met Dr. Alfred DeBard and they were married (see DeBard family).

Mary Elizabeth, another daughter of Dr. Ambrose Seaton, came to Greenup to live with her sister's family, the DeBards, in 1860. She was an accomplished musician and had the first piano in Greenup. She taught the Spalding and DeBard children and gave music lessons at the home on Front Street.

Dr. Ambrose Seaton was quite a musician and was organist in the Old Stone Church in Boston. He died in Greenup in 1863.

A brother of Samuel and Dr. Ambrose Seaton was Nathan, who lived on the corner of Main and Cedar Streets in what is known as the old Dr. Ellis and Schmutz home. It is where the county school superintendent's office is now located.

SELLARDS

Hezekiah Sellards, a Scotch-Irish Presbyterian, migrated to Pennsylvania about 1732. He continued southward to the Shenandoah Valley of Virginia and settled in Augusta County some time before 1750. His children were Jennie, Elizabeth, John, and Samuel. From Augusta County they followed the New River into southwest Virginia and on into the Big Sandy Valley of Kentucky, where the Jennie Sellards Wiley Indian Captivity was a much-told story for a century or more (Ref. *The Sellards Through Two Centuries*, p. 41).

The Greenup County Sellards family descends from Andrew Jackson Sellards (1806), the third son of John and the grandson of Hezekiah Sellards. In his teens, or about 1820, he left his father's home on Buffalo Creek in Floyd County, Kentucky, and came sixty miles to Greenup County, where he found employment on the farm of John Hartley. In 1830 he married Mary Elizabeth Hartley and they established their home one mile from Oldtown, later moving to Carter County. The death of

Andrew Jackson Sellards in 1859 left to his widow the responsibility of rearing the large family of children, eight sons and three daughters, all of whom, under her wise guidance, became honored and useful citizens. Six sons fought in the Civil War and four of them became practicing physicians, while three became farmers in Lewis and Carter Counties.

Sarah Elizabeth Sellards (1831-1911) married John Henry Lewis and they lived on Tygart Creek; Mary Elizabeth (1840-1890) married Ezra Antis and her descendants live in Oklahoma; Clara May (1856-1914) married Allen Fields Kitchen.

Dr. John Thomas Sellards (1830-1882) married Mary Elizabeth Woodrow of Carter County. He practiced in Powellsville, Ohio, and it is said that in those days he wore a stove pipe hat, and a fresh white linen suit each day, and drove coal black horses with a Negro driver. Of his six children, Andrew Jackson William Sellards became a doctor and practiced in Greenup, succeeding his uncle, Abram Goble Sellards. His career was cut short by his death at the age of thirty-three. The children of this family were Clotine, who married John Peddicord; John Armstrong, deceased; and William Heine, who married Hannah Harris and lives in California. Two other sons of Dr. John Thomas Sellards, George and Thomas, both became doctors. Dr. George married Laura ———— and they had no children; Dr. Thomas married Dr. Dorothy Davis and their children are George Davis, who lives in Ann Arbor, Michigan, and Paul. The only daughter of Dr. John Thomas Sellards, Lucy Lilly (1864-1940), married Charles Fremont Taylor (see John Taylor family). She was born in Powellsville and came to Greenup at the age of six. Two other children died.

Abram Goble Sellards (1838-1921) married Theresa Woodrow of Carter County. He taught school for two years and, following the Civil War, he served as deputy clerk of Greenup County for two years. He was graduated in medicine in 1868 and practiced with his older brother, John, in Powellsville, Ohio, until 1872, when he located in Greenup. In 1893 he moved to Portsmouth. His eldest son, Dr. Howard Conger Sellards (1866), who married Bertha Lee Welker, lived in Portsmouth, and their son, Abram Goble Sellards, is a physician in Joliet, Illinois. Other children of Dr. Abram Goble Sellards were Margaret Forsythe; Dr. Ernest Moxley Sellards, who married Nannie Warnock and lived in Ashland; Bessie E.; and William, a druggist, who married Grace McAfee and lived in Portsmouth.

As it was the custom of the time for a young doctor to connect himself with some older and experienced doctor, two younger brothers, Archibald and Andrew Watson Sellards, also began their practice of medicine with their older brother, John Thomas, at Powellsville. Later Dr. Archibald Sellards practiced four years at Hunnewell Iron Furnace. He married Barbara Miller of Powellsville, and Dr. Andrew Watson Sellards married Martha Elizabeth, daughter of John Taylor Lawson of Gray's Branch. Both of these families and that of another brother, Wiley William Sellards (1834-1888), who married Sarah Minix and was a farmer in Carter County, went to Scranton, Kansas, in the early 1880's. Their descendants still live there.

The name Abram Goble, which appears in several generations, came from Mary Elizabeth Hartley Sellards' mother, Sarah Goble, who was the granddaughter of Abraham Goble, a Revolutionary soldier in Virginia.

The Sellards were pioneers in the settlement of the United States and have crossed the continent from east to west and from north to south during their five generations in America.

SMITH

ELMER SMITH

The Elmer Smith family lived at Plum Grove, where Mr. Smith was a farmer. The children of this family were John, George, Elmer, Jr., Polly Womack, Elizabeth West, and Tennessee Hike. Of these, John married (1) Anna Callihan of Plum Grove and their children were Bertice H., Florence, and William E., the last a resident of Washington, D. C. He married (2) Belle, daughter of John Crawford of Riverton, and they had two sons, Earl and Le Roy, both of Greenup. Mr. Smith had a store at Riverton and at Greenup. He was assisted, and later succeeded, by his son, Bertice H. Smith.

Bertice H. Smith married Frances, daughter of Wilbur and Mary Walton Waring Tinsley of Lynn. They are the parents of two sons, Bertice, Jr., and Dr. Vernon Smith, who is practicing his profession in Cincinnati, Ohio. Mr. Smith is deceased.

Florence Smith married Samuel Robb and they make their home in Portsmouth (see Robb family).

GODFREY SMITH

Godfrey Smith was born near Redstone, Pennsylvania, in 1752. He enlisted in the Patriot Army of Virginia, commanded by Colonel Buford, in 1779. In 1780 he reenlisted and was in the Battles of Camden and Eutaw Springs, South Carolina. He served five years altogether in the Continental Army. After the war he married Margaret Hoover of Pennsylvania and they had six sons and three daughters. Jacob, the eldest son, was born in 1785.

In 1810 the family moved to Greenup, coming down the Ohio River in flat boats. He settled on a branch below Greenup and both the settlement and branch took his name. In 1819 he received a pension for his services in the Virginia Army, and died in 1847.

Jacob, the eldest son, married Elizabeth Gray of Greenup County, in 1824. Cynthia married James Littlejohn of Tygart Valley. Another son, Benjamin, of Greenup, operated the Little Sandy Ferry in the early days. Sarah, daughter of Benjamin Smith, married Frank York and they had three children: Charles, who went to Colorado; Sallie, who was a teacher in Greenup for many years; and Belle, who married William Cochran of Ohio.

MARTIN SMITH

Martin Smith brought his family from Prince Edward County, Virginia, and settled near the present site of Wurtland, about 1800. He was wealthy in money, land, and slaves, owning more slaves than anyone else in the county. His wife, Nancy Price, was a first cousin, and she inherited from her father, Pugh Price, one thousand acres of land across the river from Greenup and above Haverhill, Ohio. Martin Smith's will, recorded in the Greenup County Court Records, bears the date of August 21, 1822. He names seven children and appoints his son, Creed, and his friends, John Hockaday, St. Levan L. Shreve, and John McConnell, as his executors. He is buried in a cemetery on the point of the hill at Wurtland across from the old John McConnell home.

The children of Martin and Nancy Price Smith were Robert, William Woodson, Nancy, Betsy, Creed, Samuel, and John.

William Woodson married Polly Ward, daughter of Jeremiah and Polly Fuqua Ward; Nancy married William Ward, son of James Ward; Betsy married John C. Kouns (see Kouns family); Creed married Elizabeth (Ward) Barnes, a widow; Samuel married Betsy Walker; and John married Elizabeth Rankin.

Three sons, William Woodson, John, and Samuel, owned farms which later were known as the Volney Thomson, Peter

Walker, and Robert Johnson farms, and also the land from there down to Mt. Zion. They sold this land and went west to Missouri. Little is known of the other children except Robert Smith, a number of whose descendants have long been residents of the county.

Robert Smith, the eldest son of Martin Smith, married Agnes Moorman in Prince Edward County, Virginia, before coming to Greenup County. He lived on a farm given to him by his father which is now known as the McClave farm, and owned land down as far as Limeville. Nancy Smith, his mother, may have died at his home, because she is buried in a little graveyard on the McClave farm, located across the railroad. Several slaves are also buried in this graveyard.

The seven children of Robert Smith were Charles Moorman, Beverly, Frederick, Eliza, Martha, Elizabeth, and Mary. Charles Moorman married Mary Ann Ratcliff; Beverly married (1) Hetty Priest and (2) Matilda ———; Frederick married Permelia ———; Eliza married William Davis of Illinois; Martha married John Lampton of Frankfort, Kentucky; Elizabeth married Scott Guilkey; and Mary married Alson Post of Winchester, Kentucky. Elizabeth and Scott Guilkey spent their last days at the home of their niece, Mrs. Amos Hill, of Gray's Branch. They are buried in the Brick Union Cemetery.

Charles Moorman Smith, born 1810, married Mary Ann Ratcliff in 1835. She was the daughter of William Ratcliff, a Methodist preacher, who was born in Baltimore, Maryland. His wife, Mary Fenton Smith, was of Pennsylvania Dutch parentage. The Ratcliff family had come to Mason County, Kentucky, in 1795. Charles Moorman and Mary Ann Ratcliff were the parents of Robert H.; John Lampton; Martha, who married Harvey Hodges (see Hodges family); Malinda L., who married Alexander Bruce; Sarah Elizabeth, who married Amos Hill (see Hill family); Charles A., who married Virginia Morton, daughter of Richard and Martha Garrett Morton; Louisa, who died in infancy (a twin of Charles A.); William Beverly, who married Harriet Everman; and two other children who died in infancy.

Charles A. and Virginia Morton Smith had two daughters, Agnes and Etta. Both taught school in the county and Etta was one of the county school examiners for eighteen years. She was the first wife of the Rev. Edward T. Waring (see Waring family).

260

SOWARDS

James M. and Anna Weddington Sowards came from Pikeville, Kentucky, to Greenup in 1878. Mr. Sowards was a merchant and built a brick building at the corner of Main and Washington Streets. He also built a dwelling just below the store. This store burned in the early 1880's and the property was sold to James Watt and John T. Womack, who rebuilt the building and conducted a general store there for almost sixty years.

In the late 1880's Mr. Sowards and the Wilsons built a flour mill on Railroad Street. Selling out his interest to the Wilsons, Mr. Sowards built a second mill on Railroad Street, which was later sold to Robert Wilson. He built a brick office building and house on Main and Washington Streets and started a bank. He sold this building to Dr. Henry Morris and went to San Francisco, California, where he was murdered. Mr. and Mrs. Sowards were the parents of two sons, William and Dr. John.

William Sowards married Frances Wilson and they were the parents of Idalaine Sterrett, Garnet Thompson, and Hugh, who married and lives in Hartford, Connecticut. Dr. John Sowards married (1) Lutie, daughter of Cobe and Georgiana Garland Robb, and they were the parents of James Sowards, who married Rebecca, daughter of Alvin and Lola Roe Morton.

James and Rebecca Morton Sowards' children are Patricia, and James, Jr., who was killed in World War II in Bastogne, Belgium.

Dr. John Sowards married (2) Grace, daughter of James and Margaret Warnock of Greenup.

SPALDING
Dr. Alfred Spalding

Much of the following material was taken from *Glimpses of a Doctor's Life in Kentucky*, which was written by Rebecca Wentworth Spalding, a daughter of Dr. Alfred Spalding. He was born in Amherst, New Hampshire, in 1815, the son of Dr. Matthias Spalding, and came to Cincinnati to attend medical school. While there he came to Greenupsburg to visit the Seaton family, who had been old friends of the Spalding family in Amherst, New Hampshire, before they came to Kentucky.

After finishing his medical course in Cincinnati he attended Dartmouth College in New Hampshire. He received his M. D. degree in 1843. He came to Greenupsburg to practice his profession and married Rebecca, daughter of Samuel and Hannah Eddy Seaton. They were the parents of Dr. George, Dr. Alfred, Jr., Helen, Rebecca, and Samuel.

From a letter, found in an old scrapbook, and written by Dr. Spalding to his son, George, who was away from home attending school, extracts are taken: "To-day I have had a hard ride on horse back (for that is the only way we could get about now) through mud nearly up to the horse's knees." He also advises his son, "Know no such word as fail."

Alfred, Jr., added a letter to his brother, George, telling him "that the track of the new railroad (Eastern Kentucky) was laid beyond Mr. Hockaday's, and that a fine locomotive had steam up but not enough to run her."

Dr. Spalding owned the Seaton farm in the rear of Greenup. He was a lover of horses and had a large stable and race track where the horses were exercised. He was a very popular and conscientious doctor, serving wherever he was needed—fording the river when it was low, or crossing in a skiff when it was full of drifting ice, to reach his patients in Ohio. Having practiced medicine in Greenup and surrounding territory, including Ohio, for thirty-four years, Dr. Spalding died at his home in Greenup in 1878. The family moved to New York, where the sons were already located. Mrs. Spalding died there in 1896.

Dr. George and Dr. Alfred Spalding were physicians in New York City. The youngest son, Samuel, married in New York, where he was a business man. Later he moved to Asheville, North Carolina, where he now resides, as does his sister, Rebecca Wentworth Spalding. She has written several books which tell of happenings in the early days of Greenup.

One of Miss Spalding's books, *Butterstamps and a Silver Snuffbox*, relates the story of a journey made by her grandfather, Samuel Seaton, his wife, and their two small children, John and Rebecca, from Greenupsburg to the old Seaton home at Amherst, New Hampshire.

William Biggs and Samuel Seaton were "Merchants and Masters" of a flatboat loaded with wheat, potatoes, apples, peach and apple brandy, leather, castings made in the iron foundries, and other products of the county, bound for New Orleans. The Seaton family made the trip on the flatboat down the Ohio and Mississippi Rivers and at New Orleans they took passage on a sailing vessel to Boston. From there they went by stage coach fifty miles to Amherst, New Hampshire. An interesting item is the fact that little Rebecca learned to walk on the sailing vessel, but she soon found the rolling gait of a sailor was not adapted to the streets of Boston, so had to learn to walk all over again.

STARK

The Stark family descended from Jon Stark of Dunbarton, Scotland, who emigrated to New Hampshire in 1720 and settled at Dunbarton, New Hampshire. He brought his son, James, aged fifteen years, with him; and later the oldest son, Archibald, who had married Eleanor Nichols of Londonderry, Ireland, came to New Hampshire. Archibald and Eleanor Nichols Stark were the parents of General John Stark of Revolutionary fame.

James Stark, who had come to Dunbarton, New Hampshire, with his father, married Elizabeth Thornton, a sister of Matthew Thornton, a signer of the Declaration of Independence. James and Elizabeth Thornton Stark moved to Stafford County, Virginia, with their eight children, and seven more were born to them in Virginia. Their eldest son, John, married Hanson Porter and they were the parents of three daughters and a son, William, who was born in 1754. Hanson Porter Stark died and John married a second time, but it was through William (1754), a son by the first marriage, that the Greenup County Stark family has descended.

James Barton, son of William and Nancy Million Stark, came from Culpeper County, Virginia, to Greenup County in 1816, and settled at Oldtown on a farm where some members of the family have lived to the present time. The children of James Barton and Nancy Million Stark were Henry, Jeremiah, William, Mary, and Cardinal Fush. Henry married Adelaide Howe of Oldtown and they were the parents of Louise, who married David Downs; Kate, who married Harvey Virgin; Nora, who married Joshua Kelly (see Kelly family); Nina, who married Amos Hartley; and James, who married Martha Jacobs of Greenup. David and Louise Downs were the parents of Bertis of West Virginia and Adelaide of Greenup. The children of Harvey and Kate Virgin were Roscoe of Florida, Edward of Ashland, and Nora Meadows, who lives on the home farm at Oldtown.

James and Martha Jacobs Stark were the parents of Henry of Ceredo, West Virginia, and Nina Warnock of Ashland.

Jeremiah married Elizabeth Ann Kouns and among their children were Jerry, Fush, and Nancy Campbell. Mark Campbell of Riverton was of this family. William Stark married Elizabeth Wigglesworth and lived at Oldtown. Mary Stark married Gabriel Anglin of Hopewell (see Anglin family). Cardinal Fush Stark married Elizabeth Lyons of Oldtown and their children were Nancy Hall Ferry, Elizabeth Reed, and Frances Belle, who married Shadrach Mitchell of Greenup (see Mitchell family).

STEPHENSON

Robert J. Stephenson was born in southwestern Virginia. He came to Greenup County, where he married Mildred Thompson, who was a native of Kentucky. They moved to Springville (South Portsmouth), Kentucky. Children of the family were: Dr. John of Ashland, Kentucky; Elmer, a prominent lawyer of Pikeville, Kentucky; and Clayton of Springville, who married Ada McQuesten of Montgomery, Alabama, and has two daughters. Clayton served seventeen years in the U. S. Navy; Emma and Ethel were unmarried; and Pauline married Renn Austin and lives at South Portsmouth.

STEVENS

The Stevens family came to Greenup about 1864, probably from West Virginia. The family consisted of the parents, Sanford and Ann Pollock Stevens, a son, Milton, and a daughter, Belle.

Milton Stevens, or Milt, as he was known to everyone, was born in Ohio County, West Virginia, in 1843. He served as postmaster in 1866 and again in 1883. He was a partner with John Edward Pollock in a hardware store for several years, and in 1888 he established a general store in Greenup. He was also a bookkeeper at the Star Furnace during the middle 1880's. His wife was Georgiana Kibby of Carter County, Kentucky, and they were the parents of four children, all of whom died in infancy.

After the death of the parents, Milt and his sister, Belle, ran the newly-built Columbia Hotel, which they continued to operate for several years. Milt Stevens never remarried and Belle never married, so this family has passed out of existence in Greenup.

STOCKHAM

William Stockham was born in Wales in 1752. He emigrated to New Jersey, in 1767, and settled at Trenton. He married Susan

Payne, a niece of Thomas Payne, the Revolutionary patriot. They moved to Pennsylvania and from there to Kentucky about 1787. They settled in what is now Greenup County, at the mouth of Tygart Creek. In 1798, they moved across the Ohio River to Lawson Run and, in 1803, went to Madison Township in Scioto County.

When William Stockham came from Trenton, he brought a clock seven and one-half feet high, which has been in the family since then.

Rebecca, a daughter of Joseph, and a granddaughter of William Stockham, was born in 1812. In 1833 she married Smith F. Hitchcock. They moved to Mt. Zion, Greenup County, in 1833. They were the parents of ten children (see Hitchcock and Lawson families).

Russell and Vesta Stockham of Portsmouth, Ohio, are descendants of William and Susan Payne Stockham

STUART

The Stuart family came from Berthshire, Scotland, and settled near Wytheville, Virginia. From there they migrated to the Big Sandy Valley and settled in Lawrence County, Kentucky. Mitchell Stuart migrated to Greenup County in 1896 and settled in the Plum Grove Community near Greenup. Mitchell Stuart, Jr., was born in Lawrence County and was sixteen years of age when the family moved to Plum Grove. His father later returned to Lawrence County, where he died.

Mitchell Stuart, Jr., married Martha, daughter of Nathan Hilton, of English descent, and he came from Carter County to Greenup about 1900. He bought a farm near McIntire Tunnel, and he also owned a farm near Puthoff Ford on Little Sandy River.

Mitchell and Martha Hilton Stuart were the parents of Sophia, Jesse, Herbert, Mary, James, Martin, and Glennis. Herbert and Martin died young. The parents had very few educational advantages, but Jesse, James, and Glennis finished college; Sophia finished high school, and had some college work. She, James, and Glennis are teaching at present. James began writing, but has given it up in favor of an educational career.

Jesse Stuart attended the Greenup County schools and finished his education at Vanderbilt University, Nashville, Tennessee. He has been a teacher, county school superintendent, principal of McKell High School, and principal of the Greenup High School.

He won a Guggenheim Foundation Award and was given a year's travel in European countries. From there he wrote many interesting letters of places he visited, notably the birthplaces, homes and tombs of famous English and Scotch poets and authors.

Greenup County had never been noted for its poets or authors until 1930, when Jesse Stuart's poems and stories began to be published in leading magazines of the country. Since then he has had several books published and the fame of his writings will be carried on into the future not only of the county but of the nation.

Jesse Stuart married Naomi Deane, daughter of Emmett and Myrtle Spence Norris, in 1939, and they have a daughter, Jessica Jane. Their home is in W Hollow not far from Greenup.

SWEARINGEN

The Swearingen family descends from Gerret van Sweringen, born in 1636 in Beemsterdam, Holland, the younger son of a family belonging to the nobility. As a young man he came to America in 1656 in the service of the Dutch West India Company, being in charge of the ship "Prince Maurice," which brought immigrants, supplies, and sixty soldiers to the Dutch Colony on the Delaware River at Amstel (now New Castle, Delaware).

In the colony Gerret van Sweringen married Barbarah de Barrette (1659), born in Vallenciennes, France. He was sheriff and held other high offices in the Dutch Colony, but after it was taken by the British the van Sweringen family moved to Saint Mary's, Maryland. In Maryland Gerret van Sweringen was active in public affairs as he had been in the Dutch Colony. The grandsons of this family moved west to Montgomery and Somerset Counties in Maryland, and also to Beaver County, Pennsylvania.

The first Sweringen of the name born in America was Thomas, born about 1665 at Saint Mary's, Maryland. His grandson, Van, born in Maryland, emigrated to Greenbrier County, Virginia, and later settled in Bath County, Virginia. Van's son, Leonard, born January 10, 1765, was the first of the name in Greenup County, where the spelling of the name became changed to Swearingen in later years.

Leonard Swearingen (1765-1842) married Mary Cole (1770-1842), moved to Greenup County soon after 1793 and lived near the present location of Argillite. Their children were William

Rufus (1788), Lucy (1793), Van (1795), Clement (1805), Samuel (1806), John (1807), and Jane (1813).

Clement Swearingen married Nancy Prichard and lived on Pond Run. Their children were William Rufus (1835-1903), Willis (1839), Clement and Nancy Henrietta (twins) (1844), James, Ella, and Elizabeth. Clement died after 1894 and is buried in a cemetery on the high hill at Argillite.

William Rufus Swearingen married Vashti Fitch, born 1840 at Gallia Furnace. Her parents died when she was five and she was reared with her brothers by an uncle, George Davidson, on East Fork. This Swearingen family lived in Greenup and the children were Robert Fulton, William Rufus, Jr., Laura Ellen, John Hoffman, and James, who died in infancy.

Robert Fulton Swearngin, age ninety-one, lives in Ashland. His wife was Nancy Williams and their children are Sallie Bierley and Lora McCoy, who live with their father; Albert, who married Pearl Dixon, lives in Portsmouth, and has two children, Helen and Ralph; Clyde, who married Georgia Patrick and lives in Ashland; Robert Kenneth, who lives in Canton, Ohio.

William Rufus, Jr., (1866-1900) married Barbara Kaut of Greenup County.

Laura Ellen (1862-1928) married Kelley Clark and their children are Roscoe, William, Edward, James, Walter, Vashti, John, George, Martha, and Clyde, all living at Flat Woods in Greenup County.

John Hoffman Swearngin (1870-1949) married Rletische Moore (1871-1947) of Tygart Valley and they lived in Greenup until 1906, when they moved to Portsmouth where they spent the remainder of their lives. The children of this family are Bessie, who married Charles Hall Fisher (now deceased) and has two sons, Charles Hall, Jr., and John Edwin; Carrie, who married Edwin W. Bowsman (now deceased), lives in Columbus, Ohio. She has two daughters, Margaret Diane Lilly, who lives in Brookline, Massachusetts, and Jacqueline Jane Owen of Columbus. A third daughter of John Hoffman Swearngin, Mabel (now deceased), married John Kayser of Portsmouth.

Willis Swearngin, the second son of Clement Swearngin, married Sarah Fitch, sister of Vashti, and they moved to Fort Worth, Texas. His daughter, Annie Wright, lives in Fort Worth and has two daughters, Helen Childers and Mrs. Ray Crowder.

Clement Swearngin, the third son, married (1) Ellen Mackintire, (2) Elsie Ellington; Nancy Henrietta Swearngin married

John Henry Nicholls (see Nicholls family); James Swearngin, the fourth son, married Lizzie Wells; Ella Swearngin married John D. Savage and moved first to Missouri, then to Oklahoma, and finally to Kansas; Elizabeth Swearngin married Charles Callihan (see Callihan family).

TANNER

The following family history was contributed by Rhoda Van Bibber Tanner Doubleday of New York City.

"Jacob Tanner, born April 21, 1774, in England, married, March 8, 1798, Lydia Passmore, in Chester County, Pennsylvania. He died in Chester County, Pennsylvania, September 23, 1805, where he is buried. His only child was John Passmore Tanner, born August 20, 1800, in Chester County, Pennsylvania, and was taken on visits to his uncle in Kentucky. May 11, 1830, he married Rhoda Van Bibber, born 1808 and died March 7, 1881, all in Greenup County. John Passmore Tanner died and was buried in the old Van Bibber-Tanner family cemetery, March 21, 1881. This Rhoda Van Bibber was named for her Aunt Rhoda Van Bibber, daughter of Captain John Van Bibber, who married Chloe Staniford, born in Cecil County, Maryland, in 1760 (see Van Bibber family). This was the Rhoda Van Bibber, born in 1768, who was killed by the Indians, and not my grandmother.

"My father, John James, son of John Passmore Tanner and Rhoda Van Bibber, was born on October 3, 1842, at his father's place near Greenup and died in New York on August 12, 1900. He married my mother, Emma Offutt Bunch, in Louisville, Kentucky, on February 21, 1876. Their home was on the corner of St. Charles Avenue and Webster Street, in New Orleans, Louisiana. My father was first buried at Greenup, Kentucky, and, following my mother's wishes, was removed to the family plot in Henderson, Kentucky, in 1936, which had been provided by her great-grandfather, Major General Samuel Hopkins, A.D.C. to General George Washington during the Revolution.

"My father enlisted in the Confederate Army in 1862 in Company C. Second Battalion Kentucky Mounted Rifles and became shortly afterward the Chief of Escort to General George B. Hodge, of the Army of the Tennessee. He saw action in all the large battles of the Civil War, was taken prisoner, and confined a year in Camp Chase, in Ohio.

"Sincerely yours,
"RHODA VAN BIBBER TANNER DOUBLEDAY,
"New York City, New York"

Lot No. 5 of Greenup on Water Street was sold to Robert Dougherty "who kept the first store, located in the lower part of the town." John Passmore Tanner married Rhoda Van Bibber and built a house on this lot where he had a furniture shop. This building burned in 1869-70 and was not rebuilt. The family moved to a farm at Palmyra. Years later James Rankins and his wife, Lois Tanner Rankins, built a house on the lot below the one where the house had burned. Their children were Emmett, Kate, Nellie, and Emma.

Children of John Passmore and Rhoda Van Bibber Tanner were John James, George W., Lois, Lydia, and Alethia. John James married Emma Offutt Bunch, daughter of a prominent family of southwest Kentucky and a daughter, Rhoda Van Bibber Tanner Doubleday, resides in New York. A recent copy of the Louisville *Courier-Journal* published an article on her family history and social activities which had much to do with English royalty. When John James Tanner died his body was brought to Greenup and buried in the Van Bibber Cemetery near Little Sandy Falls. When his mother died in the early 1870's her body was brought to the Christian Church in Greenup for services. She was taken on the ferry boat "Royal" up the Little Sandy River to the Van Bibber Cemetery to be buried. This is remembered by one, who, as a girl, went with her father to the funeral. She says the smokestack of the ferry had to be lowered to pass under the old wooden bridge across Little Sandy and it could not have gone up the Little Sandy at all, except that the river was unusually high at that time.

A second son of John Passmore Tanner was George W., who married in Ohio and lived at the Tanner farm at Palmyra for many years. He bought the Moses Mackoy farm at Siloam and his son, William, moved there. When the Chesapeake and Ohio Railroad purchased this farm in 1915, the family moved to Greenup. A daughter, Mary, married Carl McCoy and they moved to Van Wert, Ohio, where some of the family reside.

A daughter of John Tanner and his wife, Lydia, married John T. King and lived on the original King farm near the mouth of Tygart Creek (see King family).

Alethia Tanner married George W. Gammon and lived on the original Gammon farm on White Oak Creek (see Gammon family).

Lois Tanner married James Rankins (see Rankins family).

TAYLOR

ELLIS TAYLOR

Ellis Taylor was the son of Edmund Taylor of Henrico County, Virginia. He came to Guyandotte, now West Virginia, where he married (1) Caroline, daughter of Jacob Baumgardner, and moved to Blaine, Lawrence County, Kentucky. In 1850 they came to Greenup County and settled on Tygart Creek at Load, and members of the Taylor family have owned land and lived in this part of the county to the present time.

Ellis and Caroline B. Taylor were the parents of two sons, William Butler and James Franklin (see their sketches under Taylor family). The wife died and Mr. Taylor married (2) Caroline Stuart. They had three children, Henry, John F., and Martha.

Henry, the eldest son, married (1) Electa McGinnis and they have two children, Nettie Johnson and Ara Cremeans; (2) Ruby Johnson and had a daughter, Lily Davis. This Taylor family moved to Illinois. Mrs. Ruby Johnson Taylor now lives in Vanita, Oklahoma.

John F. Taylor, the second son, married Arabella (Kit) Gray of Tygart. They moved to Fullerton, where he was engaged in the lumber business. There were three children in the family: Grover of Cincinnati, Lyman of Fullerton, and Winifred Carrigan of Ohio.

Martha, the third child, married Gilbert Nichols and they were the parents of Dr. Ellis Nichols, John, Gilbert, Edith Curry, Nancy Curry, and Martha Bradley.

WILLIAM BUTLER TAYLOR

William Butler Taylor, the eldest son of Ellis and Caroline Baumgardner Taylor, was born in 1848 at Glenwood, Lawrence County, Kentucky. He was five years of age when the family came to Greenup County and settled on Tygart Creek. In 1872 he married (1) Lydia A. Clifton of Tygart, and they lived on a farm at Load until 1882, when he moved to Greenup. In 1883 he was elected deputy sheriff of the county and in 1887 sheriff. He served four years. From 1891 until 1904 he operated the Taylor Meat Market in Greenup and then went into the furniture and undertaking business until 1929. He died in 1937.

The children of William Butler and Lydia A. Clifton Taylor were Robert D., William Butler, Jr., James Franklin, Charles, Monds Clifton, and Lona. In 1902 William Butler married (2) Ella Meadows Scott and their children were Homer, Edwin, and Frank.

Robert D. Taylor married Nancy Winn Alexander of Greenup and they moved to Ashland. William Butler, Jr., married Eunice, daughter of Dr. Alfred and Augusta Seaton DeBard of Greenup. They moved to Gallipolis, where after a few years Mr. Taylor died and Eunice returned to the DeBard home in Greenup with the children, Charles and Eunice. When the children were grown the family moved to New York City to live. James Franklin Taylor, the third son, married Royina, daughter of Thomas N. and Ellen Humphreys Biggs of near Greenup, and they made their home near Columbus, Ohio. Mr. Taylor died and Mrs. Taylor, with the children, Jack, James, Margaret Ellen and Mary Lou (twins), now live at Lewis Center, Ohio. Charles Taylor, the fourth son, died at the age of nineteen years. Monds Clifton Taylor married Alice Wall and lives in Columbus, Ohio. They have a daughter. Lona Taylor, daughter of William Butler and his first wife, married John Kinner and lives in Greenup. They are the parents of Robert (deceased), David B., and Elwood.

JAMES FRANKLIN TAYLOR

James Franklin Taylor, the second son of Ellis and Caroline Baumgardner Taylor, was probably born in Greenup County on Tygart Creek, about 1850. He married Mary Ann (Molly), daughter of John and Elizabeth Tate Guilkey Holbrook, and they lived on a farm near Leatherwood in Tygart Valley. Their house burned and they moved to the Holbrook home on a high hill near Tygart Creek at Warnock, where they spent the rest of their lives. A son, Ottis, and family live there at the present time.

The children of this family are Shannon, Effie, Bertha, Ottis, Golda, Bessie, John Ellis, and James Doval, who died in childhood. Shannon married Emma Warnock and is now deceased. Effie married Davis Womack and their children are Alta, Edna, wife of Charles Griswold, Lucy Lee, and Mary Elizabeth. Bertha married William I. Meyers of Greenup and she is deceased. Ottis, who lives at the home place, married Lucy, daughter of Newton and Matilda Baker Crisp of Tygart. Their children are Cleo Hensley, Robert Shannon, James Newton, Callie Szegedi, and Joseph. Golda married Warren McGinnis of Tygart and their children are Ivalee Yoder and Taylor. This family moved to Illinois. Bessie married Isaac W. Ferguson and they moved to Scioto County. Later they moved to London, Ohio, where Mrs. Ferguson and her younger son, Philip Lewis, live. The older son, James Maxwell, lives in Athens, Ohio, where he teaches in the schools. The daughter, Pearl Eugenia Gardiner, lives in Gallipolis, Ohio. John Ellis Taylor married Mollie Faris, daughter of Ransom and Harriet Elanor Pogue Cooper of Coopersville, in 1896, and moved to New Boston. The children were Walter Kenneth, Ernest, and James Franklin. Three children of this family died in infancy.

Walter Kenneth married Alma Oakes in 1920 and lives in Portsmouth. Their only child, Betty Jane, served as a nurse in World War II and married Dr. George Franklin Owen, Jr., of Durham, North Carolina, where they make their home.

Ernest married Helen Holcomb, and James Franklin married Christine Nash.

JOHN TAYLOR

John Taylor, born in England in 1835, came to America to construct grist mills operated by water power. He died from an accident while constructing a mill at Argillite in 1867. Mr. Taylor married Caroline Plowman, who was born in Pennsylvania and died in Ashland in 1857. The children of this family were Absolum Plowman, James J., William, David, Annie, Ianthia, Xminia, John, who lived in Ironton, Ohio, and Charles Fremont.

Absolum Plowman Taylor operated a lumber mill at Whetstone, and was also interested in the Myers mill at the head of Front Street. He built a large frame house in East Greenup and lived there several years with his wife and daughters, Minnie and Effie. In 1880 he sold his home to J. Watt Womack and moved his family to Tennessee.

James J. Taylor (1855-1940) was the pilot on the ferry at Springville in the 1880's. He married Ellen, daughter of Nelson and Eliza Gilmore Pratt, in 1876. Their children were Mary Jane Kennedy; Bertha Lee Hennessy of Washington, D. C.; Ethel Sellards; Hazel Dell Hensel; Carl Pratt of Roanoke, Virginia; Esther May McClury of Lancaster, Ohio; Annie, who married Mr. Davidson and whose children were Margaret, Rose Burkamp, Mattie, and Ina, all living in Cincinnati; Xminia, who married Harry Pratt; and Charles Fremont (1857-1936), who married Lucy Lilly, daughter of Dr. John Sellards.

The children of Charles Fremont and Lucy Lilly Taylor were Carmen, who married John W. Bronaugh, and had a son, John Charles Taylor; Benton Sellards Taylor, who married Jennie Alexander and whose children are David Alexander and Ellen Linden.

Charles Fremont Taylor was a clerk in the hardware store of Stevens and Pollock. Later he and Charles Schmutz became partners in a store which was known as Taylor and Schmutz. He served as postmaster and he built and ran the theater in Greenup. Mr. and Mrs. Taylor lived all of their married life in Greenup. They helped to organize the Greenup Chapter of the Eastern Star, he being the first Worthy Patron and she the first Worthy Matron. Mr. Taylor was a member of the Greenup Masonic Lodge for fifty-five years.

THOM

Nicholas Fisher Thom, born in Hull, England, in 1815, came to America in 1833. He probably came almost directly to Greenup County as his name appears on the records of Siloam Christian Church as a member in 1836. He was a carpenter and built the Siloam Church building in the 1840's, and he served as a deacon of the church in 1846.

Mr. Thom married Lois Van Bibber Rawlings, daughter of John Rawlings (see Rawlings family), and they lived on Tygart Creek. Later they moved to Short Branch. There were fourteen children, but seven of them died in infancy. Those living were Rhoda, John, Clark, Doyle, George, Annie, and Alfred. Clark married Tillie Kilgore and George married Nancy, daughter of Jack Worthington of Little Sandy Falls. The daughter, Annie, married Scott Colegrove of Short Branch, and the youngest son, Alfred, never married.

Rhoda Thom married Frank York, whose first wife, a granddaughter of Godfrey Smith, had died leaving him with three children, Charles, Sallie, and Belle. Frank and Rhoda Thom

York were the parents of one son, John Frank, and they lived in Greenup. Mr. York died and the older children went to live with the Benjamin Smith family. Rhoda and her son went to live with the Thom family at Short Branch. John Frank York was a merchant in Russell for many years.

John Thom married in 1872 Mary Jane Wills, daughter of William and Mary Jane Richards Wills, and their children were Orville, Erma, Lois, Charles, and Adria. Erma married John Edward Lewis in 1901 and lives on a farm at Riggs. Their children are Ernest Van, who served in World War II, married Mae Stephens, and lives at Riggs near his parents; and Mary Frances, who married Raish Blankenship and lives at Yatesville, Kentucky. Charles Thom married Ann Wilks and lives at Charlestown, West Virginia. Lois and Adria are deceased.

THOMSON

The Thomson family has a long and distinguished line of ancestry in Scotland, England, and Virginia. They are descended from the Clan Campbell in Argyle, Scotland, and members of the family emigrated to England, Ireland, Wales, and finally to America. Sir William Thomson, a Scotch-Irishman, was a noted scientist and another of the name was a delegate to a Continental Congress. Five presidents descended from the Thomson family that emigrated to Virginia. They were James Madison, Zachary Taylor, the two Harrisons, and John Tyler.

William, a son of Robert Thomson, emigrated to Virginia in the seventeenth century and his daughter, Martha, married James Taylor of Orange County. They were the grandparents of James Madison and Zachary Taylor. Frances Thomson married Anthony Armistead and they were the ancestors of the Harrisons and John Tyler. Stephen Thomson, a brother of William, had a daughter, Ann, who married Colonel George Mason, and they were the parents of the patriots, George and Thomas Mason.

During the seventeenth century the Thomson and Waddy families were neighbors and relatives in New Kent County, Virginia. Mary Thomson married Samuel Waddy and the family became known as the Waddy-Thomsons, whose ancestors were David and Robert. Other members of the family were Maurice, Colonel George, and William. Colonel George Thomson was a member of the Virginia House of Burgesses in 1629, and he also fought against the Indians. He returned to England and fought in the war against King Charles. This family has a coat of arms with the motto "In Lumine Lucem."

Waddy Thomson, son of David and grandson of Robert of New Kent County, was born in Hanover County, Virginia, in 1725. He married (1) Elizabeth Anderson, and after her death in Albemarle County, Virginia, he married (2) Mary, daughter of Colonel Robert and Jane Meriweather Lewis of the same county. Mary Lewis was the widow of Samuel Cobb and she had several children. Waddy and Mary Lewis Cobb Thomson lived in Albemarle County, where he died in 1801.

The children of Waddy Thomson and his first wife, Elizabeth Anderson, were Nelson, who remained in Virginia; David, who married Eleanor Thomson, a cousin, and moved to Kentucky; Anderson, who married Ann Anderson, a relative; Waddy, who married (1) a Miss Anderson, (2) a Miss Ormsby, and moved to Kentucky; Susanna Rodes Kerr; Elizabeth; and Sarah Lewis.

The children of Waddy Thomson and his second wife, Mary Lewis Cobb, were Ann, Mary, Waddy, and Robert Lewis Thomson.

The first Thomson of the name in the Greenup County Court Records is that of Waddy Thomson, whose will was recorded February 6, 1832, with Anthony Thomson as administrator of the estate and David Thomson as guardian of the Waddy Thomson legatees.

Another grandson of Robert Thomson of New Kent County, Virginia, was Anthony of Hanover County, Virginia. who received grants of land in various parts of Kentucky for his military services in the Revolutionary War. He settled in Woodford County, Kentucky, on one of the grants. His wife was Ann Bibb of Louisa County, Virginia, and their children were Eleanor, who married her cousin, David Thomson, son of Waddy and Elizabeth Anderson, and also came to Kentucky; Elizabeth Blanton; Ann Adams; Mary; Waddy; Judith; Sarah; William; David; Louisa; and Henry Bibb Thomson. Judith married Thomas, son of Thomas and Elizabeth Weir Bell. The parents both died in Woodford County, Anthony in 1794 and his wife in 1798.

Anthony II, son of Reuben Thomson, was born 1799 and died 1850. He married Sarah Thomas (1808) and lived in Greenup County. They were the parents of fourteen children: George Washington (1809) (see George Washington Thomson family), Reuben (1811) (see Reuben Thomson family), Eleanor (1812),

Cynthia (1813), Louisa (1814), Anthony III (1816), Nancy (1817), Sarah (1820), Winifred (1821), Anderson (1823), Elizabeth (1827), Mary (Polly) (1828), David (1829), and John Tom (1830), who never married.

Cynthia married Robert Thomas; Anthony married Mary Fuqua, daughter of Moses Fuqua, Jr.; Sarah married John Bagby; Winifred married Matthew Thomson; Anderson married Catherine Fuqua; and Mary married Robert Thomson. Several of these children lived in Franklin and Woodford Counties in Kentucky.

ANTHONY THOMSON III

Anthony Thomson III (1816), son of Anthony II (1799) and Sarah Thomas Thomson, married Mary Fuqua, daughter of Moses, Jr., and Cynthia Collins Fuqua.

Children of the family were: Cynthia, who married Amos Thornsbury of Greenup and moved to a farm near Fort Worth, Texas; Sarah Catherine, who married Zachary Taylor King and lived at the Fuqua homestead at Mt. Zion and whose children were Nathaniel Thomson and Harry A. (see King family). Other daughters were: Mary Agnes, who married William McCall of Portsmouth; Eliza, who married Harry Martin of Portsmouth and moved to Buffalo, New York; Lou, who married Hoyt Williams. Hoyt and Lou Thomson Williams were the parents of Edward, who married Hattie Callihan of Boyd County, and Mary, who married Vergne Darragh of Vanceburg. They live in Portsmouth and have a daughter, Mary Ann.

Sons of Anthony and Mary Fuqua Thomson were Andrew Washington and John Tadge. Andrew Washington married Mollie Zuhars of Springville and their two sons, Lester and Arnett, died when children. John Tadge married Mary Smith, a daughter of Captain William Smith, of Ohio and Mississippi steamboat lines.

David Thomson, another son of Anthony (1799), married Elizabeth Thomas and lived in Lewis County.

GEORGE WASHINGTON THOMSON

George Washington Thomson was a farmer and owned a large tract of land below Springville, which was a part of the land originally belonging to Patrick Henry of Virginia. Some of this land is still owned by descendants of the Thomson family.

George Washington (1809) married Perlina Malvina, daughter of Nathaniel T. and Frances Major Thomas, in 1831. Their children were Nathaniel, Maria Louisa (Ludie), Anthony Wayne (Dick), George W., Volney Europe, Frances, Malvina (Pet), Ella, Sarah Elizabeth, and Cynthia. The father died as a result of a fall from his horse just below Springville while en route home from Portsmouth.

Nathaniel married Virginia, daughter of Benjamin and Nancy Mackoy King, of Mt. Zion. Their children were Benjamin and Lucy, both of whom died unmarried; and Stella, who married Matthew Hanson and lived in Springville. Their children were Virginia and Hubert.

Maria Louisa (Ludie) married Erastus Burr Gates of Portsmouth, and their children were Lizzie, wife of James Hill of Gray's Branch; Callie, wife of George Fisher, who lives in Colorado; Eggleston, who married Sallie Davis of Portsmouth and had two sons, Charles and Harry; and Low, who died unmarried.

Anthony Wayne (Dick) was thrown from a horse and killed when a young man. He was never married.

George W., Jr., married Emma Slemp Ferguson of Ohio and their children were Nettie, Philip, Charles, and Myra. Nettie married John T. English and their children were Avis Van Bibber, Jean Bagby, Sarah Bentley, Perlina Sizemore, Cynthia Lockland, Katherine Spiers, Charles and John (twins), Owen, and Arthur. Philip married Olive Roe of Tygart Valley and their sons, Volney and Philip, live near Columbus, Ohio. Charles married Alice Williams of South Portsmouth. Myra married Frederick Cunningham and their son, Paul, married Anna May Stansbury. They lived at Lima, Ohio, when Paul died, leaving a son, Frederick Paul.

Volney Europe married Nancy Sheets, daughter of Robert and Catherine Lawson Johnson of Mt. Zion, and they lived on a farm in that neighborhood. Their children were Dr. Robert Thomson, who married Miranda Spears of Lexington, Kentucky, and located in New Mexico; Perlina, who never married; Edgar, who is married and lives in Los Angeles, California; Taylor Lawson, deceased; and Volney Wayne, who never married.

Frances married James Parker and the family moved to West Virginia.

Malvina (Pet) married a Mr. Veach of Frankfort, Kentucky. When he died she returned to the Thomson home at Springville.

Sarah Elizabeth (Hun) taught school for fourteen years. She and her sisters, Ella and Cynthia, died unmarried.

REUBEN THOMSON

Reuben Thomson (1811) was the second son of Anthony Thomson II. He married (1) Nancy Scott and they had a son, Amos. He married (2) Frances A. Waring of Tygart Valley and they were the parents of James Hollyday, Anthony Wayne, and Sarah.

James Hollyday Thomson married Margaret Maupin and their children were Jessie, who married John Rottinghaus of Portsmouth, James E., and Edward.

Anthony Wayne married Nellie O'Neill, and their children were Frances, who died in infancy, and Anthony Wayne, who is a prominent attorney in Lexington, Kentucky. He was a colonel in World War II.

Sarah married Joshua Lawson of Mt. Zion, who was a merchant and the postmaster at Springville for many years. They were the parents of Reuben, Nettie, and Anna. Reuben married (1) Belle Brown of Springville and (2) a Miss Burke of Ohio. Nettie married David Miller (see Miller family). Anna married Richard Wilson, a telegraph operator for the Chesapeake and Ohio Railroad at South Portsmouth.

TIBBETTS

Crawford Tibbetts came from Maryland to Greenup County and farmed the Eastern Kentucky Railroad land. He married Fannie Duke and they were the parents of Ona, Lula, and Stanley, none of whom married.

Mr. Tibbetts raised small fruits in the 1890's and was noted especially for his fine strawberries.

TIMBERLAKE

The Timberlake family were very early residents of Greenup County. On a plat of Greenupsburg recorded June 20, 1815, Lots Nos. 60 and 61 were owned by the Timberlake family. These lots lie on the south side of Main Street between Harrison and Washington Streets. The jail, built in 1811, was on the north side of Main Street across from the Timberlake lots. Oba Timberlake was jailer from 1813 to 1816. At the November 1816 term of court Oba Timberlake is "permitted to keep tavern at his dwelling house for one year from date hereof."

The early marriage records of the county show that Harry Timberlake married Jane Reed in 1836; Jane Timberlake married Harvey Campbell in 1836; Mary Timberlake married Cyrus Van Bibber in 1821; Thom Timberlake married Margaret Cussins in 1841; and Thomas Timberlake married Alice Howland in 1832.

Pleasant Timberlake, born 1836 and died 1919, was a resident of Flat Hollow for many years. He served in the Twenty-second Kentucky Regiment in the Civil War. He was twice married, his first wife being Ann E. Reeves, and their children were Matilda, Burl, Maggie, Abigail, Martha, Simon, and Peter. Of these seven children only two are now living, Abigail, who lives in Cincinnati and is seventy-nine years old; and Maggie, who lives in Dayton, Ohio, with her daughter and is eighty-one years old. Maggie married Sigmund Burkhardt and they lived in Portsmouth for sixty-three years. Their children are Carl of Portsmouth, Edgar of Florida, and Katherine McFarland of Dayton, Ohio.

In 1877 Mrs. Timberlake died, and Pleasant married as his second wife, Syntha Middaugh. There were seven children in this family: James, Dora, Lavinia Dugan, Florence, Bradley, Sheridan, and Mary, all living. James married Mary E. Smith and had six children. One of their sons, Floyd, married Geneva Adams and lives at Fullerton. Dora married J. H. Clark; Lavinia Dugan married Ellis Bryant; Florence married Alex Hunt; Bradley married Essie Jones; Sheridan married (1) Nancy Dortch and (2) Rebecca Harr; Mary married (1) Mr. Ruley, (2) Fred Newsome, and (3) William Mullins. All of these Timber-lakes live in Greenup County except Mary, who lives in Scioto County, Ohio.

TINSLEY

Wilbur Tinsley was a descendant of the Fennell family of Pennsylvania and Virginia. He came from Virginia to Greenup County and married Mary Walton, daughter of Roger Walton and his third wife, Mary Carnegy Philips Waring of Lynn. The Tinsley family went to West Virginia, where they lived several years and then returned to the farm on Tygart Creek. The children of the family were Wilson, Irene, Stephen C., Mary Agnes, Sally Waring, Frances, Walton W., and Edward.

Irene married William Dickinson and moved to Portsmouth, Ohio. Their children were Maud, Howard, and William. Mary Agnes married Monroe Allen of Zanesville, Ohio, and they had a son, Samuel. Since Mr. Allen's death, Mrs. Allen and Samuel continue to reside in Zanesville. Sallie Waring Tinsley has been a teacher in the schools of South Charleston, Ohio, for many years. Frances Tinsley married Bertis H. Smith, a merchant of Greenup (see Elmer Smith family). Walton Tinsley married Sara Frizzell of Vanceburg, and they moved to Covington, Kentucky, where he is employed in the electrical department of the Chesapeake and Ohio Railroad. They have a son, Walton Eugene. Edward Tinsley married Viola Veach, of Lewis County, Kentucky, and they were the parents of Harold and Joseph (twins), Mary Frances, and Marion. Edward Tinsley was sheriff of Greenup County for eight years. The family were residents of Greenup until a few years ago, when they moved to Columbus, Ohio, where Mr. Tinsley died. The family continues to reside there.

TONG

The Tong family emigrated from Devonshire, England, to Maryland about 1651, as shown by records there of land transactions at that time. The first of the name in America was John Tong, who lived at White Sulphur Springs, Virginia. Evidently he went from there to Ohio, for he died at Bainbridge, Ohio.

John Tong's son, William W., born in 1797, went to Adams County, Ohio, and from there to Mason County, Kentucky, in 1842. Sometime in the 1840's he came to Greenup County and located near the present site of Limeville. He built a lime kiln and the business was called the Greenup Lime Works. He also had a blacksmith shop where the schoolhouse was built later, and in this schoolhouse the post office is now located. William W. Tong married Mary Kellum Bishop, probably in Adams County, Ohio, and they had four children: Henry, Nancy Caroline, John, and Mary Jane.

Henry married Mary Ann Kennedy and their children were George W., Louella, Kathryn, Virginia, Ruth, and John Bishop. Mr. Tong was a captain on the steamboats for many years until the loss of his eyesight forced him to retire. George W. married Frances E. Oldaker and lives in Colorado; Louella married Wayne Allen and is deceased; Kathryn married Walter Franz and lives at Raceland; Virginia married Gordon Marquette of Portsmouth, Ohio, where they reside; Ruth married Harry Williams and lives at Russell; John Bishop married Marie McAllister and lives at Riverton.

Nancy Caroline Tong married Peter Dutiel Andre of the "French Grant," Scioto County, Ohio, in 1854. They made their home there throughout their entire lives and reared a family of six children. A daughter, Elonia Andre, is still living in Michigan. She is a retired teacher of the Detroit schools.

John Tong married Mary E. King, daughter of Thomas B. King of Greenup County, and they went to Missouri, where they spent their lives.

Mary Jane Tong married (1) Nicholas A. West and they lived in Illinois. He died, leaving his wife and three children. Ella, the first child, died at the age of seventeen; James W., the second, married Emma Anderson of Springville, and their children are Charles and Tong. Charles, who has a store and is postmaster at Tongs Post Office, married Edith Craft of Greenup; and Tong, who is a merchant in Greenup, married Doris Ruth Zimmerman of Portland, Oregon. Both of these families have their homes on the original Tong land. Charles Wesley Tong, another son of Nicholas and Mary Jane Tong West, went to Kansas City, Missouri, where he died in 1941.

Mary Jane Tong West married (2) Cyrus Cartwright (see Cyrus Cartwright family).

TOOLEY

Samuel and Eniza Adkins Tooley came from Wayne County, Virginia, to Greenup County in 1860. Their children were Lafayette, John, Perlina, and Jimmerson. John married Eliza, daughter of Smith and Rebecca Stockham Hitchcock of Mt. Zion. They were the parents of Lola, Susan, Samuel, and Eniza (twins), Carrie, Cora, Clarence, Ruby, and Willard.

Lola married Anthony (Tone) Davenport of Mt. Zion (see Davenport family); Susan married Robert Bush of Siloam (see Bush family); Samuel married May Bruce of Lewis County and they made their home there; Eniza married Edward Jones of Lewis County and they had a son, Paul, who lives in Portsmouth; Carrie married Henry Smith and they had three daughters, Eliza, Marie, and Henrietta; Cora married Edward Bennett; Clarence married Bessie Burgess of South Portsmouth, and was killed at Russell while in the employ of the Chesapeake and Ohio Railroad; Ruby married Vernon Loudenbach and they had a son, Clifford; Willard, the youngest son, died unmarried

TRIMBLE

David Trimble was born in Frederick County, Virginia, in 1782 and graduated from William and Mary College in 1799. He studied law and began practicing at Mt. Sterling, Kentucky. He served in the War of 1812 and later was elected to the legislature from Greenup County, serving from 1836 to 1839.

In 1818 David Trimble, John Trimble, and Richard Deering built Argillite Furnace, the first one to be built in Greenup County. David Trimble bought four lots on Water Street in Greenup, extending from Washington and Elizabeth Streets to Cedar Alley, and here he built a large frame house on Lot No. 1. He laid off the other lots in gardens and planted them with trees and flowers. In 1883 he and others built Raccoon Furnace. Mr. Trimble died in 1842, at his home in Greenup, or at Trimble's Furnace (Raccoon).

Charles Wilson, perhaps a relative, was the next owner of the Trimble home in Greenup. He sold it to Cardinal Fush Stark in 1858, and this was the home of the Stark family for many years.

VAN BIBBER

The Van Bibber family came from Pennsylvania to Greenup County in the very early days, and they seem to have been closely associated with the Boone family. Captain John Van Bibber's wife, Chloe Staniford, was born in Cecil County, Maryland, in 1760. They were the parents of James, Jacob, and a daughter, Rhoda, who was killed by the Indians. James married Lois Reynolds and their children were Albert, John (1797), Sydney, Missouri, Rachel, and Dr. James, Jr. Dr. James, Jr., married Naomi Barton White and they were the parents of Cyrus, Eliza Naomi, and Rhoda.

Chloe Van Bibber, who may have been another daughter of Captain John Van Bibber, had married Jesse Boone before coming to Greenup County and they were the parents of two children, Harriet and Alphonso. A third child, Minerva, probably born in Greenup County, married Wynekoop Warner in 1817.

Peter Van Bibber (parents not known) lived in the "French Grant," Scioto County, Ohio. He married Nancy Devore in Greenup County, in 1815. James Gilruth states in his letters that Peter had four sons, Jesse, Jacob, John, and Tyce. Also that a niece, Olive Van Bibber, who lived with them, married

Nathan Boone, a son of Colonel Daniel Boone. This couple went to Missouri with the Daniel Boone family in 1820.

Jacob Van Bibber, probably the son of Captain John, had three daughters, Ruth, Maggie, and Nancy. Early marriage records of the county state that Jacob gave his consent to the marriage of each of these daughters. Ruth married George Hensley in 1815; Maggie married David Kouns in 1834; and Nancy married Moses Haney in 1827.

Cyrus Van Bibber, son of Dr. James Van Bibber, Jr., married Rachel Timberlake and they lived on a farm near Little Sandy Falls. Their children were Cyrus, Jr. (1826-1900), Caroline, Charles, Obadiah, Sydney, Mary Ann, and Harvey. Cyrus, Jr., married Sophia Baker; Caroline married Dr. William Smith Kouns (see Kouns family); Charles married Carrie ———, a teacher in the Greenup County Schools in the 1870's; Obadiah lived in Cincinnati, Ohio, and died there a bachelor; Sydney married in Cincinnati and had two children, Jessie and Cyrus; Mary Ann married (1) Pearson McCoy of Ohio, and (2) the Rev. Jeremiah Farmer; Harvey, a bachelor, committed suicide by shooting himself on the streets of Greenup.

Eliza Naomi, daughter of Dr. James Van Bibber, Jr., married William King Boal, and her sister, Rhoda (1808-1881), married John Passmore Tanner in 1830 (see Tanner family).

Cyrus Van Bibber, Jr., and his wife, Sophia Baker (1834), were the parents of Marshall (1856), Lamard and Lemara (twins), Fannie B., Henry, and Thomas. Marshall married Hattie Ghent in Colorado; Lamard married Annie Hill, daughter of Amos and Elizabeth Smith Hill of Gray's Branch; Lemara died when a child; Fannie B. married Roger Waring; Henry married Lucy Berry in Colorado in 1888; and Thomas married Inez Johnson in 1890.

The children of Charles Van Bibber and Carrie, his wife, were Cyrus D. and Rachel. Cyrus D. married Lucy E. Hockaday, daughter of James and Ann Eliza Biggs Hockaday, and they moved to Huntington, West Virginia, where their children married and now live. The children are Ann Eliza Recard, Cyrus Biggs, who married Florence Lee Holliday; Laura Bixby; and Rachel Holderby (see Hockaday and Biggs families). Rachel, the sister of Cyrus D. Van Bibber, died when a young woman.

Lamard, son of Cyrus, Jr., and Sophia Baker Van Bibber, and his wife, Annie Hill, always lived in the Tygart Valley, where they reared a family of twelve children. These children have married and have families of their own. A few of them have gone to Ohio and other places, but for the most part they are the Van Bibber families of Greenup County now. The children of Lamard and Annie Hill Van Bibber are Maurice, Fred, Homer, Ferris, Cyrus, Amos, Raymond, Vernon, Bess, Ruth, Eunice, and Anna Louise. Maurice married (1) Carrie Fields, and (2) Minnie Bole of Bracken County; Fred and Homer never married; Ferris married Bess Belford; Cyrus married Lorena Warnock; Amos married Edna Meadows and lives at the Cyrus home; Raymond married Chlotine Burgess and lives in Washington, D. C.; Bess married Owen Kendall of Greenup; Ruth married Arthur Garvey of Siloam; Eunice married Mr. Slater; and Anna Louise is deceased.

NOTE: Other Van Bibber marriages in the court records are: Hanna married Joshua Rawlings (Rollins) in 1815, with the permission of her father, James Van Bibber; Elizabeth Ann married David Millirons in 1834; Cyrus Van Bibber married Mary Timberlake in 1821.

The following is taken from notes from *Trans-Allegheny Pioneers* and *Van Bibber Family* by Mrs. Miriam W. Donnolly.

"Peter Van Bibber, with his young son, Jesse, and his two brothers, John and Isaac, a Baptist minister, fought in the battle of Point Pleasant, October 10, 1774. They came with the army from Greenbrier and afterwards settled in the Kanawha Valley, where they became the ancestors of a large and prominent family. Peter distinguished himself for bravery in this battle so that he was promoted on the battlefield. His implements of warfare with which he fought so bravely are preserved in a case in historical rooms at Charleston, West Virginia.

"Peter's son, Jacob, was captured by the Indians near Point Pleasant in 1789 and made prisoner. He made his escape, however, and got home about two years later. He was afterwards with General Wayne in his memorable campaign of 1794. He and his wife died in Missouri.

"Peter's daughter, Olive, was married at Point Pleasant in 1799 to Colonel Nathan Boone, the youngest son of Daniel Boone. It was at their home on the Teme-Osage River, in Missouri, that Daniel Boone died in 1820.

"Jesse Boone, eldest son then living of Daniel Boone, married Chloe Van Bibber, daughter of John Van Bibber, brother of Peter Van Bibber.

"CHILDREN

"Jesse (1759), Peter, Matthias (Tice) (1772), who married Margaret Gardner, Jacob (1775), who married (1795) Sarah

Miller (1776-1843), Olive, and James, who married Jane Irvine. There may have been other children, Joseph, Nancy, Sophronia, and Ellen."

VIRGIN

Three brothers, Ebenezer, Samuel, and Jeremiah Virgin, came from England to America. Ebenezer, with one hundred families, settled at Concord, New Hampshire. Samuel, a sea captain, was drowned at sea. Jeremiah settled in Virginia and his son Jeremiah married Lucy Dickinson about 1735. Their children were Reason (or Rezin), Brice, Kinsey, John, Thomas, and Lucy. The five sons were in the Revolutionary War, four being officers. Rezin and Kinsey were captains, Brice a lieutenant, and John a drummer boy. Rezin was appointed captain of militia in Ohio County, Virginia, in 1777.

In 1780 Captain Rezin Virgin located on four hundred acres of land in Washington County, Pennsylvania. He married Jemima Arnold, who was born in Virginia, the daughter of Jonathan and Rachel Scott Arnold, the latter of Talbot County, Maryland. Their children were Lucy (1769), Rachel (1771), Kinsey (1773), Eli (1775), Cassandra, Rebecca, Hannah, and Eleanor. In 1790 the family moved from Uniontown (Beesontown), Pennsylvania, to Limestone (Maysville) and from there to Cincinnati, where, under a license issued by General Arthur St. Clair, Governor of the Northwest Territory, Lucy was married to John Downs. About 1807 John and Lucy Virgin Downs moved to Oldtown, where Captain Rezin Virgin and family had come about 1800. Rachel married David Enslow; Kinsey married Hannah Tygart; and they moved to Scioto County, Ohio; Eli married Nacka Hyatt; Rezin, Jr., married Polly Ann Lyons; Cassandra married Hezekiah Lyons; Rebecca married John Wells; Hannah married Ephraim Goble; and Eleanor married Moses Everman.

Lieutenant Brice Virgin went south, and John, the drummer boy, went to Illinois.

Rezin, a grandson of Captain Rezin Virgin, married (1) Lydia Meadows, of Tygart Valley. Their children were Henry, Elza, Robert, Butler, Virgil, Lucy, Laura, and Tempa. He married (2) Ann Nichols, and their children were Catherine, Rosa, Florence, and George. Of this family, Virgil lived all of his life on the original Virgin farm and several of the other members of the family lived near Oldtown. Virgil married (1) Dolly Bays, and their children are Orin, Martha, Mary, and Fay. He married (2)

Della Bays, a sister of his first wife, and their children were Harry, Charles, Clotene, Howard, Vera, and Billy. Orin married Sadie May, Martha married Victor Wells, Mary married John Allen, Fay married Don Oney, Harry married Martha Hicks, Charles married Minnie Fannin, Billy married Miss Scott, and Vera and Howard are unmarried. Children of Victor and Martha Virgin Wells are Dorothy Major, Norma Wright, and Robert, all of whom live at South Shore.

Butler Virgin married Pearla Burton and lived near Oldtown for many years, moving later to the western part of the county. Their children were Ben, Edward, Reason, Mamie, Sylvia, Oscar, and Flora. Ben married Fannie Belle Morton; Edward married (1) Eva Lamblin and (2) Emma Taylor; Reason married Gladys Wells; Mamie married Terry Scaggs of Indiana; Sylvia married Thomas Bailey, and they live in Washington, D. C.; Oscar married (1) Virginia Burns and (2) Ada Swamberger; Flora married Everett Hitchcock. Of the above families, Ben, Edward, Reason, and Flora live in Ashland, Kentucky, and Oscar at Portsmouth, Ohio.

WALCOTT

Sylvanus Howe Walcott was born at Marietta, Ohio, in 1820. The Walcotts were of English descent. His mother was a member of the Howe family, one of whom, Elias, invented the sewing machine. Mr. Walcott came to Greenup County when a young man and taught school. He was married in 1860 in Greenup to Carrie Virginia Sweetland, who was born in Virginia in 1835. They lived all their married life in Greenup. Mr. Walcott was deputy county clerk under William Corum and he was also county surveyor for many years.

Children of the Walcott family were William L., Albert S., Viola Lee, Mattie Walker, Alanson Howe, and Ella Van Meter. William L. was employed in the office of the Eastern Kentucky Railroad at Riverton in 1880 and later went to Coalton, West Virginia, as an agent for the Chesapeake and Ohio Railroad. Albert S. died when a boy. Viola Lee married Martin Wilson, of the Wilson Milling Company in Greenup and they resided in Greenup until the death of Mr. Wilson. She has made her home in late years with a daughter, Carrie Sweetland Allen, of Huntington, West Virginia. Other children of Martin and Viola Lee Wilson were Robert Jennings and Loring Martin Wilson. Mattie Walker Walcott married Emory W. Foreman, a railroad man, in 1888. Alanson Howe Walcott went to New Orleans in 1895 where he married Daisy Bachelor, and they had two children. Ella Van Meter Walcott married Lucius Roberts and went to New Orleans to live.

William and Ella Van Meter Walcott were brought to Greenup after they died, and were buried in Riverview Cemetery.

WALKER

James Walker married Nancy, one of the seven daughters of Aaron and Mary Clingman Kinney of Portsmouth, Ohio. They owned a farm on the Ohio River below Siloam and here they built a large brick house, which was very modern for that time. It had a basement kitchen and sliding doors between the rooms on the first floor. The children of this family were William, Samuel, Mary, and Peter Kinney. William married Ella, a daughter of John and Lydia Tanner King. He died of typhoid fever in 1885, leaving his wife with two small children, Roy and May. Samuel married Lizzie Bahner; Mary married William (Dock) Burns late in life and they went to California, as also did the William Walker children; Peter Kinney Walker (named for his uncle, Colonel Peter Kinney) married Mary Warner and they moved to Louisville, Kentucky.

The farm owned by the Walker family was sold to William Harper of Portsmouth, and he with his family lived there a number of years. The homestead and part of the farm is now owned by one of William Harper's daughters, Mrs. Lillian Tracy, of Portsmouth, Ohio.

WARE

Elias Ware came from Dublin, Ireland, to Maryland. Two sons, Asbury and Elias, came from Maryland to Greenup County. Asbury married Sarah Catherine, daughter of Moses, Jr., and Cynthia Collins Fuqua, pioneer settlers in the western part of the county. The young couple settled on Tygart Creek near Mt. Zion. They were a very religious family and were active members of the Mt. Zion Methodist Church. Mr. Ware was a carpenter as well as a farmer. The children of the family were Anna, Frances, Elizabeth, Edward, John, and Jane. Anna married Dr. Theodore Davidson (see Davidson family); Frances married Henry Davidson of Greenup; Elizabeth married (1) Samuel Hill of Gray's Branch and (2) James P. Winters of Greenup; John and

Jane never married, and Jane went to live in California; Edward married Julia Allen of Tygart Valley and they had three children.

Elias Ware, the brother who came with Asbury Ware to Greenup County, married as his second wife (her second husband) Mrs. Lavinia Mackoy Dugan of Siloam, where they lived until his death. He died of a heart attack while looking at his rabbit traps one morning. He is buried in the Siloam Cemetery.

WARING

Thomas Waring came from Maryland to Mason County, Kentucky, in 1784, bought one thousand acres of land within a few miles of Limestone (Maysville), and built Waring's Station for protection and defence. He had served as lieutenant and captain in the Maryland Militia in the Revolutionary War. In Kentucky he was appointed justice while it was under Virginia Government. In 1792 he was a member of the convention in Danville which formed the first constitution of the state. Several of his brothers and their families joined the Waring settlement in Mason County later in the 1780's. Among these were James Haddock and Leonard Waring.

In 1799 Judge Thomas Waring bought from the Government one thousand acres of land on Tygart Creek near the present location of Lynn and he was probably one of the earliest settlers in that section. He had an important part in formulating the plans for the organization of the new county of Greenup in 1803; he helped to lay out the county seat; served as a justice in the first Court of Sessions in 1804; and was assistant judge of the first circuit court in 1806. One son, Francis, served as sheriff in 1818, and another, Thomas Truman Greenfield, was a member of the Kentucky Legislature in 1819. "These brave settlers transmitted to their children a character as staunch as the hills —strong powers of mind and body, irreproachable integrity, and an energetic disposition which surmounted all difficulties." (Waring Family History). The Warings were people of education and refinement, and their influence was always for good. These traits have been outstanding in the family even to the present generation. The Rev. Edward T. Waring of Florida says, "Each generation has produced a minister of the gospel."

The Warings had large families. Much repetition of given names and intermarriage of the families has caused such confusion that genealogists have found it no easy task to trace one particular family line.

288

Judge Thomas Waring, born 1752 in Prince Georges County, Maryland, was the son of Major Francis and Mary Hollyday Waring. She was a direct descendant of Leonard Hollyday, Lord Mayor of London. Judge Waring married Lydia Walton, daughter of Roger Walton of Philadelphia, and their children were Francis, James, Roger W., Thomas Truman Greenfield, Basil, Mary Hollyday, Dorcas, Lydia, and Sarah Whitehead. Many of the family are buried in the Waring Cemetery at Lynn, which is located on their original land. The inscription on Judge Waring's gravestone reads: "In memory of Hon. Judge Thomas Waring. Born in Prince Georges County, Maryland. Emigrated to Kentucky in 1784 and died in Greenup County, January 15, 1818, in his 67th year."

Roger W. Waring, third son of Judge Waring, died in Ohio in 1816, and his daughter, Mary Hollyday (1808), was adopted by Francis and Mary Hollyday Waring, her uncle and aunt who lived on Tygart Creek.

The fourth son of Judge Waring, Thomas Truman Greenfield, born 1778 in Maryland, married Nancy Mefford (1782), daughter of George Mefford of Mason County. He served as field officer in the Kentucky Militia from 1802 to 1818 and is listed as a major in 1815. According to his will, dated 1865, his children were Basil; James; John; Truman Greenfield; George; Leonard; Thomas; Nathan; Francis; Lydia, wife of William Fuqua; Mary, wife of Richard Fuqua; Dorcas, wife of Charles Barrett; Sarah Ann, wife of James H. Waring; and Martha, wife of Edmund L. Phillips. The Lydia Waring Fuqua family went to Missouri. A great-granddaughter, Mrs. Emma Kidd Hulburt, of Oak Park, Illinois, a writer of children's books, has collected much information on the Waring family and has furnished some material for this sketch.

Basil, eldest son of Thomas Truman Greenfield Waring, married Mary Hollyday, his cousin, in 1827. The children of this family were Francis, Basil Alvin, Roger T., who married Fannie Van Bibber; Martha, who married Richard Dupuy; Mary Hollyday, who married the Rev. C. C. Armstrong and went to Texas; Jane, who married Van Bartlett; and Ella M., single.

The children of Francis and Jennie Stewart were Lucy, Leona, Margaret, Ada Mefford, Francis B., Edward Taylor, Agnes, Jennie M., Lawrence, and Mary. Francis B. Waring lived in Piqua, Ohio, where his daughter, Mrs. Nellie Killen, still lives;

his son, James Leonard Waring, has distinguished himself as a leader in Y. M. C. A. work. The Rev. Edward T. Waring married (1) Etta Smith, one of the best known teachers of the county, and their children are Charles Edward, of Baltimore, Maryland, a vice president of the Davisson Chemical Corporation, and Virginia Smith Waring. The Rev. Waring married (2) Louverna Hill Bennett, a cousin of his first wife. He served several large Methodist churches in Ohio and, since his retirement, lives in Lakeland, Florida.

Basil Alvin, second son of Basil and Mary Hollyday Waring, married Nancy Bell. He lived in Portsmouth for a number of years and then moved to Lynn, where he operated a general store. The children of this family were Ida, wife of Edward Howland (see Howland family); Clarence Bell, who married Daisy Laura Wood; and Maurice, who married Elizabeth Greenslate and is a resident of Greenup County. Mrs. Ida Howland is the last of the Warings to own a farm in Tygart Valley, where at one time they owned land for twenty-five miles.

The gravestone inscription of the youngest son of Judge Thomas Waring reads: "General Bazel Waring, born Mason County, Kentucky, May 11, 1794, died in Greenup County, Kentucky, August 31, 1844." (The title of general may have been received while serving in the War of 1812.) On this same stone are names and dates for his three wives and several of their children. He married (1) Sarah, daughter of John Mackoy of Siloam, (2) Jane A. R. McCall, who was probably from Adams County, Ohio, and (3) Tabitha, daughter of James Mackoy of Mason County. The surviving children were those of the third marriage. Mary Lovina married Thomas Lee Jordan and her grandson, Robert Pearce, now lives at Crestwood, Kentucky; James Edward died when a young man; Sarah (Sallie) Lydia married W. Boyd Wilson, at one time publisher of the Louisville *Courier-Journal*, and has two daughters living at Anchorage, Kentucky—Mary, wife of the Rev. John E. Travis, and Agnes Mackoy Wilson; Agnes Basil married Stephen Carnegy and they lived in the Basil Waring homestead on Tygart Creek.

James Haddock Waring, Jr., (1785), born in Prince Georges County, Maryland, was the son of James Haddock, Sr., and Ann Boone Waring, who came to Mason County in 1786. He married his first cousin, Lydia Walton, daughter of Judge Thomas Waring. He was a successful farmer and built the large brick house on Tygart Creek at Lynn. The children of this family were Ann Boone Newcomb; Eliza Lydia Stewart; Thomas, who married Mahala Howland; Roger Walton, who married three times; James H., who married his cousin, Sarah Ann, daughter of Thomas T. G. Waring; Sarah, who married James Mackoy of Mason County, and whose granddaughter, Mary Virginia Mackoy Grossenbach, still lives there; Frances May, who married (1) John King and (2) William Flowers; Henry Ellis Green, who married twice; and Leonard, who married Priscilla Stevenson.

Roger Walton Waring married (1) Eliza Philips in 1844, and they had no children; (2) Amelia Ann Philips in 1848, and they had no children; (3) Mrs. Mary Eliza Carnegy Philips in 1852, and their daughter, Mary Walton Waring, married Wilbur S. Tinsley (see Tinsley family).

Henry Ellis Green Waring married (1) Louisa Hanks, daughter of Abraham and Polly Ann Wigglesworth Hanks, and settled at the old homestead on Tygart Creek. Their five children were Agnes, James Marshall, Mary Ann, Louise Nutter, and Henry Allen; (2) Mary Ann Fox (1868), daughter of Patrick and Eliza Tierney Fox, and their children are Frances Mary, who married Andrew Jackson Henry Lewis and lives in Ashland; Albert Thomas, who died when a child; Eliza Lydia, Edward Stephen, and Sarah Nancy, wife of Frank Alexander Livingston, all of whom live in Columbus, Ohio. Mr. Livingston has a very complete history of the Waring family and furnished much of the material for this sketch.

CLEMENT H. WARING

There is little known of a Waring family that lived at Gray's Branch. The gravestones in the Brick Union Cemetery read as follows:

Clement H. Waring, born June 24, 1781, died May 28, 1853.

Mary Waring, born August 7, 1783, died January 21, 1861.

His will names these children: James Lawrence, William, Hollyday, Melvina, Thomas, Barton, Richard, and Elizabeth. Melvina married (1) John B. Powell in 1833, (2) Obadiah Fuqua Mackoy (see his sketch under Mackoy family). She is buried in the Brick Union Cemetery. Members of this Waring family went to Illinois.

Clement H. Waring was one of three men who organized the Greenup Union Presbyterian Church. He was also justice of the county from 1839 to 1845.

WARNOCK

The history of the Warnock family dates back to Scotland when three brothers, like many other people, took arms to defend the Presbyterian form of church government. They were bitterly persecuted and fled to Ireland, where they found refuge. James, one of the three brothers, became a merchant of prominence in Inneskillen, County Tyrone. He died in 1667.

Attracted by the promise of religious freedom, several Warnock brothers came to America before the Revolutionary War and some of them served with the colonists. Members of the family settled in Pennsylvania, Maryland, Virginia, and North Carolina. Among these were William James, born in County Tyrone, near Londonderry, who married Elizabeth Carlisle. He was with Daniel Boone in 1774 when he came with forty men from North Carolina to Kentucky, and he was in Greenup County before it was organized.

When the town of Greenupsburg was platted, eight of the sixty-four lots sold were bought by the above James Warnock. Two of these have always been owned by members of the family. The four sons of James Warnock were James, Johnson, William J., and Samuel.

James Warnock, Jr., married Rebecca Howe, the daughter of John Howe, an early pioneer of the county, in 1800. His will, dated 1856, names these children: John W. Howe, William Howe, Matthew, James Wesley (see their sketches following), Sallie, wife of James Alexander, and Cynthia. The sons are the ancestors of the Warnock families best known in the county. It would be impossible to write of all their descendants and connections. James Warnock owned a large tract of land now called Warnock, on Upper Tygart Creek. He was a lover of poetry and wrote poems for his own and his family's pleasure. Among these, he wrote a tribute to Robert Burns, in the poet's own style and dialect. Several of Mr. Warnock's descendants have inherited a talent for writing, painting, and other arts.

In 1813 Johnson Warnock, the second son of James Warnock, built a house on Lot No. 12 in Greenupsburg, and as he married Betsy Forester in June of that year, they probably went to housekeeping there. In his will he names these children: Carlisle, Robert, James, Martha, Lavina, and Malinda Elizabeth. Martha married her cousin, James Warnock.

Little is known of William J., the third son of James Warnock. He married Lucy Forester, probably the sister of his brother

Johnson's wife, and his children were Andrew, who married Miss Colter; James Carlisle, who married (1) Miss Hunt and (2) ———; Ann, who married George Howland (see Howland family).

Samuel, the fourth son, mentions in his will, dated December 1846, his wife, Rachel, and these children: Jackson, William, James Carlisle, Mahala Reaves, Mary Brooks, Elizabeth Huffman, Sara Huffman, Jane Bradshaw, and Lavina Crawford. The son, William, married Ann Littlejohn Craycraft in 1846, and their children were Laken Samuel, John William, Lyda, who married William Lee, and Ada, who married Dock Stepter. Laken Samuel married Martha Morton, daughter of Henry Clay Morton, and their children are Lowery Morton, who married Hattie Wear; Nathaniel Gwinn, who married Etta Pitts; and Fannie, who married Lafe Jordan. John William, the second son of William and Ann Littlejohn Craycraft Warnock, married Sarah (or Sadie) Nickell and their children are Charles Byron, who married May, daughter of Claude and Ella Hill McClave and lives in Portsmouth; Amy, who married Chester Imes and lives in Sciotoville; and Louis, who died when a child. This William Warnock family lived on a farm at Bennett's Mill.

JOHN W. HOWE WARNOCK

John W. Howe Warnock (known as Uncle Johnnie), eldest son of James Warnock, Jr., married Grace Guilkey and lived in Greenup many years. He was very active in the affairs of the county, was part owner of Old Laurel Furnace, and had a library of many valuable books. The children of this family were James (known as Red James), Edward, Matthew, Benjamin Franklin, William, Elizabeth (Betty or Betsy Ann), who married her cousin, Basil Warnock, and Rebecca, who died young.

James (Red James) married his cousin, Margaret, daughter of Matthew and Lydia Warnock, and they were the parents of Winfield, Willard, Catherine Holbrook (see Holbrook family), Grace, wife of Dr. John Sowards, Mary, and Lulu, wife of Walter Greenslate.

Edward, who lived on Tygart Creek, married Mary Mearns and their children were Cora Brady, Maud Heisel, Grace Huffman, Ernest, and Frank. Edward Warnock served with his cousin, John Dock Warnock, as road commissioner, and made possible many good roads throughout the county, including

Raccoon Hill, which was given special attention, and made into a good road.

Matthew married Elizabeth Breeding and their children were Grace, John Denny, and Fannie. Grace' died as a child. John Denny, who married Lyde Fullerton, daughter of Harvey and Mary Terrell Fullerton, served as mayor of Greenup, as police judge, and was secretary of the Masonic Lodge for thirty-six years. Fannie Warnock married Elwood Kinner of Greenup, and their son, Matthew, married Mabel, daughter of Ward and Gertrude Curry Womack of Oldtown and Florida.

Benjamin Franklin married (1) Faith Frailey and their children were Finley, Edward, Harry, Alfred, Paul, Grant, and Ella, who went to Texas; (2) Mary Ellis (Mollie) Ramey, and their children were: Jessie, who never married; William, who married Elizabeth Frailey; Sallie, wife of Carl Finney; Lorena, wife of Cyrus Van Bibber (see Van Bibber family); and Faith, called Fay, living in Portsmouth.

William, the youngest son of John Howe Warnock, married Mary (Mollie) Deering and their children were Dr. Horace H., Edward T., Nannie, wife of Dr. Ernest Sellards (see Sellards family), Wirt, Bessie, and John W. H., called Herbert.

WILLIAM HOWE WARNOCK

William Howe Warnock, the second son of James Warnock, Jr., owned many acres of land on Tygart Creek and also land in Carter County, where the Carter Caves are located. He married Emma Duzan Ratcliff, daughter of Samuel Ratcliff, in 1835. They were the parents of John Wesley (known as John Dock), Samuel Price, Richard Matthew, James Warren, Francis Marion (Slick), William Lindsey, Taylor (Whig), Julia Hall, and three who died in infancy.

John Wesley (John Dock) married Martha Clark of Lyon County, Kentucky, in 1864, and lived in the Warnock neighborhood on Tygart Creek. In 1897 the family moved to Fullerton and built a new home in the eastern part of the village. The children of this family were Clark, Walter, Lyman, Elizabeth, and Fred. Clark married Margaret Meadows, of Tygart Valley, and they were the parents of Ward, Wade, Eunice Nichols of East Greenup, and Blanche of Fullerton; Lyman married Edith Roe and their children are Raymond, Ruth Ensor, Helen Griswold, and Ethel Smith; Elizabeth married Charles Holbrook (see Holbrook family); Walter and Fred died at the home in Fullerton.

Samuel Price Warnock married (1) America Alexander, (2) Mary Nancy Morton, daughter of Henry Clay Morton, and their children were Nellie, Charles R., Samuel B., Sallie, and Albert. Of these children, Nellie married (1) Edward Meadows and has a daughter, Olive, (2) Arthur Winkler. Charles R. married Lucy Montgomery and their children are Richard and Eugenia Vincent. Samuel B. married Hattie, daughter of Henry Sloan and Emma Riffe Curry, of Hopewell, and they have two sons, Vernon Clay and Phineas Glen, both of South Carolina. Sallie married George Wear and their children are Virginia Rush, Charles R., Marynelle Literal, Olive Lindeman, and Morton, who married Nina Lou King. Albert married and has three daughters, Helen, Hazel and Mildred.

Richard Matthew Warnock (known as Dick Matt) married Adeline (Addie) Morton, daughter of James Morton, and their children were Alvin Morton, Emma, Lovina, Lillian, Leslie, Elmer, Nancy, and Ollen. Alvin Morton Warnock married Ruby Helen Withrow, daughter of William Withrow; Emma married (1) Shannon Taylor and (2) Dan Withrow; Lillian married John Ratcliff; Elmer married Lillian Abdon; Nancy married Leslie McGinnis; Ollen married Willie Womack and their children are Howard and Louise.

James Warren Warnock married Julia Bartlett Morton, daughter of Henry Clay Morton, and their children were Allen Bartlett, Bess, Don, who died as a young man, and William, who married Margaret Harper of Siloam. Allen Bartlett Warnock married Zona Wolf of Mason County, and their children are Audrey, wife of Harma Hammond; Paul, who married Bertha Dotson; Leah; and Don, who married Nelle Major, all living in Cincinnati; Bess married Price Taylor and has three sons and two daughters.

Francis Marion (Slick) Womack married Sarah Jane Breeding (Duck) and they were the parents of Ury, who died, and Elizabeth, wife of Edward Womack of Greenup (see Womack family). Francis Marion Warnock lived at Tygart Valley and later in Greenup. He served as postmaster twenty years and also as deputy clerk of the county.

William Lindsay Warnock married Mary Susan Traylor and their children are David, Nora, Amanda, Agnes, Addie, and Henry.

Taylor Warnock (Whig) married Catherine (Kit), daughter of Richard and Martha Garrett Morton, and their children are: Myrtle Belle, the wife of John Plymale; Lulu, the wife of Dahl Green of Adams County, Ohio; Edith, the wife of Bert Trickler; Elby, who married Laura Fultz; Dr. Clarence Woodson, who married Thelma Burns and lived in Huntington, West Virginia; and Etta Morton, wife of Albert Hilliard.

MATTHEW WARNOCK, SR.

Matthew Warnock, Sr., the third son of James Warnock, Jr., married Lydia Warnock, daughter of William Warnock, and their children were: Elizabeth, who married James Clifton; James, known as "Black Jim," who married Miss Bradshaw; Polly, who married Dr. Secrest; Margaret, who married James Warnock, son of John W. H. Warnock; John Tug, who married Kate Eifort; Basil, who married Betsy Ann, daughter of John W. H. Warnock; Matthew Scott, Jr., who married Emma Gibbs; Charles, who married Cassie Roberts; America, who married Benjamin Franklin Meadows (see Meadows family).

The children of Matthew Scott Warnock were Clara Kinner of Louisa, Kentucky, Edith Kinner of Greenup, Earl, and Doris.

JAMES WESLEY WARNOCK

James Wesley Warnock, the fourth son of James Warnock, married his cousin, Martha, daughter of Johnson Warnock, and their children were: Robert Johnson, who married America Batman; Scott, who married Miss Batman; Price, who never married; and J. C., who married Mabel Gannon. The children of Robert Johnson and America Batman Warnock were: John Wesley, who married (1) ——— and whose children were Dennis, Ralph, Hubert, and Elma, and (2) Lora Swearngin; Millie, who married Newton McGinnis; Ella Virgie, who married John William Miller in 1854 and whose children are Robert O., Glen Earl, Madge A., and Russell O.; Alma, who married (1) Dave Holbrook (see Holbrook family), and (2) Thomas Swearngin; Margaret, who married Owen Hopkins and has two sons, Homer and Robert.

WHITE

The greater part of this history of the White family is taken from Evans' *History of Scioto County, Ohio*. Not many families can trace their ancestry, as do the Whites, back to the landing of the "Mayflower" in 1620 in the harbor off the coast of Massachusetts.

William White and his wife, Susanna Fuller White, came to America on the "Mayflower." They had two sons, Resolved and Peregrine. Peregrine White was born on the "Mayflower" December 10, 1620. He married Sarah Bassett, daughter of William Bassett, who came to Plymouth on the "Fortune" November 10, 1621. Their children were Daniel, Jonathan, Sarah, and Mercy. Daniel (1649) married Hana Hunt at Duxbury, Massachusetts, August 19, 1674.

Children of Daniel and Hana Hunt White were John (1675), Joseph (1678), Thomas (1680), Cornelius (1682), and Eleazar (1686). Eleazar married Mary Doggett and they had nine children. Nehemiah was the eldest and his children were Philip (1732), Nicholas (1734), and Seth (1737). Seth was born at Woodstock, Connecticut, moved to New Hampshire, and from there to Kentucky in 1779.

The children of Seth were Seth, Jr., (1759) and Abel. Abel came with his father, Seth, Sr., down the Ohio River on a raft with their household goods and families, and landed about two miles below Greenupsburg. Abel had been a soldier in the Revolutionary War and was discharged in 1777. He married Sarah Comfort and they had ten children. His will is on record in the clerk's office at Greenup and is dated October 3, 1823. It names the following children: Seth, Susannah, Abel, Jr., Sabina, Rebecca, Polly, Daniel, Anna, John, Asie, Jeremiah, Joel, and Sally. Witnesses were John Fuqua, James Osborn, John Craycraft, and James L. Hyde. Daniel White was named executor of the will.

Daniel White married Sarah Osborn of Greenup County, September 22, 1814, and they were the parents of eleven children. The third child, Osborn, married Maria Chamberlin and their children were Anson, Abraham, Daniel, and Sarah Cooper. Daniel was born October 4, 1842, on Dogwood Ridge, Scioto County, Ohio. He married (1) Eliza Noel in 1866 and had one son, Frank, a jeweler in Portsmouth for many years, and (2) Belle Wilhelm and they had a son, Abraham. Frank White married Carrie Sprinkle of Greenup County and they were the parents of a daughter, Pearl, and a son, Leslie, now a resident of Lucasville, Ohio.

WILLIAMS

James Madison Williams and his wife, Sarah Brower, came from Adams County, Ohio, to Greenup County about 1834. He was born in Pennsylvania in 1778, the son of James Williams,

Sr., who served in the Revolutionary War both in Maryland and Pennsylvania, and came to Adams County before 1800. James Madison Williams served in the War of 1812 from Ohio.

Henry (1815), son of James Madison Williams, seems to be the only child that came to Greenup County with the parents. The others remained in Adams County. Henry married Jane Anderson in Adams County in 1834. She was born in Lancaster County, Pennsylvania. Both families settled on Coal Branch, where the men worked as colliers. Later they moved to Pond Run and lived on a farm. They were always furnace people and they worked at Amanda Furnace a long time.

The children of Henry and Jane Anderson Williams were: Julia (1835), who married Abraham Hamor (see his sketch under Hamor family); Sarah (1836); Mary (1839), who married Alexander Savage (see Savage family); Elizabeth (1841), who married John Patterson of Russell; John (1843); James (1848); Naomi (1850); and Henry A. (1851) (see his sketch following).

Sarah Williams married James Hoop, who had also come from Adams County, where he worked at the furnaces. They lived at Argillite and he worked at Pennsylvania Furnace. Their children were Clara, Jane, and Peter. Clara married Henry Heine and lived at Argillite; Jane (Jennie) married Olin Dickey of Greenup, where they lived for some time and then moved to Portsmouth. Their two sons were Fairfax, who married Charlotte Lewis of Portsmouth, and James, who was a graduate of West Point Military Academy and lost his life in Argonne Forest in World War I. The James Dickey Post, American Legion, in Portsmouth is named in his honor. Peter Hoop never married. Mrs. Hoop lived over ninety-nine years and was well preserved for her age. She died in 1937.

John Williams married (1) Margaret Black and had two children, Arthur and Jessie, (2) Mary De Murd, and their children were Charles, Gertrude, Sadie, Frank, Clarence, Hoop, and Lottie and Lettie (twins). Arthur Williams married Josephine, daughter of Samuel Patterson, and lived in Portsmouth, where his son and daughter, Leslie and Mildred, still reside, and have the Wilmere Tea Room.

James Williams married Mary Gilford and their children are Bertha, Olive, Gilford, Alonzo, John, James, and Margaret. Of this family, Gilford, Alonzo, John, and James went to Portsmouth to live. Miss Maybelle Williams, daughter of Gilford, is assistant librarian in the Portsmouth Public Library; Mrs.

Hortense Williams Burris, daughter of Alonzo, teaches in the city schools.

Naomi Williams married James Farmer of Greenup and they lived for a time in Haverhill, Ohio, later moving to Portsmouth. Their children are: Henry; Myrtle, wife of Oscar Shoemaker; Mary, wife of F. E. Bower; Sarah, and Elizabeth. The last three live in Columbus, Ohio.

HENRY A. WILLIAMS

Henry A. Williams, born at Pond Run in 1851, was the youngest child of Henry and Jane Anderson Williams. In 1875 he married Margaret Patterson, daughter of Samuel Patterson of Wurtland, and their children are Samuel, James, George, Hamlin, Chester, Orville, Patterson, Harry, and Amanda, wife of John Artis. Samuel married Mattie Clark and lived in Russell, where he was president of the bank; James married Bertha Chinn; Chester married Jennie Smith; Patterson married Nancy, daughter of Colonel William J. and Lucy York Worthington of Greenup, and they have four children, Patterson, Lucy, Margaret, and Adelaide. Patterson Williams worked for the Chesapeake and Ohio Railroad and later in partnership with his father in the hardware business in Russell. Later he moved to West Virginia.

Henry A. Williams aided in the affairs of Russell when it was a new town. He was director, stockholder, and vice president of the First National Bank and was associated with the Russell Coal and Mining Company.

The inscription on a stone in the Caroline Furnace Cemetery reads: "James Williams, 1778-1873. Served in the War of 1812." Also "Wife of James Williams, died in 1862, age 78." Henry and Jane Anderson Williams and their daughter, Julia Williams Hamor, are buried in the same cemetery, three generations of the same family representing three centuries of time.

WILLIS

(PALMYRA)

Three brothers, Jacob, Ambrose, and Simeon Willis, of Irish descent, came to Virginia. From there they came to Greenup County, and settled at what is now Palmyra, near the Little

Sandy River. Jacob and Simeon married there, but Ambrose went to Carter County. Jacob married Barilla, daughter of Seymour and America McCallister Hardin. The Hardin family were early settlers of Palmyra and were descendants of John Young, who settled there in 1784.

Children of Jacob and Barilla Hardin Willis were Seymour, Edward, and Sallie, who married Daniel Callihan of Palmyra. Seymour married Clara Belle Hern and they were the parents of Hubert, Ollie, Proctor, Anna, Otis, and Cecil. Hubert married Mamie, daughter of Dr. William Tiernan of Ashland; Ollie married Nathaniel Collins, Jr.; Proctor married Carrie Lafferty of Mason County; Anna married Mr. Waggoner of Charleston, West Virginia; Otis married Sarah Maud, daughter of Joshua and Nora Stark Kelly, of Laurel Furnace; and Cecil married Eunice Anderson.

Edward Willis, second son of Jacob, married Helen Corum of Greenup and they were the parents of Jacob, Edith Tanner, William, and Viola Callihan. William married Sallie Forte of Argillite.

Simeon Willis married a Miss Lyons and their home was at Palmyra.

Jacob Willis was a preacher and he built a Baptist Church on his land near Young Ford of Little Sandy. This church was named Palmyra from the East Indian palm trees, the wood of which is very strong. The village took its name from the church. When the Eastern Kentucky Railroad was built through the village, the station was named Laurel for Laurel Furnace. The iron products of Laurel Furnace were hauled to this place.

NOTE: Early marriage licenses of the Willis family are dated 1808 and 1811. One of McCallister in 1810 and one of Hardin in 1820.

JOHN H. WILLIS

The John H. Willis family came from Scioto County, Ohio, to Greenup County in the early 1890's and members of the family resided at Springville until 1920. The ancestors of this family settled in Virginia in Colonial days and several served in the Revolutionary War. The father of John H. Willis was born in Greenbrier County, Virginia, and during the Civil War he was the captain of a company of which his son, John H., was the corporal.

John H. Willis (1836-1908) married Abigail Slavens (1841-1900) in Ohio and their children were John, William, Edward, Gard F., Elizabeth, Amy, Harvey, and Simeon S.

300

John, the oldest son, went to the State of Washington to live. Gard F. lived at Springville until 1904, when he went to Riverton and then to Greenup as a telegrapher for the Chesapeake and Ohio Railroad. He is retired and lives in Greenup with his wife and his daughter, Mrs. Nellie Sturgill. Elizabeth married Mr. McNeal, now deceased. She and a son, Gard W., live in California. Amy married Ira F. Buffington, of Portsmouth, Ohio, and moved to Ocean Park, California, where their daughter, Mrs. Bingham, also resides. Harvey was a telegraph operator for the Chesapeake and Ohio Railroad and was well known in offices in Greenup and Lewis Counties. He was in the Signal Corps of the Army and was at Springville on a furlough when he died in 1918.

Simeon S. Willis was born in 1879 in Lawrence County, Ohio. After the family moved to Springville, he attended the graded school and also a normal school for training teachers, which was conducted by Professor Daniel H. Wade, who is now a resident of Ashland. In 1898 Mr. Willis was a teacher and later a principal of the Springville School. During his teaching years he studied law and was admitted to the bar at Greenup in 1901. He practiced his profession in both Greenup and Boyd Counties. He was a judge of the court of appeals at Frankfort from 1928 to 1932 and was elected the forty-ninth governor of Kentucky in 1943. He was the sixth Republican governor in the one-hundred-and-fifty-one-year history of Kentucky. Greenup County is proud of the fact that she produced a man who had only the advantages of a village school, yet received the highest honor our great Commonwealth can bestow.

Simeon S. Willis married Ida Millis of Ashland and they have a daughter, Sallie Leslie, who married Henry Meigs II in Frankfort while her father was governor. Mr. Willis has returned to Ashland and resumed his law practice since retiring from the governorship.

The parents of Simeon S. Willis, John H. and his wife, Abigail Slavens Willis, are buried in the Christian Church Cemetery at Siloam, Greenup County. The inscription on their stone reads:

John H. Willis, born July 1836 and died April 5, 1908
A Union Soldier Company E, Fifth Regiment West Virginia
Volunteer Infantry 1861-1866
Abigail Slavens, born May 22, 1841, and died Sept. 4, 1900

WILSON
JESSE WILSON

Jesse D. Wilson came to Greenup County from Allegheny, Pennsylvania, about 1844, probably with the James McMullan family, as he had married in 1840 Susan Marie, daughter of James and Tryphena Smith McMullan. The Wilson family had two sons, James McMullan Wilson and Thomas Jefferson Wilson.

Jesse D. Wilson died in 1845 and his wife, Susan Marie, married "Jack" Stewart, a widower with a family of ten children. They had one son, William Stewart. Mary, one of the ten Stewart children, married Feurt Boynton, of Haverhill, Ohio, and her daughter, Nancy, married Terry Davenport of Mt. Zion (see Davenport family).

James McMullan Wilson married Mildred, daughter of Archer and Miriam Kouns Womack, and they had no children. Thomas Jefferson Wilson married Susan Hornbuckle, and their children were Nettie, Jesse, Ellis, James, Susan, and Ernest. Nettie married Mr. Lane of Huntington, West Virginia. Jesse married Dale Brickey, whose father and brothers were well known bricklayers of Greenup County. Their son, Thomas, lives in the old home on Main Street in Greenup. Ellis was killed by a train; James never married; Susan married Edward Snyder; Ernest had a son, Alva, who married Mary Bergmeyer, daughter of Ulrich Bergmeyer.

Jesse Wilson was serving as marshal in Greenup when he was shot while discharging the duties of his office. He recovered but was crippled so that he could not work at his trade as a carpenter. Most of the Wilson men were carpenters.

ROBERT WILSON

The Wilson family was originally from Culpeper County, Virginia. Robert and Mahala Van Meter Wilson came to Greenup from Huntington, West Virginia, in 1881. He was a miller and had operated mills in Pt. Pleasant, Buffalo, and Huntington, West Virginia. When he came to Greenup he bought the old Myers Mill at the head of Front Street and operated it until it was destroyed by fire several years later.

In April 1888 Rebecca Spalding made a deed to Robert Wilson, Sr., and James Sowards, Sr., for a tract of land on Railroad Street. They built a mill on this ground and the firm was known as the Rebecca Milling Company. In 1889 William T. Hord entered the firm, buying the J. M. Sowards interest. Later

Robert Wilson, Sr., and his sons purchased the Hord stock and changed the name to the Greenup Milling Company. Members of the Wilson family have operated the mill to the present time. In 1948 Robert E. Lee Wilson, Jr., observed the sixtieth anniversary of the business and more than one hundred customers from the surrounding counties were present for a dinner meeting.

Robert and Mahala Van Meter Wilson were the parents of William, Charles, Martin, Robert E. Lee, and Fannie. William married (1) Nancy Roe and (2) Daisy Wilson. Charles married Lula Marshall. Martin married Viola Lee Wolcott and their children were Jennings and Sweetland. Robert E. Lee married (1) Allie Hope Powell, and had a daughter, Lucille, who married Charles Bentley Bennett (see Joseph Bennett family); (2) Lenore Hertle, and had a son, Robert, and a daughter, Frances, who is the wife of George Corum; (3) Chloe Ripley of Ripley, West Virginia. Fannie, the only daughter of Robert and Mahala Wilson, married William Sowards and their children were Idalaine Starrett, Garnet Thompson, and Hugh, who lives in Hartford, Connecticut.

NOTE: The Van Meter family emigrated to the Shenandoah Valley of Virginia, where two brothers, John and Isaac, secured large grants of land.

WINN

John Winn came from Virginia to Greenup when a young man. Stopping at the Kouns House Tavern, he met and married Nancy, daughter of Major John C. and Elizabeth Smith Kouns. He became the proprietor of the tavern and kept it until his death. John and Nancy Kouns Winn were the parents of Dr. John, Edward, Hattie, Kate, Sallie, and Captain George.

Dr. John Winn married Sarah Chillison and located at Hanging Rock, Ohio. Later he located near Chillicothe, Ohio. Edward married Emma, daughter of Judge James and Parthenia Bryan, and they moved to Texas. Hattie married Hugh Alexander and their daughter, Nancy, married Robert Taylor, who moved to Ashland. Kate married a man named Williamson, of Ohio, but, not liking farm life there, she returned to Greenup.

Kate and Sallie, daughters of John Winn, continued to operate the hotel until their deaths. Sallie never married. Captain George Winn operated the ferry between Greenup and Haverhill. He married Emma, daughter of Frank and Sarah Bennett, and they went to the new town of Fullerton to live. He moved the ferry from Greenup to Fullerton, where it ran between Fullerton and

East Portsmouth until his death in 1902. George and Emma Bennett Winn had a daughter, Kate, who married (1) Hager Davis and (2) William Cotton. She is the fourth generation of the family to own the Kouns House.

WINTERS

James Parker Winters was born in Franklin County, Kentucky, in 1828 and came to Greenup County to live, probably in the 1840's. He was a saddler and a harness maker by trade. In 1854 he married Louise Rankins, daughter of Alexander and Elizabeth Saunders Rankins. They were the parents of three children, William, Mollie, and Sallie.

William married Lizzie Stricklett of Lewis County, Kentucky, and they moved to Colorado. Mollie married Albert (Ab) McCoy, son of Pearson and Mary Van Bibber McCoy, and they had four children: Pursell, who married Louise Taylor; James, who married Irene Biggs; Carl, who married Mary Tanner; and Helen, who married Harvey Elam of Greenup. Sallie, the youngest child of James and Louise Winters, lived with her nephew, Pursell McCoy, in East Greenup.

James Parker Winters was made a member of the Masonic Lodge in 1856 and was a member of the Maysville Commandery No. 10, Greenup Lodge No. 89, F. and A. M., and Apperson Chapter of Ashland. He was a member of the Methodist Church for fifty years, serving as superintendent of the Sunday school and leader of the prayer meeting for many years. Mrs. Louise Winters died in 1884 and Mr. Winters married as his second wife Elizabeth Ware Hill of Mt. Zion. He died in 1897.

WOMACK

The *History of Prince Edward County, Virginia*, lists, on page 33, the name of one Archer Womack as a representative to the House of Delegates and Senate in 1809-1810. The Womack family came from Prince Edward County, Virginia, to Greenup County about the time of its organization and settled at Oldtown. There were four brothers in the family, and of these Archer married Miriam Kouns of Oldtown and settled on Little Sandy two miles south of Greenup; Allen married Lucy Osenton and lived all of his life at Oldtown; William went to Carter County; and Samuel went to Morgan County. A sister, Nancy Womack, married William Kouns of Oldtown and they were the parents of John

William Kouns (Billy), who was sheriff and judge in the 1880's and 1890's.

The children of Archer and Miriam Kouns Womack were Archer, George, William A., Charles, James Watt, Benjamin, Mildred, Miriam, and Elizabeth. William A. married Ann Elizabeth Lyons and they lived at Oldtown the greater part of their lives. In 1853 they, with their baby, James Watt, moved to Three Prong on Tygart Creek, where they lived until 1863. Mr. Womack was taken prisoner by the "Home Guards" as a Secessionist during the war and was confined in Camp Chase, Ohio, for almost a year. When released he moved his family to Greenup, where he kept a store until 1867. Later he moved to Oldtown, where the Womack children grew to manhood and womanhood.

At Oldtown William A. Womack went into the store business with his brother-in-law, Billy Kouns, also operating a grist mill and a tannery. This store was operated by Cardinal F. Stark in 1845 and has been in the Womack family ever since that time, being operated now by Walter Orin Womack. The site of the building has been changed to where the mill and tannery were formerly located.

Children of William A. and Ann Elizabeth Lyons Womack were James Watt, Elizabeth, Charles, Mary Frances, John Thompson, Willa May, Alma Ann, Benjamin Ward, Walter Orin, and Edward Reason. Two children, Alice and Emma, died when young (see sketch of James Watt Womack); Elizabeth married Joshua Kelly of Laurel Furnace; Mary F. married Robert A. E. Leslie of Big Sandy Valley (see sketch of John T. Womack); Willa May married John Bowers of Houston, Texas; Alma Ann married Dr. William Morris of Fullerton; Benjamin Ward married Gertrude Curry of Hopewell and they live in Florida; Walter Orin married Mary Carnahan of Oldtown; and Edward Reason married Elizabeth Warnock of Tygart Valley and they have made their home in Greenup.

Allen and Lucy Osenton Womack were the parents of George, Josephus, Davis, and Daisy. George married Alice Jones and they lived in Huntington, West Virginia; Josephus married Mary Anglin of Hopewell; Davis married Effie, daughter of James and Mary A. Holbrook Taylor of Tygart Valley; and Daisy married Travis Kendall (see Kendall family).

Of the other children of Archer and Miriam Kouns Womack, Samuel married Emily McAllister and lived on Little Sandy;

Benjamin married Mollie Dortch of Little Sandy; Mildred married James Wilson and lived in Greenup. The children of George Womack were Archer, James, and Georgiana.

Charles Womack, a relative in Virginia, owned five thousand acres of land on Little Sandy in the early days. He was a bachelor and left his land to a nephew, Charles Womack, of Virginia, who sold his inherited land to Ward and Orin Womack, and they in turn sold it in small tracts.

JAMES WATT WOMACK

James Watt Womack, born at Oldtown November 24, 1852, was the son of William Archer Womack (1828) and his wife, Ann Elizabeth Lyons (1835), both of Oldtown. When Watt Womack was six weeks old his parents bought a farm on Three Prong and they lived there until 1863, when they moved to Greenup. He was ten years old at that time and attended the Greenup schools until 1867, when the family moved to the old home at Oldtown. Watt returned to Greenup to attend school and then he clerked in the Womack and Kouns store at Oldtown. For one year he was a clerk at the Laurel Furnace store.

In 1874 Mr. Womack came to Greenup as deputy sheriff under Basil Warnock and served from 1875 to 1876. He also served as deputy under J. W. Kouns from 1879 to 1882, and he was elected high sheriff in 1883. He served two terms and has a record of serving as sheriff more terms than any sheriff Greenup County has ever had. He had the love and the respect of all citizens, regardless of party. A lifelong and staunch Democrat, he has voted the ticket straight ever since he was of voting age. In 1896 and 1897 he was elected representative, and in 1912 he was elected county judge, serving four terms with honor.

Besides his numerous public activities, Mr. Womack was the senior member of the Womack Brothers Store for sixty-three years, the junior member being his brother, John Thompson Womack, who died in 1946. After the death of his brother, Mr. Womack decided to sell the store, which had been outstanding for honest dealing in all of its sixty-three years.

In 1883 Mr. Womack married Miss Ida Osenton of Wheelersburg, Ohio. The Osentons were an old family of Greenup and Carter Counties (see Osenton family). Mr. and Mrs. Womack had no children of their own, but reared a niece of Mrs. Womack's, Mabel Osenton, who married O. W. Stennett of Russell. They have a daughter, Ida Louise. Mr. Womack makes his home with Mrs. Stennett on Main Street.

James Watt Womack joined Lodge No. 89 of the Masons at Greenup on April 8, 1876, and he has held every office available in the lodge. Many years ago he received the fifty-year gold pin and certificate and is well along toward a seventy-fifth anniversary. It is hoped that Mr. Womack may live many more years of his long and useful life.

The *Masonic Journal* of September 15, 1949, gives the following: "Watt Womack is probably the seventh oldest Mason in the world." The first seven living Masons are:

1. John J. Ray, Dublin, Texas
2. William J. Burwell, San Diego, California
3. Robert J. Watchorn, Merrickville, Ontario
4. Frank W. Carpenter, Maiden Rock, Wisconsin
5. James R. Rash, Madisonville, Kentucky
6. Not known
7. James Watt Womack, Greenup, Kentucky

JOHN THOMPSON WOMACK

John Thompson Womack, a brother of James Watt Womack, was born January 26, 1863, on Tygart Creek and came to Greenup when a young man. He was deputy sheriff under Butler Taylor in 1887-1890 and high sheriff in 1891-1892. He was a partner with James Watt Womack in the Womack Brothers Store for sixty years.

In 1887 John T. Womack married Lydia Connor, daughter of Thomas Naylor and Ellen Humphreys Biggs. They made their home at Greenup in the William Kouns house on lower Main Street.

Mr. and Mrs. Womack were the parents of two daughters. Xina (deceased) married James Oney of Huntington, West Virginia. Their son, James, is married and lives in Charleston, West Virginia. The other daughter, Anna Laura, is the wife of Buford Myers and they reside in the John T. Womack home on Main Street, in Greenup.

WORTHINGTON

William Jackson, John (Jack), and Charles Worthington were three brothers who went from West Moreland County, Pennsylvania, to Ohio, and later to Greenup County. William

Jackson Worthington was captain of Company B of the Twenty-second Kentucky Volunteer Infantry, in the Civil War. He was commissioned a major and later a lieutenant colonel, and was with Grant at the siege of Vicksburg and the Battle of Cumberland Gap. Also he was under the command of General Burnside on the Red River expedition at New Orleans. After the war he bought the Raccoon Furnace land for a stock farm and lived there many years. He studied law, was admitted to the bar, elected county judge, state representative, and senator. In 1895, during the administration of William O. Bradley as Governor of Kentucky, he served as lieutenant governor. He was born in 1832 and died in 1914.

He was twice married and had five children by his first wife: Anna, Agnes, Finley, Thomas, and William. Anna married Charles Dickey of Greenup, and they went to Montana to live; Agnes married George Callihan of Danleyton, where he was a farmer; Finley and Thomas went to Alabama when they were young men; William studied and practiced law in Lexington, Kentucky, where he married Addie Norwood.

Later in life Colonel Worthington married Lucy York of Hunnewell, and by this marriage he had two daughters, Mrs. Patterson Williams of Russell, and Mrs. James Collins of Greenup.

In the early 1880's John (Jack) Worthington built a home at Little Sandy Falls and here the family lived for many years. The children of this family were Ona, wife of David Vallance; Sarah, wife of Mr. Davisson; Nancy, wife of George Thom; Tempa, wife of Uhl McCoy; James; John; and Charles.

Charles Worthington, brother of Colonel William Worthington, married Nancy Holbrook of Tygart Valley. He kept a store on Tygart, which the family still own and operate.

WURTS

The Wurts family came from Wurtenburg, Germany, and settled near Philadelphia, Pennsylvania. In 1847 three brothers, William, George, and Samuel Grandin Wurts came to Greenup County to engage in the furnace business. With them was Benjamin King, who had married Ann Wurts, a sister of the Wurts brothers. They built Pennsylvania Furnace in 1847 and Laurel Furnace in 1848. The families lived at Laurel, which they operated for about twenty years. They sold Laurel Furnace to Robert and Thomas Scott, of Ironton.

William Wurts went to Maysville, where he married late in life. There were other members of the family also living at Maysville. George Wurts married Mary Ann Peters of Ironton, Ohio, and settled at what was called the Fulton Oil Works. He bought the Hon. John McConnell farm and lived there until he died. The name Fulton was changed to Wurtland. Children of the George Wurts family were George, Rebecca Wallingford of Maysville, Mary Pelham Peters of Ironton, Sarah Russell of West Virginia, Alice Biggs of Wurtland, Ann, and John, who never married.

Samuel Grandin Wurts married Matilda Cartright. A daughter, Mary, married John Hamon Chinn, Jr., of Wurtland. Lilly, another daughter, married William Walker, and Lucy married George Paull Walker, Jr., sons of George Paull Walker and Helen Marr Nicholls. A daughter, Virginia (of the Walker family), married Joseph Savage of Wurtland. A descendant of the John Hamon Chinn family is Wurts Chinn, a merchant of Wurtland.

Benjamin and Ann Wurts King were the parents of Samuel Grandin, Marinus, Maurice, Rebecca, Sarah, and Mary. Samuel Grandin married Caroline Poage Kinkead and they had a son, Benjamin, who is a resident of Fort Myers, Florida; Rebecca married William Biggs and lived at Mt. Zion (see William Biggs, Jr., family); Sarah married Richard Prichard of Ironton. They moved to Gate City, Alabama, and she was killed in a cyclone. After her death Mr. Prichard married her sister, Mary King.

YOUNG

John Young, born in Virginia, August 24, 1764, was a son of Reuben Young, and served as a dispatch rider in the Revolutionary War, in Virginia. He married Mary Moore, in 1785, and came with his family and four negro slaves to what is now Palmyra. He patented a large tract of land lying along the Little Sandy River.

On record are the marriages of his five daughters: America to James McCallister in 1810; Arimathia to Lewis Reason in 1811; Jane to Gabriel Harmon in 1812; Polly to Benjamin Aills in 1814; and Nancy to Benjamin Powell, in 1817. Mrs. Lucille Bennett, of Greenup, is a descendant of Benjamin and Nancy Young Powell. The Willis and Hardin families of Palmyra descend from the John Young family.

November 7, 1842 John Young appeared before the court as a resident of Greenup County, gave account of his services in the Revolutionary War, and made application for a pension.

ZUHARS

Five members of the Zuhars family came from Leba, Germany, to Greenup County about 1852. These were four brothers, Theodore, Alfred Ferdinand, William, and Frederick, who came with their uncle, George Anderson Zuhars. Their parents were Frederick Christopher and Wilhelmina Zuhars, natives of Leba. The father was a fisherman on the Baltic Sea and the sons were sailors. Luella McMullen, a granddaughter of Alfred Ferdinand, well remembers hearing him tell of his experiences when he ran away from home at the age of fourteen years and went with an uncle on a sailing vessel to Sydney, Australia. It took one year to make the trip of 19,200 miles.

William Zuhars went to Kansas and settled, while Frederick settled in Scioto County, Ohio. Theodore, Alfred Ferdinand, and the uncle, George Anderson Zuhars, settled in Beattyville in Greenup County and, having been sailors, they naturally turned to the river for their livelihood. They owned and operated a line of barges, at one time twenty-six in number, carrying merchandise to Cincinnati, Louisville, and Cairo. Their cargo consisted of lime stone from Limeville, pig iron from Hanging Rock, Ohio, fire clay, tanbark, and other products from the county.

When they retired from the river traffic, Alfred opened a store in Beattyville, where they had built their homes, which were among the first in the village. They were charter members and loyal supporters of the Springville Methodist Church.

About the time the Zuharses came to Beattyville, the Arnold family came to Greenup County. Sylvanus and Eliza De Bliss Arnold brought their family down the Ohio River by boat from Honesdale, Pennsylvania. The Zottman family came on the same boat and both families settled in Portsmouth. Later the Arnolds moved to Beattyville, where the two daughters, Mary and Almira De Bliss Arnold, met and married Theodore and Alfred Ferdinand Zuhars.

Alfred Ferdinand Zuhars

Alfred Ferdinand Zuhars, born in Leba, Germany, in 1833, was nineteen years old when he came to Greenup County. In 1862 he married Almira De Bliss Arnold, born in 1842, and they

310

spent their entire married life in Beattyville. Their children were Emma A., Lewis A., who died in infancy, Charles W., Sylvanus Arnold, Martin Timmonds, Anna Eliza, and Mary Elizabeth.

Charles W. married Nancy Biggs, daughter of Benjamin Biggs, and their children are Alfred, Chester, Rudolph, Mundane Miller, Margaret McAninoh, and Veva Cox. Sylvanus Arnold married Eva Hanners; Martin Timmonds married Mary Hanners; Elizabeth married (1) Alex Brown and their children are Robert, Grace, and Charles, (2) Ernest Stockham and their children are Pearl and Clyde; Anna Eliza married William H. McMullen (see McMullen family).

THEODORE ZUHARS

Theodore Zuhars married Mary Arnold and they also lived in Beattyville. Their children were: Mollie, wife of Andrew Thomson; Myrtle, wife of Frank Moore of Mt. Zion; Warren, who married Julia Kopensparger of New Lexington, Ohio, whose children are Edith McCall, Hazel, Edwin, Raymond, and Clifford, all living in Portsmouth.

OTHER SETTLERS

There are many names of early settlers of whom we have no record. Some of these became residents of the new counties taken from Greenup. The Canterburys, Shortridges, Ellingtons, Shannons, and Burnses became residents of Lawrence County; the Ruckers, Kibbys, and Tyrees, of Carter County; and later, the Geigers, Prichards, and Kitchens, of Boyd County.

Early residents of Little Sandy were the McCallister, Hardin, Cane or Cain, Lowry, Gholson, Crump, and Barney families; and on East Fork, the Davisson and Clark families. The Jacob Everman family settled on Sandy in 1800 or earlier. In 1806, a marriage license was issued to Ann, a daughter of Jacob Everman, and Walker Cummings. When Carter County was formed in 1838, members of the Everman families became residents of each county.

On White Oak, Schultz, and Lower Tygart Creeks settled the Lee, Meeks, Clary, Hunt, Dortch, Roberts, Anderson, Hardin, and Bush families. Of these, a marriage license was issued in 1817 to James Meeks and Mary Greenslate. Richard, a son of Wilson Lee, married Jane Meeks. Children of the Lee family were William, James, and Jennie, who married Henry Bush (see Bush family). Carlyle Hunt lived on Schultz Creek. A daughter of Jackson Hunt, Melvina, married Hiram Hunt in 1845. Of the Dortch family, Martha married Abraham H. Bryson and Frances married Andrew J. Bryson (see Bryson family).

Families of Upper Tygart Valley were Miller, Stewart, Duncan, McGinness, Huffman, Traylor, and Abdon. James McGinness was one of the first jurymen of the county in 1804.

CARTER COUNTY

Carter County was formed from a part of Greenup County in 1838. It was named for William G. Carter, who was state senator from Greenup County from 1834 to 1835. The county seat was named for Alfred Ward Grayson, a prominent man in the early affairs of Greenup County.

Early families who became residents of Carter County in 1838 were Rucker, Goble, Kibby, Osenton, Deatly, Ward, Davis, Burns, Powers, Scott, Jones, Bagby, Prichard, Everman, Strother, Womack, Hord, Tyree, Wilhoit, and Kitchen.

Early furnaces of Carter County were Mt. Savage (1848), Boone (1856), and Iron Hills (1873).

CATLETT SETTLEMENT IN GREENUP COUNTY (CATLETTSBURG)

Andrews

George and N. P. Andrews came to the Settlement in 1851 and carried on a general mercantile business.

Canterbury

The Canterbury family settled in the eastern part of Greenup County very early. Benjamin Canterbury married Susanna Huson January 6, 1806. Reuben Canterbury was sheriff of Greenup County, 1816-1817. He married Elizabeth Lycan September 19, 1808. John Canterbury married Nancy Lycan September 18, 1809. This family became residents of Lawrence County when it was formed from Greenup and other counties.

Catlett

Alexander (Sawny) Catlett came from Virginia across the Big Sandy River with his family and slaves, and settled near its mouth in 1800. John Savage and Charles Smith had received a military grant of twenty-eight thousand acres from Virginia in 1772 and this land was sold by their heirs. Alexander Catlett came into possession of it and the settlement became known as Catlettsburg. Horatio, a son, was tavern keeper, ferryman, storekeeper, and he also handled the mail. The Catlett Tavern was a stopping place for the stage coach that ran from Lexington to Charleston, West Virginia, and which was ferried across the Big Sandy River. Andrew Jackson and Henry Clay were distinguished passengers traveling this route. The Catlett family broke up and a man named Fry inherited the title to the estate.

CECIL

Kinzy Cecil, of English descent, settled in the valley at an early date. Cob, a grandson, became a prominent business man in the Settlement.

FRY

The Fry family that had acquired the title to the estate of Savage and Smith lived in the Catlett Settlement for many years. For a long time the family would not sell the land nor lay it off into lots. In 1849 James Wilson Fry laid off a part of the town, from Catletts Creek to the present Division Street. In 1851 he sold land to a company composed of William Hampton, John Culver, William Campbell, and Frederick Moore. This company laid off that part of Catlettsburg above Division Street.

GALLUP

Colonel George Gallup came to the Settlement in 1850. He taught school and studied law. He was a lieutenant in the Fourteenth Kentucky Regiment, became colonel, and was made a brigadier general.

GEIGER

David Geiger was an early settler of the Catlett Settlement. He bought land from James Wilson Fry and built a house which he later sold to Captain Wash Honshell.

HAGER

The Hager families of Ashland are descendants of John and Mary Shafer Hager of Maryland and Virginia, who were of German descent. They settled in the Big Sandy Valley at an early date with three sons, of whom Daniel became the ancestor of the Ashland families. John F. and Edgar Hager were prominent lawyers of Ashland. A daughter of Daniel married Dr. Martin, a well-known physician of Ashland.

HAMPTON

The Hampton family came from Virginia to the Big Sandy Valley. Henry Hampton was the ancestor of those who came down the valley and settled at Catlettsburg. His son, William, had a large family of boys, among them John W., who became a prominent lawyer of Ashland. Hampton City was named for William Hampton, who owned a great deal of land at the mouth of the Big Sandy River. He probably inherited this land through his wife, Melinda, daughter of Colonel John Shortridge.

KINCAID

Dr. John D. Kincaid came from Virginia in 1847, and practiced his profession in the Catlett settlement for forty years.

MARR

The Marr family is of French descent, having come to Maryland before the Revolutionary War. The grandparents of Thomas Marr of Catlettsburg came to the valley before 1800. Thomas Marr married the daughter of Benjamin Williamson.

McCOY

James McCoy, a wagon maker, came to the Catlett Settlement from South Point, Ohio, in 1847. His parents were of Irish descent and settled in Lawrence County, Ohio, in 1817.

The wagon shop, which was a busy place in those early days, was located on North Street. The McCoy family lived for more than seventy-five years in the large home which he built on the opposite side of North Street from the wagon shop.

James McCoy married Delilah Kouns of Lawrence County, Ohio, and had a family of six daughters: Catherine, Effie, Sarah, Belle, Elizabeth, and Jennie. Elizabeth married Frank French, who edited the first newspaper in Ashland soon after he returned from the Civil War. In the 1880's the French family moved to Kansas, where Mr. French edited one of the early newspapers of the state. Of the seven French children four are still living: Susie, widow of Edwin Word, of Higgins, Texas; Ethel, wife of Bert Osborn of Lakin, Kansas; Hal of Temple, Texas; and Frank, now retired, after long association with the Gulf Lumber Company of Galveston, Texas.

MIMS

John D. Mims became a resident of the Catlett Settlement in 1852. He was a merchant and also operated a tannery.

MOORE

Frederick Moore came from Pennsylvania to the Big Sandy Valley in 1815. He was a merchant and became identified with the early affairs at the mouth of the Big Sandy. A son, Laban T., was a colonel in the Fourteenth Kentucky Regiment, and later became a prominent lawyer of Catlettsburg. A daughter, Sarah, married (1) John Poage and (2) Pleasant Savage.

PATTON

James Patton came to the Catlett Settlement in 1850. His sons, George, James, and William, established a thriving drug business.

RICHARDSON

James N. Richardson came to Greenup County from Pennsylvania in 1833. In 1852 he took a position at Pennsylvania Furnace. He later went to what is now Ashland and, with R. D. Callihan, built a grain mill which was afterward sold to the Poage family.

SHORTRIDGE

Colonel John Shortridge was of English descent, his ancestors coming to Virginia at an early date. He served in the Revolutionary War, and came to Greenup County in 1792. One of the first suits tried in the court of October 1804 was that of Hugh McGary against George Shortridge for four hundred fifty pounds ten shillings with interest from 1787. The Shortridge family lived in the eastern section of the county and owned all land located two miles below the mouth of Sandy River between Horse Branch and Campbell's Branch.

STEWART

John F. Stewart was principal of the Academy at the Catlett Settlement in 1857. He was born and educated in Pennsylvania. He studied law and located in Lawrence County.

SUTTON

Dr. William Sutton was born in 1791 and in 1818 he became a practicing physician in the settlement. He studied his profession at Maryland Medical College. He married Mary Belle, daughter of Sawny Catlett.

THORNTON

Ezra Thornton came to the settlement in 1851 from New York. He founded the Thornton Academy and edited the first newspaper in the county in 1854.

ULEN

Benjamin Ulen was one of the earliest settlers of the county. He was deputy sheriff under Josiah Davidson from 1804 to 1805. In 1816 he married a widow, Eleanor Cornelius, and lived on Ulen's Branch. A son, Elba, was deputy sheriff under John Brown in 1850. In 1852, when the dreadful Brewer murder occurred, Elba Ulen and his wife took two of the Brewer children, William and Annie, into their home and reared them. Elba Ulen lived continuously in Catlettsburg from its beginning, and was always ranked as one of its useful and prosperous citizens.

VINSON

James Vinson, who came from South Carolina, was the ancestor of the family. In 1800 he came to the Big Sandy Valley with Benjamin Sperry, Peter Loar, and William Artripp of Virginia. He married a daughter of Benjamin Sperry. His sons, William and Samuel S., were lumber dealers, the latter being a member of the firm of Vinson, Goble, and Prichard of Catlettsburg. Z. C. Vinson, son of William, was a prominent business man of the settlement. Fred Vinson, Chief Justice of the Supreme Court of the United States, is a member of the valley family. Shannon Vinson married Rebecca, daughter of Congressman Joseph B. Bates, and resides in East Greenup.

WILLIAMSON

The Williamson family is of Welsh descent, and settled in Pennsylvania before the Revolutionary War. They moved to Virginia and from there to the Big Sandy Valley in 1795. Descendants were Benjamin, Wallace, and Mrs. Thomas Marr, all of Catlettsburg and Ashland. The Williamson family owned a boundless tract of land where the town of Williamson, West Virginia, is now located. The town takes its name from this family.

Conclusion

When planning a compilation of past events of Greenup County, we intended to use only material of the first one hundred years, from 1803 to 1903. But such a wealth of material came to us—much of it extending into the years beyond the time limit—that it became a problem to know where to stop.

We gathered statistics of the past to the best of our ability. We contacted many folks, most of whom responded with some knowledge of the county. We wrote many letters and received many gracious replies from interested people, many of them from far-away places. We endeavored to write a true and kindly history of Greenup County. We realize that we do not have a complete history of families. To have written of all these would have taken years and would have filled more than one book. This book may inspire someone to continue the work begun, thereby encouraging families to acquire and preserve records for generations to come.

THE AUTHORS

INDEX

323

Cole—*continued*
 Mary, 266
 William, 35-67-142-247
Colegrove, Family, 142
 George, 97
 Henry, 97-142
 Nathan, 142-143
 Perla, 248
 Scott, 143-273
Coleman, Henry, 14
 John R., 106
 Sarah, 189-210
 Widow, 246
Colley, Ellen, 232
Collins, Cynthia, 3-165
 Family, 143
 John, 3-38-131-143-186-189
 Joseph, 41
 Lewis, 74-143
 Mary, 78-143-189
 Mattie, 207
 Nathaniel, 143-300
 Retta, 223
 Rose, 178
 Sibbie, 143-184
 William, 143-183
Colson, Everett, 193
Colter, Sallie, 190
Colvin, John, 84
 Stephen, 11
 Vincent, 31
Colwin, Hon. John, 21
Comelius, Roland, 38
Comfort, Sarah, 297
Compton, Caroline, 242
 Elizabeth, 207
Condit, Rev. J. H., 73
 William, 73
Connor, William, 41-67
Conroy, Mary, 160
Cook, Benjamin, 14-164-198
 Jane, 137
 Nancy, 14-164-198
 Sallie, 198
Cooper, A. S., 41-61-63
 Della, 249
 Elizabeth, 249
 Family, 144
 Frances, 217
 Mary, 144-272
Corum, George, 35
 Family, 145
 Helen, 300
 Jesse 33 - 34 - 41 - 52 - 57 - 60 - 62 -
  78-145
 Rebecca, 60-145-180

Corum—*continued*
 William, 31-32-33-35-36-37-50-60-
  61-79-119-145
Coshow, Lucy, 116
Cottingham, Mary, 177
Coulter, S. E. M., 79
County, Clerks, 35
 Judges, 35
Courtney, Louise, 198
Covert, John, 210
 Larkin, 250
Cowper, Hulda, 134
Cox, Charles, 167
 Verda, 234
Coyle, Maude, 149
Craft, Edith, 281
Craig, John, 4
 Lewis, 4-6-7
Crank, William, 38
Cravens, Rev. Nehemiah, 169-215
Crawford, Belle, 145-258
 Family, 145
 Samuel, 53
Craycraft, Ann, 293
 Charles, 146-195
 Family, 146
 Garfield, 133
 Hugh, Family, 147
 James R., 133
 Malvina, 188
 Mary Ann, 115
 Oscar, 218
 Reuben, 146-174
 Sarah, 146-147-190-209
 Walter, 231
 William, 115
Craynon, Family, 148
 Hugh, 49
Creel, George, 62
Crisp, George, 38
 Joel, 85-117
 Lucy, 85-272
 Matilda B., 85
 Newton, 85-117
Croghan, Col. George, 83
Crooks, Abraham, 34
Cross, Annie, 179
Crosset, John, 212
Crum, Thelma, 200
Crump, Ambrose, 190
 Lucinda, 131
 Richard, 52
 Turner, 26
Culp, Catherine, 162
Culver, Ann, 125
 John, 37-73-77-79-125

324

Culver—*continued*
  Romulus, 37-168-204
Cunningham, Fred, 277
Curry, Dove, 200
  Family, 149
  Gertrude, 305
  Hattie, 295
  Hugh, 79
Cussins, Margaret, 279

D

Damron, Family, 150
  Solomon, 216
Danner, Melville, 250
Darlington, George, 32-33-37-50-60
Darragh, Vergne, 276
Daugherty, Lydia, 183
  Robert, 11-27-57-84
  Thomas, 20-21-67
Davenport, Eva, 87-151
  Family, 151
  Sarah, 236
  Terry, 151-302
Davidson, Annie, 77-79-89-152
  Charles, 35-152
  Edward, 152-230
  Family, 153
  Henrietta, 143
  Henry, 152-156-287
  Jeremiah, 52-67-79-80
  Jesse, 31
  Joseph, 31
  Josiah, 3-11-19-20-36-84
  Matilda Hood, 2-186
  Rebecca, 143
  Robert, 20
  William, 150
Davis, Capt. Geo., 49-105
  Capt. Geo., Family, 152
  Capt. John, 49
  Chrisanna, 160
  Cora, 217
  Dr. Dorothy, 257
  Eliza, 153
  Geo. N., 25-26-27-28-34-36-37-73-95-106
  Geo. N., Family, 152
  Hazel, 153-178
  Ida, 208
  James, 37-41-153
  John, 135-153
  Lucy, 124
  Matilda, 158
  Reason, 47-84
  Robert, 153
  Russell, 200

Davis—*continued*
  Sally, 277
  Samantha, 138
  Samuel, 232
  T. P., 137
  William, 153-260
Davisson, Daniel, 131
  John, 20
  Lewis, 20
  Matt, 78
  Susan, 79-131
Dawson, Asa B., 187
  Reuben, 10
  Robert, 21-22
Day, John, 57-70-132
Deane, Mary, 232
Deatly, John, 38
  Polly, 253
Deavers, Bonnie, 151
DeBard, Dr. Alfred, 64-127-154
  Eunice, 271
  Family, 154
  Harriet, 78-154
Deering, Family, 155
  Mary, 156-294
  Nancy, 153-156
  Richard, 27-103-108-155
Degman, Rev. Thomas, 70
DeMurd, Mary, 298
Demint, Samuel, 24-68-71-72
Dempsey, Dorothy, 197
Deterla, Frank, 210
Devereau, Mr., 215
Devore, Nancy, 282
  Sarah, 99
Dickey, Charles, 229
  Fairfax, 298
  Jane, 92-298
  Mary Dulin, 229
  Olin H., 82-298
Dickerson, Sarah, 188
Dickinson, Lucy, 285
  William, 279
Diedrich, Henry, 97
  Irene P., 205
Diehlman, Martha, 128
Diggins, Emma, 209
Dillon, Thomas, 146
Dinwiddie, Gov. Geo., 164
Dixon, Piety, 249
  Thomas, 93
  Unity, 249
  William, 249
Doggett, Mary, 297
Donahue, Ann, 238

Donaldson, Lucy, 116
Donathan, Margaret, 10-183
Doran, Family, 156
Dorn, Edith, 207
  Nicholas, 97
Dorsey, George, 69
  Julia, 183
Dortch, Frances, 135
  Luella, 135-214
  Martha, 135
  Mollie, 306
  Nancy, 279
  Pet, 163
  Rebecca, 117
  Sarah, 117
  Susan, 117
  William, 163
Dotson, Bertha, 295
Doubleday, Rhoda V., 268-269
Douglas, Rebecca, 117
Dowdy, Family, 157
  Sophia, 138
Downs, David, 158-263
  Family, 157
  Lucy Virgin, 74
Drury, Elizabeth, 98-175
  James H., 198
  Millard F., 193
Duduit, Elsie, 138
  Eva W., 46
Dugan, Fannie, 45
  Thomas, 45-216
Duke, Fannie, 278
Dulin, Edward, 41-61-63-67-80
Duncan, Carrie, 144
  Edward, 144
  Harriet, 184
  Hattie, 144
Dunn, Drexel, 163
  Dr. Lewis, 176
  Elijah, 204
  John, 32
Dunnaway, Benjamin, 174
Dupuy, Family, 158
  Jesse, 33-160
  Moses, 37-159
  Rev. B. N., 158
  Richard, 289
  William, 20 - 26 - 28 - 48 - 71 - 77 -
    79-159-160-165
Dusenbury, Caleb, 150
Duval, ——, 107
Duzan, Emma, 245
  Peter, 144-237
  Rachel, 144-237

E

Eads, Fannie, 245
Eakman, Cyrus, 79
Earson, Barbara, 204
  Susannah, 204
Earwood, Clyde, 149
  William, 209
Eastham, Emma, 116
  Henrietta, 231
  Samantha, 149
Eberwine, Caroline, 184
Eddy, Hannah, 255-262
Edmonston, William, 118
Edwards, Emily, 65
Eifort, Kate, 296
Elam, Bert, 222
  Davis, 201
  Family, 160
  Harve, 38-160-304
Elkins, Laura Ellen, 161
Ellington, David, 20
  Elizabeth, 240
  Elsie, 267
Elliot, Brunette, 199
  Octavia, 199
Ellis, Dr. Samuel, 41-59-64-120
English, Eunice, 200
  John, 277
Enslow, David, 285
Ensor, George, 180
  Iowa, 180
Erb, Dr. Albert, 176
Evans, Jefferson, 41-169
Evrett, Hannah, 233
Everman, Harriet, 260
  Jacob, 156
  Moses, 285

F

Fagan, William, 226
Fagins, C. H., 91
  William, 91
Fannin, Beulah, 161-206
  Ella, 161-210
  Family, 161
  Lena, 190
  Minnie, 286
  Rev. Isaac, 70-161
  Sarah, 188
Fansler, Edward, 173
Farley, Hannah, 203
Farmer, James, 299
  Jeremiah, 283
Faucet, Armstead, 48
Fenton, Mary, 260

Hamilton, David, 250
Hammon, William, 94
Hammond, Harma, 295
Hamor, Family, 177
Hampton, Charles, 220
  Henry, 314
  John, 190
  Richard, 27
  William, 34
Hancock, Lee, 195
Haney, Moses, 283
Hanks, Louisa, 291
  Mary Ann, 117
Hannah, Alexander, 115
  Caroline, 248
  Charles, 178
  C. W. G., 41
  Family, 178
  James, 41, 178
Hanners, Benjamin, 195
  Eva, 311
  Mary, 311
Hanson, Matthew, 277
Harbison, James, 35
Harbour, Rev. C. F., 71
Hard, Charles E., 213
  William, 213
Hardia, Elizabeth, 215
Hardin, Barilla, 300
  Fielding, 33
  Seymour, 300
Harding, Seymour, 109
Hardman, Bertha, 189
  Virginia B., 159
Hardwick, George, 19-34
  Henry, 31
Harmon, Gabriel, 309
Harper, Margaret, 295
  William, 206-287
Harr, Rebecca, 279
Harrie, Ann, 116
Harris, Hannah, 257
  John, 114-232
  Robert, 172
Harrison, Gen. W. H., 95
  Robert, 34
Harsin, Deborah, 68
  Garret, 68
Hart, Mary Lou, 126
Hartberger, Jack, 210
Hartley, Amos, 253
  Family, 179
  John, 31-171-179
  Lucy, 79
  Mary, 64-180-256
  Myrtle, 79-179

Hartman, John, 240
Harvey, John, 13
Hatfield, Emzy, 248
  Martha, 179
  J. N., 79
Hawkins, William, 248
Hayward, Sophia, 222
Heine, Henry, 298
Heisler, Edwin, 60-180
  Family, 180
Hellinger, John, 254
Henderson, C. J., 150
  Robert, 23-24-27-29-34-37
Henry, Patrick, 13-276
Hensley, George, 283
Hern, Clara, 300
Herbert, Smith, 71-181
  Susie, 181
Hertel, Charles, 57
  Nora, 78
Hiatt, John, 131
Hicks, Martha, 286
  Parthena, 249
  Sarah, 160
Higley, Julius, 165
Hill, Amos, 106-181-260
  Annie, 283
  Elizabeth, 181-304
  Family, 180
  Faris, 106
  Florence, 106-182
  Hazel, 150
  John, 106-180-181
  Joseph, 204
  Lena, 199
  Louis, 106-181-195
  Samuel, 287
Hilliard, Albert, 296
Hilton, E. R., 41
  Miranda, 175
Hinton, Martha, 265
  Miranda, 175
  Penelope, 227
Hitchcock, Eliza, 281
  Everett, 286
  Family, 182
  Joanna, 228
  Smith, 86-265
Hobbs, Benedict, 57
Hockaday, Edwin, 62
  E. J., 31-76
  Family, 182
  George, 62-183-202
  Irvine, 183
  Isaac, 20-35-182

Ireland, Family, 190
  W. C., 34
  William, 41-58-67-190
Irvin, Henry, 232
  Rev., 73
Irvine, Jane, 285
Irwin, Alexander, 149
  Barr, 149
  Nancy, 200

J

Jackson, Gen. Andrew, 95-202
  Henry, 149
  Walker, 246
Jacobs, Charles, 185-191
  Henry, 104-191
  Jackson, 104
  Jackson, Family, 191
  John, 104-191
  Martha, 191-263
  William, Family, 191
James, Ephraim, 135
Jayne, Beulah, 159
Jeffers, Josephine, 160
Jennings, Maude, 175
Jewell, Nellie, 197
Johnson, Charity, 133
  Dora, 188
  J. W., 200
  Levi, 25
  Mary, 206
  Richard, 11
  Robert, Family, 191
  Ruby, 270
  Sophia, 204
Johnston, John, 94-111
  John, Family, 192
  John Brisco, Family, 193
Jones, Addie, 77
  Alice, 79
  Catherine, 170
  Edward, 281
  Elizabeth, 174
  Essie, 279
  Griffith, 170
  James, 249
  John, Family, 194
  John Paull, 162
  Loue A., 79-195
  Mary, 69-209-243
  Martha, 69
  Oratio Nelson, 69-70
  Rival D., 69-165
  Richard, 41
  Samantha, 242
  Samuel, 194

Jones—*continued*
  Thomas W., 73
  Thomas W., Family, 195
  William, 31-194
Joplin, Charles, 225
Jordan, Lafe, 293
  Thomas, 290
Judd, Don, 79
Justice, George, 134

K

Kane, Mary, 2-9-186
Kaut, Barbara, 267
  George, 98
  John, 59
  Malinda, 97
Keeton, Jefferson, 34
Kegley, Henry, 41
Kehoe, Charles T., 132
Keister, John, 121
  Rella, 199
Kelly, Family, 195
  Joshua, 56-195-263-305
  Mary, 189-240
  Nora, 196
  Sarah, 189-196-300
  Gen. W. H., 8-13
Kendall, Elizabeth, 255
  Family, 196
  Jefferson, 121
  Louisa, 167
  Milton, 167
  Owen, 197-284
  Travis, 115
  Virginia, 65-139-197
  Gen. William, 133
Kennedy, Mary, 280
Kenton, John, 14
  Simon, 2
Kenyon, Professor S. T., 77-79
Ketter, Grace, 218
Kibby, Amos, 21-25-171
  Georgiana, 264
  Moses, 20-82
Kidd, George, 186-187
Kidwell, Benjamin, 76-197
  Family, 197
Kilgore, Minnie, 163
  Tillie, 273
Killen, William, 203
Kimball, Amos, 25
Kincaid, Dr. John, 314
King, Benjamin, 31-34-65-71-125-
  199
  Clyde, 105-199
  Family, 198

McKee—*continued*
  Samuel, 23-35
  William, 49-62
McKenny, Nancy, 38
McKenzie, Delbert, 38
  Earl, 38
McKinster, Rev., 70
McLain, Sherm, 231
McMullan, Isaac, 91
  James, 31-58-61-91-247
  James, Family, 212
  Susan, 302
McMullen, Luella Barton, 213
  Sydney, 213
  William, Family, 213
McNeal, Family, 214
  Thomas, 70
McQuestin, Ada, 264
McVey, William, 171
McWilliams, Maude, 214

M

Mackintire, Ellen, 267
Mackoy, Family, 214
  Harry B., 215
  Henry Clay, Family, 217
  James, 3-193
  James B., 106-217
  John, 3-20-69-70-165-198
  John L., 48-77
  Judith, 215
  M. E., 106
  Moses, 70
  Moses, Family, 216
  Obadiah, 31-48
  Obadiah, Family, 215
  Thomas, 48
  William, 86
  William Hardia, 215
Madison, President James, 274
Major, Buela, 190
  Frances, 277
  Nelle, 295
Mallory, Rev., 71
Malone, Elizabeth, 159-160
  George, 59
Mantle, Agnes, 178
Marquette, Gordon, 280
Marr, Thomas, 314
Marshall, Lula, 303
Martin, Family, 218
  Harry, 276
  James, 18-83-186
  Oliver, 33-37
Mason, George, 14-274
  Maude, 198

Mason—*continued*
  Peter, 14
Massie, Hattie, 231
Matthews, Eliza, 246
  Mrs. Albert, 193
Maupin, Julia, 231
  Margaret, 278
May, Alfred, 162
  Nell, 214
  Sadie, 286
Mayhew, Elisha, 94-156
  Malinda, 38
Maynard, Fred, 79
Mayo, Sarah A., 207
Mead, A. H., 31
  Benjamin, 109
  Elizabeth, 109-176
  Elizabeth B., 88
  Emmoline, 141
  Family, 219
  Henry, 72
  Sarah, 243
  Sophia, 88
Meadows, Benjamin, 41
  Edna, 284
  Edward, 295
  Family, 220
  Lydia, 285
  Margaret, 294
  Matthew, 105-185
  Nora, 86
Means, Family, 221
  John, 123
Mearns, Mary, 66-293
Mears, Susan, 212
Mebane, Rev., 73
Medford, Bessie, 118
  George, 120
  Sarah, 120
Meek, Caroline Burns, 93
  James, 174
  Mary, 98
Meeks, ——, 118
Mefford, George, 120-244-289
  Nancy, 120-289
  Sarah, 120
Menach, Hannah, 172
Merce, Albert, 222
Meriweather, Jane, 275
Merrill, Family, 221
  John, 71-79-107-122
  Josiah, 181-215
  Mattie H., 106
Metz, Edward, 204
  Phoebe, 204
Michael, John, 208

342

www.ingramcontent.com/pod-product-compliance
Lightning Source LLC
Chambersburg PA
CBHW031115020426
42333CB00012B/100